DISASTER DRAWN

DISASTER DRAWN

VISUAL WITNESS, COMICS, AND DOCUMENTARY FORM

HILLARY L. CHUTE

THE BELKNAP PRESS of HARVARD UNIVERSITY PRESS
Cambridge, Massachusetts | London, England
2016

Library of Congress Cataloging-in-Publication Data

Chute, Hillary L.

   Disaster drawn : visual witness, comics, and documentary form / Hillary L. Chute.

      pages cm

   Includes bibliographical references and index.

   ISBN 978-0-674-50451-6 (hardcover : alk. paper)   1. Comic books, strips, etc.—History and criticism.   2. Nonfiction comics—History and criticism.   3. Graphic novels—History and criticism.   4. Psychic trauma in literature.   5. Storytelling in literature.   6. Narration (Rhetoric)   I. Title.

   PN6714.C487 2016

   741.5'9—dc23   2015017876

For my parents, Richard and Patricia Chute,
the two people I respect and admire most

———————————————

And for Shahab Ahmed

CONTENTS

A NOTE ON THE FIGURES

All images presented here as figures appear at or close to their actual size. I have not enlarged any images, although some by necessity (double spread pages, for example) appear smaller than they do in print.

Every effort has been made to trace copyright holders and to obtain their permission for the use of copyrighted images. I would be grateful to be notified of any corrections that should be incorporated in future reprints or editions of this book.

DISASTER DRAWN

INTRODUCTION
SEEING NEW

Form is the record of a war.
—NORMAN MAILER, *CANNIBALS AND CHRISTIANS*, 1966

My interest in comics as nonfiction—as a form of documentary, as a form of witnessing—began with realizing how comics as a medium places pressure on classifiability and provokes questions about the boundaries of received categories of narrative. In 1991, cartoonist Art Spiegelman's *Maus II: A Survivor's Tale*, a work about his Polish father's experiences during the Holocaust that depicts Jews as mice and Nazis as cats, made the *New York Times Book Review* best-seller list, on the hardcover fiction side of the ledger. Spiegelman wrote in a letter to the *Times:* "I know that by delineating people with animal heads I've raised problems of taxonomy for you. Could you consider adding a special 'nonfiction/mice' category to your list?"[1] Apparently editors at the *Times* were debating after receiving the letter whether or not to move the book, and one of them said, "Hey, let's go down to Soho

1

and ring Spiegelman's doorbell. If a giant mouse answers, we'll put it in nonfiction." Clearly a mouse was not going to answer the doorbell, but in an unprecedented act the *Times* published Spiegelman's letter and moved the book to nonfiction. This series of events indicates the discomfort that people have with the notion of drawing (and its attendant abstractions) as possibly "true" or "nonfictional"—as opposed to writing, a system of communication seen to be more transparently true or accurate.[2] In 1992, the *Maus* series was awarded a Special Pulitzer Prize, because the committee was not sure into which category to place a comics work about the Holocaust that pictured Jews as mice and Nazis as cats. While *Maus's* animal metaphor put the book's nontransparency on the surface (Spiegelman then proceeded to rupture his own visual conceit in all sorts of ways), it only amplified what many took to be the subjective quality of drawing that ought to keep it out of nonfiction categories anyway. Comics narrative, however—which calls overt attention to the crafting of histories and historiographies—suggests that accuracy is not the opposite of creative invention.

Why, after the rise and reign of photography, do people yet understand pen and paper to be among the best instruments of witness? There are many examples of the visual-verbal form of comics, drawn by hand, operating as documentary and addressing history, witness, and testimony. Today, figures such as Spiegelman, whose two-volume *Maus* (1986, 1991) cemented comics as a serious medium for engaging history; Joe Sacco, a self-described "comics journalist"; and a growing number of others all over the globe seize public and critical attention with hand-drawn histories and accounts from Auschwitz, Bosnia, Palestine, Hiroshima, and Ground Zero (see Figure I.1). The essential form of comics—its collection of frames—is relevant to its inclination to document. *Documentary* (as an adjective and a noun) is about the presentation of evidence. In its succession of replete frames, comics calls attention to itself, specifically, as evidence. Comics makes a reader access the unfolding of evidence in the movement of its basic grammar, by aggregating and accumulating frames of information.

Disaster Drawn: Visual Witness, Comics, and Documentary Form explores how the form of comics endeavors to express history—particularly war-generated histories that one might characterize as traumatic. For that reason, it is centrally about the relationship of form and ethics. How do the now-numerous powerful works about world-historical conflict in comics form operate? To what end, aesthetically and politically, do they visualize testimony? How do they engage spectacle, memory, and lived lives—as well

Figure I.1 Joe Sacco, cover to *Palestine* comic book #4, 1993. *Palestine* was a series before it was collected as a single book volume in 2001. (Used by permission of Joe Sacco.)

as extinguished lives? While the works I discuss here are each rooted in a different way in traumatic history, they all propose the value of inventive textual practice to be able to express trauma ethically. (By "textual practice," I refer to the space of the comics page in its entirety—that is, to work in both words and images.)

I have written on comics's visual form as an ethical and troubling visual aesthetics, or poetics, in *Graphic Women: Life Narrative and Contemporary Comics.* That book takes up the question of ethics in relation to notions of self-constitution in the face of trauma. The most relevant sense in that book in which I was interested in comics texts as ethical is expressed by Lynne Huffer's posing of the ethical question as "How can the other reappear at the site of her inscriptional effacement?"[3] Graphic narratives that bear witness to authors' own traumas or to those of others materially retrace inscriptional effacement; they repeat and reconstruct in order to counteract. In this book, as before, I am fascinated by how comics positions and enacts itself as a form of counterinscription. Like the works I investigate in *Graphic Women,* many of the documentary comics I explore here, most notably those by Keiji Nakazawa and Spiegelman, are also narratives of the self that, however complex, are united by the fact that they are genealogical narratives of family history, or by the weight of history on family structures.

Two features of the medium particularly motivate my interest in how comics expresses history. First, comics is a drawn form; drawing accounts for what it looks like, and also for the sensual practice it embeds and makes visible, which I treat here as relevant to the form's aesthetics and ethics. Second, the print medium of comics offers a unique spatial grammar of gutters, grids, and panels suggestive of architecture. It presents juxtaposed frames alternating with empty gutters—a logic of arrangement that turns time into space on the page. Through its spatial syntax, comics offers opportunities to place pressure on traditional notions of chronology, linearity, and causality—as well as on the idea that "history" can ever be a closed discourse, or a simply progressive one. While Rosalind Krauss laments that contemporary art has entered the "post-medium condition," attention to comics reveals a form that is deeply rooted in the specificity of its medium as a source of cultural, aesthetic, and political significance.[4]

In asking why there are so many difficult and even extreme world-historical conflicts portrayed in the form of comics, and how it came to be a site of documentary that is expanding as I write, this book is centrally occupied with the question of how war generates new forms of visual-verbal witness. It is not an accident that after 9/11 and the commencement of wars in Afghanistan and Iraq, there was an increase in attention to documentary experimentation—just as there was also during the period of the Vietnam War, both in visual realms (such as film and photography) and in prose (with the era's deep innovations in reporting). Indeed, the author of a recent study of 9/11 literature wondered if the enterprise of fiction could withstand the public appetite for documentary after the 9/11 attacks.[5] We are now in a kind of golden age of documentary, in which attention to myriad forms of recording and archiving is greater than ever, and the work of documentary is central to all sorts of conversations (as, perhaps, the *New York Times*'s recent "Op-Doc" category indicates).[6] But despite the fact that the hand-drawn form of comics has emerged afresh as a major location for documentary investigation—and that there is a wealth of very widely known, acclaimed graphic narratives that pivot on the figure of the witness—there has not until now been a sustained critical study of documentary comics.[7]

Disaster Drawn analyzes the substance and emergence of contemporary comics; it connects this work to practices of witnessing spanning centuries. In placing earlier documentary traditions in conversation with those of modern comics, I focus on contemporary cartoonists who work within well-established cultural traditions of comics writing and reception. (The United States, Japan, and France have the longest of such codified traditions, identified in Japan as manga and in the French or Franco-Belgian tradition as *bande dessinée*.) All of the artists I examine—Callot, Goya, Nakazawa, Spiegelman, Sacco—visualize war and death. Graphic narratives, on the whole, have the potential to be powerful precisely because they intervene against a culture of invisibility by taking what I think of as the risk of representation.[8] Specifically, in comics produced after World War II, despite the prevailing views of representing trauma after the Holocaust, we see that trauma does not always have to be disappearance; it can be plenitude, an excess of signification. All of the creators I discuss here engage traumatic history, and all grapple with what it means to "picture" suffering and trauma.[9]

This book makes two historical arguments, claiming that the forceful emergence of nonfiction comics in its contemporary specificity is based on a response to the shattering global conflict of World War II—and also that we need to see this work as adding to a long history of forms. *Disaster Drawn* seeks to provide a longer genealogy than is usual for nonfiction comics and also to assess what is happening now. For that reason, Chapters 1 and 2, short opening chapters, focus on selective histories of visual-verbal witnessing going back to the Thirty Years' War and on the expansion of comics in the nineteenth and early twentieth centuries, particularly in Europe and in the United States, when the form established the conventions recognized widely today.

Second, I investigate the social and psychic pressures that impelled the form's reemergence after World War II, and the formal innovation across national boundaries—along with the global routes of circulation—that comics took and created.[10] The contemporary cartoonists who have changed the nonfiction field most drastically are a Japanese artist (Nakazawa) and two European immigrants to America (Spiegelman and Sacco), each profoundly motivated by world war (Spiegelman was born Itzhak Avraham ben Zev). In Chapters 3 and 4, I analyze the work of two cartoonists creating comics at the same moment in Japan and the United States about World War II: the eyewitness Nakazawa and the secondary witness Spiegelman. In 1972, with their germinal, respective early works *I Saw It* (a stand-alone comic book) and "Maus" (a three-page comic book story), these artists invented nonfiction comics afresh, responding to a world gripped by the Vietnam War and saturated with its constant stream of televisual images.[11] Attentive to the ontology of different media forms, I argue that we can understand the return to a tradition of "drawing to tell" against the backdrop of this saturation and the discourses of technological power that shaped the atomic age, and specifically the Vietnam War, during which time, as Michael Herr writes, nuclear war loomed in the background and an "empty technology" characterized the institutional temperament of the war.[12]

Finally, in Chapter 5 and the coda, the traditions of visual witnessing this book traces culminate in the body of work known as comics journalism, featuring Sacco, its contemporary innovator, and others. "It's very unusual for this kind of art, this comic art, to become testamentary," Michael Silverblatt mused about *Maus* in a 1992 interview with Spiegelman.[13] Almost twenty-five years later, one might say the opposite is true. Work that is historical and specifically "testamentary" or testimonial is the strongest genre of comics. (And sometimes where to find testimony and memory is ambiguous; Phoebe Gloeckner, whose project in progress on serial murders in Juárez, Mexico, I treat briefly in the coda, focuses in depth on *non*-survivors, chasing down the particularity of life and death occurring outside of the public eye.) The form of comics has taken center stage among a range of documentary forms—moving forward, say, from the era of New Journalism and cinéma vérité—that innovate the parameters of documentary, investigating historical trauma and even the concept of history itself. Functioning conspicuously in two different narrative registers, the word-and-image form of comics expands the reach of documentary, recording facts while also questioning the very project of what it means to document, to archive, to inscribe. Pitting visual and verbal discourses against each other, comics calls attention to their virtues and to their friction, highlighting the issue of what counts as evidence. (The concept of "evidence," as with "fact" and "proof," has discipline-specific valences and a long history; in one commonplace view, as Lorraine Daston points out, evidence indicates "facts with significance.")[14]

The past century's debates about documentary have been almost wholly about theorizing the filmic and the televisual—or the photographic. (One recent exception is Lisa Gitelman's *Paper Knowledge*, about how genres of the document such as the photocopy and the PDF become epistemic objects.)[15] Stella Bruzzi's oft-cited *New Documentary* (2006) is entirely about cinema and television—as are, in essence, Michael Renov's *The Subject of Documentary* (2004) and John Ellis's *Documentary: Witness and Self-Revelation* (2012), each of which also includes a smattering of photography and video analysis.[16] And works such as William Stott's classic *Documentary Expression and Thirties America*, on documentary photography of the 1930s—the period when the concept of "documentary" gained shape in the United States—are crucial precursors to the parameters of contemporary debates.[17] "Documentary," like "witness," is a nontransparent concept, or group of concepts, with a history and a set of debates attached to it. But what it has not recently landed on in critical discourse is drawing—the hand-drawn document.[18] As Bruno Latour glosses a predominant view in *Iconoclash*, "The more the human hand can be seen as having worked on an image, the weaker is the image's claim to offer truth."[19] In *Disaster Drawn*, I work against this idea, as do Latour and others, by exploring comics's documentary properties and aspirations.

War Comics

Disaster Drawn is the first book to present a substantial historical, formal, and theoretical context for contemporary comics that seek to document histories of war and disaster.[20] The visual depiction of war and the circulation of such depictions are, of course, not new.[21] Attic black- and red-figure vases of the Archaic and Classical periods, for instance, portrayed scenes from the *Iliad*. This book is interested, however, in war in the context of print, and how at every turn war spurs formal innovation. Editions of Robertus Valturius's *De Re Militari (Art of War)*, identified by the Museum of Modern Art as "the first illustrated book about the science of war," appeared at Verona in 1472, offering variously sized woodcuts portraying machinery (Figure I.2). William Ivins, in *Prints and Visual Communication*, characterizes its importance as a form of documentation: "This was not edification at all, and neither was it mere decoration. It was the deliberate communication of information and ideas. The historians have concentrated their interest," he continues, on technicalities of printing and who designed the woodcuts. "But they have unanimously overlooked the importance of these illustrations as the first dated set of illustrations made definitely for informational purposes."[22] The urgency of documenting practices of war had produced a new visual idiom.

As the movement of its chapters makes clear, this book traces a history that understands contemporary comics as part of a long trajectory of works inspired by witnessing war and disaster—works that in turn created new idioms and practices of expression. It considers visual-verbal forms of witnessing war going back to the influential French printmaker Jacques Callot, whose enigmatic 1633 *Les Grandes Misères et les Malheurs de la Guerre* series, inspired by the Thirty Years' War, was not commissioned, and appeared with verse inscribed below its etched images. Moving across a fine art context, it lingers especially on Francisco Goya, who was directly influenced by Callot and worked on *Los Desastres de la Guerra*, his famous series of eighty-three captioned and numbered etchings of the Spanish War of Independence, from 1810 to 1820. Goya witnessed at first hand many, although not all, of the subjects depicted in the *Disasters of War*. Some of the etchings, those completed during the war, produce an account of the present, while others function to produce the recent past and perform the work of countermemory. A textured subjectivity emerges in the space of the relationship of caption to image, even as the images, many of which are of actual historical record, flag themselves as doing the work of reporting. The captions appearing below the images are not simply descriptive; some are sarcastic, and some work against the fact of presentation of the image itself, such as in plate 26, whose caption simply states, "One cannot look at this" (Figure I.3).

POSTEA quidam faber tyrius nomine phefarfemenos hac rati-
one;& inuentione inductus malo ſtatuto 'ex eo alterum tranſuerſũ
uti trutinam ſuſpendit xt in reducendo & implendo uenientibus
plagis deiecit Gaditanorum murum.

Figure I.2   Robertus Valturius, from *De Re Militari*, 1472.

Figure I.3 Francisco Goya, "One cannot look at this," plate 26, *The Disasters of War,* 1810s, published 1863. (Image courtesy of Dover Publications.)

A new category of artist-reporter essentially developed in relation to war, in particular the Crimean War (1853–1856). This was despite the fact that war photography, such as that of Roger Fenton, considered one of the first war photographers, was also developing during the Crimean War, as well as during the American Civil War.[23] The role of the artist-reporter arose in periodicals in the 1840s, a time when, as Paul Hogarth argues, "the new picture papers were . . . providing artists with their biggest audience since the Middle Ages."[24] Later, avant-garde experiment following the devastation of World War I, by figures such as George Grosz and Otto Dix, offered new idioms for reporting in a spate of new publications. Dix, who had been a machine gunner in the war, produced the disturbing series of fifty etchings *Der Krieg* (*The War*) in 1924, modeled after Goya. And in the specific context of the emergence of comics as a commercial form—which happened close to the turn of the twentieth century in sensational American newspapers—war played a defining role. The history of the Spanish-American War, often referred to as the first press war, is deeply imbricated with the history of comics. In the earliest years of comics, the conventions of the form were being laid down in Joseph Pulitzer's *New York World* and William Randolph Hearst's *New York Journal*, among other papers; comic strips were a circulation booster as Pulitzer and Hearst sought to claim new, largely immigrant readers. What is widely recognized as the first American comics work, Richard Felton Outcault's *The Yellow Kid* (or *Hogan's Alley*), appeared in 1895 in the *New York World*; Hearst soon stole the cartoonist away from Pulitzer, giving rise to the term "yellow journalism."

This is a period in which the appearance of comics in newspapers, taking on a range of genres, was developing concurrently with the press itself in reporting war, and reporting it visually, displaying its graphic information.[25] Hearst sent Frederic Remington to Cuba to sketch the rebellion against Spain's colonial rule. After Remington had telegraphed his boss in 1897, "Everything is quiet. There is no trouble here. There will be no war. I wish to return," Hearst is alleged to have instructed the artist, "Please remain. You furnish the pictures, and I'll furnish the war." This famous exchange, first reported in 1901, and even referenced in *Citizen Kane* but never verified, has been most recently debunked by Joseph Campbell; whether or not it happened, the sentiment it expresses is a valid and instructive description of the times and the importance of warfare for this emerging documentary medium.[26] Conventional comic strips and cartoons were being formed in their earliest years on newspaper pages together with visual—and sensational—war reportage. An 1898 editorial cartoon from the caricature periodical *Vim* even critiques Pulitzer and Hearst by portraying them both as the Yellow Kid, in his yellow nightshirt, tussling over building blocks that spell "WAR" (Figure I.4). At every corner of its history, comics, or its antecedents, takes shape in conversation with war.

During World War II, fictional comics in the form of comic books, a format that began in 1929 as bound, floppy commercial inserts, were at an all-time high, selling at one point 15 million copies a week. It is worth noting that plenty of fictional comics arose explicitly in the context of the war; comic books dominated by genre conventions strove to incorporate history into their plotlines.[27] In a famous example, the cover of the

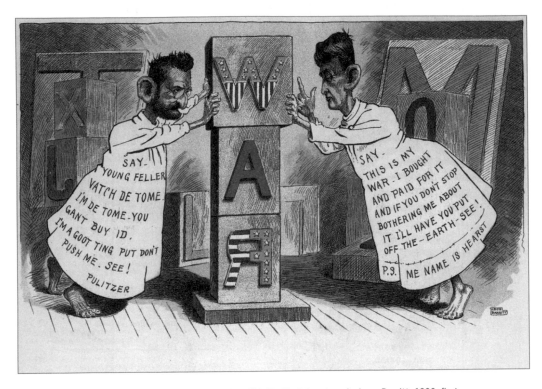

Figure I.4 "The Big Type War of the Yellow Kids," editorial cartoon by Leon Barritt, 1898, first published in *Vim* magazine, vol. 1, #2.

March 1941 issue of *Captain America* shows the titular hero punching Hitler in the jaw after raiding Nazi headquarters. (This image is the inspiration, in part, for Michael Chabon's 2000 novel *The Amazing Adventures of Kavalier and Clay*.) This kind of superheroic take on World War II history lasted for decades, as we also see in stories such as the 1968 *Sgt. Fury* title "Triumph at Treblinka!," whose cover pictures prisoners lined up behind a concentration camp barbed-wire fence. There was also a whole spate of comics grappling with mushroom cloud imagery, like the *Action Comics* issue from 1946 that shows Superman hovering in the air, filming an atom bomb test, which is pictured exploding with a huge red and white mushroom cloud spanning the cover's height (Figure I.5). Comics had

Figure I.5 *Action Comics*, #101, October 1946. Cover by Stan Kaye and Wayne Boring. (From: "Action Comics" #101 © DC Comics.)

been for decades focusing on nuclear futures; as Ferenc Morton Szasz points out, in August 1945 American papers noted that the atomic bomb felt like the comics coming true.[28] And, less explicitly but perhaps no less forcefully, as Spiegelman has suggested, we might consider the EC horror comics that bloomed in the 1950s as a secular American Jewish response to Auschwitz—as in the gory 1953 *Vault of Horror* issue whose cover depicts passengers on a subway staring at a disembodied arm and hand gripping a hanging strap (Figure I.6).

It is striking that there were so many comics about the war that sought to engage deadly serious subject matter.[29] And it is particularly striking that many of these images, like Superman filming an atomic bomb and subway passengers gaping at a detached hand, are actually themselves about the act of witnessing. The desire to grapple with the war through images was powerful and inchoate, and many works engaged iconography obsessively but history indirectly. It was not until 1972 that comics itself became a form for witnessing in any kind of nonfiction context. (Japanese American artist Miné Okubo's *Citizen 13660*, a 1946 narrative about her experiences in internment camps that was illustrated with pen-and-ink sketches, is one among many important precursors.) In the case of Spiegelman and Nakazawa, the obliteration wreaked by World War II, which each of them approached from a different cultural starting point, led to a new phase in the creation of visual-verbal forms of witness. And if, as critics and Spiegelman himself have pointed out, there would be no "Maus" without cartoonist Justin Green's inaugural American comics autobiography *Binky Brown Meets the Holy Virgin Mary* (from earlier in 1972), I argue there would also be no "Maus" without survivor Paladij Osynka's 1946 hand-drawn pamphlet *Auschwitz: Album of a Political Prisoner*, which Spiegelman's mother, Anja, a survivor of Auschwitz, brought from Poland to Sweden to the United States after the war. It is exactly these traditions of drawn witnessing, seen in postwar pamphlets and other survivor—and nonsurvivor—art, that opened up the creation of today's comics field.[30]

Framing Documentary

I am interested in comics as a visual-verbal narrative documentary form, one that, significantly, is also a print form, trafficking in the presentation of the stationary framed image (and perhaps in that way akin to

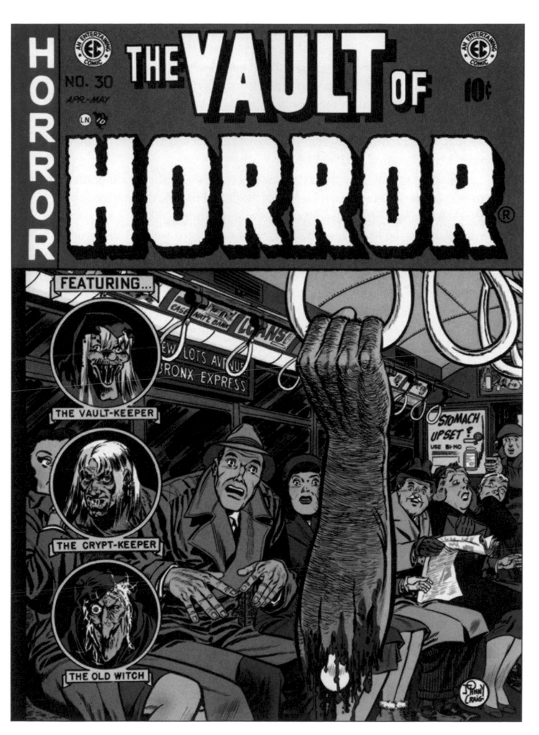

Figure I.6   EC Comics, *Vault of Horror,* vol. 1, #30, April 1953. Cover by Johnny Craig. (Copyright ©
1953 William M. Gaines, Agent, Inc., reprinted with permission. All rights reserved.)

photojournalism). Comics is composed in hand-drawn frames that exist in meaningful fixed spatial relation to each other: they are typically juxtaposed on the page in between strips of space known as the "gutter." The gutter is where readers project causality from frame to frame; comics, then, is at once static and animate. It paradoxically suggests stillness (the framed moment inscribed in space on the page) and movement (as the viewer animates the relationship between the frames that indicate time to create the sequential narrative meaning of the page).

This level of engagement is the reason that Marshall McLuhan named comics, which he designated "a highly participational form of expression," a cool medium in his classic *Understanding Media* (1964); this is also the reason narratologist Seymour Chatman takes up comics in his own classic *Story and Discourse* (1978), in which he demonstrates how comics reading is a kind of "reading out," as opposed to ordinary reading, because it "[leaves] the burden of inference to the reader."[31] In *Disaster Drawn* I discuss the specific relation of documentary and witnessing to drawing—which itself presents a kind of animation, even without the multiplication of frames; as renowned South African artist William Kentridge explains, "I see drawing as inherently animated."[32] I also address the unique and related grammar of comics, which addresses itself to the concerns of documentary in its most fundamental syntactical operation, of framing moments of time and mapping bodies in space.

In its multiplicity of juxtaposed frames on the page, comics operates differently from other documentary images in print, such as the single, information-dense or evocative photograph, or even photo essay, conventionally delivered by photojournalism. Do more frames indicate more evidence? Comics, with its proliferation of frames, suggests plenitude. In this sense, comics is about the fullness of what can be crammed into the frame to display. Spiegelman compares the work of creating comics panels with being taught to pack an emergency suitcase by his Auschwitz-survivor father: comics can be about packing the space of the panel as tightly as possible.[33] We see the power of marking out sequence to present the density and accumulation of evidence, especially evidence of horror, in famous works of visual-verbal art that remain influential for cartoonists: Callot's seventeenth-century *Miseries of War,* and Goya's nineteenth-century *Disasters of War,* both of which I analyze in Chapter 1. These foundational works about seeing trauma are, it is important to note, series.

But comics further inscribes the logic and practice of seriality on every page in its most basic narrative procedure.

In this, as with other features of its form, comics establishes itself suggestively as a rich location for the work of documentation, always calling attention to the relationship of part to whole, to the self-conscious buildup of information that may or may not coalesce into meaning. For if comics is a form about presence, it is also stippled with erasure—in the interruption provided by the ambiguous spaces of the gutter, its spaces of pause. My interest in comics is motivated in part by how these works push on conceptions of the unrepresentable and the unimaginable that have become commonplace in discourse about trauma—what W. J. T. Mitchell calls "trauma theory's cult of the unrepresentable."[34] Movingly, unflinchingly, comics works document, display, furnish. They engage the difficulty of spectacle instead of turning away from it. They risk representation. They also refigure representation, in Peter Galison and Lorraine Daston's sense of the contemporary movement from representation to presentation—the shift from "image-as-representation to image-as-process."[35] Comics is about contingent display, materially and philosophically. It weaves what I think of as interstice and interval into its constitutive grammar, and it provokes the participation of readers in those interpretive spaces that are paradoxically full and empty. To the extent that comics's formal proportions put into play what we might think of as the unresolvable interplay of elements of absence and presence, we could understand the gutter space of comics to suggest a psychic order outside of the realm of symbolization—and therefore, perhaps, a kind of Lacanian Real.[36] Comics openly eschews any aesthetic of transparency; it is a conspicuously artificial form.

As I have suggested before, while all media do the work of framing, comics manifests material frames—and the absences between them. It thereby literalizes on the page the work of framing and making, and also what framing excludes.[37] While it has become commonplace to identify and praise a work's self-reflexivity, the textual feature of self-reflexivity is not necessarily a value in and of itself. Comics offers attention both to the creation of evidence and to what is outside the frame. It invokes visual efficacy *and* limitation, creating dynamic texts inclined to express the layered horizon of history implied by "documentary." Stella Bruzzi suggests that documentaries are "performative acts" and that a documentary is constituted by "results of the collision between apparatus and subject."[38] The self-reflexive awareness of apparatus—drawing—is definitional to comics form. Its hand-drawn enclosures create diegetic space. And while the form, which rejects the verisimilitude of mechanical objectivity and presents in turn a succession of little drawn boxes, reveals its own process of making, it is also forcefully invested in detailed documentation—of place, of duration, of perspective, of material specificity, of embodiment. That is to say, while comics is a form that is constantly aware of its own mediation, that is by no means the most interesting aspect of its form. Rather, what is most interesting is *how* it displays, inscribes, and marks.

Maus, for instance, troubles the link between the traditionally conceived categories of documentation and artistic practice in particularly obvious ways because of the visual abstraction of its animal metaphor. As Marianne Hirsch's important 1993 essay "Family Pictures" demonstrates, comics can raise the question of how "to produce a more permeable and multiple text . . . that definitively [erases] any clear cut distinction between the documentary and the aesthetic." (Hirsch first developed her widely influential and generative concept of "postmemory," now canonical in trauma studies, in relation to *Maus*.)[39] While Hirsch sees that critical discourse on the Holocaust in its aftermath resulted in renewed effort to distinguish between "documentary" and "aesthetic" forms, this tension existed earlier; it was distinctly in play during the period in which "documentary" gained force as a concept, as we see in James Agee's famous injunction in 1941's *Let Us Now Praise Famous Men:* "In God's name don't think of it as Art."[40]

My sense of documentary, sympathetic with Bruzzi's definition although not encompassed by it, is that documentary operates as a set of practices that is about and instantiates the presentation of evidence. As Lisa Gitelman points out, documenting is "an epistemic practice: the kind of knowing that is all wrapped up with showing, and showing wrapped with knowing."[41] Stott, who notes that documentary can take shape in any medium, calls it "a genre of actuality."[42] John Berger's comments are instructive here in understanding how comics functions as documentary: of a Vermeer painting of Delft, he writes it has "*a plentitude of actuality*," although one ought not suppose "this has to do with accuracy: Delft at any moment never looked like this painting. It has to do with the density per square millimeter of Vermeer's looking, the density per square millimeter of assembled moments."[43] If we can consider documentary, then, along these lines as a set of evidential practices and a genre of actuality (or, as John Grierson famously suggested in the early 1930s, "the creative treatment of actuality"), it is my assertion that comics is currently expanding its reach, range, and depth.[44]

Stott's first chapter opens with the following epigraph: "*Documentary . . .* pertaining to, consisting of, or derived from documents."[45] This description usefully points to a functional description of documents themselves. Stott begins his book by identifying two kinds of documents: "official" and "human," with the latter being "the opposite of the official kind," offering a method of "[dramatizing] the human consequences of a few facts."[46] The *Oxford English Dictionary*'s primary definition of *documentary* is similar: "Of the nature of or consisting in documents." The second common definition listed here allows *documentary* less range than Stott does: while he mentions its manifestation "in film, photograph, writing, broadcast, or art," the *OED* specifies "a film or literary work" for the adjective form, and adds "broadcast" to the list of two in the noun form. *Document*, however, has a capacious definition that invokes a range of media and materials: its current *OED* usage is "something written, inscribed, etc., which furnishes evidence or information upon any subject, as a manuscript, title-deed, tomb-stone, coin, picture, etc." Francis Wharton's *Law of Evidence* from 1877 appears as an example: "A 'document' is an instrument on which is recorded, by means of letters, figures, or marks, matter which may be evidentially used."

Through marks, comics is a form that is able to combine both official and human documents. We see this in works heavily driven by reconstituting archives, such as Alison Bechdel's *Fun Home: A Family Tragicomic* (2006) and, as I will discuss here, Spiegelman's *Maus* and Sacco's *Footnotes in Gaza*. (The most important page of this last, bearing the title "Document," palimpsests those that are both "official" and "human.") And while *Maus* is on every level about presenting archives, it is also, in its function as a "human document," about the concomitant absence of archives—a whole line of Spiegelman's family who were obliterated, along with their effects, in the Holocaust. Spiegelman formulates his work and Sacco's, in a description apposite to Stott's above, as invested in "showing a fractal."[47]

Comics, Photography, Film

Comics, both in its autographic aspect and in its constant juxtaposition of word and image, reveals a form that takes up the problem of reference as central. In recent times it has been more typical to think of "documentary" practices as what can be generated by "mechanical objectivity"—or otherwise by prose, a system of recording and communication that is ideographic like drawing but is seen to be more transparently true than drawing, so evidently a trace of the body of the drawer. A comics text has a different relationship to indexicality than, for instance, a photograph does. Marks made on paper by hand are an index of the body in a way that a photograph, "taken" through a lens, is not. Galison and Daston point out how "objectivity," a fully historical, nineteenth-century category, is understood to be the removal of constraints such as the "personal." We see this, for instance, in André Bazin's famous 1945 essay "Ontology of the Photographic Image," a foundation for his prominent later film criticism, which rejoices in the idea: "All art is founded on human agency, but in photography alone can we celebrate its absence."[48]

Conversely, drawing's connection to "reality" is perceived as immeasurably weaker than the photograph's, which is often understood to be an index of a certain truth because it possesses mechanical objectivity.[49] Bazin, for one, understands the mechanical image to ease a kind of burden of resemblance for painting, because in his view the object photographed and the image itself are ontologically equivalent, "like a fingerprint"; the image shares in the being of the model.[50] While recent readings of Bazin have suggested a more flexible belief in porous realisms based on an actual tension between style and ontology, what his writing nevertheless provocatively brings to the foreground is the productive divide between what is captured with a lens and what is captured by hand.[51] Bazin's first footnote in "Ontology of the Photographic Image" addresses itself precisely to the topic of this book: he muses that it would be "interesting" to compare the rivalry in the illustrated press in the period 1890–1910 between photographic reportage (then in its infancy) and drawings. Noting the discursivity (and historicity) of different media platforms, Bazin observes that "the sense of the photograph as document emerged only gradually" and also that in France in the 1940s, because of "a degree of saturation," there was a return to drawing.[52]

In a 1975 essay on documentary and indexicality, Joel Snyder and Neil Walsh Allen warn, "The naïve belief that photography lies outside the sphere of other representations can lead to a misunderstanding of the 'documentary' questions we ought to ask."[53] There remains, however, a strong impulse to see the work of recording as happening transparently through the camera, as opposed to the pen.[54] Susan Sontag takes this on in *Re-*

garding the Pain of Others, a book about photography whose most celebrated figure is Goya. She does not find it odd that photographs such as
Alexander Gardner's were staged (in his Civil War album *Gardner's Photographic Sketch Book of the War*), but she does find it odd that people are
surprised and disappointed that they are staged.[55] Comics texts, on the other
hand, while many of them are deeply invested in the work of documentation, eliminate the question of "staging" entirely: they are evidently staged,
built, made images as opposed to "taken" ones. In Bazin's ontological arrangement, since photographs "achieve identity with the model" as painting
never can, painting, a defeated rival, is consequently enabled to fully "trans-
form itself into an object."[56] Comics, too, evidently is not a duplicative
form; its drawings may refer to reality, but they constitute their own separate functioning model. Comics calls attention to images as material objects and not just as representation.

Comics diverges from the more common documentary mediums of both
photography and film in its temporal dimension. Drawing, through its
manifestation of marks, as I will discuss further, offers its own kind of thicket
of time. Berger writes of drawing as "[forcing] us to stop and enter its time.
A photograph is static because it has stopped time. A drawing or painting
is static because it encompasses time."[57] In addition to the temporality implied by the act of drawing itself—which Berger suggests is about a quality
of *becoming* rather than *being*—comics is also, as I have noted, a form that
is characterized by its complex temporal and spatial features.[58] Through
its frame-gutter architecture, which implies duration and is also the basis
for many experiments with collapsing distinct temporal dimensions, comics
is about both stillness and movement, capture and narrative motion.

Like Berger, Roland Barthes, in his famous *Camera Lucida*, writes of the
frozenness of the photograph, which he suggests aligns it with death.
(Sontag similarly writes of the "embalmingness" and "foreverness" of photography.) Unlike the cinema, the photograph represents "Time's immobi-
lization" and arrest, and hence its "strange stasis": it is "*without a future*
(this is its pathos, its melancholy); in it, no protensity."[59] And while cinema
is protensive—is about duration—and is not "motionless" in the way of the
photograph, its feature of controlling time and pace for the viewer, as a
medium that exists for its audience *in time*, makes it categorically different
from comics, a form in which the reader controls the pace of reading, looking
at images, and assembling sequence. Comics traffics in time and duration,
creating temporalities, and often smashing or imbricating temporalities on

the page, but it is not a time-based medium, one that has duration as a fixed dimension.[60] The film theorist and historian Tom Gunning, writing in a special issue of *Critical Inquiry* on comics and media, sees that while "the art and concept of animation always shadows the comics, the relation between them is hardly one of larva to butterfly, as if comics simply awaited the fullness of time and technology to deliver them from an unwilling immobility." Gunning writes that "the power of comics lies in their ability to derive movement from stillness—not to make the reader observe motion, but rather participate imaginatively in its genesis."[61]

Cartoonists cede the pace of consumption to the individual viewer—an issue of ethical significance when the work in question is visual and traumatic, as is all the work I analyze here. The freedom to control one's pace in comics presents an important distinction from film, in which, say, an image of death—something every cartoonist in this book includes—may either go by too quickly, obviating scrutiny and attention, or linger too long on the screen, forcing an uncomfortable (and even perhaps manipulatively so) confrontation for the viewer. Spiegelman discusses how cinema, along with theater, "straps the audience to a chair and hurtles you through time."[62]

Yet if the danger of the photograph is that it feels aoristic, and the danger of film is that it moves relentlessly, sweeping one along (which is, of course, part of its pleasure), comics is a form in which stillness and motion exist together. Barthes's essay "The Third Meaning," which is largely about filmmaker Sergei Eisenstein and the quality Barthes identifies as "the filmic," offers a remarkable footnote on comics (see Figure I.7).[63] Barthes notices that the form of comics in particular produces the "third meaning"—a level of meaning fruitfully "inarticulable" or "obtuse," which subverts not the content but rather "the whole practice of meaning."[64] The third meaning, writes Barthes, is "evident, erratic, obstinate." It is not "the message," nor is it symbolic, dramatic meaning; rather, it "exceeds the copy of the referential motif."[65] Barthes observes: "There are other 'arts,' which combine still (or at least drawing) and story, diegesis—namely the photo-novel and the comic-strip. I am convinced that these 'arts,' born in the lower depths of high culture, possess theoretical qualifications and present a new signifier. . . . This is acknowledged as regards the comic-strip. . . . There thus may be a future—or a very ancient past—truth in these derisory, vulgar, foolish, dialogical forms of consumer subculture."[66]

Elaborating on the art of the pictogram—what he calls "obtuse meanings placed in a diegetic space"—Barthes continues, identifying comics in

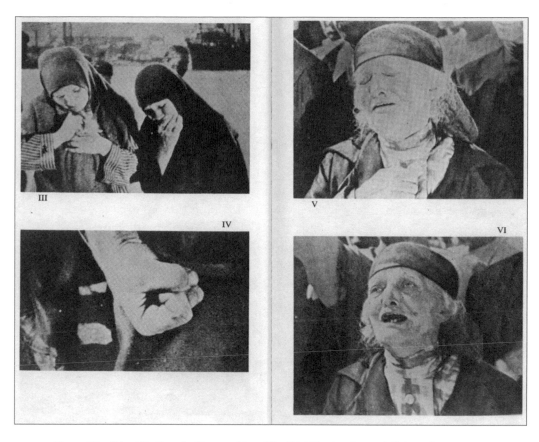

Figure I.7   Roland Barthes, double spread from "The Third Meaning: Research Notes on Some Eisenstein Stills," 1970. (Copyright Éditions du Seuil.)

a list of similarly constructed forms: "This art [is] taking place across historically and culturally heteroclite productions: ethnographic pictograms, stained glass windows, Carpaccio's *Legend of St. Ursula, images d'Epinal*, photo-novels, comic-strips."[67] The feature generative of comics's third meaning, and thus its ability to function as a "future" or "ancient past" truth, is its specific form of narrative movement: its combination of the still ("or at least drawing," as Barthes says above—but comics furnishes *both* in its drawn stills) and its unfolding diegesis. In particular, as I will discuss further, much of the language Barthes uses to express the third meaning, such as "useless expenditure," is apt to describe the gutter effect in comics.[68] The gutter is the space that keeps panels discrete (and hence still), but it is also the space that marks expenditure in opening up meaning infinitely without the possibility of closure. Writing in 1970, before any critical appreciation of comics in the U.S. academy, Barthes identifies comics as a form that opens up the field of meaning through its dual inscription and mobilization of time.[69]

Drawing History

With characteristic frankness, Michael Taussig points out the apparent conflict that undergirds Barthes's discussion in "The Third Meaning": Barthes's essay, subtitled "Research Notes on Some Eisenstein Stills," concerns "film stills, in other words a photograph ripped out of a stream of photographs making a moving picture. The still, [Barthes] asserts, is the truly filmic aspect of film (well, there's a contradiction for you)." This conflict at the heart of Barthes's essay is also at the heart of his brief strong claim for comics's potential. Taussig's contribution in *I Swear I Saw This: Drawings in Fieldwork Notebooks, Namely My Own*, one of the best recent books on drawing, is to focus intently on the difference that drawing creates for the third meaning—and for documentation as a general practice and witnessing as a specific one.[70]

In the drawn line itself, Taussig argues (unlike in a symbol that becomes timeless), images both flow and arrest: "Images that inhabit time—the recursive time of rereading—are historical, in a peculiar way. Being recursive, they flow with time yet also arrest it. . . . Chronology is grasped and analyzed in a spatial image, as with the tunnels and freeways of modernity, at once mythic and profane."[71] I am precisely interested in images that inhabit time, especially in endeavoring to document, to become a certain kind of "data," and even to testify. Taussig is keenly aware of drawing's demotion—aside from in the art world—in relation to reading and writing in Western culture, and he is intent on bringing it into fresh focus across a range of practices (including his own anthropological field notes).[72] Indeed, Kentridge, perhaps today's most globally acclaimed artist, claims *drawing* as his primary medium; he is known as a *drawer*.[73] The (re)appearance of comics today is part of a general renewed attention to the myriad registers of mark-making. But with some exceptions, including Sontag's *Regarding the Pain of Others* and Taussig's suggestive *I Swear I Saw This*, contemporary studies about documentation and witness have ignored the hand-drawn.[74] And the often compelling body of critical writing about contemporary drawing more generally, despite copious attention to, say, Kentridge as a mark-maker, has not incorporated attention to the conspicuous prominence of graphic narrative—it has not, as Taussig indicates, expanded outward from the art world. Critical insight on drawing has not often been applied to comics (and conversely, this writing has not been considered in the context of articulating the principles of this rigorously hand-drawn form). While Krauss notes in 2000 that the "joint presence of [Raymond] Pettibon and Kentridge within the art practice of the 1990s demonstrates . . . [t]he upsurge of the autographic, the handwrought, in an age of mechanization and technologizing of the image via either photography or digital imaging," it is striking that her account of the upsurge of drawing does not mention the conspicuously increasing field of comics.[75]

The subject of this book, at its most basic, is the relationship of drawing to history. What does it mean to draw history, to bear witness through the mark? What is the *difference* of narrative embodied as drawing, as marks on the page? In *The Body in Pain*, her 1985 book about torture as a structure of unmaking, Elaine Scarry also analyzes structures of making, particularly bodily creation and the production of the artifact. She identifies marking as the crucial and basic urgency of any culture to make. Comics is made up of marks (what Walter Benjamin calls the medium of the mark) and displays the impulse toward materiality and the made object.[76] Scarry writes that "a made object is a projection of the human body" and that artifacts—marks, for instance—might most accurately be perceived as a "making sentient of the external world," as themselves "a materialization of perception."[77]

Materializing

There is one particular aspect of drawing—of comics—that I never fail to find fascinating, and which accounts in large part for my interest in the form. It is articulated by Spiegelman in what remains one of the most compelling academic essays on *Maus*. Writing in a history journal about *Maus* as "a work of history" that is "about the presentation of history," Joshua Brown cites Spiegelman's use of the verb *materialize*. Brown's brief series of sentences caught my awareness immediately: "Consider the challenge Spiegelman faced. He had to 'materialize' Vladek's words and descriptions, transforming them into comprehensible images."[78] Later, while editing

Figure I.8   Philip Guston, with Clark Coolidge, 1972. From *Baffling Means: Writings/Drawings by Clark Coolidge and Philip Guston*, Stockbridge, MA, o•blek editions, 1991. (Used by permission of Clark Coolidge and Peter Gizzi.)

MetaMaus (the book Spiegelman and I collaborated on, about the aesthetic, historical, and family research that went into the thirteen-year process of making *Maus*, his Pulitzer Prize–winning book about the Holocaust), I found one of Spiegelman's unpublished notes about *Maus* that worries about creating his father's experiences in visual form, comparing the process of drawing his father's history—bringing it into a material form on the page—to creating material for a suit. What does it mean to materialize history? What does it mean to mark out of a desire to render history concrete? Kentridge has repeatedly discussed the internal projection of a single mark, its quality of animation and movement. He asserts of drawing, "I have come to think of drawing as a form of projection. So it isn't really a matter of making drawings of things in preparation for something else, but of *making drawing literally into other things*."[79] Clark Coolidge and Philip Guston put it another way in one of their collaborative poem-pictures:

"To draw is to make be" (Figure I.8).[80] Drawing is not just mimetic: it is its own artifact, substance, thing, phenomenology.

"Materializing" history through the work of marks on the page creates it as space and substance, gives it a corporeality, a physical shape—like a suit, perhaps, for an absent body, or to make evident the kind of space-time many bodies move in and move through; to make, in other words, the twisting lines of history legible through form. Berger writes, "Out of the artist's mind through the point of a pen or pencil comes proof that the world is solid, material. But the proof is never familiar."[81] W. J. T. Mitchell calls attention, as do other theorists of drawing such as J. Hillis Miller and Barthes, to the desire that inheres in making marks: "Drawing itself," Mitchell writes, "the dragging or pulling of the drawing instrument, is the performance of a desire. Drawing draws us on. Desire just *is*, quite literally, drawing, or *a* drawing—a pulling or attracting force, and the trace of this force in the picture."[82] Comics amplifies a feature Mitchell identifies as "the fundamental ontology of the image": the "dialectics of life and death, desire and aggression. . . . The Freudian fort-da game of appearance and disappearance, the endless shuttling between presence and absence, duck and rabbit [that] is constitutive of the image."[83] In the logic of boundedness it enacts through its frames, its boxed moments of time, comics traffics in the ascesis (dialectic of binding and unbinding) Mitchell attaches to a Deleuzian form of desire. But it also longs for an object in the terms he characterizes as Freudian, and it consistently expresses the propulsive structure that registers lack and longing.[84] Activating the past on the page, comics materializes the physically absent. It inscribes and concretizes, through the embodied labor of drawing, "the spatial charge of a presence," the tactile presence of line, the body of the medium.[85] The desire is to make the absent appear.

The compelling recent writing about drawing has largely been about figures like Kentridge and Pettibon and not about comics. But these visual artists and the contemporary cartoonists I write about here share figures such as Goya and William Hogarth as common inspiration, revealing how lineages of drawing today connect the work of the hand across differently marked spaces (Spiegelman calls comics a medium that "talks with its hands").[86] Describing his influences, Kentridge explains that Goya and Hogarth "had engaged drawing and printmaking as singularly important and valid media. They employed what many people think of as intimate and supplementary media to make significant statements, not just formally but politically."[87] These two artists, along with William Blake, have provided the explicit inspiration for many, if not all, of the contemporary cartoonists I analyze. All three of these figures were invested in some way, as I will discuss further, in what Benjamin Buchloh calls "a type of drawing that could be defined as both communicative and reproducible."[88] And all three created word-and-image works that are connected—especially in Goya's case, but demonstrably with each one—in forms of witness.

Discussing concentration camp survivor drawings and surviving art from World War II, Spiegelman observes: "Those drawings were a return to drawing not for its possibilities of imposing the self, of finding a new role for art and drawing after the invention of the camera, but rather a return to the earlier function that drawing served before the camera—a kind of commemorating, witnessing, and recording of information—what Goya referred to when he says, 'This I saw.'"[89] Spiegelman here refers to one of Goya's most famous prints from *The Disasters of War*—which has come to stand in for the project of the entire series—whose caption simply reads "I saw it" (#44). This etching features fleeing citizens, including a woman and a small child in the right foreground, who look fearfully, their faces frozen with terror, toward a coming force that is out of the frame. Drawing is laced with urgency to communicate. In *Regarding the Pain of Others*, about the history of images of atrocity, Sontag barely has a single compliment to dispense, as I mentioned, until she gets to Goya roughly fifty pages in. The handmade aspect of his *Disasters of War* etchings, in her view, constitutes their power, as against what she wants us to recognize today as the "camera-mediated knowledge of war," which weakens war's force for her.[90]

Sontag's appreciation of Goya's series of war images lies in how they bear witness to atrocities perpetrated by French soldiers in Spain—by, in her opinion, eliciting responsiveness, by assaulting the viewer, by inviting one to look while signaling the difficulty of looking. She critiques the notion that only "photographs, unlike handmade images, can count as evidence." ("Evidence of what?" she asks, questioning this legal structure and the commonplace view of photography as "a transparency of something that happened.")[91] *Disaster Drawn* raises the question of what it means to witness in drawings, and why witnessing takes this shape.

Witness, Reference, Presence

"Witness," like "documentary," is a concept with a history that has been used in different ways by many different people, and is today sometimes taken for granted. *Witness* in the barest-bones *OED* sense of the term means "attestation of a fact, event, or statement." While *Disaster Drawn* is indubitably about witnessing trauma, it does not posit that witnessing must be determined by trauma. Nakazawa, Spiegelman, and Sacco all bear witness, in distinct ways, to extraordinary and devastating wartime events—to take Nakazawa's case, the dropping of the atomic bomb on Hiroshima in August 1945. However, while their works are driven by such traumatic events, these events are not isolated; their works also bear witness through words and images to the everyday—to the ordinary and to the scenes of enunciation that produce the acts of witness. These are works in which the objects of witness operate on scales both large and small. Motivated by crisis, they bear witness to lived experience that is often shaped by crisis but is not necessarily fully dictated by it. Nakazawa's work, for example, is highly attuned to the rhythms of daily family life both before and after the bomb. These are also works focused on different kinds of witnessing: being a witness to oneself, a witness to the testimony of others, a witness to the process of witnessing. Joe Sacco's drawings, for instance, make us take stock of the research ritual as part of his own acts of bearing witness to the experience of others. The idea behind witnessing is the attestation of truth, even if that truth, as many have discussed in trauma studies, is elusive or "unclaimed."[92]

Witnessing, in my account, then, is not necessarily didactic. The photographer Gilles Peress, speaking at a symposium on memory, recently posited that when photography is done right, it does not fall into the category of "bearing witness," for propaganda is not as interesting as images.[93] I am sympathetic to Peress's weariness around conventional notions of "bearing witness" that suggest the transparency of images and their polemical truth-value, as opposed to work with a deeper aesthetic valence whose images are allowed their ambiguity, and their nonideological desire, as images. Unlike Peress, however, I do not shy away from the category of "bearing witness." Acts of eyewitnessing that find testimonial form in comics, or acts of bearing witness to the experiences of others in comics, are rarely accorded the transparency that photographs are. And they are always operating with what

Peress identifies as the essential interestingness of images that are not predictable.

The contemporary figure of the witness emerged as a social force around the trial of Adolf Eichmann in 1961, an event for which 111 witnesses testified in court in Jerusalem with a global audio and television audience. Annette Wieviorka identifies this moment as "the advent of the witness."[94] Hannah Arendt and others criticized the organization of the Eichmann trial—for which the prosecutor carefully prescreened and selected witnesses from hundreds and hundreds of people who wanted to testify—for its overdetermination and its presentation of witnesses not directly related to Eichmann's crimes. The works I analyze here operate in an extrajuridical realm. They are not invested in a statutory conception of rights, or, for that matter, in lobbying for justice—they are invested in a *narrative* elaboration of witnessing that unfolds conflicts and interpretations, and probes their particular human effects through soliciting testimony and communicating its dialogical contours. Although its attention to the globally disenfranchised may seem to rhyme with current human rights discourse, Sacco's work is not about a vocabulary of rights.[95] In Sacco's work one registers a kind of *haunting* by the other that does not end, that cannot be accounted for by rights talk.[96]

My interest in how witnessing operates, then, is more closely related to Taussig's, when he writes—of a drawing he made of people sewing themselves into a bag in a tunnel in Medellín, Colombia—that "to witness . . . is that which refuses, if only for an instant, to blink an eye."[97] In Taussig's account, the act of witness gains power as witnessing the shock of shocking things passing from horror into banality; to witness is to arrest this transformation, even momentarily, in drawing. An artist such as Sacco is doing connected work: showing us the everydayness of horror, and trying to turn the banality itself back into something horrific.

Asserting the connection between witnessing and drawing, Taussig writes: "The drawing got drawn as if I needed not only to swear to the veracity—this *did* happen, this *is* the truth—but needed to make an image so as to double the act of seeing with one's own eyes. . . . Doubling the image through drawing, stroke by stroke, erasure by erasure, amounts to a laborious seeing. Eye and memory are painstakingly exercised or at least exercised in new ways. History is repeated in slow motion and the clumsiness of the artist adds to this *seeing seeing*."[98] In tracing the connection between seeing and drawing as a doubled, duplicative process that calls attention to the work of vision and memory, Berger's comments are similar: "To draw is to look, examining the structure of appearances. A drawing of a tree shows, not a tree, but a tree-being-looked-at. . . . This is how the act of drawing refuses the process of disappearances and proposes the simultaneity of a multitude of moments."[99] The form of drawing in these accounts is revealed as apposite to acts of witnessing, to testimonial form. These features—what Taussig calls the quality of *seeing seeing*, present even when the artist is not clumsy—are related to what Viktor Shklovsky, writing in 1925, named the fundamental device of art: permitting a "new seeing" of reality instead of mere "recognizing" or "acknowledging."[100] Through their wide range of aesthetic experiments with word and image, mark and line, comics sets new terms for visual-verbal reports, accounts, and histories. Driven by the urgencies of re-seeing the war in acts of witness, comics proposes an ethics of looking and reading intent on defamiliarizing standard or received images of history while yet aiming to communicate and circulate. Comics picks up steam as this new seeing at every turn in its history, but with particular force after World War II and the broad silence that surrounded the war in America and in Japan.

Scholars across many fields, but especially those attuned to witness and trauma, are frequently concerned with spectacle and spectacularization. When a work is praised, it is often in the context of its avoiding or sidestepping spectacle, as in Krauss's positive concluding assessment of Kentridge's work that it "attempts to undermine a certain kind of spectacularization of memory."[101] Some even want to define witnessing itself as against a certain kind of spectacle: Wendy Kozol writes of how "scholars often define witnessing as politically engaged practices distinct from media portrayals characterized by a focus on violent spectacle." Such claims, Kozol points out, "presume that a spectator gazes passively at violence, whereas a witness undertakes an ethical look that mobilizes the viewer's sense of responsibility."[102] While I am interested in the productive power of witnessing, I do not believe that witnessing must have an ethical value—nor do I believe that "spectacle" ought always to be avoided. Jacques Rancière puts it well when he advocates for the role of the new "emancipated spectator" who rejects the opposition of viewing and acting. Sontag reserves one of her iciest comments for famous critics of spectacle such as Guy Debord. She writes, "To speak of reality becoming a spectacle is a breath-taking provincialism. . . . It has become a cliché of the cosmopolitan discussion of images of atrocity to assume they have little effect, and that there is something innately cynical about their diffusion."[103]

The works I treat here face and engage spectacle and presence, neither attaching themselves pruriently to spectacle nor avoiding it. Brief attention to a paradigmatic debate that centers on the portrayal of traumatic history in film clarifies how, in turn, the drawn medium of comics mobilizes the visual work of witness. Today's two most famous verbal-visual texts—aside from *Maus*—that represent Holocaust history are Steven Spielberg's fictionalized Hollywood narrative *Schindler's List* (1993) and Frenchman Claude Lanzmann's independent nine-and-a-half-hour documentary *Shoah* (1985).[104] *Schindler's List* is most profoundly disparaged for its representational indulgence in images.[105] On the other hand, it is common to heap praise on *Shoah*, a film honored by many, as Shoshana Felman puts it, as "more than the film event of the century . . . not simply a film, but a truly revolutionary artistic and cultural event."[106] Lanzmann, among many others, represents today's dominant mode of theorizing trauma; he formulates his ethical "refusal of understanding" as a "blindness."[107]

In contrast, not only are the hand-drawn texts of witness this book examines explicitly driven by the desire to understand (even if they recognize and even foreground how the project of understanding is not fully possible), but they also involve—thematically and formally—what Caruth calls "literal seeing." Miriam Hansen adroitly questions the cultural bases for evaluating the two films in the essay "*Schindler's List* Is Not *Shoah*." *Maus*, I would like to add, is not *Shoah* either. *Maus* transvalues the putatively exclusive categories of "presence" (criticized in *Schindler's List*) and "absence" (praised in *Shoah*). In so doing, it travels beyond, in Andreas Huyssen's words, the now "rather confining issue of how to represent the Holocaust 'properly'"—and here, I would add, how to express traumatic history generally—"or how to avoid aestheticizing it." All of the works in *Disaster Drawn* dare to explicitly "bank" on the power of images.[108]

Drawn texts of witness complicate, and perhaps even integrate, the opposing aesthetic agendas that Hansen also aims to refigure.[109] In Hansen's argument, the elitist critique of *Schindler's List*—a narrative that does not seek to negate the power of the representational—"reduces the dialectics of the problem of representing the unrepresentable to a binary opposition of showing or not showing—rather than casting it, as one might, as an issue of competing representations and competing modes of representation."[110]

This assessment is directly relevant to the works of visual witness this book engages. Like the popular *Schindler's List*, *Maus* represents horror. Unlike *Schindler's List*, a classical Hollywood film in the realist tradition, *Maus*, in its experimental comics form, develops a unique idiom for representation (even as it exploits and draws on genre material, including references to popular film and Disney comics). Spiegelman, Nakazawa, and Sacco's texts work in the space of the popular, yet they reject the verisimilitude that constitutes the agenda of popular film. Operating in between the poles that Spielberg and Lanzmann represent on the cultural and aesthetic spectrum, these works of witness eschew the seamlessness that has been criticized in popular narratives such as *Schindler's List*, while they also eschew the obsession with invisibility and unrepresentability that characterizes such lauded avant-garde films as *Shoah*.

Disaster Drawn suggests that comics has peculiar connection to expressing trauma—that there are potent reasons acts of witnessing and testimony are created and find shape in this form. Felman, who focuses in *Testimony* on the imbrication of politics and form, is correct to point out that for works that represent traumatic history, the context of the text must be part of the *reading* of the text. She writes that her project is to analyze "how issues of biography and history are neither simply reflected, but are reinscribed, translated, radically rethought and fundamentally worked over by the text." Felman, then, in a formulation crucial for how this book chooses to focus on traumatic history, identifies the most compelling work of a text as its "textualization of the context." She explains: "The empirical content needs not just to be *known*, but to be *read*. . . . The basic and legitimate demand for *contextualization of the text* itself needs to be complemented, simultaneously, by the less familiar and yet necessary work of *textualization of the context*."[111] Graphic narratives accomplish this work with their basic hand-drawn grammar—frames, gutters, lines, borders—rendering this textualization graphically, conspicuously manifest.

The parameters of disputes about trauma and form provoked by the Holocaust reverberate widely to this day and shape how the figure of witness has developed (along with concomitant issues of creativity and address). Felman links a work's textualization of its context to Adorno's demand in *Negative Dialectics*—in the section titled "After Auschwitz"—for "thinking that thinks against itself," asserting that in Adorno's "radical conception, it is, however, not . . . simply lyric poetry as a genre, but all of thinking, all of writing that has now to think, to write *against itself*."[112] Further, as Felman and others have pointed out, it is Adorno's revision of his famous dictum, in his later "Commitment," that is valuable as a hermeneutic: "I have no wish to soften the saying that to write poetry after Auschwitz is barbaric," Adorno maintains. "But [Hans Magnus] Enzensberger's retort also remains true, that literature must resist this verdict." In struggling against the verdict, literature must struggle against itself—formally, textually, and aesthetically. Adorno, then, invests hope and responsibility in "the uncompromising radicalism of . . . the very features defamed as formalism."[113]

This challenge to literature to struggle not despite but even through its "formalism" not only is demonstrated legibly in graphic narrative texts but also accounts for why the doubled, multiply layered form of comics has become the site of so much wrestling with history. Like Felman, I am interested in works of art writing against themselves—what Adorno in "Commitment" affirms as art's *inscription* of politics, its textual resistance to his own earlier verdict. "Inscription" is writ large in comics. The comics form is poised to make an intervention in literary and historical fields because its formal possibilities are so rich as to be able to accommodate, and even redefine, this doubled act of narration and expression suggested by writing writing against itself. This is evident in how the authors deploy divergent styles, revealing how the question of style functions not as a mere representational register but as a narrative and political choice. This is also evident in how the authors embrace textual collision between styles, codes, and narrative modes, foregrounding and problematizing reference and transparency. And it is evident in how comics mobilizes verbal and visual discourses, as well as in how it makes readers aware of the space *between* word and image.[114]

The composition of comics in words and images lends itself to witness and testimony, a form that "seems to be composed of . . . events in excess of our frames of reference."[115] The hybrid form of comics, then, engages presence in active and important ways, while also leaving itself open to the provisional, partial, and disjunct. Comics's word-and-image hybridity, as I have written elsewhere, is clarified by Lyotard's notion of the *différend*: necessarily set into play by the nonunity of language, the *différend* represents the impossibility of bridging incommensurate discourses.[116] Taussig, for one, notes of the text-image interchange that "this twofold, generative character of complementary opposites expresses itself *as an act of bearing witness*."[117] Comics form moves along the axis of this generative friction. The issues of taxonomy, classification, and reference that comics pressurizes are a register not only of documentary innovation (and its attendant epistemological inquiry) but also of the complexity of witnessing and the forms that shape its iteration. The spatial features of comics, such as its activation of the space between word and image and its erection of literal drawn frames alongside its breaking and violation of them, presents a grammar that can inscribe trauma not just thematically (as in Adorno's "helpless poems to victims of our time") but also powerfully at the level of textualization in words and images. We see this, to name one instance, in the element of comics known as the gutter.

The Gutter

Comics's gutter is a feature Scott McCloud claims is not duplicated in any other form.[118] This blank space, which translates as *blanc* in its French usage, is constitutive of comics logic and grammar. It is where a reader, conventionally, projects causality, and where the division of time in comics is marked, providing a constant source of tension, a constant proffering of the unmarked in spaces that are carefully bounded and marked out. At the heart of the attention to the gutter is the fact of its *constitutive* absence. It is not merely like a seam or a margin (although it bleeds out into margins often, suggesting a kind of narrative ceaselessness, an unendingness); rather, its present blankness, often implying duration, is laid out for readers as part of the narrative encounter. Taussig writes of what he calls drawing's ability to "hold the communicable in fruitful tension with the incommunicable," a feature that also constitutes the frame-gutter dynamic that creates comics form.[119] The gutter might be, as I earlier suggested, the figuration of a psychic order outside of the realm of symbolization, a space that refuses to resolve the interplay of elements of absence and presence. One can also understand the space-time of the gutter as Henri Bergson's unquantifiable *durée*, an experience of the ineffable. The gutter could be understood as a breath (a notion suggested to me by a musicologist colleague), a pause that conditions, or is disruptive of, the parts that make a crafted sound. Thinking of architecture, one might conceive the gutter as the space in between walls.[120]

The gutter is both a space of stillness—a stoppage in the action, a gap—and a space of movement: it is where, in a sense, the reader makes the passage of time in comics happen. Kentridge explains that "the perfect point" for him and many visual artists "is that point between stillness and movement." The gutter is certainly this point, both literally still and possibly a space of movement, often a gesture to experience interval between frames of presence.[121] (The gutter could also leave one spiraling out into endless duration.) And the gutter, to return to the notion of form struggling against itself, is a thread of erasure inscribed in a sequence of repletion. Comics texts can capture, can textualize, the context of bearing witness to trauma, the context of an articulation that also carries its own inchoate parallel, its own inarticulate shadow. "Erasure and the traces it leaves are about the passage of time, and hence about memory," as Kentridge points out. His comments on erasure and drawing reveal a feature that is built into the structural form of comics, and which the gutter makes legible across comics pages: "The image comes as much from what I'm taking away as what I'm putting down," he says. "Erasure becomes a kind of pentimento, an element of layering as you get in painting, but it is more ghostly in drawing."[122] This principle is also spread across the surface in comics, written into the space of the gutter. And erasure, Kentridge avows, "gives you a sense of the process of both making and thinking, which is not linear but a series of advances and reversals and lateral moves. Erasure begs the question of what used to be there."[123] In comics, this question can be prospective, too: what could *never* be there, in the gap space? As noted previously, comics calls attention to its own additive nature, to its accretion or accumulation of evidence—and also to what it subtracts, or refuses to measure and materialize, in the spaces between; in this, comics is a recursive form.

There are many who see the rise of comics as a sign of the replacement of real literacy with an all-too-easy, subpar visual literacy—Harold Bloom, for instance, cautioned students in a *New York Times* op-ed in 2009 that "undergraduate education should be a voyage away from visual overstimulation into deep, sustained reading."[124] However, comics texts often require an active and complicated literacy—one to which those making comics, and writing about them, attribute a slowed-down engagement: "It seems to me that comics have already shifted from being an icon of illiteracy to becoming one of the last bastions of literacy. If comics have any problem now, it's that people don't even have the patience to decode comics at this point. . . . I don't know if we're the vanguard of another culture or if we're the last blacksmiths," Spiegelman says.[125] This is in part due to how comics can retrack narrative, confuse the eye, offer multiple directions of reading (say, horizontal or vertical, as we see in Spiegelman's *In the Shadow of*

No Towers). Texts that incorporate word and image create a spatial and temporal depth on the page that lends itself to formal experimentation—understanding that term in Marianne DeKoven's fundamental sense of it as "the obstruction of normal reading."[126] Joe Sacco calls his work "slow journalism."[127] His investment in slowing readers down and asking them to grapple with producing meaning is a deliberate technique positioned against the unremitting speeding up of information that characterizes today's hyperactive media landscape.

Comics can slow time and thicken it through the rhythms it establishes in panel size, shape, and arrangement. In its composition, then, it underlines the link between duration (both readerly and represented) and narrative surface. In its form one recognizes the potential of comics to suggest the slow reading (and "surface reading") that many have discussed with particular fervor in the past ten or so years.[128] While a visual rhythm is sometimes established (through panelization, through color) as regular in these texts, it is just as often not, and the intervals between regularity can be striking for their deviation from a measured flow, just as, in some cases, the very regularity established can stand apart as discrete. There are two broad senses of rhythm at work here: the rhythm of the reader's acquisition of the text, and the material, visual rhythm of the created page, in which a trace of the imaginary, projected regularity of the grid is always present. (The traditional grid of the comics page, for instance, is constantly open to meaningful de- and reconstruction.)[129] Panel shape, size, and sequence on a page create and also disrupt rhythms, evoking formal features often used to describe music and poetics, such as pacing, tempo, phrasing, stress, and alteration.

Specifically, as I mentioned earlier, work that approaches trauma, and seeks to approach histories of trauma, raises the issue of pace. In a discussion of No Towers, which details his eyewitnessing of the fall of the World Trade Center towers, Spiegelman noted that the kinds of work he is interested in making are "things where there are giant ellipses."[130] What does it mean to read texts with "giant ellipses"? While experimental narration in comics, made possible by the form's spatiality, can only gesture at the duration of reading, it is crucial, especially with texts that devolve upon violence and trauma, that comics leaves the question of pace open. When comics evokes the traumatic, the reader engages the form through a participatory mode of agency that film, for instance, structurally eschews.[131] As Sacco understands the issue of pace: "[In my work], it's up to the reader how long he or she wants to dwell on a particular image. A reader can make his or her experience either easier or more relentless in that way."[132] This is an integral aspect of the texts this book groups together, which are often replete with horror. While the composition, the ruffled surface of comics pages, may gesture at a certain response—Sacco discusses adding drawings to a page so that the reader experiences the passage of time, for instance— the reader, unforced, may pace herself, look as little or as long as she wants. Film, on the other hand, "washes over you," Sacco contends.[133]

––––––––––

Comics raises productive issues of taxonomy and classifiability, and the next relevant question, as Galison and Daston indicate at the end of *Objectivity*, is not "Is it true?" but rather "How does it work?" So while Michael Rothberg in *Traumatic Realism* recounts a Holocaust historian claiming at a seminar that he "wouldn't touch *Maus* with a ten-foot pole," one of my favorite assessments of *Maus* comes from historian Hayden White. In his essay "Historical Emplotment and the Problem of Truth," White writes of Spiegelman's book, admiringly, "*Maus* manages to raise *all of the crucial issues* regarding the 'limits of representation' in general."[134] White notes that *Maus* is "one of the most moving accounts of [the Holocaust] I know, and not least because it makes the difficulty of discovering and telling the whole truth about even a small part of it as much a part of the story as the events whose meaning it is seeking to discover."[135] As with Barthes's footnote—in a moment that is almost an aside—White notices that the comics form forcefully instantiates the dynamics of expression and signification he articulates across his work on discourse, history, and form. Articulating presence and facing spectacle in time and space while underlining gaps and frictions, comics texts give shape to lost histories and bodies. Through the practice and aesthetics of materializing history in the mark, with their hand-drawn words, images, frames, gutters, tiers, balloons, and boxes, they offer a "new seeing." Extending forward from a rich tradition of forms, comics has reemerged after the age of the camera through urgent acts of witness.

| 1 |

HISTORIES OF
VISUAL WITNESS

*I tried to explain that . . . history was far too important to leave solely
to the historians.*
—ART SPIEGELMAN, *METAMAUS*, 2011

Disaster Drawn places contemporary comics of witness in conversation with
earlier traditions of visual—and, specifically, visual-verbal—witness that
clarify their aesthetic, historical, and political outlook. It addresses the
stakes surrounding the right to show and to tell history, examining hand-
drawn works of visual witness before the age of the camera, and after. This
chapter traces a selective history of terrain-shifting works of witness and
documentary form created by hand, disseminated by print, and spurred by
the ravages of war: Jacques Callot's *Les Grandes Misères et les Malheurs de
la Guerre*, created in 1633, and Francisco Goya's *Los Desastres de la Guerra*,
created between 1810 and 1820. Although Goya (1746–1828) was directly inspired by Callot (1592–1635), both series of etchings, which portray aston-
ishing bodily suffering, created new typologies of expression. Callot and

Goya are today known as foundational artist-reporters—as, in distinct ways, are the twentieth-century cartoonists Keiji Nakazawa, Art Spiegelman, and Joe Sacco, who, inspired by the challenges to expression brought by war, also have changed the possibilities of visual-verbal witness.

In the past few decades, as attention to the figure of the witness and concern with the ethics of war have increased, Goya's work, and to a lesser extent Callot's, has been the object of interest from a range of discourses and locations that mark its continued relevance. Twentieth-century theorists and critics on vision, ethics, and violence, most notably Susan Sontag—who writes about Goya extensively in *Regarding the Pain of Others*, her history of images of atrocity—have been drawn to Goya and have claimed him as an important figure for addressing witnessing, reporting, and the value of art. Goya's etchings continue to animate conversation around war reporting in general and war photography specifically. A foreign correspondent for the *New York Times* declared in 2014 of Goya's *Disasters of War*, in a review of an exhibit titled "The Disasters of War, 1800–2014": "As someone who has covered wars closely over the course of 14 years, I found the engravings a true revelation." In her book *Goya's War*, Janis Tomlinson quotes famed photojournalist Don McCullin, who has covered wars globally from Vietnam forward: "When I took pictures in war I couldn't help thinking of Goya"—particularly, he notes, "when people are about to be shot."[1]

And while among art historians and critics recent attention to Goya has focused on his role as an inspiration to the contemporary fine arts world, such as in the provocative adaptations by Jake and Dinos Chapman, his idiom of witness has also had profound reverberations for contemporary cartooning—a demotic form, as with Callot and Goya's etchings, itself meant for print.[2]

Goya's effect on the world of comics has been profound. Robert Crumb, perhaps the world's most famous cartoonist—and one whose dark, taboo visions of America in the late 1960s inaugurated the underground comics movement with *Zap Comix*—notes Goya's impact, and one can see that "Goya's sense of monstrosity," as one art critic puts it, inspired the comics underground to take shape.[3] Goya's name appears in Crumb's image "R. Crumb's Universe of Art!," in which the cartoonist pictures himself sitting at a table in front of a blank page (thinking, "Draw or die!") with a list of his most profound influences behind him. And Art Spiegelman and Françoise Mouly's 1987 *Read Yourself RAW: The Graphix Anthology for*

Damned Intellectuals, a collection of work from their field-defining maga-zine *RAW* (1980–1991), where Spiegelman's *Maus* was first serialized, is dedicated in part to Goya.[4] Working to express the trauma of war in hand-drawn forms, cartoonists such as Nakazawa, Spiegelman, and Sacco, who openly acknowledge the artist's influence, regenerate Goya's own groundbreaking language of expression for contemporary times.

   Callot and Goya today offer insight as documentarians of wartime atrocity, artist-reporters at the juncture of the history of art and the history of journalism, and figures marking turning points in the history of thinking about the relation of ethics and vision. (While through a late twentieth-century lens one can understand their work as being about witness, this concept obtained differently in seventeenth-century France, for instance.)[5] This chapter sets up their work, along with other, later manifestations of the artist-reporter, to be in conversation with related twentieth- and twenty-first-century comics work. I am interested not only in presenting lines of influence (although they are present, and sometimes unexpected) but also in using the vocabularies and concepts that the older and newer forms—all violent, serial, visual-verbal, handmade, and meant to circulate—establish in order to shed light on each other, asking what each can help us see in a chain of key developments in documentary form.

Callot's *Les Grandes Misères et les Malheurs de la Guerre* is a series of eigh-teen numbered, titled, and captioned prints widely recognized as one of the most powerful extant works of art about war—and expressions of wit-ness to its depredations. Published in Paris in 1633 in the midst of the Thirty Years' War (1618–1648), *The Miseries of War* (as it is commonly known in slightly abbreviated form) is physically small—each print is less than three inches tall and eight inches wide—but its influence and its force of vision, especially in revealing atrocity, are gigantic. Callot is one of the masters of printmaking in the history of European art. He was famous in his time for, among other innovations, developing the use of the *échoppe*, an implement designed to create both slim and swelling lines.[6] And while he is commonly known as the "father of French etching," A. Hyatt Mayor, the late art his-torian and Metropolitan Museum of Art curator, points out that Callot was "the first inventive international printmaker."[7] Callot's etchings inspired a range of artists, including Rembrandt, Hogarth, and Goya, whose *Disas-ters of War*, composed roughly 180 years later, acknowledges its debt to

Callot in its title. As Edwin de T. Bechtel points out, Callot has also fascinated writers such as E. T. A. Hoffman, who described one of his novels as
a "Capriccio in the manner of Callot," and composers such as Gustav
Mahler, whose "Dead March in Callot's Manner" is the third movement
of his Symphony in D Major, No. 1.[8] Callot was hugely prolific and his work
enjoyed robust circulation: he created more than 1,400 plates before his
death at age forty-three, including scenes of everyday life and comic images,
such as his widely popular *Gobbi* (hunchback) series (1622), alongside important military scenes such as the commissioned six-part, four-foot-tall
panoramas *The Siege of Breda* (1628) and *The Siege of La Rochelle* (1631).
But the uncommissioned *Miseries of War* broke from his previous work and
established a new idiom.

A bifurcation in images of war emerged in the mid-sixteenth century, as
historian Theodore Rabb argues in his recent study of art and war: one traditional, evoking "honor and triumph," the other critical, evoking "horror
and mayhem."[9] For Rabb, this bifurcation appears in two representative
paintings less than a decade apart—Titian's *Allegory of the Battle of Lep-
anto* (1575) and Pieter Brueghel the Elder's *Massacre of the Innocents* (1567).
And then, as he writes, the 1630s—when the Thirty Years' War was at its
"most ferocious"—became the decisive decade in which the rift widened
dramatically. "The first blow was struck by a Frenchman, Jacques Callot,"
he declares. Rabb notes the long history of the "documentary style" of
representation of military events, including in medieval manuscript illu-
mination and even in Callot's earlier work—a style he terms "relatively
dispassionate and neutral."[10] The shift Callot enacted with the *Miseries*,
then, is that while it is conspicuously about war, as its forcefully simple title
declares, the series moves beyond the previous idiom of articulation that
Rabb calls a visual "description" or straightforward "record of event" (as if,
as Rabb knows in his use of the modifier *relatively*, this could ever really
be neutral). Rather, *The Miseries of War* fully inhabits itself, instantiates
itself, as a work of witness to war: to war's unleashing of pervasive, ubiquitous violence for which no political framework can account. *The Miseries
of War*, then, documents *and* witnesses. Rabb notes that Callot's series
must have been a "shock to his patrons."

Callot was born in Nancy, the capital of Lorraine, an independent duchy
between Germany and France; although it was French-speaking, its his-
toric affiliations were as much with Germany as with France.[11] Callot grew
up in comfortable circumstances, familiar with court life: his father, a

nobleman who passed the rank along to his son, became the herald at arms to Duke Charles III when Callot was a child. Callot took up an apprentice-ship with the court goldsmith before leaving at age sixteen to study etching in Rome, working for a French engraver; it was there he learned the craft of a printmaker. Unlike Goya, his artistic descendant in so many ways, who resides firmly in the category of a "painter who also etched," as William Ivins puts it, Callot was a professional etcher.[12] He went on to an appointment in the Florentine court of Grand Duke Cosimo II de' Medici, where his reputation blossomed, but after Cosimo's death Callot returned to Nancy to become the official artist to the court of Lorraine. The Thirty Years' War pitted the Duchy of Lorraine against the French king, and Callot witnessed, as Sarah Kirk points out, three sieges on Nancy in as many years.[13]

In Mayor's portrayal, when Callot came back to Nancy in 1621 "he re-turned to random destructiveness—to the impersonal suffering of the Wars of Religion that seesawed back and forth across Lorraine, inflicting everyday lootings, beheadings, and hangings."[14] In September 1633, the French, led by Louis XIII and his minister Cardinal Richelieu, finally entered and oc-cupied Nancy; when the king subsequently requested Callot etch the siege of Nancy, he staunchly refused, but he did proceed, independent of any commission, to etch *The Miseries of War*.[15] This series, which became his most celebrated, presented a new mode of expression. As Antony Griffiths, the former keeper of prints at the British Museum, writes, *The Miseries of War* offered a "striking innovation in subject matter": "no series of such a subject had ever been seen in art before, neither in printmaking nor painting."[16]

The Miseries of War has much in common with the etchings in Goya's *The Disasters of War*, as I will discuss—and also with the twentieth-century comics about World War II and more recent wars this book later explores. The points of connection include defining features such as its seriality, its creation and circulation as a printed object, its word-and-image form, and its combination of spectacle and intimacy. In offering a loose narrative arc across its frames, the *Miseries* in particular resonates with later narrative work in comics. The *Miseries* is, most conspicuously, a series—and one with a narrative order that unfolds in sequence, in frames, on printed pages. The images are individually titled, and each is numbered below its bottom right-hand edge, an element that underlines the work's sequential form. As I suggest in the Introduction, Callot's accumulation of evidence responds to the declaration of the title: each frame could be thought of as (at least) one misery, adding to the pile while also furthering the story. To borrow Tom Gunning's language on comics, the sequential form of *The Miseries of War* asks one to be aware of it as both "succession and composite."[17]

There is, as with all engravings, no "original." The *Miseries* was meant to circulate. Although Callot drew preparatory sketches and studies (which exist as singular objects) for his images before etching them on the surface varnish of the copper plate, the series is indissoluble from its print form. The set of the *Miseries* was conceived and sold as a small book in which eighteen sheets were stitched together at the left side.[18] And for each print after the title page, Callot's small oblong image is accompanied immediately below by six lines of French rhyming verse, divided into three sections of two lines each.[19] The verses are traditionally attributed to Michel de Marolles (1600–1681), the Abbé de Villeloin, a famous collector, prolific poet, and friend of Callot's; they would have been added by a specialist writing engraver underneath the designs.[20] Callot approved the verses, as Diane Wolfthal points out, although he did not compose them; he originally left a blank margin at the bottom of the prints to accommodate them.

Also known as *The Large Miseries of War*, to distinguish it from a preliminary, six-plate rehearsal series etched at an even smaller scale, the *Miseries* suite opens with an elaborate, densely decorative title plate.[21] Within the frame, eight people—six men and two boys—stand on either side of a large, central ornate placard, holding pikes, halberds, swords, shields, and other weapons of war. Almost all of them stare out directly at the reader, with expressions bordering on the cheerful. Ceremonially festooned with emblems of war, the placard, taller than the gallant soldiers, reads vertically down eleven separate lines, each in script full of flourishes: "Les MISERES ET LES MAL-HEURS DE LA GUERRE. Representez Par JACQUES CALLOT Noble Lorrain. ET mis en lumiere Par ISRAEL son amy. A PARIS 1633 Avec Privilege du Roy."[22] *Mis en lumiere*, literally "brought to light," means "published"; Israel Henriet, whom Callot had known from their Nancy boyhood, had become, in Paris, Callot's partner and publisher; *avec privilege du roy*, "with the privilege of the king," signifies that copyright had been granted.[23] Unlike every other tightly contained plate in the series, on the title page the images spill out of their rectangular frame: the emblems of war, including drums, cannons, and a crown, bulge out of the bottom border to surround the appearance of the title within. The tone and content of the image feel almost facetious, given the declarative, negative title around which the military men (and their succeeding generation) approvingly crowd. Their outward gaze, however, suggests a mode of acknowledgment and engagement with the gaze of the reader, a feature not often replicated across the series. This attention to practices of looking, in the exchange of gazes, signals the work's aspirations to reveal through its images, to do the countering work of looking at war stripped of the ceremony.

In its time, *The Miseries of War*, in addition to its given title, was referred to collectively as "The Soldier's Life": depicting scenes from a history of war in minute detail, its images also suggest a narrative thread.[24] The seventeen images of the *Miseries* following the title page show the broad arc of a soldier's life, without specifying any individual protagonist. The prints are characterized by what Callot scholar Wolfthal names the hallmarks of the artist's style: clear daylight, meticulous drawing, and a wide-angle perspective.[25] The first two plates portray what Wolfthal calls "war in the narrow sense of the word": the image "The Recruitment of the Troops" is followed by "Battle Scene." The next five plates, however, depict atrocious crimes the troops proceed to commit against civilians: ruthless pillaging, rape, and murder. They plunder a farmhouse, destroy a convent, and burn a village, mercilessly ransacking and attacking anything and everything they encounter. In the ninth plate they are caught by a camp marshal, and the ensuing five plates, "The Strappado," "The Hanging," "The Firing Squad," "The Stake," and "The Wheel," show equally atrocious physical punishment meted out to the soldiers—all of which involve torture and execution witnessed as a spectacle by readers as well as by plentiful crowds within the frame: we watch and watch others watching. The series ends with three plates that portray the misfortunes of soldiers—injured at the hospital, dying in poverty, the victims of revenge by enraged peasants. A concluding image, "Distribution of Rewards," echoes the first in its presentation of a controlled world of order, featuring a generic king dispensing rewards to virtuous soldiers.[26] This print has often been described as satirical.[27]

Most scholars do not mention the verses of *The Miseries of War* at all, as Katie Hornstein has recently pointed out.[28] But its words are key to its creation of an intimate idiom of witness that draws a reader into the world to which Callot testifies on the page. Their presence and their link with the images of the *Miseries* mark the work as different from the impressive and impersonal military chronicles that Callot had etched on commission, or the much larger-scale single-frame paintings that Rabb notes preceded

Callot in the history of changing images of war.[29] Susan Sontag, in her brief discussion of Callot, calls each six-line poem a "caption" that is a "sententious comment in verse on the various energies and dooms portrayed in the images."[30] The voice of the verses takes on an observational tone that also characterizes Callot's controlled rendering and wide-angle views: "Those whom Mars nourishes with his evil deeds, treat in this manner the poor country people," reads plate 7. The verses often refer to their awareness of the images with which they share space with demonstratives ("this manner") and deictic words such as "here" (see plate 6).

Callot's artistic independence in expressing the miseries of war led him (in collaboration with Marolles) to the cross-discursive, to producing visual and verbal accounts—and the gaps in between them. The verses become part of what Paul Hogarth, in his important book *The Artist as Reporter,* deems Callot's "completely new factor of the artist's personal vision."[31] Callot's use of the space and proportion of print to cohabitate words and images underlines the idiosyncratic vision of his work. *The Miseries of War* presents itself as about evidence and apprehension—about modes of looking and absorption. Unfurling horizontally in groups of three couplets per page, the verse heightens one's awareness of one's own processes of reading and looking at atrocity. The prints' rectangular shape "creates an elongation of the pictorial field that promotes a scanning mode of viewing," as Hornstein points out. "Moreover, the text below the image, also oriented horizontally, enforces this directional viewing as the eye moves across the printed sheet from left to right. The broad, full landscape pictured in each image draws attention to the general actions of a large number of people as opposed to a few detailed figures."[32] The verse works with the images' composition to emphasize the large scale of information contained within the tiny frames; one's eye takes in the masses of bodies in orderly or terrifyingly disorderly formations as one reads each couplet. As the verse spreads out under the long image and draws readers across the space of the page, it also often forces one to encounter and absorb the detail of the image sitting directly above its lines. As the art critic Jed Perl, who writes of Callot's "genius for the tiniest etched line," points out, when Callot etches a figure "less than half an inch high, we see a person with a particular physique and demeanor."[33] The presence of the verse also asks readers to consume the image itself as a sequential three-part narrative, soaking up intricacies of detail.

The Miseries fashions its style of witness through its use and awareness of the frame. In "Scene of a Pillage" (plate 4), soldiers whose own bodies are mostly cut off by the right-side vertical border charge forward with pikes across the space of the page, a dramatic presentation of threat and impending death via weapon—a trope that Goya eventually adopts in *The Disasters of War.* "Plundering a Large Farmhouse" (plate 5) is one of the series' most haunting images—one whose violence corresponds closely with primary testimony from all over Europe during the Thirty Years' War (Figure 1.1).[34] One looks into the central interior of a farmhouse, populated by approximately thirty-five people, victims and perpetrators both, swarming across its packed, detailed spaces. On both the left and right sides of the frame a woman is being violated by a soldier; for the latter, we must see into a bedroom. (Callot often uses repoussoir figures on the sides of his images, as Wolfthal notes, to set off the frontal plane.)[35] In the left foreground, a soldier's sword is raised and is about to plunge into a supine victim who holds his arm up in protest. In the left background, soldiers drain casks; dead animals are scattered throughout. In this image, the upper border of the frame, which Callot blends with the ceiling of the farmhouse, creates a stage that presents the action within. Pots and pans hang from the ceiling, appearing to hang from the edge of the frame itself; they are dark and shaded, like the ceiling, and evoke in their different coloration a kind of embellished stage curtain. This use of the frame as a pictorial element makes even more horrifying what is also hanging within it, rendered in lighter, fainter lines: a man, tied at the feet, hangs upside down from an interior beam in the right background, being burned alive over an open fire. One's eye is first drawn to the objects hanging before one recognizes the human hanging.

Hanging is a motif throughout the *Miseries*, and Callot uses the borders of the frame to powerful effect. "The Hanging," plate 11, is the series' best-known image. Twenty-one hanged men—punished soldier-marauders—dangle from a large, dark oak tree that grows off the page in its center (Figure 1.2). The verse opens, "Finally these ignoble and abandoned thieves, hanging from this tree like ominous fruit." Another man is forcibly dragged by his neck up the ladder resting on the tree's thick tall trunk as a priest below scrambles up with him trying to administer last rites. In the right corner, another priest, his face turned toward readers, gives last rites to the next soldier in line. On the left side of the frame, and all around the oak

269 Plundering a Large Farmhouse. The poem reads: "Here are the fine exploits of these inhuman hearts. They ravage everywhere. Nothing escapes their hands. One invents tortures to gain gold, another instigates his accomplices to perform a thousand misdeeds, and all with one accord spitefully commit theft, kidnapping, murder and rape."

Figure 1.1   Jacques Callot, "Plundering a Large Farmhouse," plate 5, *The Miseries of War*, 1633. (Image courtesy of Dover Publications, from *Callot's Etchings: 338 Prints*, ed. Howard Daniel [1974].)

tree, large groups of people are assembled to watch the hangings, and stare intently at the action. Below the tree, amid others waiting to die, a small group of men casually gambles on a drum. All of these elements are horrifying. But the tree itself, with its spooky leafy branches, is the most appalling. It stands in iconographically for what the image's elements add up to: the awfulness of prurient interest in suffering, the awfulness of complete disregard for suffering. The tree is growing, literally and graphically, as if it cannot be contained by the page; its upward expansion while littered with dead bodies indicates how atrocity begets—grows—atrocity.

Callot's *Miseries of War*, like Goya's *Disasters of War*, is not polemical or even partisan. The story it presents, like the one Goya will later present with his own series, depicts violence as total and pervasive, not attaching only to one set of actors but rather entirely permeating the world of warfare. The force of its mode of witness is in its attention to observing and revealing endemic suffering on all sides of war: some of the most painful-to-behold prints in the series, as in "The Hanging" and "The Wheel"

275 The Hanging. The poem reads: "Finally these ignoble and abandoned thieves, hanging from this tree like ominous fruit, show that crime (horrible and black spawn) is itself the instrument of shame and vengeance, and that it is the fate of vice-ridden men to experience the justice of Heaven sooner or later."

Figure 1.2 Jacques Callot, "The Hanging," plate 11, *The Miseries of War*, 1633. (Image courtesy of Dover Publications, from *Callot's Etchings: 338 Prints*, ed. Howard Daniel [1974].)

(plate 14), are those of the ruthless soldiers being subjected to atrocious acts as punishment for committing atrocity. *The Miseries of War* is about the miseries soldiers inflict on civilians, and also the miseries of the life of a soldier. It examines, as Hornstein argues, "the nature of warfare in general, without recourse to the sorts of polemic questions normally taken up by propagandistic images from the period"; it transcends propaganda.[36] Rather, Callot testifies to the existence of calamity, and he blends artistic devices with meticulous historical detail, such as weapons, costumes, and military techniques.[37] Certainly, Callot would have been "long familiar with the atrocities of troops, whether provincial or mercenary," as Bechtel notes.[38] While Wolfthal claims that Callot never portrayed specific historical events, showing instead generalized crimes and punishments (certainly based on the Thirty Years' War, however), she also reminds us that "all the kinds of events Callot depicts actually happened: peasant revolt, severe punishments, troops out of control," and Perl argues that some of the prints are "surely made from direct observation."[39] Writing on the

Miseries, the curator Hilliard Goldfarb states simply, "The subject matter itself was one at the heart of daily life in Lorraine."[40]

"Callot was a master of capturing spectacle," Wolfthal declares.[41] The *Miseries* is a fascinating instance of how witnessing evokes spectacle and intimacy at once, a combination it seems to have pioneered, at least in documentary form, and which is recognizable hundreds of years later in the printed form of comics, whose small, intricate drawn boxes also often seek to document atrocity. Callot's etchings, many of which might be more comfortably observed with a magnifying glass than with the naked eye, demand scrutiny—the kind of scrutiny that is also so much a part of reading the dense, detailed, black-and-white comics work of Joe Sacco, which I will discuss in Chapter 5, and the meaningfully crowded comics work of Art Spiegelman, who likens comics frames to tightly packed suitcases. Perl acknowledges "there is something uncanny in the experience of Callot's etchings, because the proliferation of tiny elements generates an image that feels extraordinarily expansive."[42]

The Miseries of War frames suffering as a spectacle. It both forces spectacle upon readers, as a historical and everyday fact, and depicts spectacle as a social phenomenon within the frame, in a sense doubling our awareness of witness and asking us to evaluate our own difference from the organized crowds. Yet despite facing and refracting massive violence and spectacle, its size and scale are modest, intimate: images with which observers can interact, images they can hold and scrutinize. Callot's work demonstrates, as Perl suggests, that printmaking "was infusing new forms of intimacy and immediacy into the visual arts."[43] *The Miseries of War* draws readers into its layered, complex spaces, proposing an ethics of attention that has had significant reverberations. In *Eyes on the World,* her study of Callot, Esther Averill, like many others, designates Callot "the first great reporter-artist" of the Western world.[44] Callot created "reporting"—and documenting—as a visual idiom that could encompass the expression of witness in addition to the vigorous chronicling of facts.

Callot directly influenced Goya, whom art critic Robert Hughes, among numerous others, identifies as "the first modern visual reporter on warfare."[45] The precedent Goya set for the hand-crafted, word-and-image work this book explores is hard to overstate. Goya, along with his predecessor but even more forcefully, inspired a legion of artists—and specifically cartoonists—whose work faces war and engages the difficulty of spectacle. Callot and Goya are foundational artists in the history of aesthetics and trauma because they produce work that, in different ways, sees trauma for a viewer and is also conspicuously *about* the force of seeing trauma. Goya's goal—to evoke and to show, with handmade images as reporting—has been crucial to contemporary cartoonists as a model for visual witnessing.

From Manet to Picasso to Otto Dix to William Kentridge to Robert Crumb and all of the cartoonists whose work I explore here, Goya's creations, specifically his prints, have been vastly significant. If Callot, inspired by the dread and violence of the Thirty Years' War, crafted a fresh genre of witness, Goya, inspired by the dread and violence of the Peninsular War, the part of the Napoleonic Wars that specifically came to be known as the Spanish War of Independence (1808–1814), took it in a new direction. Also a court artist, Goya worked in a mode similar to Callot's in his own document of the dark, shattering warfare of his time: his uncommissioned *Disasters of War*, like *The Miseries of War*, is captioned and numbered, a series of eighty-three etchings of atrocities that Goya in many cases saw with his own eyes. In Goya's case, however, distinct from Callot's, the first-person voice at times enters into the legends, giving the work an even more intimate mode of address in the expression of witness. Each etching has a caption such as, simply, "This I saw" (plate 44) or "That is how it happened" (plate 47).

Although they both trained in Rome as young men and went on to become highly productive artists in their native countries, Goya, unlike Callot, was a major painter in Spain in addition to being a printmaker.[46] Goya generally painted according to commission. He was first court painter, the highest cultural office in visual arts, to the Spanish crown in Madrid for thirty years, serving three Spanish kings (and one French puppet king, Joseph Bonaparte), for whom he executed famous portraits. But Goya was used to working with the reproducible in mind: for eighteen years, from 1775 to 1792, he turned out paintings and cartoons that served as designs for tapestries for the Royal Tapestry Factory of Santa Bárbara. *Cartoon* comes from the Italian *cartone*, meaning "cardboard"; it denotes a drawing for a picture historically intended to be transferred to tapestries or frescoes. Later, *cartoon* came to indicate a sketch that could be mass-produced, an image that could be transmitted widely, as in the case of the contemporary cartoonists I discuss here, who value the term's mass-medium connotations.[47]

Goya painted more than sixty cartoons for the royal factory, full-size and in color. His designs depicted life in Madrid and the countryside, and featured types like the *majo*, who was seen to represent Spanish nature; Goya developed what we might think of as a comics lexicon of typological essences. And he was attracted to printmaking, although Spain at the time had a sparse culture of reproduction; having previously learned engraving, he taught himself to etch by copying, with royal permission, Velázquez paintings in the royal palace, for there were then no public museums. (A show at the Museum of Fine Arts in Boston in 2014 displayed his etched copy of Velázquez's famous 1656 *Las Meninas*.) At least from the early 1790s, Goya had access to an unusually extensive collection of thousands of prints amassed by his friend Sebastían Martínez, including works by English artists such as William Blake and caricaturists James Gillray, Thomas Rowlandson, and William Hogarth, whose work influenced Goya's first set of prints, *Los Caprichos*.[48] In the *Caprichos* (1799), an uncommissioned, published suite of eighty numbered and captioned etched and aquatint prints, Goya made sure to call attention to his more artistically elevated status as a *painter*: the first print is a self-portrait with a legend that identifies him as "Fran.co Goya y Lucientes Pintor." The independently executed *Caprichos*, however, as Hughes points out, was meant to be popular art. A sometimes fantastical send-up of Madrid society, it demonstrates Hughes's point that Goya allowed himself to flourish as a critic in small-scale work such as drawings, prints, and small paintings, while his large, commissioned paintings adopt, no less authentically, a more reverent tone toward their subjects.[49]

   The Disasters of War was conceived of in 1808, the year that the Spanish *pueblo* rose up against their French occupiers and the brutal War of Independence began. The insurrection was sparked in the morning of May 2, 1808, in Madrid, and occupation troops endeavored to quash the insurgents, quickly rounding up and killing every Spaniard suspected of rebellion. One mass execution took place at the Mountain of the Príncipe Pío, a small hill not far from the apartments where Goya then lived.[50] *The Disasters of War*, like the *Caprichos*, offers Goya's unique combination of etching and aquatint, a technique for achieving tone that roughens the copperplate to catch ink. It was created for "no audience of whom he could be certain," as Thomas Crow puts it.[51] Goya began completing plates in 1810—for each, he did preparatory drawings, many in red chalk, some in ink—and he worked on the series until 1820. It was not published, however, until 1863, thirty-five years after his death.

Initially called *The Fatal Consequences of the Bloody War in Spain with Bonaparte*, *The Disasters of War* has three identifiable parts, although these are not separated within the set: it opens with a long section of reported war scenes (plates 2–47), moves into recording the famine that ravaged Madrid in 1811–1812, killing 20,000 (plates 48–64), and concludes with a small group of allegorical subjects relating to war, which Goya called "emphatic *caprichos*" in his original title (plates 65–80). Goya likely recognized that his cycle of etchings would have an incendiary effect in its depiction of the political and moral chaos on both sides of the exceptionally violent war, the first war to popularize the term *guerrilla* (little war), which referred to the fighting Spaniards, many of whom were enraged civilians and for whom no rules of conduct applied.[52] (Both Callot and Goya depicted pre-professional armies.) When Goya left Spain for France in 1824, as Janis Tomlinson explains, he gave the copper plates and the trial proofs for the *Disasters* to his son Francisco Xavier.[53] In 1854, Goya's grandson Mariano inherited these, and put them up for sale; they were acquired by the Royal Academy of San Fernando in 1862. The following year, the Royal Academy printed the first edition for purchase. As early as 1819 Goya had given his friend Juan Agustín Ceán Bermúdez a full set of working proofs with each sheet numbered and captioned in pencil; this provided the model for the order and the manuscript captions for the work's publication in 1863.[54]

The word-and-image presentation of *The Disasters of War* is one of the signal features of what Hughes, hardly alone in his appraisal, calls "the greatest anti-war manifesto in the history of art."[55] Across Goya's work one notices inventive attention to the relationship of word and image. Take, for instance, his most renowned *Caprichos* print, *The Sleep of Reason Produces Monsters* (plate 43). It gains its spooky power from the unstable connection of word and image: Goya here removes the caption from the margin, atypically for this series, and places it within the diegetic space of the frame. The declaration of the title appears, then, facing outward at readers, on the front of the writing desk at which a man lies asleep, surrounded by bats and owls, his head buried in his arms, his paper and implements laid out in front of him. The dramatic placement of the writing within the frame, at the physical scene of composition, suggests the blurring of interior and exterior realities, a sort of "mystic writing pad," to evoke the title of Freud's essay—or an ominous conscious statement, a graffiti message for oneself.[56] And in the celebrated painting *The Duchess of Alba* (1797), in which the imperious titular duchess is pictured standing, she points, wearing a large ring spelling "Alba," down to the ground, where in front of her delicate feet someone has inscribed *Sólo Goya*, "only Goya," in the sand.[57] Even in his public paintings, where he had less freedom to experiment, Goya uses short phrases to re-create purely visual spaces as ones marked by the fuller friction of word and image as signifying systems. In *The Disasters of War*, as Philip Shaw puts it, the negation we see in the images of war is "redoubled by the semiotic disturbance" of Goya's words.[58]

Goya carefully created the captions for *The Disasters of War*. In what has come to be known as the Ceán Bermúdez album—which remains the only complete record of Goya's intentions for a published version of *The Disasters*—Goya wrote the captions for each etching by hand in pencil under the printed proof. The title page of the Ceán Bermúdez album, as Juliet Wilson-Bareau points out, even contains under Goya's own hand-written title a handwritten note by Valentín Carderera, the collector who was eventually given the album by Ceán's daughter, stating that the manuscript titles are in Goya's own hand.[59] For Goya, the visual-verbal play of layering both image and word to record history and experience had become a way of thinking and observing (something that may have been connected to his own disconnection from the aural as a functionally deaf person from 1793 onward). Before the *Disasters*, Goya used captions and images together in the *Caprichos* and also, significantly, in many of his own sketchbooks—for instance, in what is known as the Madrid Album (1796–1797), and later in others, from the period he worked on *The Disasters* and after.[60] Goya established for himself two artistic practices that have profound connections to the contemporary world of comics: he was the first Spanish artist to consistently use word and image together, and he was the first Spanish artist to keep a sketchbook, where we now can see many of his unpublished word-and-image drawings.[61]

In *The Disasters of War*, Goya innovates the relationship of word and image for the act of documenting atrocity. Viewers of *The Disasters of War* become aware of their own processes of perception in the quick cognitive impulse to match caption to image—one looks for explanatory confirmations from each that often do not exist, so that one is frequently aware of the space between word and image, their nonredundancy. The captions, most of which are short, register the immediacy of shock; as Alison Sinclair suggests, "the individual and cumulative effect of these titles is that they highlight Goya not just as an artist, but as a horrified witness."[62]

A subjectivity emerges in the space of the relationship of caption to image, lending the prints a quality both reportorial and intimate. The captions' punctuation gives the prints a conspicuously observed quality, as though we as readers and viewers are witness in real time to Goya encountering and exclaiming upon the scene that presents itself to us on the page. "This is too much!" readers learn in plate 31, in which two men hang from a tree, their corpses soon to be further desecrated by troops wielding swords. The two plates that follow, also depicting the mutilation of corpses, both end with question marks: "What more can one do?" Goya asks despairingly in 33, in which the genitals of a stripped dead man who is suspended upside down are sliced off by a group of soldiers with a large sword; the black gulf between his legs, held wide open by French troops, pulls our eye in, as the direct center of the page above the caption. "Barbarians!," "Great deeds! Against the dead!," "A cruel shame!," and "Unhappy mother!" are examples of the cycle's exclamatory, immediate captions in prints whose mode of testifying is generated by the relation of word to image.

As we see in its captions, *The Disasters of War* is also profoundly aware of sequence even if its images do not complete a continuous narrative, à la Hogarth's *Rake's Progress* (published in 1735), or a narrative arc even in the loose sense of the shorter *Miseries of War.* In 1806, Goya painted what Hughes calls "a narrative comic strip"—a six-painting oil-on-wood sequential narrative about the capture of Pedro Piñero, nicknamed "El Maragato," a widely known bandit who earlier that year was apprehended by a friar who shot him in the behind at point-blank range.[63] Each small painting is framed and carries a distinct subtitle describing the action. *The Capture of the Bandit El Maragato by Friar Pedro de Zaldivia* was one of a small number of Goya's "unofficial" paintings, which he completed on his own time in the years around the turn of the century; it shows his flair for visualizing news and also for capturing historical events in sequence, in frames—whatever the medium they enclose—that exist in meaningful relation to each other. The *Disasters* makes us aware of movement and sequence as it draws us across frames in its captions, some of which are linked and indicate continuity in referring to one another.

The second plate of the cycle, for instance, "With or without reason," which shows a fatal confrontation between two groups about to pike and bayonet each other, connects to the third, whose caption reads, referring back, "The same thing" under an image of a peasant standing above a tangle of bodies, axe raised, about to swing at a protesting French soldier.

In plates 9 through 11, the words of each caption work together as the three scenes differ. The effect is conspicuous aggregation of horror under one pronouncement, as if Goya's is a roving eye accumulating the diverse iterations of brutality: "They do not want to" appears under a rape scene, followed by "Nor do these" under a mass of killed bodies, and "Or these" under the portrayal of another rape. Throughout, small clusters of sequence emerge from the incoherent violence; captions begin with coordinating conjunctions that refer to the last one: "They'll still be useful" is followed by "So will these"; "Everything is topsy-turvy" gives way to "So is this." The effect underlines the artist-reporter's roaming, all-seeing eye, making accretion his form of witness, collecting and arranging images.

The view that Goya presents in the *Disasters*, which is modestly sized but larger than Callot's *Miseries*, with each etching roughly six inches high and eight inches long, is much closer than Callot's wide-angle perspectives—the bodies, both alive and dead, do not appear distant at all. If Callot's work is about what Perl calls an ethics of vision and I call an ethics of attention in the apprehension of large assembled scenes of atrocity that are horribly, massively peopled and full of dense swarming action, Goya's prints take us up close to violent action among groups of fewer agents. And while Callot's prints are rigorously formalist in their patterning and repoussoir effects, Goya's oblong images also present sturdy, rigorous compositions usually based on strong geometrical lines. And yet what we often see—and what is part of the series' own ethics of ambiguity—is a snarl of bodies in which one cannot distinguish French from Spanish, "bad" from "good," one side from the next. The very terms of opprobrium and approbation are confused. The inconclusivity at the level of the corporeal is profoundly unsettling; Goya calculatedly courts confusion and the cognitive effort produced by trying to pick out corpses in a pile. However, Goya also delivers ghastly images with precise clarity, such as the truly awful "Great deeds! Against the dead!" (plate 39), which horrifies viewers by presenting the deliberately disarticulated body arranged as a specimen to create fear and terror (Figure 1.3). Here, in a barren landscape, assorted bodies and body parts are stuck to and spaced out across a shattered tree, including a decapitated head spiked on a branch, a lone pair of arms, and a headless torso.

The *Disasters* etchings "created a form of their own," which Hughes identifies as "vivid, camera-can't-lie pictorial journalism before the invention of the camera." It is also true, he explains, that if Goya had been present

39

Grande hazaña! Con muertos!

Figure 1.3   Francisco Goya, "Great deeds! Against the dead!" plate 39, *The Disasters of War*, 1810s, published 1863. (Image courtesy of Dover Publications.)

at some the events he depicts, he would not have escaped with his life.[64] It is uncertain which among the etchings Goya witnessed firsthand and which he visualized based on newspaper accounts, other printed matter (such as government decrees), and eyewitness reports.[65] Goya almost certainly witnessed some of what appears in the *Disasters* with his own eyes; he lived in Madrid in May 1808, during the uprising and the ensuing war, and he likely would have seen the executions and/or their aftermath on Príncipe Pío hill, near his home. Although they are unconfirmed, Hughes reports sightings "of Goya with a loaded blunderbuss in one hand and a little sketchbook in the other, sitting down to draw the piles of corpses by lantern light in the darkness and confusion of the Madrid night, and it doesn't seem wholly implausible."[66] During the early stages of the war in 1808, Goya also traveled to Zaragoza, in the province of Aragon (where he was born), at the invitation of the Spanish general Palafox to document the devastation, which one imagines contributed to the stuff of the *Disasters*.[67] He certainly had opportunity to witness the ruin and barbarity of the war. One might understand the specificity of the caption "I saw it" (plate 44)—a simple, powerful declaration that inspired a range of journalistic and artistic output in the centuries to come, confirmed by the succeeding plate, "And this too" (plate 45)—as Goya marking out, in a literal sense, that he actually saw some of these things with his own eyes, but perhaps, it follows, not all of them.

In his close, immediate portrayals of war's atrocities, Goya makes his viewers themselves become witnesses to the scenes he depicts, regardless of whether or not he himself was an eyewitness to each event he materializes. It is in this sense that Sontag declares that the *Disasters* is "fashioned as an assault on the sensibility of the viewer."[68] The *Disasters* evokes a doubled act of witnessing in some cases, as is underscored by the captions: in "One cannot look at this" (plate 26), one of his savviest prints in the cycle, mentioned briefly in the Introduction, the "one" collapses to be both the artist-reporter himself, the viewer he addresses, and the eight victims huddling in a cave, about to be killed, averting their eyes, staring at the ground praying, covering their faces with their hands. Eight bayonets menacingly collect on the right side of the frame, as if piercing through the border from the margin into the space. The executioners' bodies are not pictured. And while Goya signals the difficulty of looking ("One cannot"), he and we, of course, *are* looking, underlining the gap between the witness, who is beholding the scene, and the actual targets of violence.[69]

This print is aware of itself as a difficult object of witness, as offering an instant isolated from a temporal sequence of horror: it captures the moment, the beat, before death. Sacco, the comics journalist, hits on this model of visual reporting describing his own work: as with Goya's example, he says, one can in comics "assemble the moment and put the reader in the moment."[70] Goya makes us aware of this through his multivalent caption and through his dramatic use of the frame in the print's visual composition. "One cannot look at this" is an example, along with "And it can't be helped" (plate 15), of Goya's "invention" of showing the length of weapons such as bayonets or rifle barrels entering the space of the scene horizontally from the frame's right side, often without the soldiers who wield them—a device he replicates in his famous painting *The Third of May 1808*

Para eso habeis nacido.

Figure 1.4 Francisco Goya, "This is what you were born for," plate 12, *The Disasters of War*, 1810s, published 1863. (Image courtesy of Dover Publications.)

(1814), which directly influenced Édouard Manet's series of paintings *The Execution of Maximilian* (1867–1869), and which Sacco imitates in his 2009 *Footnotes in Gaza*, as I will discuss.[71]

The Disasters of War compels an encounter with the idea of the *act* of looking and witnessing. Across its plates the series endeavors to make one aware of processes of seeing in its documentation of the relentless, mutual atrocities of war. This can be magnified by the address of the pithy captions, especially when there is also a multivalent "you" invoked, as in the haunting "This is what you were born for" (plate 12) (Figure 1.4). The print depicts a man stumbling across the frame, through the bleak landscape, coming upon and vomiting upon a thick tangled pile of corpses; the audience sees the ghoulishly hard-to-distinguish chaotic heap of organic and inorganic matter, and sees his act of seeing (and involuntary physical response). Who is the "you"? Were "you" born for vomiting on mangled corpses? Were "you" born to die ignominiously and then be vomited on? Were "you" born for drawing such horrible realities? Were "you" born for having to look at drawings of such existentially bleak realities? Sontag chooses an etching from the *Disasters*, "Not [in this case] either" (#36)—its caption refers to the previous etching, "Nobody knows why" (plate 37)—to grace the cover of her *Regarding the Pain of Others*. The image Sontag chose, in classic Goya fashion, illustrates her title through the triangulated ethics of vision I have been describing: it makes us aware of ourselves as viewers, looking and looking at others looking upon horror.

In this print, we regard the pain of the man hanged from a shattered tree, his head, full of dark hair, flopping downward, his pants pulled to his ankles. And we also regard a seated, smug French soldier, hat on his head—conspicuously, luxuriously attired, in contradistinction to the dead man—gazing happily, almost fondly, at the corpse, perhaps his own hand-iwork, at the side of the frame. An inverse of "This is what you were born for," this print, proffering greedy elective looking, is a particularly powerful example of what all of Goya's *Disasters* prints do, which is to make one aware of oneself as a seeing subject, to make "witnessing" not transparent, but rather a process of encountering presence, however difficult.

Above all, Goya wants us to look upon extremity without turning away. In his beautiful, terrifying painting *Witches in the Air* (1797–1798), which to me, in its content, feels the most connected among his commissioned work to the *Disasters*, three witches, who have spirited away a man, hover in the air holding him, gobbling away at his flesh vociferously; his arms are outspread and we see his anguished face (Figure 1.5).[72] On the ground, people refuse to look: one man lies facedown, covering his head and ears, while the other makes a sign to ward off evil but pulls a sheet over his head, hurrying past: they will not engage with the suffering of another. In *Witches in the Air*, Goya stages the refusal to witness—to even look. It is this desire to avert one's eyes that he counters in the visceral, tricky aesthetics of the *Disasters*, enfolding an acknowledgment of that desire into his idiom of documentation.

Both Callot and Goya created visual-verbal series about the nature of war—particularly its physical ravages on the human body—that were received as documents of the time, as reports (however delayed the publication) from the front lines of a specific war: the Thirty Years' War in Callot's case, the Spanish War of Independence in Goya's. Yet in neither series is any group of soldiers or battling civilians named. Entirely at the level of

Figure 1.5 Francisco Goya, *Witches in the Air*, 1797–1798. (© Madrid, Museo Nacional del Prado.)

the image, one deciphers the action by guessing at origin, position, and type of person pictured through details such as costumes and uniforms, as in the recognizable uniform of French Napoleonic soldiers. Often this code is clear, as in the leering soldier and non-uniformed Spaniard appearing paired in "Not [in this case] either." And sometimes it is unclear who is the murderer and who is the victim in the *Disasters*, just as the tortures Callot depicts run in all directions. In "Mob" (plate 28), for instance, Spanish peasants torture a bound man one might assume from his lack of uniform to be a Spanish civilian but a French sympathizer: one person aims a sickle into his anus while another bashes him with a pole.[73] The refusal to mark and name sides—which we notice in part through what is often the confusion of bodies in the frame, something to unknot and decode—underscores how both series ask us to look and to acknowledge history, but how both step away from soliciting our pity or engaging the didactic. While Callot and Goya's work is intimate in different ways, both use their etched lines ultimately to *observe*, and hence they are part of a long tradition of documentary: their mode of witnessing is *witnessing*, in fact, because it attests to facts rather than enlisting those facts for a polemic. In Goya's art, as in Callot's, no remedy is posed.[74]

Goya in particular enacts this moral ambivalence in an evocative style linked to the febrile lines of his contemporary cartoonist inheritors. Callot's tiny, virtuosic scenes and minute figures demand interaction with the space of the frame, close attention as an ethic of engagement with atrocity. We see some of this in Goya, too, especially with the visual disentanglement of forms his drawings provoke, but aesthetically Goya turns Callot's idiom inside out—at least its visual surface. He makes the urgency and horror sit right on the surface, both in the close view and in the visceral and spontaneous quality of the line. Goya's drawings "exalt the scribble, the puddle, the blot, the smear, the suggestive beauty of the unfinished," as Hughes aptly describes his hand.[75] The urgency and immediacy of testifying, and even some of the indeterminacy, are instantiated in Goya's rendering. This line is sketchier and looser than we see in Callot; it is closer to the work of cartoonists such as Spiegelman in *Maus*. The *Disasters*, as with the most successful comics also testifying to war, have a gestural style even as their compositions are tightly organized. Further, Goya encodes a kind of grammar we might now recognize as a comics grammar into the forms of his images, playing detailed articulated spaces and forms off bare ones. The landscape in the *Disasters*, as Sontag points out, is an atmosphere, a darkness, barely sketched in.[76] In its attention to the interplay of filled spaces and spaces of the unfilled, *The Disasters* adopts an aesthetic practice characteristic of the comics I treat here, both recording information and allowing blank spaces to become spaces onto which a reader can connect and project.

The path that takes us from Callot and Goya to the present proceeds by way of the rise of the professional category of the artist-reporter. If Goya worked privately on *The Disasters of War*, another vein of visual reporting—the commercial tradition of illustrated newspapers, which started in 1842 with the weekly *Illustrated London News*—posited artists as reporters.[77] Each issue of the *Illustrated London News* offered twenty to thirty engravings; it was the most popular news periodical in Great Britain. Its model spread internationally, with titles such as *L'Illustration* (Paris), *Illustrierte Zeitung* (Leipzig), and *La Ilustración* (Madrid) appearing in the 1840s, and *Le Monde Illustré* (Paris), *Frank Leslie's Illustrated Newspaper* (New York), and *Harper's Weekly* (New York), among others, appearing in the 1850s. (*Harper's*, now a monthly magazine, still publishes graphic journalism, as in Joe Sacco's 2007 report of his embedment with the Iraqi army.)[78] There were artist-explorers, who illustrated voyages; artist-naturalists; social satirist artist-observers; and then artists out in the field— "news illustrators."

A category of artists called "Special Artists" emerged specifically to report on war; these were an international brigade of artists who were more or less permanently employed as journalists.[79] These war correspondents were often conspicuously engaged in reporting as a form of witnessing. Constantin Guys, a war correspondent who covered the Crimean War and who later became the subject of Baudelaire's essay "Painter of Modern Life," created the sketch *Our Artist on the Battle-Field of Inkerman*, which was published as an engraving by the *Illustrated News* in 1855 (Figure 1.6). (To ensure the shortest possible delay, artist-reporters often sent sketches that would be filled in by staff artists before publication.)[80] It features an image of the artist himself walking his horse through a battlefield strewn with corpses. (One recognizes the visual insertion of self, a demystifying device that calls attention to the mechanism of reporting and witnessing, in the

OUR ARTIST ON THE BATTLE-FIELD OF INKERMAN.

Figure 1.6 Wood engraving after Constantin Guys, *Our Artist on the Battlefield of Inkerman, London Illustrated News,* February 3, 1855.

contemporary work of Sacco.) As John Stauffer notes in the example of Guys, "Its message seems clear: the war artist must bear witness to the terrible realities of war. Crimea was the first war covered by civilian reporters, and this image was one of the first to depict someone on the battlefield who was an independent eyewitness reporter."[81] And Scottish artist William Simpson was famously assigned to sketch the Crimean War in 1855—images that one can see in the books *The Campaign in the Crimea* and *The Seat of War in the East.* Celebrated photographs exist of the Crimean War, too, most notably early war photographer Roger Fenton's controversial "The Valley of the Shadow of Death," from 1855, which shows a road in Sebastopol littered with cannonballs.[82] But for roughly fifty years artists provided the primary visual depictions of war because of the *efficiency* of drawing, especially on the battlefield. Carrying the equipment that photography then required was possible but not optimal.

Further, periodical publications were unable to reproduce the tonal qualities of photography until the halftone printing method became viable in the 1880s. During the American Civil War (1861–1865), particularly, the pictorial press was a force in reporting; artists working for *Harper's Weekly*, such as Alfred Waud and Winslow Homer, were embedded with troops and created sketches of war, which were sent to staff artists and copied onto woodblocks for electrotyping and reproduction.[83] *Harper's Weekly* announced in July 1861 it would have artists in the field (Confederate states had no similar pictorial magazines). Homer was both salaried and freelance for *Harper's* in his time with the magazine; his Civil War images include a mix of timely documentary sketches based on eyewitnessing, drawings composed from earlier sketches and reports in the press, and images created from memory and invention. During this period photography and drawing were in meaningful conversation; the unposed motion that sketching captured, for instance, led Civil War photographers to stage similar informality in their own images.[84] And Special Artists also sometimes created their drawings for venues like *Harper's Weekly* as adaptations—as their captions would announce—from specific photographs. In-house staff artists at illustrated newspapers sometimes drew images on woodblocks as direct copies of photographs, by, say, Mathew Brady.[85]

By the early part of the twentieth century most dailies and older illustrated weeklies used photographs. The appearance of the commercial box camera in 1889 had made photography a more convenient and cheaper form for reporting. But for World War I (1914–1918), newspapers on both sides resorted to "illustrating the news" because of the affective resonance of drawn images and the emotional visual languages they could produce. In the decade following the war, avant-garde aesthetics motivated by the crisis of World War I established the role of the artist in the context of a crucial new kind of visual journalism, allowing figures such as George Grosz and Otto Dix—both significant influences on contemporary cartoonists—to report on war and its aftermath in Europe in the 1920s. Both Grosz and Dix had served in the war for Germany—Grosz in 1914–1915 and Dix as an infantryman in 1915 and 1916, after which Dix was wounded in the neck, was awarded an Iron Cross, and then worked his way up to lance-sergeant.

Publications such as *The Cudgel* (1922–1928) in Germany, which reported on postwar life, had contributors such as Grosz, Dix, John Heartfield, and Frans Masereel (whose 1918 woodcut novel *A Passionate Journey* is considered by many the first twentieth-century graphic novel). The 1920s, when Berlin in particular was home to a profusion of important Dada-inspired journals and bulletins, was "a decade in which avant-garde idioms at last established the role of the artist in the context of enlightened journalism," as Paul Hogarth suggests.[86] Grosz's portfolios of drawings expressed his harsh views of war and its ravages, often in the context of biting satire, as in the drawing "Shut Your Mouth and Keep on Serving" (from the 1928 collection *Background*), which pictures Christ on the cross wearing a gas mask, and earned Grosz an official charge of blasphemy.

Dix's *The War* (1924), a cycle of fifty etchings, is evocative of Goya's *Disasters of War*, by which it was inspired. In fact, a recent exhibit and book titled *Disasters of War: Callot, Goya, Dix* call these artists' work "links in a chain."[87] *The War* is the most forceful example of what Thomas Compère-Morel argues is the theme of all Dix's work across different avant-garde movements: the discourse it develops around war.[88] *The War* was published by Dix's Berlin dealer, Karl Nierendorf, in five linen-bound portfolios of ten prints each (this edition was a colossal commercial failure, selling one of seventy copies).[89] Dix had sketched profusely while enlisted, making more than three hundred on-the-spot drawings with charcoal and pencil, often on postcards, in France, Russia, and Flanders.[90] In 1923, he drew and etched what he had seen and experienced in the violent trauma of war for publication; Philippe Dagen reminds us that the etchings are the product of direct recollection, "an attempt to give visual form to something that had remained impressed" in the artist's mind.[91] Each of the etchings is accompanied by a title, which sometimes editorializes and often carries a date and specific location (Figure 1.7). All unremittingly dark, some of the etchings strike an observational tone, as in "Gas Victims," and some produce a tone of surreal horror, as in the swirls of facial flesh overtaking the frame in "Shot to Pieces."

Photojournalism picked up and solidified in the 1940s; many, many photographs were taken worldwide covering World War II. However, magazines such as *Fortune* and *Life* maintained their reputations for visual fascination by offering pictorial variety: photographs alongside drawings and colorful reproductions of reportorial paintings.[92] Hence Philip Guston's three *Fortune* painting portfolios from 1943–1944, and reportorial drawings by the artist Ben Shahn, among work by many talented and later famous others working for *Fortune*.[93] *Life* maintained a working team of twenty-eight war artists during World War II.[94] But by and large, at least in the mainstream press, reportorial drawings were at a bare minimum in the postwar period of the 1950s. Drawing, with some exceptions, was

Figure 1.7 Otto Dix, "Gas Victims (Templeux-La-Fosse, August 1916)," *The War,* 1924. (© 2015 Artists Rights Society [ARS], New York/VG Bild-Kunst, Bonn.)

supplanted as normative practice by photography (and film) in the realm of the documentary. As we can recognize, however, across these selective, necessarily brief histories that connect Callot, Goya, and Dix to the later work of Nakazawa, Spiegelman, and Sacco, the shattering of forms of expression produced by war and trauma opens a space for the primal immediacy of the hand-drawn to reemerge as a form of witness.

Sontag claims that 1945 was the year "when the power of photographs to define, not merely record, the most abominable realities trumped all the complex narratives . . . with the pictures taken . . . at Bergen-Belsen, Buchenwald, and Dachau . . . and those taken by Japanese witnesses . . . following the incineration of the populations of Hiroshima and Nagasaki."[95] But it is precisely the catastrophic global conflict of World War II, of 1945, that gave rise to the hand-drawn form of comics in its contemporary specificity. Art Spiegelman exactly documents the Nazi camps his parents lived through, and Keiji Nakazawa, in his comic book *I Saw It,* offers the phenomenology of the atomic bomb from the perspective of someone hit by the blast on Hiroshima city ground.

| 2 |

TIME, SPACE, AND PICTURE WRITING IN MODERN COMICS

Comic books are to art what Yiddish is to language—a vulgar tongue that . . . talks with its hands.
—ART SPIEGELMAN, 2002

By pinpointing important work created in distinct word-and-image formats— some weird, new, unassimilable, and off to the side—this chapter pulls to- gether strands that only seem disparate in order to create a story of the growth and impact of a form that now speaks to readers across fields and disciplines. This chapter ranges selectively over significant works from the 1830s to the 1970s that have established what one can think of as the po- etics of comics through their formal experiment. The poetics of comics that emerges from this account reveals the features relevant to comics' doc- umentary propensities—those that incline the form to the expression of witness, to picturing subjectivity and the paradox of history's layered spaces and temporalities.

The work I engage here presents substantial differences in cultural context, format, and genre. Most of the works themselves created new formats, genres, and aesthetic modalities—whether they were composed in commercial contexts, such as Harvey Kurtzman's invention of a fresh mass cultural genre for media aesthetics and comic book production with *Mad*, or in private ones, such as Henry Darger's unrecognized work in his one-room apartment on his epic *In the Realms of the Unreal*, painted on butcher paper.[1] From nineteenth-century "engraved novels" to newspaper comic strips, "wordless novels" to print-culture-obsessed word-and-image fantasies, mass comic books to radical left comics commentary, short modernist compositions to darkly political satire, each of the narratives on which this chapter alights exhibits a formal vocabulary, however distinct, that connects comics to the practice and possibility of witness, to the expression of realities of lived life and history. One sees this in the profound proliferation of time and multiplication of space in comics, in its refusal of linearity and regularity in its narrative movement. One also sees this in its immediacy-provoking insistent positioning of the body, whether reflexively through the mark itself or through the location of bodies in time and space on the page. And, significantly, one sees this in comics' awareness of its own properties, which constantly marks attention to the acts of spectating and perception, both within and outside the frame.

Comics is a form that Art Spiegelman calls "picture writing" and the Iranian cartoonist Marjane Satrapi, author of *Persepolis*, calls "narrative drawing": the narrative, or the discourse, moves forward in time through both its words and its images. Swiss schoolmaster Rodolphe Töpffer (1799–1846) is the inventor of modern comics conventions, and his two central innovations underscore the concept of picture writing. Töpffer was the first artist to create word-and-image stories and to handwrite his own captions—employing the same implement and the same mark for both his words and his images. He also invented the first stories to combine word and image that use multiple panels on one page, experimenting with the expression of time through space and its subdivision. "If for the future, he would choose a less frivolous subject and restrict himself a little, he would produce things beyond all conception," Johann Wolfgang von Goethe proclaimed of Töpffer.[2] This was notable approbation from someone with a well-known contempt for what he saw as the socially divisive malice of caricature.[3] In contradistinction to caricature, which was mostly single-frame, Töpffer created a sequential narrative that he called a pictorial language. While

Töpffer's work was largely satirical, in its creation of a handwritten language of comics we can recognize how he laid the groundwork for the work of the hand to emerge as a feature of comics of witness. Töpffer demonstrates how comics unites elements of the haptic and visual—a crucial connection for witness—that is recognizable in the idiom of "firsthand" information, a claim that generally indicates direct visual apprehension.

Töpffer created eight *histories en estampes* of forty to ninety pages each— witty, amusing, and textured works that were known as "engraved novels" or "picture-novels." He sketched his first picture-novel, *Les Amours de Mr. Vieux Bois*, in 1827; the English-language edition, translated as the *Adventures of Mr. Obadiah Oldbuck*, subsequently became the first graphic novel printed in the United States, in 1842. In the succeeding years after *Vieux Bois*, Töpffer self-published his picture-novels and circulated them privately, although later he published in established venues, such as in *L'Illustration*, based in Paris, which serialized his *Histoire de M. Cryptogame* to great acclaim in 1845. Earlier, in 1830, Töpffer had managed to get *Histoire de M. Cryptogame*, which he completed that year, to Goethe through Frédéric Soret, Goethe's friend and translator, and had earned Goethe's admiration. The ultimate success of *Cryptogame*, as art historian David Kunzle argues, had "tremendous consequences for the character and diffusion" of comics.[4]

Töpffer invented comics to be a form that is about its own "handedness," to make use of a suggestive contemporary phrase from Arthur Danto, by handwriting his captions along with his images. Inscribing his own handwriting on the page along with his images instead of a typeface, Töpffer set the possibilities for an essential feature of comics: the presentation of a unity of marks that evoke and create a world. Even the element of the frame in Töpffer's comics becomes pictorial, as Kunzle affirms, clearly created by hand in his "trembling, quirky frame line."[5] Today, one way critics discuss the division between "commercial" or mainstream comics, published by big companies, and "literary" or "independent" comics involves that most basic of elements, the frame: if the borders are hand-drawn, the work is likely independent. Töpffer, the first comics auteur, created this signifier of the auteur creating a world, and literally enclosing it, a "visual and psychological unity" with one set of marks for all elements on the page.[6]

The expressive, even impulsive quality of Töpffer's particular mark, across text and drawing design, calls attention to its own fabrication. As Kunzle notes, "Philosophically, Töpffer was averse to the straight line."[7]

Töpffer's style, which employs line only, is wavery, even sometimes abstract in its vitality and its evocation of the spontaneous. Doodling was the cornerstone of Töpffer's art theory, as Thierry Smolderen, among others, suggests; what Töpffer constructed, Smolderen writes, is "a sophisticated semiotics of anti-academic drawing, as a form of art."[8] One of today's most heralded cartoonists, Chris Ware, admiringly deems Töpffer's style "rough-hewn" and "loosely doodled"; a poster by Ware made for an international comics conference in 2012 describes the conference as addressing "the art of the empathetic doodle."[9] Töpffer called his own work, among other things, a scrawl. A picture-story, he writes in his 1845 "Essay on Physiognomy," is a series of sketches in which visual "accuracy is unimportant but, on the other hand, a clear, rapid expression of the essential idea is imperative."[10] Comics is not illustration—it is not about accuracy in rendering—but rather is a type of expressive language.

Töpffer was able to suggest the reading of image as word, and word as image, because he adapted an early version of offset lithography that allowed him to draw "right reading," unlike engraving, in which he would have had to inscribe backward (this usually required, as in Callot and Goya's etchings, employing a calligraphic specialist trained in mirror writing). As Spiegelman frames Töpffer's legacy, his lithographic process meant that a cartoonist could be making the same kinds of marks for his writing as for his drawing.[11] Töpffer called this practice "auto-lithography." It involved direct drawing with a pen, typically a steel-nibbed one made from a watch spring, onto special transfer paper spread with a layer of glue starch before transfer onto the stone, resulting in a double reversal back to the original direction when printed.[12] In Geneva, where Töpffer lived, this practice previously had been used for commercial ephemera, such as advertising circulars and grocers' bills, while in England it was known as "transfer lithography."[13] In his "Essay on Autography," from 1842, Töpffer discussed his "invention" and revealed the practical "secret" of the reproductive technique. In Töpffer's concept of autography, one notes the early instinct to self-publish inexpensively; at the time, printing cost little more than the paper did, and Töpffer himself paid for 800 copies of his *M. Pencil*. (The impulse to self-publish work made by hand recurs at the end of this chapter with the American underground comics of the 1960s, inaugurated by Robert Crumb's *Zap*, which he sold to passersby on San Francisco's Haight Street out of a baby carriage.) And, crucially, Töpffer proposed narrative as constituted by a series of irreducible marks, whether word, image, or perhaps both.

The artist claimed to be inspired by two forms—the novel (one assumes Laurence Sterne's *Tristram Shandy*, among others), and the picture-story, as in Hogarth, about whose influence he was explicit.[14] Many histories of comics begin with Hogarth's sequential pictorial narratives, as in his *A Harlot's Progress* (1731), which initially unfurled a narrative through a sequence of frames hung side by side on a wall, and later in collated portfolios of engravings. As Stephen Burt puts it in a recent issue of *Artforum*, Hogarth "set a precedent for serial art at once popular and complex."[15] In bridging the novel and Hogarth's visual narratives, Töpffer was able to express temporal development in spatial terms on the page, and experiment with the presentation of time, changing the size and shape of panels.

Töpffer established techniques of perspective that preceded the camera but have come to be associated with film, such as cross-cutting (see, for instance, Figure 2.1).[16] Working in the 1830s, Töpffer "anticipated cinematic cross-cutting before there was anything like a movie camera. He was able to capture multiple moments of time," as Spiegelman observes.[17] Kunzle, a student of E. H. Gombrich, Töpffer scholar, and author of two magisterial volumes of the history of the comic strip starting from 1450, describes Töpffer's work as "a battery of montage devices."[18] Montage is about proliferating temporalities but also about holding time in suspension, in the space between frames and cuts, an evocative poetics that captures the subjectivity of the individual experience of time. Goethe noted how Töpffer's new form allowed one to follow movement, how it "freezes and unfreezes as it were in the spirit of imitation."[19] He cannily observed in Töpffer's picture-novels, in other words, the paradoxical stillness and movement at the heart of comics. As film and media theorist Tom Gunning writes, "Rather than ignoring time, comics opens up new modes of representing it."[20]

One of the central practitioners of expressing comics time in the twentieth century, Winsor McCay (1867–1934), exemplifies in his oeuvre the contradictions of comics: it is frozen and in motion, high and low, driven by fantasy and governed by regulation, both forward-moving and disruptive or recursive, regular and irregular, "art" and entertainment, field-defining and ephemeral. McCay, who started publishing comics in 1903, "developed a creative language that set the foundation for the medium," as one critic puts it succinctly.[21] That America's first decade of the twentieth century and on into the teens represents an aesthetic benchmark for the sophistication of comics is widely acknowledged; this is the

Figure 2.1 Rodolphe Töpffer, page from *Monsieur Pencil*, 1840. Reprinted and translated in Kunzle, *Rodolphe Töpffer*. (Used by permission of David Kunzle.)

era when comic strips flourished in newspapers, particularly in Sunday supplements.[22]

In McCay we see comics that present and disrupt linear time and motion both thematically and formally. Comics, even comics that predate the high modernist moment, have often been discussed as a reference point for the modernist avant-garde (Duchamp's 1917 readymade urinal *Fountain*, one of the most famous works of art in the world, is, after all, signed "R. Mutt," a reference to Bud Fisher's *Mutt and Jeff* comic strip).[23] Adam Gopnik and Kirk Varnedoe claim, "When art in the later teens and twenties began to include images from the comics, it was informed by [the] sense of the comic strip as the popular embodiment of avant-garde values."[24] While Gopnik and Varnedoe stress their point from the perspective of the avant-garde, my emphasis here is on the cultural and aesthetic landscape that comics themselves produced. This can be inclusive of the kind of formal experimentation we find in the visual and literary avant-garde, but it embraces a functional populism most often absent from the avant-garde's aesthetic oppositionality. The early newspaper comics—the first major appearance of comics in the United States as a commercial and cultural phenomenon—were formally experimental while they yet inhabit their popular, reproducible status.

McCay helped to establish and develop both comics and animation in the early years of the 1900s. An artist renowned for his printed work and also for his wildly popular stage appearances, he was a minor celebrity in his lifetime. McCay's work had what a contemporary critic might call a "transmedia" aspect. His most famous comic strip, *Little Nemo in Slumberland*, appeared weekly in the *New York Herald* starting in 1905, inspired a Victor Herbert operetta of the same name on Broadway in 1908, and also inspired an early animated film of the same name in 1911, which McCay incorporated into the vaudeville shows he performed all over the country. McCay innovated principles and practices that continue to epitomize the form—and its dynamic conversations with other media forms.

McCay's practical training came from drawing caricatures for money at a dime museum in Detroit and from working as a poster painter for Cincinnati's Vine Street Dime Museum, a permanently installed "freak show," before becoming an artist-reporter for the *Cincinnati Enquirer*. In 1903 he arrived in New York to work in the art department of the *New York Herald*. The weekly Sunday comic strips he started creating shortly after his arrival are all remarkably dark.[25] *Little Sammy Sneeze* (1904–1906), which always features six frames in a fixed perspective, is about a boy who wreaks considerable havoc with his powerful sneeze, disrupting all manner of bourgeois life. The incredibly strange *The Story of Hungry Henrietta* (1905) is about a female infant to whom no one pays attention except to overfeed her. Most episodes end with the child enclosed alone in the frame, eating. The strip featured twenty-seven installments at three-month increments in Henrietta's life; as she grows bigger, her family keeps on stuffing her with food. Both *Sammy Sneeze* and *Hungry Henrietta* have a set structure for each installment: the expulsion and the intake, respectively. As one McCay scholar notes, "Sammy is an engine of destruction; Henrietta of consumption."[26] Henrietta is being destroyed, the strip implies, by her negligent family members, who are too distracted and embarrassed to deal with any real problems and instead feed her; they create her hunger in order to satiate her easily. But Henrietta, set on her path, becomes a scarily voracious consumer.[27] McCay's children are always losing control: Sammy can't help but sneeze, as the tagline to his strip every week reads: "He just simply couldn't stop it / He never knew when it was coming."

McCay started his disturbing *Dream of the Rarebit Fiend* series in 1904; it became his longest-running comic strip. *Dream of the Rarebit Fiend* has a simple premise: a shifting cast of characters who have recently eaten a meal of Welsh rarebit (melted cheese) are plagued by nightmares, which include scenarios such as the dreamer dismembered by traffic on a city street, helplessly buried alive, or suffocated in sleep by small animals. *Rarebit Fiend* imagines a huge host of nightmares; at the conclusion of each panel, the dreamer wakes up in bed. The more overtly sanitized *Little Nemo in Slumberland* appeared the following year, and it had the exact same structure as *Dream of the Rarebit Fiend*: each weekly installment reports on the dream state of a character—in this case, a child named Nemo—who wakes up, disoriented, in a concluding frame. McCay's two most significant strips show an obvious attachment to the principle André Breton articulated almost twenty years later in his 1924 definition of Surrealism: belief in "the omnipotence of the dream."[28] It is for this reason that popular culture scholars such as Thomas Inge and comics scholars including John Canemaker have suggested the link between McCay's work and Surrealism.[29] The most powerful way to think through how we can understand McCay in the context of modernist practices, however, is through attention to the formal language of comics, which is defined by its approach to time. McCay developed a language of formal expression that set the terms for the best comics works in the twentieth century and beyond, across genres. The push and pull of the regular and irregular in McCay, of control and fantasy, reflects comics' attempt to refashion perception and inscribe modern contradictions, commenting on and re-visioning contemporary experience.

Comics is a form that fundamentally relies on space—the space of the page—to represent the movement of time; it presents a temporal map, juxtaposing frames on the page. McCay boldly experiments with the spatial and temporal conventions of comics form, complicating the constraints of this map and showing, even in gimmicky newspaper series, how profound comics could be for expressing temporal disjunction and proliferation tied to historical realities—and anxieties. Even in his short-lived *Little Sammy Sneeze*, a feature that would seem one-note, he played with the conventions of the medium. In one famous installment, Sammy's disruptive sneeze first breaks and then fully shatters to pieces the black square frame that encloses him (September 24, 1905). McCay announces his presence in this episode, his adoption and violation of the rules of his medium; he intrudes on the fantasy world he creates. McCay's comics comment on their own panelized representation, on the exigencies and problems of comics form. If comics is supposed to be composed of discrete, bordered images that each represent a punctual temporal moment in the unfolding thread of a story, McCay breaks the order that is one of the form's strictures. In other words, the fantasy in McCay's work registered its disruption not only as content but also more significantly as form. So while the film and media theorist Scott Bukatman, who has written extensively on McCay, sees that chronophotography in roughly the same period, such as the work of Eadweard Muybridge, mapped the body "onto the regulated spaces of industrial culture," he sees that comics, and particularly McCay's work, represents a counterlogics that marks "disorder in a time of insistent regulation."[30]

We see throughout McCay's work how the rhythm of efficient motion—and a view of the body's connection to linear time—is subverted. Many of his strips, as Bukatman points out, function as a response to chronophotography and its scientific tracking and recording of motion. *Little Sammy Sneeze*, with its same-sized fixed-perspective frames, is a reference to film and to chronophotography—specifically, to the 1894 Kinetoscope five-second film *Fred Ott's Sneeze*. The first motion picture to be copyrighted, the film was produced by Thomas Edison's studio and was printed as a gridded graphic of same-size frames in *Harper's* magazine.[31] In McCay's

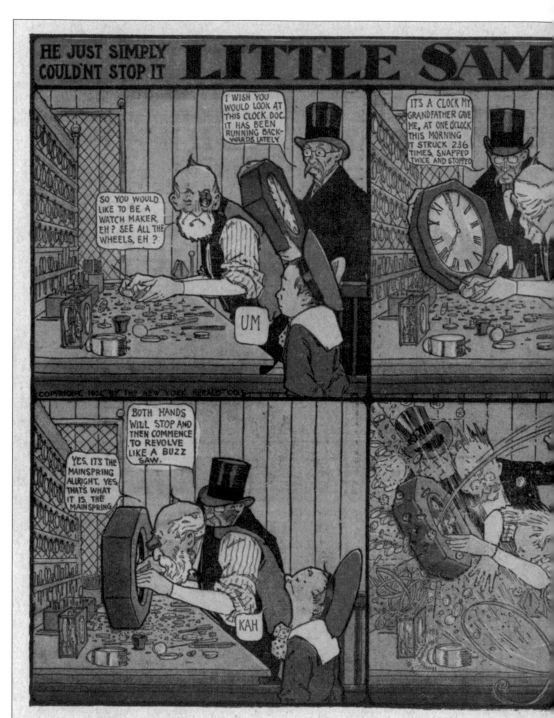

Figure 2.2 Winsor McCay, *Little Sammy Sneeze, New York Herald*, September 18, 1904. (Image courtesy of Peter Maresca and Sunday Press.)

comics response to the gridded diagram, Sammy's sneeze upsets time's orderly division and its documentation. One of *Sammy Sneeze*'s earliest installments depicts how Sammy's sneeze disrupts the work of a watch and clock repairman who is trying to fix a handsome clock that has literally "been running backwards" (Figure 2.2). Sammy's sneeze disperses the clock's parts; he is ejected with lovely Art Nouveau curlicue motion lines, flying out of the strip in its conclusion toward the reader, while the clock remains scrambled. The unruly motion he generates from his body, visualized through winding ribbons, is the motion that guides the strip—not the logic of mechanized clockwork.

Sammy's shattering sneeze also often conspicuously occurs on moving transport, such as subways and trains. Trains and the speed of modern life in general feature heavily in *Dream of the Rarebit Fiend* as a horror in which forward motion is activated and cannot be stopped.[32] In one visually powerful example, also from 1904, a woman on a walk with her dog halts an oncoming train by head-butting it (Figure 2.3). "Let us go on," implores the train's engineer. Trains that will not stop moving abound, framed in a perspective that makes them careen toward the reader (a technique also evocative of famous perspectives in early film, such as the Lumière brothers' *Arrival of a Train*, and many early American examples). Similarly, cars and other vehicles that simply will not cease moving are also frequently seen (if "it would only stand still a minute," the protagonist of a 1907 strip laments). These forms of efficient movement are frightening in McCay's dreamworlds, a logic to be escaped; McCay's protagonists are terrified of propulsive, uninterrupted movement.

And they are also troubled, as all of McCay's work suggests on a larger formal level, by the fixing of time implied by photography, the fixing of bodies in space. Conspicuously, both Hungry Henrietta and Sammy Sneeze are children positioned against photography, and they share prominent rejections of being photographed. The inaugural episode of *Hungry Henrietta* sets the terms for the bad psychic structure the family plays out with their baby when they take her, at three months old, to a photography studio (January 8, 1905). As five adults fuss over Henrietta's pose—"just fix her this way," one man says—she starts to protest and wail, is given a bottle, and the pattern begins. It is a comic strip whose platform is rooted in a critique of freezing time and bodies in a still image, of capturing the single perfect shot (Figure 2.4). Likewise, it is not a coincidence that Sammy con-

Figure 2.3   Winsor McCay, *Dream of the Rarebit Fiend*, *New York Herald*, December 15, 1904.
(Image courtesy of Ulrich Merkl.)

Figure 2.4   Winsor McCay, *The Story of Hungry Henrietta, Chapter One*, *New York Herald*, January 8, 1905. (Image courtesy of Peter Maresca and Sunday Press.)

spicuously destroys a camera with his sneeze: in the 1904 strip in which his mother takes him to a photography studio, the very first frame has a photographer imploring him to "hold still" for the pose, prompting Sammy to sneeze and break the camera and knock over the studio layout. Sammy's logic, as with the clock, refuses a certain kind of regulation and mechanization, the recording of his "still" body. McCay, whose work is intensely bodily, wants to loose modern bodies from their frames.

As Bukatman argues, "Comics inherit the techniques of chronophotography but frequently deploy them to parodic effect, and this tendency continues to subtend their existence through the next century."[33] Motion through and with time and space is the implicit and explicit subject of all of McCay's strips, and the forward march or the fixing of bodies in space is often thwarted. One particularly lovely color *Dream of the Rarebit Fiend* satirizes a bit of both, as one notices in fixed, Muybridgian perspective the bodily movements of a man "not moving an inch" despite his rush to go forward (Figure 2.5). But even more than parody (and as Bukatman also points out), comics offers an aesthetic system that pushes back on both progressive linear movement and the freezing of time. Comics provides an experience and view of time in which it is tensile and layered, proliferative instead of linear, dispersed rather than propulsive.

Little Nemo in Slumberland (1905–1911), McCay's best-known comic strip, is about its own recursive procedure, the constant repetition of a child dreaming and waking up. Despite the idea of the charming sleeping boy at its center, *Little Nemo*, whose title character's name is Latin for "no one," is not a character-driven strip. Its recursivity may suggest an escape from the marching forward of mechanization and commodification, or the bourgeois tyranny of "regular" time. In *Little Nemo*, McCay plays with the idea of rhythm, manifest across a range of textual practices; he defies the strip's traditional arrangement of panels, stretching them horizontally, and also vertically, as in his famous "Walking Bed" episode (July 26, 1908), in which the panels grow with Nemo's expanding bed. As I discuss in the Introduction, in the material, visual rhythm of the comics page, a trace of the imaginary, projected regularity of the grid is always present. Without shattering the frames, as in *Sammy*, McCay yet deregularizes the procedure of his medium through experimenting with panelization.

In McCay's work, which never resolves itself, the normal ruptures back at the dreamworld: at the end of every episode, for example, Nemo's dream is disrupted, usually by one of his parents, and he wakes up in or near the

Figure 2.5 Winsor McCay, *Dream of the Rarebit Fiend*, February 9, 1913. (Image courtesy of Ulrich Merkl.)

embedded bourgeois domestic frame of his bed, itself a kind of panel enclosure. In this reciprocal rupture, this self-contradictory setting into play of oppositional elements, we may recognize an aesthetic politics of modernist form, which sought simultaneity—an alternative to dualism that maintains difference while denying hierarchy.[34] One may understand *Little Nemo* as simultaneous both figuratively and literally. Its simultaneity is an alternative to a dualism that might ultimately decide in favor of the rational or the irrational. And it was the first comic strip to be profoundly, evidently simultaneous in the sense of presenting comics' "all-at-once-ness": it gave readers panels to be read in sequence, and also to be seen as one integrated image (what Spiegelman calls comics' "symphonic effect"). The architecture of early comics, then, makes legible and material its approach to modern experience. Comics suggests the proliferation of perspectives and temporalities—simultaneity, escape from "exclusive linearity."[35]

Even when it is pressurizing its own expected patterns, McCay's work presents a formal architecture—its attention to the total visual space of the page as the essential unit of information. McCay developed the comics page to function as a complex narrative unit with subdivided panels that chart temporal movement, and also simultaneously as an abstract graphic whole. McCay's comic strips make legible comics' poetics of simultaneity: they present both a sequence and a surface that can be read as a graphic unity. His visual architecture offers a formal layer to the page that is extrasemantic, an element that is independent of the action happening within the strip. As John Fell observes, distinguishing comics from film in writing on McCay: "Even after the reader has proceeded from picture to picture, the panels continue to relate to one another on the page in a kind of spread-out, timebound Cubism."[36] Spiegelman maintains that he could not have composed *Maus*, his account of his father's Holocaust testimony, without McCay's "architectonic rigor." Tom Gunning claims that "comics offer simultaneously two alternative regimes of reading: an overall one that grasps the page as a total design and a successive one that follows the order of individual frames one at a time." Comics, he argues, is not only "an art of succession" but also "a medium of new processes of reading."[37]

McCay's creation of the comics page as succession and as composite, in Gunning's terms, "[seizes] . . . awareness of its unending play between different states."[38] In many ways, then, McCay's work suggests how comics might fruitfully join critical conversations around kinds of reading that are exemplified by, say, Sharon Marcus and Stephen Best's recent call for "surface reading," which seeks to understand the complexity of literary surfaces they feel are under critical erasure.[39] I want to suggest, further, that part of the effect of McCay's awareness of artifice and architecture is to call attention to comics as literally "spectacular," offering dream stories but also demanding that we pay attention to the process of visualization, a key facet of work expressing the experience of trauma.

War shaped one of McCay's biggest formal innovations directly: he created the first animated documentary to have a commercial feature release, the critically underexamined *The Sinking of the Lusitania* (1918). In *The Sinking of the Lusitania*, techniques from McCay's comics join work that is explicitly documentary. The RMS *Lusitania*, a British luxury passenger liner, had been torpedoed by a German submarine off the Irish coast on May 7, 1915, on its way from New York to Liverpool; approximately 1,200 civilians, including 128 Americans, were killed. McCay's film, his fourth animated film, or "pen picture," and a two-year effort, was released by Jewel Productions on July 20, 1918, more than a year after the United States joined the war (McCay's son and son-in-law served in the armed forces). An early example of cel animation, *The Sinking of the Lusitania*, which unfolded almost in real time (the vessel sank in eighteen minutes), proposed itself as a work of witness to an event for which no archival footage existed; it was received as such.[40] Its images were drawn by hand on pieces of celluloid acetate in white and black India ink and then individually photographed at Vitagraph Studios. *The Sinking of the Lusitania* was said to re-create events of the disaster as told by survivors; it was advertised as "Winsor McCay's Blood Stirring Pen Picture—the World's Only Record of a Crime That Shocked Humanity!"[41] McCay forcefully staked a claim in drawing's power to document, continually flagging the word *record* ("From here you are looking at the first record of the sinking of the *Lusitania*") in the intercut title cards.

The Sinking of the Lusitania is a fascinating hybrid object that shuttles back and forth between drawing and a photographic register (as, for instance, does the acclaimed 2008 animated documentary *Waltz with Bashir*, which is also about war). McCay made 25,000 drawings for *The Sinking of the Lusitania*. The look of the documentary, as Annabelle Honess Roe points out, resembles nonfiction media of the time, such as editorial illustrations and newsreels. Its renderings of objects, particularly the *Lusitania* and the German U-boat, are detailed, proportional, and realistic, a feature for which it was widely admired.[42] But *The Sinking of the Lusitania* opens with a live-action prologue of sorts, an embedded mini-documentary, that depicts McCay's research and work on the film, including receiving details of the sinking from a Mr. Beach—a Hearst correspondent, August F. Beach, who was the first newsman at the scene of the disaster.[43] It also shows McCay presiding over a team of artists in his studio, suggesting a proliferation of hands. While with the earlier animated film *Gertie the Dinosaur* (1914) McCay had joined his body with Gertie's in the graphic space of the film when it was shown in his famous vaudeville presentations, as Daniel McKenna points out, here he crosses the other way and makes animation take over and represent the physical realm.[44]

Through its conspicuous attention to and mixing of different media, all under the auspices of creating a record, *The Sinking of the Lusitania* takes on what may seem a contradiction: McCay foregrounds his own presence as an artificer, and his own research (making viewers a witness to that, too—a feature we see in later work by Joe Sacco).[45] While McKenna understands that McCay's presence indicates that he himself must act as a form of evidence, a witness-body testifying metonymically to the veracity of his created images in place of photographs, my view is different. McCay's foregrounding of his own live-action body is actually a way of underscoring the handicraft of the film and thus calling attention to the action of (dying) bodies within its diegetic space. One sees this in McCay's typical emphasis on the movement of bodies—the procession of tiny light-colored lemminglike bodies jumping off the listing ship in the film's haunting long shot sequences, or the mother pushing her baby dramatically to the surface of the ocean with one arm as she slips underwater in one of its closing episodes.[46] In a film about the disappearance of bodies, McCay asks us to connect to processes of embodiment through attention to drawing. The first commercial animated documentary depicts a traumatic historical event—it is a registration of drawing's desire to compensate for and connect to lost bodies.

As one recognizes in McCay's work, comics inhabits, and produces, tensions between low and high modes, between appeals to mass readerships and a commitment to experimentation with its own formal grammar as a register of history and experience. This dynamic is legible in a different way in the rich tradition of visual storytelling offered by the socialist "wordless novels"—also known as "woodcut novels"—of the 1920s and 1930s, which enacted new structures of experiment with time and space based on a modern book format.[47] Wordless novels, catalyzed by silent film, were Expressionist and largely composed in black and white with stark contrasts in color. The tradition includes the work of Frans Masereel, the Belgian who invented the form; Otto Nückel, a German; and the Americans Lynd Ward and Giacomo Patri.[48] The midwesterner Ward's six wordless novels, which he published between 1929 and 1937, are emblematic of this mode of storytelling and its seemingly contradictory cultural embrace, as with McCay, of craft and commerce. As Eric Bulson points out, "There was no established generic category for the kind of book Ward had made."[49] *Gods' Man: A Novel in Woodcuts*, composed of 139 pictures rendered by wood engraving, was published by the house of Jonathan Cape and Harrison Smith and appeared the week of the Black Tuesday stock market crash in October 1929. It was a critical and commercial success.

Ward was influenced by Hogarth, Callot, Honoré Daumier, Goya, Käthe Kollwitz, and others with a "sympathetic response to the idea of pictorial narrative."[50] He discovered Masereel as an art student in Leipzig. Masereel produced more than twenty wordless novels; Ward believed he was the first artist to go beyond Hogarth.[51] A pacifist, a political cartoonist for *La Feuille*, and an illustrator of the works of Tolstoy, Zola, and Wilde, among others, Masereel published his inaugural book, *A Passionate Journey: A Novel Told in 165 Woodcuts* (German title: *Mein Stundenbuch*) in 1919. Thomas Mann—greatly invested in the possibilities of what he recognized as a new art form—wrote an appropriately passionate introduction. As with Töpffer and Goethe, one sees how new narrative visual forms, as their conventions were being created, were actively received as part of a conversation with literature. Mann writes that the reader will be "captivated by the flow of the pictures and . . . the deeper purer impact than you have ever felt before." He also lauds the populist contours of Masereel's picture-novel, arguing that Masereel's work "relies so little on a culture which is not . . . a product of ordinary democratic education."[52]

In a key repositioning, Ward, who forcefully brought the wordless novel tradition to the United States, became the first graphic author to have a Library of America volume of his work appear, in 2011 (Spiegelman introduced and edited the collection). Modernist and mass-produced, Ward's *Vertigo* is an experimental, political work that was published by Random House in 1937 and printed and marketed as a conventional novel around the same time that the first comic books appeared on newsstands.[53] It is an important expression of historical trauma in a then-uncharted graphic form. In *Vertigo*, composed of 230 woodblocks, Ward plays with the rules of panelization, arranging its narrative in four distinct panel sizes (small, medium, large square, and jumbo rectangular).[54] No one frame of reference, Ward seems to suggest, is fixed; there is no one "normal" view of the world. *Vertigo* also bears the influence of visual modernism in its Cubist and Futurist images. In some instances Ward "works within an idiom of almost pure abstraction and pattern," as Michael Joseph, his most suggestive commentator, observes.[55] Yet *Vertigo* was sold in bookstores—a fact crucial to my interest in comics as a "popular embodiment of avant-garde values."

The Girl, The Boy, and An Elderly Gentleman structure *Vertigo*, a narrative free of words except for those carried on signs within individual panels, such as "Fight for the Union—The Union Fights for You." Desperation and cruelty are the novel's guiding themes. An immigrant father-daughter family is at the story's center: the father tries to commit suicide by shooting himself in the head so that his daughter, The Girl, an aspiring violinist, might be able to collect his life insurance. The Boy, destitute, surrenders his blood—literally—to the character An Elderly Gentleman (the implication, of course, being that there are many such privileged and disinterested elderly gentlemen), a person who brings in National Guardsmen to bayonet his workers when they strike.

One of *Vertigo*'s most important features, as with all comics, is its thematization of time as space. *Vertigo* offers only one panel on each page, like most wordless novels, printed on only one side of the leaf. In this "triadic novel," the whole schematic revolves around time.[56] Time is theorized in both content and form: the narrative gives us Section One, "The Girl," divided into seven chapters, 1929 through 1935; Section Two, "An Elderly Gentleman," is divided into twelve chapters, January through December; and Section Three, "The Boy," is divided into seven chapters, Monday through Sunday. Years, months, days: while *Vertigo*'s time unwinds in smaller and smaller denominations, we are presented with an alternate temporality in opposition to An Elderly Gentleman's tyrannical, linear clock time (he is often featured with conventional clocks).[57] In this alternate temporality, visual details are repeated—analogous, perhaps, to lexical repetition in the work of modernist figures such as Stein—and exact images are offered twice, or more.[58] The result of this nonlinear movement is that, as Joseph puts it, "the reader's experience of the meaning and relationship of non-contiguous parts of *Vertigo* is shaped by a continual process of revision and renewal."[59] The book's last image—The Boy and The Girl on a downward-spiraling roller coaster—itself spirals back to the book's beginning, when they had visited an amusement park together (Figure 2.6).

Figure 2.6 Lynd Ward, last page of *Vertigo*, 1937. (Used by permission of Robin Ward Savage and Nanda Weedon Ward.)

The book's title, writes Ward, "was meant to suggest that the illogic of what we saw happening all around us in the thirties was enough to set the mind spinning through space and the emotions hurtling from great hope to the depths of despair."[60]

In his book *Graphic Storytelling*, cartoonist Will Eisner names Lynd Ward "perhaps the most provocative graphic storyteller in this century."[61] Against these sharp drops and hurtles, *Vertigo* encourages slowness and dwelling as a practice of reading and looking. In his introduction for the Library of America edition of Ward, Spiegelman declares that the secret "locked inside all wordless novels" is flipping pages back and forth.[62] With each image "floating in open space," as Eisner comments of *Vertigo*, the amount of action that transpires between scenes takes considerable input from the reader to comprehend.[63] Joseph highlights the book's dialectical means of graphic narration: its evident political message, on one hand, and on the other the fact that its form makes us decide "for ourselves how and where *Vertigo* ends."[64] And while the crafted *Vertigo* is visually elegant, as McCay's pages also never failed to be, Ward emphasized in a letter that its very form is connected to the "great violence" of the period in which it was composed: "Why this form was somehow most productive when used to develop themes related to the cataclysmic world we lived in through the Depression may be related to the violence those experiences did to our sense of the world."[65] Artistically and commercially, Ward's approach to narrative demonstrated "the viability of graphic storytelling" in America and suggested myriad possibilities for comics as a formally refined and yet urgent comment on contemporary circumstance, particularly in immersing a reader in its proliferative and disorienting timescapes.[66]

Approaching history from a different angle, but one connected to Ward's sensitivity to the ubiquity of great violence for the ordinary American, is the visual-verbal output of Henry Darger (1892–1973), a Chicago janitor whose wildly imaginative and often lovely, if terrifying, narratives were unpublished in his lifetime. Darger is often considered an "outsider artist," assigned to that tricky and basically incoherent category; in an autobiography he composed in the last years of his life he wrote firmly,

"I'm an artist, been one for years."[67] Since Darger's death and the discovery of his complete oeuvre inside his one-room Chicago apartment, he has been claimed by the art world on a national and international scale, with posthumous gallery exhibits and museum purchases; the largest public repository of his work is owned by the American Folk Art Museum in New York City, which describes Darger as one of the most significant self-taught artists of the twentieth century.[68]

Darger's work has also been claimed by the comics world as kin; it provides a fascinating example of inventive—and lengthy—serial visual storytelling (as well as itself drawing inspiration from newspaper comics, among other sources). One of the first venues to print Darger was Mouly and Spiegelman's *RAW*, in 1990, where an excerpt of his work alongside a selection of his autobiographical writing appears directly after a chapter of *Maus*. Darger's most significant work is his 15,000-plus-page *The Story of the Vivian Girls, in What Is Known as the Realms of the Unreal, of the Glandeco-Angelinian War Storm, Caused by the Child Slave Rebellion*—a meandering, gruesome, gorgeous tale of war featuring seven little girls as heroines. Darger wrote the narrative from about 1908 to 1938, after which he spent several decades vividly illustrating and continuing the story.[69] (It has been called the longest novel ever, and it may be also the longest original graphic novel, if one wanted to apply this terminology.) *In the Realms of the Unreal*'s images—watercolor and collage paintings—feature photographs traced from newspapers and magazines, among other sources, and Darger's own distilled and evocative line drawing.[70] Among Darger's characters in his vast visual narrative are mixed-sex children, many of whom, enslaved, appear naked (and always angelic). The visual world of Darger's story balances the beauty of his lovingly rendered children and his colorful patterned landscapes with the horror of war waged by the fictional Glandelinians on an innocent child population.

While Darger's work has often been understood as creating a fantastical (and creepy) escape world for a lonely person officially branded "feebleminded," Michael Moon's recent *Darger's Resources* makes the important point that Darger, in his massive lifelong art practice, instead "took on the role of witness to the terrible ordinariness of violence in the history of the twentieth century."[71] Darger, in his own official introductions to *In the Realms of the Unreal*, which he bound into thirteen volumes, adopts a somber rhetoric of bearing witness, writing about the difficulty of expressing war and trauma and offering statements that underscore the accuracy of his detailed report. He states, "Readers will find here many stirring scenes that are not recorded in any true history"; calls it "the complete and most accurate account"; and avows that the narrative is "perfectly reliable in every way," so "editors of great experience will be in due time allowed" to verify dates and occurrences.[72] Darger's suggestive writing about his story mixes the laying out of his fictional civil war (which is, after all, instigated by slaves righteously rebelling; he makes references to its nineteenth-century roots) with the naming of historical realities; he calls Glandelinia's government "worse than Communistic."[73] Darger's proliferatively serial work provides an idiom, however fantastical its content, for witnessing history; it relentlessly returns to scenes of war, massacre, and atrocity. Moon reads this as a "profound fidelity" to expressing "the place of just such forms of extreme violence, often perpetrated against highly vulnerable populations, in the history and development of the Americas down through Darger's own lifetime."[74]

Indeed, as his introductions also make clear, Darger's work is about witnessing and trauma—about visual apprehension and expression (in his writing he often calls the atrocities of war indescribable). In one fascinating painting, the caption-title appears within the space of the frame: "Vivian Girl Princesses are forced to witness frightful murder massacre of children—Vivian Girls not shown in this composition" (Figure 2.7). Directly above the cluster of words, in the left foreground, Glandelinian soldiers chat and smoke while absentmindedly strangling a child.[75] The word-and-image relation demands attention to the story's heroines not only as escapees but also as witnesses. Further, it indicates that the eyes of the reader—also "offscreen" apprehending the violence—have merged with the eyes of the witnessing Vivian Girls; they are our eyes, and we are theirs, looking upon this horrible scene.

While at midcentury Darger worked alone in his Chicago apartment bearing witness to the trauma of everyday violence in endlessly unfurling epic fantasies, in the commercial publishing industry new forms and modes of comics flourished. Across formats, comics integrated features of high and mass, modernist and lowbrow, mixing stark oppositionality with mainstream cultural appeal, antirealist aesthetics with popular narrative convention. Bronx-born cartoonist Harvey Kurtzman started *Mad Comics* (later *Mad* magazine) in 1952; it was a comic book self-reflexively concerned with comics aesthetics and the aesthetics of media (in his *Picture*

Figure 2.7 Henry Darger, "Vivian Girl Princesses Are Forced to Witness the Frightening Murder Massacre of Children." Date unknown. (© Kiyoko Lerner/Artists Rights Society [ARS], New York.)

Theory, W. J. T. Mitchell analyzes the incisive cultural force of *Mad* through the lens of the "metapicture").

Kurtzman, who was in the military, had illustrated training guides for the Army Informational Division during World War II.[76] His Korean War–focused series *Two-Fisted Tales*, first published in 1950, called "the most historically accurate war and adventure books ever made," portrayed "war and fighting men so accurately that they became 'anti-war' comics."[77] One sees this in stories such as his dark 1952 "Corpse on the Imjin," about the Korean War, and the important 1953 story "Atom Bomb!" Kurtzman engaged in "orgies of research" in the New York Public Library, in the words of comic book historians Michael Barrier and Martin Williams, among others who cite Kurtzman's zealous investigations. In a famous example of his obsession with accuracy, he sent an assistant down in a submarine so that onomatopoeic words he used to represent the sound made by a submerged submarine would be accurate.[78] The trajectory of Kurtzman's career reveals a crucial dual impulse—the impulse to research and represent the demands of historicity, and the impulse to satire—that now, routinely integrated, characterizes so much contemporary work: he went from meticulous representation of then-contemporary historical wars to establishing *Mad*'s satirical send-ups.

Kurtzman's later *Mad Comics: Humor in a Jugular Vein* attacked the mainstream American mind-set, and media culture, by offering a conscious "devaluation of American secular mythology" in a mass cultural genre: the comic book.[79] With *Mad*, Kurtzman realized "comics as a place outside consensus culture," as Gopnik and Varnedoe put it.[80] From 1957 to 1971 there were thirty-six FBI files on *Mad*, Paul Buhle reports.[81] Because it rejected "*everything* sacrosanct: television, advertising, Mom, Christmas, Hollywood, apple pie," as De Haven argues, *Mad* was a direct inspiration for underground comics, or "comix," in the late 1960s and early 1970s; indeed, "*Mad invented* the 60s," he avows.[82] J. Hoberman pronounces Kurtzman a "vulgar modernist," in the same category as T. S. Eliot and the sometimes Dadaist German collage artist Kurt Schwitters, other influential modernists sharing *Mad*'s argument that Western civilization is a clutter of cultural detritus.[83]

What is evident in comics—especially in the 1930s, and in the anticipation of the countercultural swell of the 1960s—is that its formal techniques were turned into specific social practices (and vice versa). *Mad* offered a rigorous self-consciousness about the comic book form; it attended to, and established, a formal self-reflexive grammar. Comics became legibly sophisticated in comic book form with *Mad*, without losing any potential for humor or bite. "I do timing, I do rhythm, I do sequence, I create movement by arranging panels," Kurtzman told the *Comics Journal*.[84] And in calling attention to its possibilities as a medium—especially in its satirical replication of the conventions of other media, such as TV, film, and advertising—*Mad* established, as Kurtzman understood it, a mode of engaging in and reflecting reality. *Mad* ushered in what Kurtzman called "the age of reality art."[85] This is "reality" not in terms of content but rather in terms of transparency, as the nontransparency of form: reality as attention to the narrative frame. In this, *Mad* created the idiom that is so common and popular today, as seen in the spate of "fake news" shows made canonical by Jon Stewart and Stephen Colbert, among others. Unsurprisingly, Kurtzman innovated another format that was slightly ahead of its time, at least in terms of commercial success: in 1959, he created *Harvey Kurtzman's Jungle Book*, a Ballantine Books paperback original offering four comics stories for adult audiences, a format not unlike Will Eisner's *A Contract with God and Other Tenement Stories*, the series of four linked vignettes that in 1978 was the first book to appear with the publisher-approved designation *A Graphic Novel*.[86]

Mad ushered in a new era for the complexity of comic books. Across Manhattan, Jules Feiffer was also observing reality—and creating comics that were explicitly adult as well as intellectual—in a different ephemeral format: his comic strip *Sick, Sick, Sick*, which ran in the *Village Voice*. The *Voice*, a weekly newspaper founded by Norman Mailer, among others, began publication in 1955; Feiffer started publishing *Sick, Sick, Sick* in 1956. Feiffer had grown up left-leaning in spite of his eager-to-assimilate parents (to them, disrespecting authority meant "you'd be on a boat back to Poland in 20 minutes," as he put it).[87] He was further radicalized by his time in the army: he was drafted in 1951, during the Korean War, but never served in Korea itself. While in the army, Feiffer began his story *Munro*, about a four-year-old drafted into the military.[88]

Feiffer's work registers an important shift in which narrative comics (as opposed to only single-panel cartoons) became literary and political in both their form and their explicit framework. His concept for his *Voice* strips was a calculated subtle one-two punch of images and words, as he explained to me: "You draw as little as possible so they don't get scared by the graphics, and you hit them with the dialogue." Feiffer had been a writer for the cartoonist Will Eisner during the commercial "golden age" of comics, and he, like Kurtzman, understood the beats and rhythm of the form. When I asked him if he knew he was inventing a new idiom, he replied, "Sure I knew. And of course, I loved that. But I didn't think that inventing a new idiom was important . . . I was saying things about the country I lived in that were terribly wrong." Feiffer was profoundly antiwar. He presented comics as a language of observation, and he crucially joined comics to an intellectual left-wing culture—and brought that culture to comics. When I inquired about this, Feiffer noted the era of the Max Eastman–helmed graphically innovative socialist magazine *The Masses* (1911–1917), when "artists and intellectuals were part of a radical group." In the post-1945 period, Feiffer's comics brought the form into the social-aesthetic fabric of those kinds of artistic and intellectual groups. And in addition to emplacing comics in such active political conversation, he opened up a cross-media investigation into form, as a screenwriter and a playwright, that only sharpened his rhythmic mode of observing and reflecting reality.[89]

Feiffer's comic strip became his expression of opposition to American policy, governmental and cultural; in his hands, comics was a pithy, trenchant, and formally sophisticated form of scrutiny attached to history. Feiffer was involved in protesting the Vietnam War and agitating for civil rights. "I was the first cartoonist to oppose the war in Vietnam," he recently claimed. "As far back as 1963."[90] Feiffer's comic strips became part of an active political conversation; he published *Feiffer on Vietnam* and *Feiffer on Civil Rights* in 1966, the latter with a foreword by Bayard Rustin, who notes, "LeRoi Jones attacks Feiffer for being a white liberal—but yesterday, and even ten years ago, Feiffer was already dissecting the phony aspects that are to be found among white liberals" (see Figure 2.8).[91] Feiffer joined *The Paris Review* set through *New Yorker* theater critic Kenneth Tynan, who wrote the glowing introduction to the British collection of *Sick, Sick, Sick* (1959); Feiffer's strip had appeared in the *Observer* in England, where Tynan previously had been the most famous theater critic in the country. "When Feiffer's cartoons started to appear in *The Village Voice*," writes Tynan, "it was immediately clear that a minor revolution was taking place in the art of drawing pictures for newspapers."[92] One night Feiffer and Tynan, as yet unacquainted, met when they both happened to be standing in line to pick up tickets for a Mike Nichols–Elaine May show at Town Hall. Tynan invited him afterward to dinner with friends including George Plimpton; Feiffer soon became friends with Tynan's crowd and with "old-time *Partisan Review* socialists" like Dwight Macdonald.[93]

Feiffer evolved to be one of the form's first public intellectuals, thus shaping comics as more open to itself being shaped by other forms in a dynamic cultural exchange.[94] As with other cartoonists discussed in this chapter, he had a key connection to a novelist—E. L. Doctorow, who closely edited his prose book *The Great Comic Book Heroes* in 1965. But while Feiffer was accepted (even, as he put it, "too accepted") at the

Figure 2.8   Jules Feiffer, strip from *Feiffer on Vietnam*, 1966. (© Jules Feiffer.)

Plimpton parties, his intellectual cohort refused the designation *comic strip*—they insisted, he recalls, that his *Voice* strip "was a column, an essay . . . I'd say, 'No, I'm a cartoonist, I do a comic strip.'"[95]

The mid-1950s also registered drastic changes in comic book aesthetics and culture—changes that directly affected the creation of the "underground comix revolution" of the 1960s and also oriented mainstream comics toward a wide range of modes, some banal and some usefully new. The heyday of the unselfconscious creativity of the "aboveground" genre comic book ended in 1954 after Senate hearings on the connection between comic book readerships and juvenile delinquency resulted in a censorious federal content code.[96] The Comics Code, which had strictures such as "In every instance shall good triumph over evil and the criminal be punished for his misdeeds," brought the comic book industry's sense of creative possibility to a halt. (How many interesting stories can happen when good always wins?)[97] The concern about the violence in comics, particularly in horror comics, some of which were quite vivid, had been sparked by the psychiatrist Fredric Wertham's 1954 best seller *Seduction of the Innocent: The Influence of Comics Books on Today's Youth*; he later testified before the Senate subcommittee.[98] Wertham's effective assault on comic books has made him a long-vilified figure in the comics world: Spiegelman collaborated on an opera about Wertham, *Drawn to Death: A Three-Panel Opera*; Michael Chabon fictionalized the hearings as a crushing blow to his central characters in *The Amazing Adventures of Kavalier and Clay*; and most recently journalist David Hajdu narrated the events colorfully in *The Ten-Cent Plague: The Great Comic-Book Scare and How It Changed America*.

EC Comics, founded in the 1940s, published Kurtzman's war series *Two-Fisted Tales* and *Frontline Combat*, along with *Mad* and a whole host of lurid titles including *Tales from the Crypt, The Vault of Horror*, and *Crime SuspenStories. Mad*, which was basically outside the scope of the code in its content as a humor title, shifted away from comic book newsprint and became a "slick" magazine in 1955, thus permanently evading any restriction and flourishing as a commercial enterprise. In the aftermath of the code, publisher William M. Gaines turned to "cleaner" stories, as did other comics publishers, resulting in new titles, some explicitly educational or bland, and some simply unusually meditative, such as EC's 1955 *Psychoanalysis*, part of its New Direction line. In 1955 New Direction also published the grave "Master Race," an eight-page story about the Holocaust, in the first issue of the brief series *Tales Designed to Carry an . . . IMPACT*. Written by Al Feldstein and illustrated with somber beauty and sophistication by Bernard Krigstein, "Master Race" involves a postwar chance encounter on the New York City subway between a mysterious man and a former Nazi perpetrator; the story then delves into flashbacks, picturing, in a crisp panel each, Kristallnacht, the Belsen camp perimeter, gas chambers, camp medical experiments, and mass graves, among other horrors of Nazism. Acknowledging Nazi barbarism and actually picturing it in comics (which was rare for the period in any form), "Master Race," which did not gain critical or popular traction at the time of its publication, demonstrates how short-form comic-book stories, even in formulaic genres such as suspense, were edging in significant moments toward an accounting with the violence of history.

Psychoanalysis, which appeared for four issues, told stories of "People Searching for Peace of Mind" (Figure 2.9). Its content is schlocky: "Into

Figure 2.9   Cover of *Psychoanalysis* (reprint of all four issues, originally from 1955), art by Jack Kamen.

his peaceful, tastefully-decorated, subdued office come the tormented," the narration unironically announces, heralding the unnamed square-jawed, bespectacled psychiatrist. But *Psychoanalysis*, representing a truly new genre, attempted to do what it has become clear today comics excel at: visualizing the workings of the individual mind on the page, especially memory as a process, and revealing the imbrication of past and present as a psychic structure through a visualized grammar. (These features are evident, for instance, in Justin Green's 1972 *Binky Brown Meets the Holy Virgin Mary*, the first work of autobiographical comics, which is about obsessive-compulsive disorder.) The series takes its rhetoric of addressing pain seriously; each issue contained several "case file" stories of patients whose progress readers follow from issue to issue; and each of those stories in part represents the past through flashback panels, marked by wavy or jagged lines, and the meaningful patterned use of color. From all cultural vantage points, whether self-consciously intellectual or "mass," comics in its various formats was inclining itself more and more to address a reckoning with war and trauma.

But while some new and unexpected comics formats and subjects emerged in the 1950s, as we recognize in the short-lived *Psychoanalysis*, the Comics Code essentially forced cartoonists interested in doing radical work in comic-book form to publish outside of mainstream strictures. Underground comics, which often reveled in breaking taboos, took shape as a reaction to several factors, one of which was the censorious code that debilitated the mainstream industry. Many if not all of the cartoonists who would go on to create the underground comics movement were devotees of *Mad* and involved in networks that had grown from communities devoted to *Mad*-inspired satire. As Spiegelman sees it, "Kurtzman is the undisputed Godfather of the underground comics of the sixties."[99] In the aftermath of the code, cartoonists were politicized by the New Left, the Vietnam War, and the underground press, and they were also unable to publish uncensored work in aboveground outlets. Underground comics, then, originated entirely with the artist, were self-published or published by loose collectives, and were distributed through nontraditional channels, such as head shops, for an exclusively adult audience.

Responses to the Vietnam War motivated the rise of underground comics and shaped profound innovations in comics form. The year that many mark as the beginning of the underground comics movement, 1968, was one of escalating numbers of American troops in Vietnam as well as the year of the war's highest casualties; the antiwar movement was at a high pitch. Nineteen sixty-seven had brought the March on the Pentagon, memorably chronicled in Norman Mailer's *The Armies of the Night* (Feiffer makes an appearance); 1968 delivered the infamous protests resulting in substantial violence at the Democratic National Convention in Chicago. The late 1960s saw comics across formats pushing at their own boundaries to take on the war. Garry Trudeau's *Doonesbury*, which began in 1968 under a different title in the *Yale Daily News* (it was first published as a syndicated daily strip in 1970), directly addressed the war, featuring the character B. D., a college student who volunteers for Vietnam; a collection appeared in 1973 as *But This War Had Such Promise*. While after the war Trudeau was honored by the Vietnam Veterans of America as "one of the most important creative voices of the Vietnam War generation," in the late 1960s and early 1970s his comic strip was routinely censored by newspapers.[100] A statement of censorship adorns the back of *But This War Had Such Promise*, quoted from the *Dallas Morning Star-Telegram*: "For the second time this month, *Doonesbury* does not appear in the comic section. Reason: it was not a comic. Instead, it was a violent editorial comment on the war in Vietnam."[101] What a comic essentially was or could be, in any publication context, was in flux, motivated by the urgencies of the war.

The underground papers publishing uncensored comix—the *East Village Other*, the Berkeley *Barb*, the Los Angeles *Free Press*, the Detroit *Fifth Estate*, and the Michigan *Paper*, which together made up the Underground Press Syndicate—instituted a free exchange of features. Publication information offered in Robert Crumb's 1971 *Home Grown Funnies*, for instance, put out by Krupp Comic Works, Inc., expresses the sustained ethos of the period: "All material herein may be reprinted for free by any underground publication or other small, independent enterprise. All fat Capitalists who reprint without permission will be sued for briech [*sic*] of copyright! Nyahh!"[102] Crumb galvanized underground publishing—and defined the phenomenon of underground comics—with his 1968 comic book *Zap Comix*, the first title to appear from San Francisco underground imprint Apex Novelties. Its publisher had traded his tape deck to borrow a friend's printing press to print *Zap*. *Zap* presented enduring characters such as Whiteman, Mr. Natural, Flakey Foont, and Schuman the Human. Crumb was, in his own words, making "a drawing of the horror of America."[103] Crumb channeled a profound and deep-seated—and perhaps, as he indicates, in his own case even partly subconscious—disgust and malaise provoked by contemporary America that translated on the sketchbook page as teeming psychedelic landscapes both amusing and frightful. The tagline on *Zap* #1—"Fair Warning: For Adult Intellectuals Only!"—boldly repositioned comics beyond mere entertainment as a sophisticated aesthetic critical practice outside of mainstream culture. The response to Crumb's work was enormous and immediate, and comix titles, as well as new issues of *Zap*, proliferated steadily.[104]

The underground comix movement is responsible for the current prospering field of literary comics; it established, as Spiegelman puts it in a 1981 image he designed for *RAW*, "comics as a medium for self expression," with work by figures such as Spiegelman, Crumb, Justin Green, Aline Kominsky-Crumb, Spain, Kim Dietch, and others harnessing that notion and inspiring today's multifaceted crop of independent artists.[105] The underground was both a movement that understood itself as modernist and a refuge for those artists still interested in the figure during the period when Abstract Expressionism was the dominant preoccupation of American art. Underground cartoonists self-identified as modernist or avant-garde, no matter that the historical period of high modernism had passed: it was their turn to meaningfully inhabit that posture. Underground comics, often deeply concerned with form, anticommercial, and oppositional to mainstream mores, were not trying to adhere to an established notion of what avant-gardism meant; rather, they sought to invent the notion of an avant-garde afresh—sacrificing none of the fascination with form in also investing in the populist idea of accessibility and inexpensive publication and circulation. This also often meant connecting to humor without abandoning intellectual or formal rigor (indeed, form is often part of the joke), an aesthetic-cultural modality seen especially in the *fumisme* of the fin-de-siècle avant-garde detailed in *The Spirit of Montmartre*, a book and exhibit that has been important to Spiegelman, whose own work emerged out of the underground.

Spiegelman's hugely significant *Breakdowns* (1978), for instance, a collection of mostly antinarrative underground comics pieces, is littered with explicit references to Winsor McCay and George Herriman, as well as to famous exemplars of literary and visual modernism such as Stein and Picasso, but its attachment to, and expansion of, modernist aesthetics resides in its experiments with how to divide time and space while still remaining narrative. Crumb published *Av'N'Gar Comix*; Spiegelman noted he was certain *Breakdowns* "would be a central artifact in the history of Modernism."[106] Both cartoonists experimented with the possibilities for offering a story that stopped or slowed time. Crumb's "Bo Bo Bolinski: He's the No. 1 Human Zero—He's No Big Deal" appeared in *Uneeda Comix* in 1970. In this one-page story, a man is seen in nine different frames from nine different perspectives; the expectation of causality or progression across frames is halted (Figure 2.10). Spiegelman calls this "turning the page into a diagram—an orthographic projection."[107] Comics in this configuration then becomes evidently about narrative space—orthogonal projections indicate a depth-oriented mapping.[108] In his dense one-page Cubist-inspired strip "Don't Get Around Much Anymore," also concerned with freezing time, Spiegelman enacts this principle.[109] There is little action or movement in the diagrammatic strip, published in 1974 in *Short Order Comix* #2. It visually implies diegetic temporal movement only once, and it disjoints word and image, unhinging reference.[110] Comics supposedly is a form built on sequence; cartoonists were dialing its properties back, toying with the expression of temporal progression. The features that today incline comics to history and documentary are seen here: formal attention to mapping, to nonlinear time, and to complicating causality and movement.

"In comics," Spiegelman says, "formal energies hadn't been tapped, although they had in all the other arts—literature, painting, sculpting, music. . . . Here was this young medium that, in a sense, was the last bastion of figurative drawing. As a result, nobody had become preoccupied with the issues that preoccupied modernist art elsewhere."[111] Comics, indeed, was a bastion of figurative drawing during a period governed by the sanctities of abstraction. The underground comics offered an aesthetic form that was both avant-garde and, importantly, figurative. *Zap* #1 included Crumb's famous three-page "Abstract Expressionist Ultra Super Modernistic Comics," which has no speech that is readable for denotative content nor any regularized panels or discernable narrative; it moves, and moves beautifully, as an arrangement of vital shapes and images that seem to burst from the page, as a pattern of vital marks. Even in the version of comics heralding itself as abstract, though, one recognizes shapes and forms, however decontextualized: a woman's body, breasts, hands, a rose, a cityscape. Comics is an aesthetic practice in this period in which figurative drawing, however experimental the frame, is legible. Several prominent cartoonists, among them Green and Kominsky-Crumb, came to underground comics specifically as an escape from their formal training in Abstract Expressionism.[112]

Figure 2.10 Robert Crumb, "Bo Bo Bolinski: He's the No. 1 Human Zero—He's No Big Deal," *Uneeda Comix*, 1970. (© R. Crumb.)

Other Abstract Expressionists also came to comics—or at least to the language of comics. One of the primary examples is painter Philip Guston, born Phillip Goldstein, who in 1968—the same year underground comics took off—abandoned the Abstract Expressionism he had earlier been celebrated for. In the wake of the endemic violence in America and overseas in Vietnam in the late 1960s, Guston turned to a vocabulary of images. Even earlier in his career he had stated, "I do not see why the loss of faith in the known image and symbol in our time should be celebrated as a freedom."[113] Guston began a relationship in his work with portraying *things*—commonplace things, although ones that could evoke uneasy histories in the post–World War II period, such as piles of shoes. "Books, shoes, buildings, hands—feeling a relief and a strong need to cope with tangible things," he wrote of abandoning his "pure" drawings that eschewed objects.[114] Guston's famous 1970 show at the Marlborough Gallery of his figurative paintings—notably of hooded Klansmen and a host of familiar objects distilled to basic cartoon shapes (lightbulbs, clocks, shoes, bottles, cars, cigars)—was roundly criticized, most prominently by the *New York Times*'s Hilton Kramer, whose headline "A Mandarin Pretending to Be a Stumblebum" became notorious. Arthur Danto calls this moment a "reflection of a deep turn in art history" and avows, "Guston was helping to consolidate a new artistic order"—one I would characterize as linking handmade images to witness, taking on the figure, and the complicated and contingent act of reference.[115]

Guston's turn away from pure abstraction and toward what he called his desire to "tell stories" in his paintings—however obscure these "stories" really are—is motivated, as with underground cartoonists such as Spiegelman and Crumb, by the need to connect with history through encountering and refracting its own set of symbols. "Our whole lives (since I can remember) are made up of the most extreme cruelties of holocausts. We are the witnesses of the hell," Guston wrote to his biographer Dore Ashton.[116] American involvement in Vietnam peaked in 1968, the year that underground comics, with its awareness of narrative time and space, and the taboo, emerged as a political force and the year that Guston broke out of what he considered an aloof engagement and introduced a new vocabulary—one based on the vernacular form of comics—to the art world. In fact, Guston and Crumb, both themselves influenced by Goya and by the American comic strip, coming at the horror of America from the distinct vantage points of their separate mediums, produced a range of similar iconography (both based on early comics, for instance from the 1920s). We see this, for instance, in conspicuously bulging shoes, often attached to puny limbs, and rubbery bodies. Bill Berkson, the poet and critic, recalls getting a letter from Guston collaborator Clark Coolidge in 1969, in which he noted Guston's imagery "looks a lot like Crumb World."[117] While critics agree—and there has been hearty speculation about this—that the two artists developed their iconographies independently, what is striking is not the possibility of influence but rather the simultaneity: both, coming from different cultural spaces, turned to creating sets of images, images of seething historical detritus, at a similar moment as a mode of bearing witness to the modern world.[118]

I want to conclude by mentioning a project by Guston completed in 1971, shortly before Keiji Nakazawa in Japan and Spiegelman in the United States kick-started the phenomenon of nonfiction comics based on the experiences of their families during World War II. Guston's book of drawings, *Poor Richard*, a riff on the Benjamin Franklin work of the same name, is a weird object—as many of the anomalous objects noted in this chapter are— that inhabits comics even more fully than his paintings, in the service of documenting history. *Poor Richard* is one of those books, one of those compelling understudied objects to emerge in recent years, that one could plausibly name the "first" graphic novel, were one in the business of adducing that particular first (which I am not). What I am interested in is *Poor Richard* as an inventive visual form of recording a sharply felt external political reality: the presidency of Richard Nixon. A series of seventy-five drawings, *Poor Richard* charts Nixon's life and coheres into a loose narrative, developed out of Guston and his friend Philip Roth's mutual obsession with the creepy pathos of the president even in this pre-Watergate moment (see Figure 2.11). Guston had been crushed by the reception of his 1970 show and retreated to Woodstock, New York, where and he and Roth became close friends and co-conspirators and he continued to make his searing figurative images.

Poor Richard is akin in form to the wordless novel tradition—one image without a caption appears on each printed page, although words often appear inside the frame. Debra Bricker Balken understands the work as part of a long line of political caricature that includes Goya's *Caprichos* and Picasso's 1937 *The Dream and Lie of Franco*, his comic-strip work that is an artifact of the Spanish Civil War, darkly protesting the Spanish generalissimo.[119] But it has a lot in common with underground comics. Its tone is

Figure 2.11 Philip Guston, title page, *Poor Richard,* composed 1971. Note Nixon's dog Checkers, referenced in Nixon's emotional 1952 televised speech that came to be known as the "Checkers speech." (© The Estate of Philip Guston.)

cutting satire, and its expressive lines and disproportionate grotesqueries of form feel very close to the spontaneous, bulbous rendering of many underground comics (Nixon's nose is generally represented as a penis and his cheeks as testicles). Guston did not publish *Poor Richard* in his lifetime, although Roth, among others, encouraged him to do so. (Balken, a curator, brought the book out in 2001.) What is striking is Guston's creation of the long-format drawn work as a record of history.

Poor Richard was a research project and not simply a series of impressions; in a talk at Yale in 1973 at which Guston showed the drawings for the first time, projected, he noted that his preparation had included reading books such as Nixon's own *Six Crises* and Gary Wills's *Nixon Agonistes*.

He described his own turn to the form as one of urgency: "In the summer of 1971, I was pretty disturbed about everything in the country politically, the administration specifically, and I started doing cartoon characters. And one thing led to another, and for months I did hundreds of drawings and they seemed to form a kind of story line."[120] *Poor Richard* may be grotesque, but it aims for incisive accuracy. In the early 1970s, artists across fields innovated comics, understanding picture writing, as Töpffer had, as a language in which the snaking lines of history could be legible.

| 3 |

I SAW IT AND THE WORK
OF ATOMIC BOMB MANGA

There's much to be done with black ink and paper.
—WILLIAM KENTRIDGE, 2014

This book proposes 1972 as the crucial moment for the global emergence of comics as a form of bearing witness to war and historical devastation.[1] In this year, some of the earliest works of nonfiction comics emerge from different "sides" of World War II: Hiroshima survivor Keiji Nakazawa's groundbreaking work of "atomic bomb manga," the comic book *Ore Wa Mita*—or *I Saw It*, a title that explicitly evokes Goya's famous caption in his *Disasters of War* series—and Art Spiegelman's pivotal first "Maus" comic, about his immigrant family's survival of Poland's death camps. While annihilated parental bodies explicitly motivate both works, Nakazawa's is an eyewitness account, while Spiegelman is a secondary witness. In the case of Nakazawa and Spiegelman, the obliteration wreaked by World War II, which each of them approached from a different cultural starting point, led to a new phase in the creation of visual-verbal forms of witness.

In thinking comparatively, which is to say in looking at the substantive innovation occurring at the same time from different sides of World War II, we can begin to paint a picture of why the early 1970s gave rise to what has become the most trenchant kind of work within the comics field: nonfiction, and nonfiction specifically expressing the realities of war. While in earlier decades in both Japan and the United States the subject of the war and the status of "survival" was largely still shrouded in silence or taboo, by the opening of the 1970s, especially after the artistic, cultural, and political upheavals of the 1960s, including fierce anti–Vietnam War movements in both the United States and Japan, the issues that had been simmering under the surface—what does it even *mean* to survive, to remember?—demanded articulation. The world was engrossed by the Vietnam War and immersed in its stream of televisual images, as its American moniker the "living-room war" indicates (a television critic for the *New Yorker*, Michael Arlen, coined the term in 1966).[2] In Japan, by the end of the 1960s, the Vietnam War—particularly its visual aspect— offered a context to revisit the Asia-Pacific War. Vietnam "saturated the media with images that resonated with Japan's wartime past," as Eldad Nakar argues, producing a reevaluation that "transformed Japan's vision" of its own history.[3] The Vietnam War was part of the Cold War and so in that sense was an extension of World War II.[4] It also suggested, in its galvanizing of antiwar affect and its full-blown media manifestation, a precondition for the visibility of earlier wartime testimony. We can understand the return to *drawing to tell*, the reemergence and creative expansion in our contemporary world of the power of the hand-drawn image, against the backdrop of this saturation of mechanical objectivity and the discourses of technological power that shaped the atomic age.[5]

Keiji Nakazawa, the innovator of documentary comics of witness in Japan, survived the atomic bombing of Hiroshima city on August 6, 1945. He was six years old. (Nakazawa died in Hiroshima on December 19, 2012, of lung cancer.) At 8:15 a.m., when the B-29 *Enola Gay* dropped the atomic bomb on the city, Nakazawa was walking to Kanzaki Elementary School from his home in the Funairi Hommachi neighborhood. Less than one mile from the hypocenter, he paused outside the schoolyard's concrete wall to

answer a question posed by a classmate's mother; when the bomb deto-
nated, the wall fell on him, deflecting and absorbing the shock and protecting him from the heat, while she died instantly. (More than 70,000
people died instantaneously, with as many perishing afterward from radiation sickness.) In *I Saw It*, his groundbreaking documentary comics about
the bomb, her instantly blackened corpse plays a central role in Nakazawa's
dawning recognition of the horror; in his later prose autobiography he
observes that "her entire body had been burned pitch black."[6] Violence so
extreme it appears abstract became Nakazawa's instant perceptual reality.

Nakazawa's father, Harumi, older sister, Eiko, and younger brother, Su-
sumu, perished on August 6. The Nakazawa house collapsed on them and
then went up in flames while Keiji's pregnant mother, Kimiyo, watched
helplessly. Kimiyo, known as Kimie, gave birth later that day on the pave-
ment, induced by shock, to a baby girl named Tomoko, who died of mal-
nutrition at four months old. Two older brothers who were not in the city
that day survived the bombing; Akira Nakazawa had been part of a group
evacuation to the country, and Kōji Nakazawa, the eldest sibling, had gone
to Kure as a student-soldier. After the bomb, Nakazawa and his mother
fled to relatives in Eba and gradually made their way back to Hiroshima.
Nakazawa created the first so-called atomic bomb manga as a cartoonist
living in Tokyo after his mother's death. *Manga* refers, as a general
matter, to comics from Japan; it translates roughly as "whimsical pictures."
Although the term is often credited to self-proclaimed "drawing maniac"
Katsushika Hokusai (1760–1849), the pen name of famed *ukiyo-e* artist
Katsukawa Shunrō, from his collection of sketches *Hokusai Manga* (which
began serial publication in 1814), the word had been introduced at least as
early as 1798 to indicate comic sketches.[7]

Shaped by the realities of war, Nakazawa's manga established a new
imaginary, and a new culture, for nonfiction manga in Japan. There had
been nonfiction manga published previously, largely in the context of political satire and current events commentary, such as in *Jiji Manga* (a Sunday
supplement that was added to the *Jiji-Shinpō* newspaper starting in 1902),
which depicted, for instance, the discourse surrounding the Great Kanto
Earthquake of 1923.[8] However, the overwhelming majority of work was fictional.[9] Post–World War II manga of the 1950s—even works classified as
senki mono (records of war)—were fictionalized: they combined historical
settings, dates, and figures with fictitious plots and details.[10] In the 1960s,
"artist manga" emerged as a genre, focusing plotlines on young, aspiring

manga artists, but these accounts were semiautobiographical—as were the works that are the closest precursors to what Nakazawa created in 1972. Earlier, proximate manga includes Osamu Tezuka's short story "Gachaboi's Record of One Generation" (1970), in which he recounts personal experiences, including during wartime; Shigeru Mizuki's "The Flight" (1970), which depicts how he lost his arm in the Imperial Army in World War II; and short stories (1971–1972) by Yoshihiro Tatsumi, eventually collected in the volume *Good-Bye*, which concentrates on postwar life in Osaka.[11] (Tatsumi is one of the progenitors of the *gekiga*—literally, "dramatic pictures"—style of alternative manga, which developed in the late 1950s; Nakazawa, although he produced dark, realistic work, worked from within a commercial idiom distinct from *gekiga*.)[12] The most directly comparable work is Kōji Asaoka's "The Tragedy of a Planet," about Hiroshima, a manga adaptation of Tatsuo Kusaka's prose memoir.[13] While these works in part focus on war and the self, they do not claim, as Nakazawa's *I Saw It* does, the status of first-person witness, proclaimed by the bold title.[14]

Nakazawa, whose deceased father had been a *nihonga* artist, a creator of traditional Japanese-style ink paintings and lacquer work, discovered manga through Tezuka's 1947 lengthy, creative *New Treasure Island (Shin Takarajima)*, a retelling of the 1883 Robert Louis Stevenson classic. Tezuka, influenced by American comics and Disney animation, widened manga's mainstream scope hugely in the postwar years, in part through his creation of longer narrative work; *New Treasure Island*, a smash hit, marks this shift.[15] (Japan's most famous modern manga creator, Tezuka is known worldwide for his Astro Boy—Tetsuwan Atomu, or "Mighty Atom"—character; in the mid-1980s he also created the series *Adolf*, a historical drama that begins before World War II and features three Adolfs, including a Jewish Adolf living in Japan.) Nakazawa could not afford drawing paper, so he tore down movie posters from city streets and hand-made books from them: he would cut them to size, sew them into a notebook, and copy Tezuka illustrations in pencil on their white backs. He was also taken with the inventive and populist visual-verbal storytelling form *kamishibai* (literally, "paper play" or paper theater), in which a traveling performer displays a series of picture boards, set in a wooden proscenium, voicing the story while showing images to collective audiences on the streets.[16] After graduating from junior high school, Nakazawa became a sign painter—a trade also practiced by his American counterpart Justin Green, who revolutionized nonfiction comics in America in the early 1970s.[17] In his private creative practices and his professional life, Nakazawa continually worked in and around the edges of handmade culture, where graphic storytelling and design intersect with the accessibility of the vernacular and the artisanal. In 1961, at age twenty-two, he moved to Tokyo with the express purpose of becoming a cartoonist. Nakazawa created a new idiom inspired by witness and established manga as a global export, achievements equaled by few other cartoonists.

The dominant mode of managing the legacy of the atomic bomb in this period was silence and disengagement. In the early and mid-1960s, Tokyo, which had been firebombed during the war, was a city Nakazawa describes "an assemblage of people from all of the country who knew absolutely nothing about the atomic bomb" and who believed rumors of the transmissibility of "atomic bomb disease," in which one could "catch" radiation.[18] There was heavy disdain for atomic bomb survivors, called *hibakusha*—literally, "explosion-affected people" (a phenomenon that, although lessened, persists to this day and also can be recognized in extant attitudes toward those affected by the Fukushima Daiichi nuclear plant disaster). Punning on the anti-genocide and atrocity catchphrase in his often quite funny prose autobiography, Nakazawa titles a section on 1960s Tokyo "Never Again Say the Words 'Atomic Bomb'!"[19] He has detailed in many different outlets the "severe discrimination" he and other bomb survivors faced.[20] Deciding to hide the fact that he was a *hibakusha*, Nakazawa resolved upon moving to Tokyo to, indeed, never again say those words; he even refused to read newspaper articles with the characters "atomic bomb."[21] Nakazawa became a paid assistant to the commercial manga artists Daiji Kazumine and Naoki Tsuji, and he made his solo debut in 1963 with the ongoing serial *Spark One*, about car racing and espionage ("one racing team was trying to steal the secrets of another racing team's car design," as he glosses it), in the magazine *Boys' Pictorial (Shōnen Gaho)*. "I did all kinds of genres," Nakazawa explains of his catholic tastes. "Sci-fi, baseball, samurais . . . I'd try my hand at anything."[22] In his early career in manga, he worked within multiple genres and mastered them.

Kimie Nakazawa's disintegrated body, her *bonelessness*, compelled Nakazawa to create comics about the bomb, a compensatory, material infrastructure. She died in October 1966 in Hiroshima, after ongoing treatment at the Atomic Bomb Hospital and suffering a cerebral brain hemorrhage. In Japanese funerary practice, after a body has been cremated, relatives pick out the major bones and place them in an urn.[23] When Nakazawa went to the crematorium to collect his mother's ashes, he was shocked that "there were no bones left in my mother's ashes, as there normally are after a cremation. Radioactive cesium from the bomb had eaten away at her bones to the point that they disintegrated. The bomb had even deprived me of my mother's bones."[24] Devastated and infuriated by the invasion of the bomb into the very foundational structure of his mother, robbing him of anything solid to recover of her, to literally hold of her, Nakazawa resolved to make the atomic bomb the central subject of his cartooning practice.

As Herbert Bix writes in *Hiroshima in History and Memory*, there was an immediate postwar censorship in Japan, imposed by the U.S. administration but endorsed by both sides, that forbade publications about suffering.[25] This predominant culture of silence persisted long past the end of the U.S. occupation of Japan in 1952. Nakazawa's early attempts, all fictional, to create narratives about Hiroshima in the late sixties were considered so politically radical that he had to publish them in an "adult"—meaning "erotic"—magazine.[26] His "Pelted by Black Rain," which appeared in May 1968, is a fictional account considered the inaugural "atomic bomb manga."[27] It was published in *Manga Punch*, a magazine for young men. In this regard, the field of production with which Nakazawa was imbricated looks much like the American comix underground, where determined political radicalism mixed with what was often the licentiousness of the taboo-shredding 1960s visionary cartoonists. An angry, hard-boiled genre story about a young bomb victim, "Pelted by Black Rain" was completed in 1966 and rejected by major commercial publishers for years until *Manga Punch* took it on despite the editor's expressed fears that both he and Nakazawa would be arrested by the CIA.[28] The "third-rate" magazines, the "lowbrows"—this is where Nakazawa was able to create a venue for circulating work about the bomb. The "black" series, presenting hard-boiled plotlines focusing on the atomic bomb, appeared in four additional installments: "The Black River Flows," "Beyond Black Silence," "A Flock of Black Pigeons," and "Black Flies."[29]

In 1970, still motivated by the urgency of addressing the bomb, Nakazawa published "Suddenly One Day," an eighty-page story about a second-generation bomb victim, conceived of as part of a "peace" series. It appeared in *Boys' Jump (Shōnen Jump)*, a boys' entertainment magazine founded in 1968 as a venue for newcomer talent, competing against the mainstream weeklies *Shōnen Magazine* and *Shōnen Sunday*, manga mainstays since the late 1950s.[30] While Yu Itō and Tomoyuki Omote write in an essay on Nakazawa that it "cannot be overlooked" that the work in *Boys'*

Jump was "at that time disdained as an extremely vulgar medium," that publication had a larger share of the market than *Manga Punch*: *Boys' Jump* sold a million copies a week in 1970. "Suddenly One Day" produced, to Nakazawa's surprise, a major reaction—he received hundreds of letters from people avowing that they had not known or understood even the basic factual parameters of the bombing that he conveyed in the fictional story.[31]

Nakazawa was both impressed and horrified by this correspondence, and depressed by the reimmersion that drawing scenes of the atomic bombing had caused him, as well as at the public backlash. Drawing and memory, particularly sense memory, became fundamentally intertwined: "When I was drawing . . . [t]he stench of rotting bodies returned to me."[32] The *Asahi* newspaper, in covering Nakazawa's controversial atomic bomb manga, publicly announced his status as a Hiroshima survivor. Nakazawa and his wife, Misayo, whom he had married in 1966, were stigmatized by neighbors, and criticized as bringing shame to their families. Misayo Nakazawa asked her husband to stop writing about the atomic bomb.[33] Nakazawa persisted in his focus on war, however, drawing eponymously titled manga about Okinawa prior to its reversion to Japanese administration in 1972 and a whole burst of fictional work about the bomb, creating a new manga field.[34] It is possible to see links between the conceptual and formal underpinnings of Nakazawa's comics and the Japanese art movements of the early 1970s, such as Mono-Ha (School of Things), particularly as a reaction to the annihilation caused by the bomb, but the growing commercial world of manga and the world of the Japanese avant-garde were then deeply stratified.

Finally, in 1972, the supportive editor of *Boys' Jump Monthly*, a supplement to *Boys' Jump*, decided to publish a series of autobiographical comics by manga artists and, knowing of his personal connection to the Hiroshima bombing, asked Nakazawa to be the first in the series.[35] As with Spiegelman in the exact same year, who initially begged off the comics story that became "Maus" for editor Justin Green, Nakazawa refused the invitation until editor Tadasu Nagano, who had published his recent fictional and controversial atomic bomb comics with enthusiasm, wore him down. For both Spiegelman and Nakazawa, these comics stories about witness necessarily involved producing, however contingently, identity affiliations connected to trauma with which both were uncomfortable. In thinking about how they overcame their mutual reluctance, the difference in the cultural contexts of their work becomes clear: the American underground comics emphasized above all artistic independence (Spiegelman, despite his initial disinclination, eventually came around on his own to a powerful idea that would drive his story), while in Japan's commercial comics industry editors often played a significant, involved role in the careers of manga artists, as in Nakazawa's case.[36] *I Saw It*, Nakazawa's eyewitness account of August 6, 1945, was published in October 1972 in black and white, as a stand-alone, forty-five-page issue of *Boys' Jump Monthly* (Figure 3.1).[37] Ineluctably inspired by the war, with this publication Nakazawa invented comics in 1972 in Japan as a form of witness. *I Saw It* was the first autobiographical comics work about the atomic bomb, and it opened up a significant cultural and aesthetic field of practice, confrontational visual idiom, and documentary imaginary.

I Saw It established a serious documentary mode for comics in Japan and was an unexpected success in the climate of the early 1970s, a time when the atomic bomb evoked embarrassment, shame, and silence. The English-language version was published in 1982 by the independent comics publisher EduComics as *I Saw It: The Atomic Bombing of Hiroshima: A Survivor's True Story* (Figure 3.2).[38] John Hersey's best-selling *Hiroshima*, in which Hersey, in economical, unaffected prose, offers the reported stories of six civilian survivors before, during, and after the bomb, is the best-known Western work about Hiroshima from a Japanese perspective; it has never been out of print.[39] Nakazawa's narrative offers a similar perspective—but, crucially, in a non-Western voice, where Nakazawa's own witnessing becomes the primary form of expression: *I Saw It* is narrated, verbally *and* visually, by someone who himself had been hit by the bomb. *I Saw It* was printed as a full-color comic book—at that time, there were not that many full-color comic books that were not superhero comics, and so *I Saw It* stood out even in its U.S. context as reclaiming comics conventions for a new subject.[40] *I Saw It* became the basis for Nakazawa's globally important book series *Barefoot Gen: A Cartoon Story of Hiroshima (Hadashi no Gen)*, a project that began in Japan in 1972 as a long serial and ultimately concluded at approximately 2,500 pages across ten book volumes. The form, content, and international reception of *Barefoot Gen* show how comics developed across continents as a documentary practice of witness in response to World War II. *Barefoot Gen* was the first book-length manga translated into English, in 1978, by an all-volunteer international group of peace activists known as Project Gen.[41]

おれは見た

Figure 3.1 Keiji Nakazawa, original cover of *Ore Wa Mita*, 1972. (Used by permission of Misayo Nakazawa, arranged with Japan UNI Agency, Inc.)

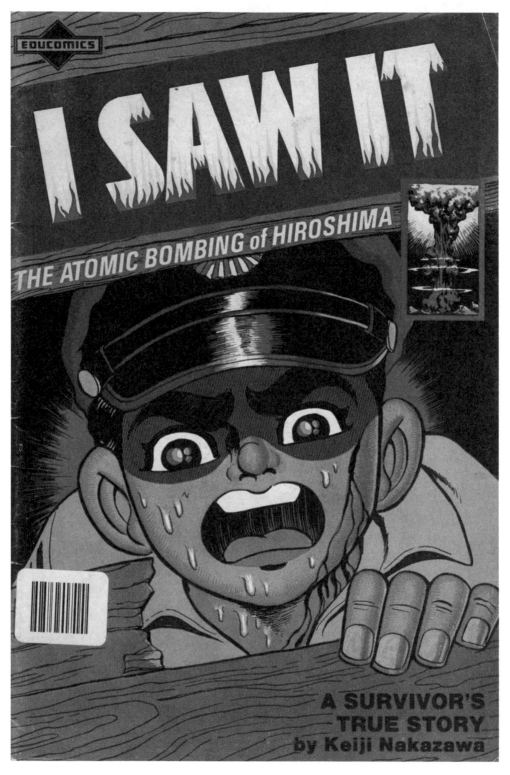

Figure 3.2 Keiji Nakazawa, cover of *I Saw It*, English-language edition (EduComics), 1982. (Used by permission of Misayo Nakazawa, arranged with Japan UNI Agency, Inc.)

The world's most celebrated cartoonist, Robert Crumb, calls *Barefoot Gen* "some of the best comics ever done."[42] *Barefoot Gen* is one of the most famous manga in Japanese history, and as historian Ferenc Morton Szasz points out, it ranks as the most popular manga in Japanese history, with sales of over eight million copies.[43] It is one of the few manga in translation worldwide, with more than twenty-one foreign editions—including *Nudpieda Gen*, in Esperanto.[44] *Barefoot Gen* was the first manga used in Japanese schools in the 1970s; it has been adapted as two animated films, a live-action film, a television series, a play, and an opera.[45] Nakazawa's graphic narrative has achieved the status of a cultural truth in Japan, but it is often rendered one-note as a polemic or a heartwarming tale of survival, rather than a work deeply engaged with remembering terror and its aftermath. In a 2005 op-ed in the *New York Times* titled "An Anniversary to Forget," Joichi Ito, a Japanese citizen and the current director of the MIT Media Lab, notes how *Gen*, which in his view is one of the few popular "meaningful references to Japan's nuclear past," has "morphed into the cultural equivalent of elevator music."[46]

A rich, weird, and much more aesthetically complicated text than its treatment as a signal work of antinuclear polemic can sometimes indicate, *Gen* offers a trenchant critique of Japanese militarism and the imperial system alongside American warfare practices. Unlike famous works of "nonpolitical" *genbaku* (atomic bomb) literature—and popular works inspired by atomic radiation such as 1954's classic film *Godzilla (Gojira)*, *Gen* names and dwells on perpetrators. Further, it is unusual in being as critical of Japan as it is of the United States for the actions that led to the bomb.[47] Nakazawa grew up in an openly antiwar family: in 1940, his father was jailed for fourteen months for "thought-crime."[48] A theme of *Gen*, for instance, is Japan's mistreatment of Koreans, both globally and locally—to name just one example, the series features the ongoing plight of the Nakazawas' Korean neighbor Mr. Pak. (Nakazawa's resistance to the idea of the nation as the traumatized body of war, in Thomas LaMarre's reading, indicates that his critique of power edges toward a biopolitical paradigm.)[49] As an aesthetic object, *Gen* has a strange serial weight and rhythm, and a striking, violent visual idiom. *Gen* is still controversial in Japan forty years after its first appearance: in August 2013, the Matsue Municipal Education Committee pulled copies of the book off library shelves in the city's primary school, due to complaints about its graphic depictions of atrocities committed by Imperial Japanese Army troops on the Chinese front—particularly images of beheading and rape (see vol. 10, *Never Give Up*, pages 19–20).[50]

While *Gen* is crucial to my view of Nakazawa's creation of a new graphic idiom for witness, I am interested in attending to the germinal *I Saw It*, a rarely analyzed work—despite being the only of Nakazawa's atomic bomb manga to announce itself as nonfiction, thus creating a new culture of documentary comics in Japan in the early 1970s. *Barefoot Gen*, which is billed as "semiautobiographical"—the protagonist is named Gen Nakaoka—and which repeats precisely many events and details of Nakazawa's earlier comic book, reveals an amplification of the themes and practices established in *I Saw It*, the work inaugurating comics as documents of eyewitnessing.

The Mark versus the Bomb as Documentarian: *I Saw It*

In *I Saw It*, Nakazawa explicitly names himself as the author and protagonist of his narrative. On page 2, the narration shifts from a sort of interiorized, contemplative mode as the protagonist remembers his mother to a scene of public address and testimony, where his body and visage turn outward to face readers and his speech balloon reads, "I am Keiji Nakazawa . . . born in Hiroshima City, March 1939 . . . [t]hird son out of five kids" (Figure 3.3).[51] Like Spiegelman in "Maus," published the same year, he introduces himself immediately as a son of war-ravaged parents. The next panel moves away from an exteriorized view of his body to a scene of his visual and aural memory, framed by the words "The earliest days I can remember were in the middle of the war that started in 1941." The postwar frames are marked by symbols of the past: the lily pads dotting the page's top panels are drawn like mushroom clouds, and the ripples in the water into which he gazes—which subsequently envelop his body, as a figure for memory—evoke the rippling out and up of the atomic bomb.[52] The nine irregular panels on the page suggest the present-day protagonist's distracted, fragmented psyche.

The page is conspicuously marked by its disarticulated body parts. Keiji Nakazawa's feet—the speech balloon looks awkwardly like it is floating up from his boots—open the page, enclosed in the panel. His mother's running bare feet, creating swift motion lines, and angled in the same direction, close the page in their own matching frame, creating a diagonal rhyme across its space; our first introduction to her is as disembodied movement. Before the graphic narrative even brings us to August 6, 1945, the perspective

Figure 3.3   Keiji Nakazawa, *I Saw It* (page 2). (Used by permission of Misayo Nakazawa, arranged with Japan UNI Agency, Inc.)

of its panels and the composition of its pages underscore an uneasy groundedness that exists in tension with the unboundedness of the sky and aerial views located from space above. This sense of ground connects to the fact that *I Saw It* is an eyewitness account from the ground, which is to say from the perspective of someone hit by the U.S. dropping of the atomic bomb. However, this groundedness does not indicate psychic or bodily coherence; rather, it suggests the body under duress.

Nakazawa is both a protagonist who speaks within the diegetic space of frames and a narrator who provides overarching narration, which appears intermittently as floating text toward the upper inside edge of panels. In *I Saw It*'s frame narrative, Nakazawa walks through the streets of Tokyo in 1971 and remembers his dead mother's suffering. Quickly *I Saw It* moves backward temporally to 1945, but it does not begin with the atomic bomb: instead, it establishes the rhythm of dailiness for the Nakazawas in Hiroshima despite hunger and air raids, presenting scenes of everyday life in the modest, jolly group, in the family business of painting wooden clogs. In this, *I Saw It*'s narrative shape resists what Lisa Yoneyama, in her classic study of testimony and memory, *Hiroshima Traces*, identifies as the problematic conventional postwar "identity of a *hibakusha* as a one-dimensional speaking subject . . . [that is] constituted by prioritizing the speaker's ontological relationship to the bomb over his or her numerous other social relationships and positions."[53] (Amplifying the concerns of the originary work, in *Barefoot Gen* the bomb does not drop until page 249.)

August 6, 1945, takes place over thirteen pages in *I Saw It*, including a tense lead-up to the bomb that includes Keiji's sighting of the *Enola Gay*; the flash of the bomb itself (many Japanese referred to the bomb simply as *pika*, "flash"); his regaining consciousness and horrified apprehension of a suddenly unfamiliar population turned into a fleet of walking dead; his encounter with a neighbor who tells him the whereabouts of his mother, who had just given birth; and his mother's account of seeing her husband, son, and daughter die pinned under their collapsed, burning home. The panels of the bombing and its immediate aftermath unfold unhurriedly, cataloguing carefully, graphically, the effects of the bomb as the child observes them, each page a fresh encounter with bodies ruined in extraordinary ways. In the temporal languidity, Nakazawa conveys how trauma radically disjoints the experience of time, and the feeling of the child observer watching what his adult narrating self describes as "an endless procession of living specters" (page 20). The languorousness of these scenes rhymes, it feels, with the terrifying visual spectacle Nakazawa chronicles of the slow hordes of burned people who move dazedly, "hunched forward, dragging their skin"—marching onward slowly and automatically (page 20). Later, his older brother returns and they ride a bicycle together through the ruins to their home to recover the bones of their father and siblings, which they bring back to their mother in a pail.

With the compression at which comics excels, *I Saw It* follows by documenting the bleak struggle to survive in the postwar days, months, and years, including the shattering death of Nakazawa's infant sister and the period when he goes back to school, where he is ridiculed, and later finds work, finally moving to Tokyo as a young man in the midst of his mother's declining health. His mother dies shortly after his marriage, and recognition of her bones' thorough decomposition is the turning point in his life that returns us to the present: he is a cartoonist giving himself his mother's bones back in comics, in a sense, by drawing them, drawing her—creating work about witnessing the atomic bomb that preserves, archives, and makes material his experience in the face of the war that decimated the very materiality of his mother. (In the later *Barefoot Gen*, Nakazawa revises his history so that Gen witnesses the deaths of his brother, sister, and father in the fallen house alongside his mother, registering the artist's desire to share the emotional—which here is to say optical—burden of the bomb with her, watching her family die.)

I Saw It is famous for visualizing the effect of the physical disfigurement wreaked by the bomb, such as bodies with flaps of dissolving skin dripping off their frames, eaten faces without eyeballs, and bald, burning women. As with many first-person comics, *I Saw It* shuttles back and forth between picturing the body of the narrator in space on the page and picturing his own optical perspective. Readers not only see Keiji witnessing but also witness his point of view—the perspective of the witness ("I saw it"). In other words, *I Saw It* produces a phenomenology of memory and trauma, both exterior and, crucially, interior; it captures both exterior and interior trauma. Nakazawa draws the enormous, overpowering, white-centered flash of the bomb in an elongated panel, with a hand-drawn time stamp in its upper right corner—8:15 a.m.—in a discursively multivalent image that catalogues witnessing both exoscopically and endoscopically, both as historical record-keeping and as an optical, embodied act. An even larger panel (and thus, perhaps, more heavily weighted) on the same tier displays a kind of expressionistic snapshot before Keiji loses consciousness: a tree breaking apart amid a sweep of flying roof tiles. The pages that follow are characteristic of Nakazawa's portrayal of the intense suffering caused by the bomb: his child character, stricken, declares that "everybody's turned into monsters" (page 13; Figure 3.4).

The kinds of images Nakazawa drew were new to Japanese culture. A few years later, in 1975—perhaps influenced by the interest in Nakazawa's drawn documents—the Japan Broadcasting Corporation (NHK) published *Unforgettable Fire: Pictures Drawn by Atomic Bomb Survivors*. Despite featuring drawings by nonprofessionals, the volume does contain some images that feel close to Nakazawa's.[54] In a survey of World War II manga, sociologist Eldad Nakar writes that *I Saw It*—which he calls "unsparingly graphic" with its "gruesome scenes"—marks a shift in that "the horrific effect of the war is no longer hidden," as it had been previously, even in manga about the war.[55] And it is worth noting that Nakar is here comparing the autobiographical *I Saw It*'s graphic violence to war-oriented work in a whole range of genres, including fiction. The framework of first-person survivor testimony *and* visual witness was also unprecedented. Iri and Toshi Maruki's famous fifteen-part *The Hiroshima Panels* (1951–1982), large paintings on traditional folding screens (roughly six by twenty-four feet), depict the aftermath of the Hiroshima bombing; the artist couple arrived in Hiroshima on August 9, 1945, and in 1950 completed the first panel, titled *Ghosts*, which bore witness to the human devastation.[56] But the Marukis' style, while portraying atrocity, has been accurately described as "poetic figurative realism."[57] In *The Hiroshima Panels*, one detects an aesthetic distance absent in the immediacy of *I Saw It*'s cruder hand-drawn images.[58]

I Saw It's mode of witnessing makes us take stock of the gross straightforwardness we might associate with science fiction—a booming Japanese genre in the era of censorship—as a genre of reality ("everybody's turned into monsters"). The grotesque clarity and directness of the comic book's images, which Nakazawa, who witnessed the fallout of Hiroshima with his own eyes, reconstructs for us here in a popular format, are an undeniable part of what makes *I Saw It* so powerful. The disjuncture, or lack of disjuncture, between the "exaggerated" rendering in the story—much of which is conventional to manga—and the real, decimating violence of the bomb throws into even greater proportion the catastrophe of "the real" in this narrative. Frederik Schodt offers a context for manga's stylistic conventions: "Japanese artists in all media have traditionally used a spare approach, concentrating on caricature or on revealing the overall 'essence' of a mood

Figure 3.4 Keiji Nakazawa, page after the bomb hits, *I Saw It* (page 13). (Used by permission of Misayo Nakazawa, arranged with Japan UNI Agency, Inc.)

or situation," he notes. "Japanese art styles can bewilder Westerners. It is common, for example, for artists to create a very serious story in 'cartoony' style, or to draw humans in an abbreviated, caricatured style against a superrealistic background."[59] In Nakazawa's re-creation of his own Hiroshima experience as a graphic narrative created in Japan's most widely popular style, he structures his text around the productive tension between form (here the overstated idiom of manga) and content (the indubitably traumatic and gravely serious subject of the devastation of the U.S. bombing of Hiroshima).

These graphic details show that Nakazawa's intervention resides as much in his visual idiom as in his political content. A text about witness that itself instantiates the "inexorable art of witness," *I Saw It* is also a graphic narrative *Künstlerroman*; it is a "manga on manga," to use the phrase of critic Kenji Kajiya.[60] *I Saw It*, like the subsequent *Barefoot Gen*, is conspicuously about mark-making. Very early in the comic book, Nakazawa presents a scene of his artist father kneeling, painting on a canvas, hand holding a brush, surrounded by dishes of ink (Figure 3.5). The son approaches his father, holding out a blank piece of paper: "Teach me how to draw a soldier, Papa!" (page 5). The blank sheet the son clasps is evident in the panel that also reveals his father's in-progress canvas as the son approaches his father's work: two frames, one blank and ready to be filled, enclosed in the comic book frame. "Don't you remember how, Keiji?" his father asks gently; the implication is that this exercise, this shared production of marks, is one the son repeats for pleasure. "All right—watch carefully now," Harumi says—and the comic closes in for four regular, tight panels on his hand, gripping a brush, inscribing the blank paper, starting with a loop that tracks the blank page. (This horizontal loop, a spiral when rotated vertically, connects with Spiegelman's memoir *Portrait of the Artist as a Young %@&*!*, which opens with a scene very similar in spirit, of the young narrator-protagonist playing the "scribble game" with his mother; as in Nakazawa, the child and parent together make a drawing of a recognizable object from an inscribed abstraction.) As W. J. T. Mitchell points out, the vortex or spiral line is "the signature of the artist since Apelles and Hogarth, the sign of transformation and empathetic doodling."[61]

Throughout *I Saw It* there is conspicuous attention to implements, to revealing and spotlighting acts of marking, to the hand. Keiji finds his father's palette in the rubble of their house when he goes to retrieve his

Figure 3.5 Keiji Nakazawa, page of father and son drawing, *I Saw It* (page 5). (Used by permission of Misayo Nakazawa, arranged with Japan UNI Agency, Inc.)

family's bones. It sits alone in a rare wordless panel—on the same page Keiji comes to hold and recognize his father's skull—and is echoed twelve pages later, in a matching placement on the page, by a panel spotlighting Keiji's first palette. In *I Saw It*, we read scenes depicting Keiji's excited reading of manga (pages 30, 31, 34), across pages in which Nakazawa portrays his love of consuming popular visual culture: he reads Tezuka, named in the text, with joyful total absorption—"there hadn't been any comics till then," the narrator explains—and he sits through his favorite movies (like *The Hunchback of Notre Dame*) repeatedly (page 31). Scenes of Keiji absorbing visual culture, crucially, alternate with scenes of him marking on paper.

One panel in *I Saw It* presents Keiji surrounded at a low desk by what seems like a fortress of paper spread out on all sides, a kind of psychic armor. Sitting in the center, pencil in hand, he marks a page of foraged scrap paper with the lines of an empty frame, comics' essential unit of grammar. Here Nakazawa reveals how Keiji begins to frame his experience by drawing it. While this page with a blank frame faces him, the only two visual images we see inscribed on paper, on the floor along with crumpled balls of paper, are a fighter plane and a space rocket. The next page depicts him—again surrounded by paper—cartooning in bed, in the act of marking the white page in front of him. *I Saw It* shows us again and again Keiji engaged in the act of drawing (pages 31, 32, 35, 40), as well as painting when he begins work as a sign painter (pages 35, 36, 39). What is notable in these numerous instances is how Nakazawa draws himself in the act of drawing, revealing his hands in front of him on the paper, grasping the implement, so that we can see the mark traveling, as it were, from hand to paper. Comics is a haptic form for both its creators and its readers, and Nakazawa visually features the act of touching involved in mark-making (hand touching pen touching paper)—the actual practice of creating itself, and not just its result—in his autobiographical depiction.[62]

This is amplified in the *Barefoot Gen* series. After the success of *I Saw It*, Nakazawa's editors, who had "paid close attention to their readers' reactions," gave him unusual free rein to create a longer series based on his personal experiences.[63] Nakazawa started *Gen* almost immediately and published it serially from 1972 to 1987, filling ten volumes (all now available in English from publisher Last Gasp).[64] In *Barefoot Gen*, which follows its protagonist's daily life in much more detail than the earlier work, there are several critical artist characters whose bodily acts of mark-making define the project that the later narrative shares with the original. (Naka-zawa asserts that the episodes in *Barefoot Gen* all "really happened to me or to other people in Hiroshima"; while autobiographical, it also takes on a collective idiom of witness.)[65]

In *Barefoot Gen*'s arc, then, a key figure is Seiji Yoshida, an artist badly burned by the bomb. Seiji is covered by maggots and pus; his relatives isolate him to one room, fearful of catching his "bomb disease." Seiji's wealthy brother hires the poor and hungry Gen, who had been hawking his services on the street in Eba, to change Seiji's bandages. In the first view of Seiji's room, his cup of brushes, pencils, and palette knives rests on a table next to a tube of paint; framed portraits—a still life and a landscape—hang on the walls, facing readers. Thick swarms of flies buzz everywhere; some rest on the paintings, blots of rot. We see in the page's last panel that the flies come from maggots hatching in Seiji's foot. Later Seiji points out poignantly, "You lose just a single layer of skin, and people start treating you like an inhuman monster" (page 51). He cannot paint with his heavily bandaged hands. And in the post-bomb world, his serene pictures, as our first view of them dense with flies indicates, are no longer relevant: in front of Gen, he slashes them violently with a knife, destroying them.[66] A sim-ilar moment of shredding pre-bomb painting, as Kajiya points out, occurs with another central artist figure of the narrative, Amano Seiga.[67] Seiga, a grandfather, painter, and atomic bomb survivor Gen meets in the country six years after his encounter with Seiji, brutally chops his many paintings (also serene landscapes and still lifes) to bits with an axe in front of Gen and his own grandson.[68] After the bomb, with its massive destruction of the Japanese landscape, not only must these representations be destroyed, but also the memory of peaceability that they provoke as objects must be annihilated: images themselves are under attack. (After this performance of rage and helplessness, Seiga agrees to teach Gen the basics of painting, and it is through conversations with him that Gen develops his aspirational slogan, fitting to Nakazawa, that "art has no borders" [page 134].)

Barefoot Gen, like *I Saw It*, ultimately spotlights inscription by hand as a form of recording through its copious attention to mark-making. In per-haps the most tellingly self-reflexive scene in *Barefoot Gen*—and one that is key to my reading of the series and Nakazawa's work in general—Gen, his adoptive younger brother Ryuta (a so-called A-bomb orphan), and Seiji set out to find wide-open space to draw. Clearly yearning for the father artist figure, Gen convinces Seiji to teach him to paint, as he also does later on with Seiga. As they come up to an embankment built around an army rifle range—the wounded Seiji in a cart pulled by Gen—they glance over the edge and realize it is a site of mass cremation and burial for bodies from all over Hiroshima. Grimly inspired, Seiji insists on "recording this" (vol. 3, page 115; Figure 3.6). Nakazawa and the figure of Seiji discursively merge in a large, tier-wide self-reflexive panel: the cartoonist Nakazawa enacts the recording vowed by the artist Seiji, as the optical perspective of the panel sweeps to the ground of the burial site, allowing Seiji's words, spoken from above the mass graves, to enter the frame and join the bodies on the ground. "I'm going to draw the suffering faces of every one of these people—turned into monsters and tossed away like old rags," the speech balloon reads, in a frame in which Nakazawa draws nine corpses, including three with large, detailed faces that seem to almost push out of the frame, their burned-out eye sockets staring at readers (page 115).

Seiji repeats his urgent need to draw the bodies, to show them—and, in the language repeatedly used in the passage, to *record* the dead: "I'm going to draw this . . . record it all" (page 120). Eliciting shocked cries from his child companions, he rolls himself down the embankment and crawls with his canvas under his arm and his paintbrush in his mouth to a heap of corpses; the brush in his mouth figures voice, the visual voice he creates and lends his subjects in the act of reconstituting them on paper. Seiji bears witness not only to mass death but also to the particularity of the people he sees. He addresses them—in their concrete, not generalized, material aspect—through his spoken interlocutory voice ("You," he addresses each, identifying features in individual bodies as he moves his eyes through the group) and through the visual voice of his drawing that bears witness to their individual existences, even evacuated of life.[69] He documents suffering on the ground, from the ground. Seiji compels the primitive body-made mark to record the devastation of war—what Nakazawa compels comics to do. Reinventing comics form, Nakazawa responds to the most high-tech of high technology, the atomic bomb, and the ominous march of technological scientific progress it represented, with the deliberately low-tech, primary practice of hand drawing.

The conceptual and material force of Nakazawa's comics inheres in how he counters the idea of the bomb as documentarian with his own form of witnessing and documentation. Following the early pages of *I Saw It* that establish the texture of Keiji's life through key vignettes, including his originary scenes of mark-making shared with his father (pages 5–6), Nakazawa

Figure 3.6 Keiji Nakazawa, page featuring Seiji Yoshida painting corpses, *Barefoot Gen Vol. 3*: *Life after the Bomb,* page 115. (© Keiji Nakazawa. Reprinted by permission of Last Gasp.)

offers a crucial statement that straightforwardly redirects the narrative to the bombing. In the top right corner of the panel that opens the page—which offers a view from below of the still-dark early morning sky—is the sentence "On August 6, 1945, when I was just a first-grader, I witnessed a holocaust that left an indelible mark on history" (page 8). Here the figuration of the atomic bombing of Hiroshima as "leaving an indelible mark" is not only idiomatic, a cliché.

Rather, we can read Nakazawa's statement as literal: the atomic bomb, which Paul Virilio refers to as a "light-weapon," acted as a camera, inadvertently documenting its own destructiveness when the light produced by radiation was blocked by a solid object, imprinting surfaces—for instance, shadows on cement (see Figures 3.7 and 3.8).[70] This marking, this imprinting, occurred on surfaces both inorganic and organic; it has been called "shadowing" or "ghosting."[71] People wearing patterned clothing when the bomb dropped had these patterns imprinted onto their bodies. "If photography, according to its inventor Nicéphore Niépce, was simply a method of engraving with light," as Virilio argues, "where bodies inscribed their traces by virtue of their own luminosity, nuclear weapons inherited both the darkroom of Niépce and Daguerre and the military searchlight."[72] The Hiroshima atom bomb, named "Little Boy"—created using uranium-235, a radioactive isotope of uranium—was the result of many years and approximately $2 billion in scientific research for the atomic bomb project (which included plutonium, used in the Nagasaki attack). Its nuclear flash both vaporized bodies en masse and left its own documentary photographic imprint.

Akira Mizuta Lippit understands the atomic blasts in Hiroshima and Nagasaki to be "massive cameras," and in turn he suggests how "the victims of this *dark atomic room* can be seen as photographic effects."[73] In *Atomic Light (Shadow Optics)*, Lippit argues, "The atomic bombing of Hiroshima and Nagasaki in 1945 initiated a new phenomenology of inscription. . . . [This was] a singularly graphic event, an event constituted graphically, which put into crisis the logic of the graphic. . . . Atomic irradiation can be seen as having created a type of violent *photography* directly onto the surfaces of the human body." The atomic bomb functioned as a camera, a documentarian; it enacted a high-technology method and devastating practice of documentary inscription. There can be no "authentic photography of atomic war," Lippit suggests, because "the bombings themselves were a form of total photography, testing the very visibility of the visual." For Lippit,

Figure 3.7 Shadow effect: Unidentified photographer, flash burns on steps of Sumimoto Bank Company, Hiroshima branch. (Courtesy of National Archives and Records Administration, Washington, D.C., photo no. 243-H-982.)

Figure 3.8 Shadow effect: Unidentified photographer, "shadow" of a hand valve wheel on the painted wall of a gas storage tank; radiant heat instantly burned paint where the heat rays were not obstructed, Hiroshima, October 14–November 26, 1945. (Courtesy of the International Center of Photography.)

the horrifying sense produced by the atomic bombs of "the world a camera, everything in it photographed," leads him to a principal theoretical premise of his book, which he describes as "avisuality" ("a visuality without images, an unimaginable visuality, and images without visuality").[74] Nakazawa's documentary practice, in contradistinction, is about its own very visible visuality, specifically as a form of counterinscription to the atomic bomb's mode of inscription (and death) by light.

I Saw It's hand-drawn form is a documentary counterinscription to the bomb as camera. A deliberately primitive technology that operates as a countermarking and countervisuality, its comics form signifies the bodily in the act of making marks against the techne of bodies marked and vaporized by the bomb's light. To the removed, clinical, superlatively high-technology mode of inscription (and one dropped from above on an unsuspecting populace), Nakazawa counters with perhaps the world's most basic technology—and one associated with the solid surface of the earth. Elaine Scarry, as I note in the Introduction, identifies marking as the most basic urgency of any culture to make. "In any culture," asserts Scarry, "the simplest artifact, the simplest sign, is the single mark on wood, sand, rock, or any surface that will take the imprint."[75] Important comics frames reveal the protagonist marking the ground in *Gen*, as when Gen writes "Mama" repeatedly in the ground during Kimie's illness and when after her death Gen carves the word *jiritsu* (self-reliance) into a rocky dirt road in enormous characters bigger than his own body.[76] This latter scene is conspicuously attentive to the manual process of imprinting (Figure 3.9). The page opens with a frame whose close view is on hands jabbing a sharpened branch into the ground. Nakazawa then lingers over the depth of the mark in two subsequent frames that focus even more closely on the implement traversing the surface. As the documentary *White Light/Black Rain*, among other many sources, shows, Air Force pilots and top brass wrote messages (on Hiroshima's "Little Boy") and their own names (on Nagasaki's "Fat Man") on the atomic bombs.[77] The hand-drawn document *I Saw It*, for which this scene in *Gen* is synecdochical, functions as a countersignature from the ground, responding vehemently to the multivalent "signature" of the bomb from above.[78]

The atomic bomb directly produced a violent photography. In some cases the record it created was of an object that remained intact through the flash, such as the hand valve, and in other cases it created a record of a human body that itself was destroyed. Comics marks both things: the indelible pres-

Figure 3.9   Keiji Nakazawa, tier of panels (drawing "self-reliance"), *Barefoot Gen Vol. 8: Merchants of Death,* page 253. (© Keiji Nakazawa. Reprinted by permission of Last Gasp.)

ence of trauma, but also its limit. In Nakazawa's phenomenology of trauma, comics is the place where the destruction gets recorded, and it is a register of something not destroyed onto which an image can be made. Nakazawa established a new idiom by documenting "the violent inscriptions of light and shadow on the Japanese body" as content in comics, in a revealing, unsparing, direct visual mode audiences had not previously encountered.[79] Further, we can understand that he was motivated by that inscription of light and shadow on the body to generate an iterative form for documentation—for witnessing—that does not replicate it. (Intriguingly, Tatsumi's manga story "Hell" registers suspicion of this technology too: published in 1971, it is about a Japanese military press photographer's radical misperception of the "ghostly silhouettes.")[80]

In Nakazawa's political and aesthetic logic, his hand-drawn images are a counterburning—a spectacle that engages, or reengages, the reader with the realities of the bomb. Nakazawa takes on burning in his work as an action upon sight, a somatic provocation. Seiji, in a climatic scene, rips off his bandages and demands to show contemptuous Japanese citizens his burned body—a spectacular act of display that Nakazawa himself enacts in his drawing of it. "I'm going to burn the sight of this ugly body into their brains," he vows (vol. 3, page 133). In Art Spiegelman's introduction to the first two *Barefoot Gen* volumes, he writes that *Gen* "burned its way into my heated brain with all the intensity of a fever-dream."[81] Spiegelman echoes this language in an interview, compellingly mixing metaphors of temperature to indicate the affective extremity of Nakazawa's work. "What comes through is so chilling and burns its way so far into your brain," Spiegelman explains of his reading experience, "that I would say the descriptions of the Hiroshima bombing are more firmly etched inside me than many of the written or photographic testaments I've seen."[82]

Plasticity and Corporeality

The mark in Nakazawa's work is both itself etched and longing to be etched, then—to burn inside a reader's brain. (As W. J. T. Mitchell asks, *What do pictures want?*) But how to describe this mark that also becomes an image, and what its shape, weight, and texture accomplish? Nakazawa's marks, or his lines, convey openness and accessibility: generally, we see black line-work alongside moderate shading and cross-hatching. This set of solid, expositional marks mixes with what can be a more detailed rendering of environments, particularly architectural or topographical in the case of Hiroshima (see Figure 3.10), and with the jumpier exuberance of lines depicting movement, from raging fires to the dripping sweat on characters' faces that is conventional to expressing emotion in manga. In *Barefoot Gen*, the conventions of boys' manga (*shōnen manga*) become amplified, particularly with the introduction of a range of slapstick movement—Gen is often leaping into the air in joy or rage, kicking up puffs of speed and vertical mobility. In one of the few substantial analyses of Nakazawa's visual style, Thomas LaMarre correctly points out, as I suggest throughout this chapter, that *Gen* defies the paradigm of trauma in which representation proves inadequate to depiction. Yet even though *Gen* "leans toward the composition of forces rather than toward the decomposition of representation," he writes, "there is a disjuncture."[83] This manifests itself in Nakazawa's style through the dynamics of the line, LaMarre argues, particularly the co-presence of what he suggestively deems the "structural line" and the "plastic line."

The cartoon line itself is generally plastic; inspired by Sergei Eisenstein's unfinished essay on Disney (composed in large part during the war years, 1940–1946), LaMarre describes it as having a plasticity that "tends to keep open the play between different levels of synthesis, such that we see and feel its dynamic across levels."[84] Cartoons, then—Eisenstein did not

Figure 3.10 Keiji Nakazawa, panel of Keiji and his brother going to collect family bones, *I Saw It* (page 23). (Used by permission of Misayo Nakazawa, arranged with Japan UNI Agency, Inc.)

distinguish drawings from animated cartoons, using the blanket term "cartoon" for both—return us to a primitive elasticity, fluidity, and flexibility.[85] The plastic line jumps out all over Nakazawa's work: in the springy depictions of Gen as boy hero (the plastic line attaches to children, LaMarre points out); in the copious gag violence of *Gen*, traditional to boys' manga; in the explosive force of Gen's roving anger at Japanese and American cultural and military practices.[86] This anger, instantiated in the plastic line, is held back by the structural line, which is a formalized, regularizing line—for instance, the rectilinear lines of a comics panel—in a dialectical struggle.[87] Focusing intently on registers of style, LaMarre understands the major question of Nakazawa's work to be: *Can there be plasticity after the bomb?*[88]

Just as Spiegelman claims that the vividness of *Gen* "emanates from something intrinsic to the comics medium itself," LaMarre reminds readers that in Nakazawa's work, "trauma is not separable from the medium of comics itself. In other words, if we simply seize upon the 'message' of trauma or its politics, we miss the tonality and the materiality of violence itself, which is related to the medium."[89] LaMarre's suggestion underlines my reading of *I Saw It* as a counterinscription, a counterburning: "the manga bomb explodes with and against the atomic bomb," he writes.[90] The persistent plasticity—unruliness, unruledness, animism—of Nakazawa's lines (or strokes or marks) is a feature of what I identify above as Nakazawa's political-aesthetic logic.

For LaMarre, similarly, we can recognize manga as a political and historical orientation. Nakazawa "spurs a commitment to following the plastic line in shōnen manga," he argues, "which is prolonged not merely into a politics of affirming or protecting life but into a politics *in which life itself emerges as radical exposure,* in which explosion of the plastic line enacts resistance at the very site where life enters politics."[91] In comics, one feels the constant tension between what can be contained within the frame and what cannot be contained within it—both in terms of historical realities and in terms of the burden of expressing those realities. Comics makes readers aware of what can be pictured and what cannot be pictured. It is a form, then, that is *about* disjuncture at its most basic: in what we see in the frame and do not see in the gutter, in what we make of the gap between word and image. The shape and textures of lines on the page, and how they interact, also produce this disjuncture, allowing readers to recognize how thoroughly Nakazawa's work takes on the post-atomic body not only as a theme but also as the structure of its iteration.

The plasticity of Nakazawa's line (a reaction, perhaps, to the "burning flat" or "knocking flat" of his native city) is an index of its signature corporeality. Across all of its aspects—in its content, what I think of as its somatic provocations, its form—Nakazawa's atomic bomb manga invokes the corporeal. One recognizes the corporeality *within* the diegetic spaces of Nakazawa's work—from its shredded, burned bomb victims to the crying, pissing, shitting, eating, pounding, and punching protagonist children carrying on in the aftermath. "What remains constant" in *Gen*, as one critic aptly puts it, "is the grotesquerie and agony of survival"—and this is a closely chronicled *bodily* survival.[92] This bodiliness, which sometimes registers as a carnivalesque excess, is not without its pleasures. Gen, a boy without sanctimony, revels in bodily revenge: he urinates on his foes, in addition to thwacking them, and even smears feces in the face of a doctor in cahoots with the Atomic Bomb Casualty Commission (ABCC), the commission established by the United States in 1947 that studied radiation effects but failed to treat survivors in Hiroshima.[93] Manga critic Bill Randall notes that the "characters have a heft and solidity, a corporeal presence. This weight stems from a combination of heavy linework, a sensitivity for motion and a profound link to the ground for all characters, something that makes Gen's perpetual leaping and dancing all too tied down by gravity."[94] The characters' relentless bodiliness, reinforced by their connection to the ground, aligns them figuratively and literally throughout with the perspective of the bombed witness, in contradistinction to the disembodied aerial perspective of the U.S. B-29s, with their target sites and aerial recordings.

In Nakazawa's manga, as in many of the comics I discuss in this book, we also recognize what Takayuki Kawaguchi identifies as the reading experience of *Gen*, one that "involves a peculiar corporeality."[95] While my own earlier writing on comics has focused on the embodiment of the creator in the act of composing comics—an act of embodiment that translates to the page—the documentary comics I explore in this book also bring the issue of the reader's embodiment to the forefront. This is due to the graphically violent nature of many of their wartime images—and also to how they propose meaning by generating readers' awareness of their own contingent, durational, embodied activity of *reading* and *looking* at the mark, the panel, the page. In Nakazawa's work, prone to a repetition that indexes trauma, the "peculiar corporeality" his comics provoke can be draining. "His images of melting skin and raw brutality exact a physical toll greater than the work of any other comic artist," Randall affirms.[96] Invoking similar language, Ma deems Nakazawa's images of maggot-ridden bodies "nauseating," and she suggests that "the rawness of Nakazawa's art still assaults our senses."[97]

———————

There are two central reasons today's form of nonfiction comics developed so forcefully out of the postwar period. The first has to do with visual witnessing, the way that comics can offer an absorptive intimacy with their narratives while defamiliarizing received images of history. *I Saw It* and "Maus" are both narratives of terror that devolve on *images* of terror: the zombielike, decomposing citizens of Hiroshima that Nakazawa witnessed firsthand; and the corpses, both pictured and implied, that people the Spiegelman son's visual reconstruction of his father's death-camp testimony. We might think of approaching World War II, after the broad silence that surrounded the war in America and in Japan, as mandating afresh Shklovsky's "new seeing" of reality. Comics picks up steam in the early 1970s as this new seeing. Motivated by the urgencies of re-seeing or re-visioning the war, comics sought to defamiliarize received images of history, and also to communicate, to circulate in realms of the popular. I do want to acknowledge a different argument, however: the Yale historian Laura Wexler argues that Nakazawa aims to *familiarize* Hiroshima by putting domestic bodies in images of the city, to counteract the cold point of view of U.S. military aerial photography of the city after the bombing.[98] In either reading—mine or Wexler's—what we see is that in the early 1970s, the emotional and intellectual exigencies of World War II had the opportunity to metabolize into formal innovation, into expanding modalities for capturing traumatic histories that were not yet part of a culture of expression.

In comics documenting war we also understand the form's ability to reconstitute lost bodies in its drawn lines. The subject of these comics, and often the procedure of composing them, is a resurrection or materialization of bodies in form in the mark on the page. (Cartoonist Alison Bechdel, for one, figures paper as skin and ink as blood.) The corporeality of the work comes to stand in for the missing corporeality of the dead parent, eviscerated by war. While both Anja Spiegelman and Kimie Nakazawa "survived" the war, the war, in a sense, killed both mothers in the late sixties: Spiegelman was a suicide in 1968, and Nakazawa died, as mentioned, from complications of radiation-induced leukemia in 1966. Like *Maus*, dedicated to Anja Spiegelman, *I Saw It* is an obituary for an absent mother destroyed by World War II.

In the same way that the irrecoverable absence of his mother's account of the Holocaust is motivation for Spiegelman to reconstruct Holocaust testimony, to make radically visible and present the narrative of his family's life as best he can, for Nakazawa the decimation of his mother's body from atomic radiation—its complete deconstitution—is also the reason he decides to embark on a career of testimonial visibility. As discussed, this is the explicit subject of I Saw It's frame narrative. Nakazawa details the painful scene of primary motivation, which is about a physical evacuation we see countered in the frames—or bones—of the comics page (Figure 3.11). Even as it depicts her ashes, this page of his encounter with her boneless-ness reconstitutes the mother's body in its own concretization; one might even understand its gutters as cartilage. (Thierry Groensteen's concept of comics's "arthrology," a way to think about layout and the relationship of elements on the page, is suggestive here because it indicates the jointing that comics pages propose.)[99] The rectangular cart onto which Kimie's ashes are delivered to her son also conspicuously frames what is left of her body in clearly bordered space, echoing the son's own hand-drawn frames that commemorate and, more important, evoke her. Framing her experi-ence, and his own, in hand-drawn comics boxes presents a psychic and material architecture of memory and history. The page becomes a foun-dation, a body, a corporeal index and archive.

I Saw It and "Maus" aspire to give voice and body to the mother's absent—decimated, wordless—body in composing a narrative form contoured by testimony so tangible, so manifest, so radically visible as to figure the rein-statement of a more intimate bodily form, the mother's body. The recon-struction of bodies on the page—what Spiegelman has called "material-izing" history—addresses this loss with visual shape; as Clark Coolidge and Philip Guston phrase a simple but powerful suggestion, "To draw is to make be."[100] There is an instantiation of the lost body on the page in comics.

Japan's comics culture grew enormously after World War II, when Western comics were imported in large number, and strong narrative struc-tures for comics developed in children's comics publications, which then claimed adult audiences, shifting the field dramatically. Modern comics as form had gained shape in large part because of the influence of the Japan Punch (1862–1887), which was based on the canonical English satire pub-lication Punch (1841–1996) and was created by Charles Wirgman, an En-glishman who arrived in Japan as a correspondent for the Illustrated London News.[101] (Wirgman never left, dying in Yokohama in 1891.) As Hiroshi Oda-giri points out, Japan's modern manga took so-called ponchi-e (Punch pic-tures) as its point of departure.[102] And Adam Kern suggests that the begin-ning of contemporary manga might be considered the serialization of a Japanese children's comic strip, Shosei and Katsuichi's Shochan's Adven-ture, alongside translated Western imports such as George McManus's

Figure 3.11 Keiji Nakazawa, *I Saw It* (page 43). (Used by permission of Misayo Nakazawa, arranged with Japan UNI Agency, Inc.)

Bringing Up Father in the *Asahi Graphic Weekly* in 1923.[103] We can note the bidirectional roots of cross-cultural exchange in Henry (Yoshitaka) Kiyama's *The Four Immigrants Manga: A Japanese Experience in San Francisco, 1904–1924*, an often humorous, actually bilingual (Japanese and English) hardcover 104-page proto–graphic novel printed in Japan and bound in San Francisco in 1931 that chronicles in a series of comic strips the misadventures of four Japanese friends in California.[104]

However, Japan's comics culture developed from culturally specific antecedents that shape its tradition, such as early picture scrolls from the twelfth century, the most famous of which is the ink-on-paper Chōjū Giga (Animal Scrolls), attributed to Bishop Sojo Toba (1053–1140).[105] The pictorial, sequential art of scrolls was often religious, illustrated by Buddhist monks, and circulated to a limited powerful audience including the clergy and aristocracy. Secular woodblock prints from the seventeenth century and beyond, however, were produced for a popular audience, such as the *ukiyo-e* illustrations that began as depictions of Yoshiwara, a decadent area of Edo (now Tokyo)—pictures of the "Floating World," a term suggestive of life's uncertainties and the search for pleasure.[106] (*Ukiyo-e*, especially with Hokusai, continued to grow more aesthetically precise and inventive.) By the mid-nineteenth century, a variety of formats of caricature and sequential art, some quite sophisticated, had proliferated across periods, including *otsu-e*, Buddhist-inspired folk art; *toba-e*, bound books of twenty to thirty witty cartoons; *akahon*, lowbrow "red books," eventually joined by black and blue books; and *kibyōshi*, yellow-covered books with strong storylines.[107] By and large the Japanese manga tradition and the U.S.-European comics tradition have developed independently, but we can see that these spaces of the popular were expanded globally, and really reinvented, in the early 1970s to address the disturbing legacies of war.

———————

There are, of course, a range of important precursors to the emergence of comics of witness, even in the framework of the Pacific War. In Miné Okubo's *Citizen 13660* (1946), illustrated with pen-and-ink sketches, the Japanese American Okubo records life in the Tanforan and Topaz internment camps, where she and thousands of others were held in "protective custody" after Pearl Harbor, and where cameras were prohibited.[108] While

Okubo's narrative combines word with image and offers a fascinating documentary model, *Citizen 13660* differs from the body of work whose postwar increase I am interested in tracing, which specifically understands itself as comics and articulating comics conventions.[109] It was not until 1972 that comics itself became a form for witnessing in any kind of nonfiction context.

However, in the United States, one might consider the foundations of comics to be built, in some way, on atomic fears and possibilities. As Szasz points out, many if not most of the form's early field-setting—and transmedia—exemplars, such as *Buck Rogers* (which began in 1929) and *Flash Gordon* (which began in 1934), have plots premised on radioactivity, as does the more recent *Spider-Man*. They were filled with references to the "atomic," a term that in context implied both a positive energy benefit and potentially devastating weapons.[110] In the interwar years, Szasz argues, comics contributed hugely—even more than professional science writing, and along with science fiction—to popular understandings of the basic framework of nuclear futures, in part because of how they visualized scientific events and possible outcomes.[111] In August 1945, the *New York Herald Tribune*, among other papers, declared that President Truman's Hiroshima press release was as if the "fantasies of the 'comic' strips were actually coming true." After the release of the bomb on August 6, *Enola Gay* copilot Robert Lewis remarked "the actual sight caused all of us to feel that we were Buck Rogers 25th Century Warriors."[112]

Szasz traces the evolution of three main types of atomic comics in the postwar period: educational comics for young people, short-lived newfangled atomic superheroes, and customary superheroes taking on the fissioned atom in their storylines.[113] While comic books created more atomic bomb stories than any other media form, Szasz confirms, and images of mushroom clouds blossomed all over the comics, what is clear is the rarity of sophisticated nonfiction accounts—and any that themselves took the form of witness.[114] As discussed in the Introduction, there were many comics about World War II that sought to engage the war, especially with abundant imagery, but which actually engaged history indirectly, even as many of them thematized the act of witnessing.[115]

And on the other end of the cultural spectrum in the 1940s, inverting the word-and-image problematic, we can see the inability—or the simple lack of desire—to grapple with images of war in the *New Yorker*, which ran John Hersey's groundbreaking "Hiroshima" as its entire issue on August 31, 1946, but which offered a cover of a New England vacation by Charles

E. Martin (Figure 3.12). *The New Yorker* indicated the enormity of its subject by transforming its own format—allowing one article to run uninterruptedly for the whole issue for the first time in its history—but it refused to tamper with its genteel visual aesthetic.[116] Five years later, in 1951, Laurence Hyde extended the tradition of the wordless novel, with its strong history of social justice, to atomic issues in *Southern Cross: A Novel of the South Seas*, which presents 118 wood engravings imagining destructive atomic bomb testing in the Bikini Atoll in 1946. While Northrop Frye reviewed it on the radio, connecting "simple" pictures with the actual recognition of nuclear reality ("man . . . can tie himself up in words"), the small-press book, now considered a classic, was an outlier, as opposed to a galvanizer.[117]

In subsequent decades, atomic anxiety and anger around models of progress attached to nuclear power shaped underground comics powerfully; the underground became a space in which political fears, including fear of the destruction of the planet, found shape.[118] An engagement with atomic anxiety is also a large feature of superhero comics of the period; two of Marvel's enduring Silver Age superheroes are Spider-Man and the Hulk, both of whom derive their powers from nuclear radiation.[119] In the underground, Ron Turner started one of the major, lasting, significant independent comics publishers and named it, appropriately, Last Gasp. Its first title, the also aptly named *Slow Death Funnies* #1 (1970), was a benefit title for the Ecology Center in Berkeley, the first of its kind. *Skull Comics*, among other gloomily named anthologies, followed from Last Gasp. Meanwhile, Rip Off Press, the other key underground outlet, published *Hydrogen Bomb and Biochemical Warfare Funnies* #1 in 1970 with the subtitle running vertically down the spine: *Apocalyptic Apocrypha for Apoplectic Apostates.*

The first story, significantly, is by Robert Crumb, whose hugely resonant comics inaugurated the underground comics movement in 1968 and gained wide recognition. Crumb's comics, as Leonard Rifas points out, repeatedly refer to nuclear destruction. In *Foo*, the comics magazine he self-published with his brother Charles in 1958, mushroom clouds appear repeatedly—including as the concluding image of the first issue.[120] In Crumb's famous *Zap* #0 (1968), the story "City of the Future" ends with the President of the World pushing "the button," producing an enormous mushroom cloud to "blow up the world!!" Helen Swick Perry, in 1970's *The Human Be-In*, analyzes forces that in retrospect one can read as an explanation of the rise of comics culture: "Two central messages seemed to emerge from Hiroshima, followed so shortly by mass television: *unless something is done*, we shall all perish by thermonuclear accident . . . *and there is nothing to do about*

Figure 3.12 Charles E. Martin, cover of the *New Yorker* ("Hiroshima" issue), August 31, 1946.
(© Charles E. Martin/*The New Yorker.*)

it, except sit in front of the picture box." She continues, "In the process of trying to escape this double message, the young in the Haight-Ashbury disavowed television as the focal point of their interest; practically none of them watched television at all. Yet in another way, the television screen had taught the young the power of a symbol, the importance of pictures."[121] What she calls this double message is registered in the creation of underground comics.

In the opening piece of *Hydrogen Bomb Funnies*, "Mr. Sketchum," Crumb offers a brilliantly succinct one-page story—four clean rows of two frames each—that expresses the fear of the end of world that fueled much underground culture and production (Figure 3.13). Mr. Sketchum, a boyish cartoonist, gets an idea at the drawing board, pencil in hand: "I'm going to send some o' my cartoons to Bertrand Russell!!" (Russell, the philosopher and famous nuclear disarmament activist, died later that year.) He walks to a mailbox with a shining sun and cityscape in the background, mails the letter, then looks up to see a bomb dropping through the sky. "What's that!" he proclaims. The clearly marked H-bomb falls to his eye level, and his pencil flies out from behind his ear. The comic pauses—stopping time, as comics does—as Sketchum mutters, "Gee . . ." before exploding. In the final frame, a speech balloon emanates from only a pair of glasses hovering in the air: "Now I'll never know if Bertrand Russell liked my cartoons." As with Nakazawa, this piece pits a cartoonist in the act of writing and drawing by hand against the disembodied technological prowess of the bomb.

Underground cartoonists, including founders of the movement such as Crumb, made comix the arena in which they could visualize disaster. Crumb explains of his Marine father: "He survived World War II and was sent in to Hiroshima ten days after the Americans dropped the atomic bomb. I can't even imagine the things he witnessed. He never talked about it."[122] World War II and its repercussions—atomic warfare, the Cold War—become visualizable, imaginable, in comics, animating a generation that in some cases was haunted even by the silence it engendered. In 1976, Leonard Rifas started the independent publishing company EduComics in order to promote nonfiction comics and specifically his underground comic book *All-Atomic Comics*, which went through five printings; he published *I Saw It* in 1982.[123]

In the United States, the underground comix movement, and even many earlier genres of comics, from comic strips to wordless novels, revealed an

Figure 3.13 R. Crumb, "Mr. Sketchum," *Hydrogen Bomb Funnies* #1 (Last Gasp), 1970.
(© R. Crumb.)

atomic haunting, an atomic imaginary, that we might say was foundational to comics at key moments. But the atomic *reality* was voiced in hand-drawn words and pictures by Keiji Nakazawa, creating a field, a movement, and a transcultural exchange. Motivated by World War II, in the early 1970s Nakazawa—and Spiegelman—invented comics afresh as a testamentary form to violence.

In 1972, "Maus" was first published in *Funny Aminals*, an underground comic book anthology edited by Terry Zwigoff and Justin Green, who stipulated only that the stories contained within must somehow be anthropomorphic. Spiegelman, born in Sweden in 1948 to Polish Holocaust survivors, produced "Maus," a three-page story employing the abstraction of an animal metaphor even as it announced itself as a nonfiction narrative. Spiegelman interviewed and taped his father, Vladek (unnamed in the piece), about surviving Auschwitz; the transmission of that testimony from father to son is the framework of the story. "Maus," unlike *I Saw It*, was received with very little fanfare in 1972; Spiegelman recounts that cartoonists, unable to assimilate the serious content, complimented his rendering of mice. Meanwhile, his father's survivor friends, unable to recognize the mice or to recognize visually shaped narrative, reacted only by situating themselves in relation to the facts presented in the story. In the Robert Crumb cover to *Funny Aminals*, in which two nattily dressed cats lust after a callipygian chicken girl, we can recognize, as with *I Saw It*'s appearance in the lowbrow *Boys' Jump Monthly*, what might seem like a discordance: serious work about the status of eyewitnessing, in an uncharted form, yet shaping and being shaped by the field of the popular. As Green explains of the ethos of underground cartoonists, "[We] all held to the ideal of reaching a common audience while reinventing the formal boundaries that defined the medium."[124]

Nakazawa and Spiegelman's foundational texts opened a new phase for hand-drawn forms of witness and the representation of war broadly—and they also generated lengthier works that circulated internationally and created a phenomenon in popular culture. *I Saw It* became the basis for the long-form graphic narrative *Barefoot Gen*, the serial that became Japan's most popular manga and a globally important book series; "Maus" became

Figure 3.14   *Left:* Keiji Nakazawa, cover of *Barefoot Gen*, first trans. 1978. (© Keiji Nakazawa. Reprinted by permission of Last Gasp.) *Right:* Art Spiegelman, cover of *Maus I*, 1986. (Copyright © 1986 by Pantheon Books, a division of Random House LLC; from *Maus I: A Survivor's Tale: My Father Bleeds History* by Art Spiegelman. Used by permission of Pantheon Books, an imprint of the Knopf Doubleday Publishing Group, a division of Penguin Random House LLC. All rights reserved.)

the basis for the long-form graphic narrative *Maus: A Survivor's Tale*, arguably the world's most famous work of comics, which first appeared serially in 1980 in *RAW* magazine and was published to massive critical acclaim by Pantheon as two book volumes in 1986 and 1991, forever altering the terrain of comics in America and worldwide (Figure 3.14). *Barefoot Gen*, as I noted earlier, was the first book-length manga translated into English, in 1978, by an international group of peace activists. Spiegelman read it that year.

| 4 |

MAUS'S ARCHIVAL IMAGES
AND THE POSTWAR COMICS FIELD

The question of images is at the heart of the great darkness of our time, the "discontent of our civilization." We must know how to look into images to see that of which they are survivors. So that history, liberated from the pure past (that absolute, that abstraction), might help us to open the present of time.

—GEORGES DIDI-HUBERMAN, *IMAGES IN SPITE OF ALL,*
2008

The year 1972 established a serious documentary mode for comics glob-ally. In the United States, autobiographical comics began in March of that year with Justin Green, who created the forty-two-page stand-alone comic book *Binky Brown Meets the Holy Virgin Mary* (Last Gasp), about his struggle with obsessive-compulsive disorder, sex, and Catholic guilt.[1] Green had been motivated by Robert Crumb's comics—"the [drawn] line . . . was like a call to action"—to drop the study of Abstract Expressionist painting at Rhode Island School of Design and move to the center of underground comics, San Francisco, to become a cartoonist; *Binky Brown* went on to influence Crumb and many others.[2] *Binky Brown* was powerful because it set the space for comics to be a realm of the intensely personal—a space to reveal, through words *and* pictures, what one might consider the purview of the especially private. In the imagistically explicit *Binky Brown*, the protagonist imagines that all remotely phallic objects emit what he terms "penis rays," which he must avoid touching. But as personal as *Binky Brown* was, its genre innovation developed directly out of the collective trauma of Vietnam.

Underground comics arose from the context of the underground press and Vietnam, as author and scholar Tom De Haven, among others, has noted.[3] Art Spiegelman agrees, explaining that underground comics were "inspired by Vietnam [even when] not *about* Vietnam."[4] While there is no explicit reference to the Vietnam War in *Binky*, Green reveals that Vietnam was "in the forefront of my thoughts prior to and during the undertaking of the work."[5] In Green's account, "Everyone I knew knew at least someone that was killed. And a couple people that were injured. There was a feeling of a real collision." That urgency meant a search to create modalities of self-expression in which the self was both conspicuously looking and looked at: "I needed to wage my own war. And so I looked within and . . . I didn't want to present myself as a hero but rather as a specimen. So the comic form gives you a multifaceted view of doing that."[6] Appearing later that same year, the first nonfiction work that was rooted in the self and yet moved outward from first-person autobiography to something approaching the documentary is Spiegelman's "Maus." This three-page story is the prototype for Spiegelman's longer, two-volume work of the same name, *Maus: A Survivor's Tale*—which one could say was motivated by two wars, and perhaps even their connection.

Green opened the floodgates for a range of nonfiction work, including "Maus," to take shape. Instead of dreaming up violence for extreme, taboo-shattering underground comics, Spiegelman explains, after *Binky* "I could now locate the atrocities present in the real world that my parents had survived and brought me into."[7] And as Spiegelman points out, Green did it both by example and by personal encouragement, inviting Spiegelman into *Funny Aminals*, the one-off anthology comic book featuring all anthropomorphic characters that was nominally a benefit for animal rights (Figure 4.1). Spiegelman initially begged off, but Green, as he recounts, "wouldn't let me off the hook," insisting on Spiegelman's contribution in a letter—Spiegelman had moved back to his hometown, New York, from San Francisco—onto which he even supportively taped two tabs of amphetamine.[8] As with Keiji Nakazawa's *I Saw It* in *Boys' Jump* the same year, Spiegelman's somber "Maus" sits awkwardly in the madcap milieu of *Funny*

Figure 4.1   R. Crumb, cover to *Funny Aminals*, 1972. (© R. Crumb.)

Aminals. While in that context "Maus" appeared as something of an aberration, when it is set next to *Binky Brown* and *I Saw It* it becomes visible as part of a subsequently profound link between witnessing war and comics form.

Featuring first-person perspectives rooted in opposing sides of World War II, both 1972 stories offer up scenes of 1945: the dropping of the atomic bomb in Japan in August, the liberation of the Buchenwald concentration camp in Germany in April. The cultural contexts of publication for Nakazawa and Spiegelman's germinal comics of witness seem to run in cultural reverse—but both generated a productively uncomfortable result, refiguring expectations for genre and form. *Boys' Jump*, with a large print run, presented the unpredictable misery of the atomic bomb to an audience typically expecting action formulas. *Funny Aminals*, with its print run of 20,000–30,000, catered to a left-wing counterculture that had an appetite for outrageous plots and images but was less accustomed to serious historical violence, especially in the "funny animals" framework. The three-page "Maus" appears before a piece about a poodle prostitute and after *Funny Aminals*'s opener: Crumb's six-page "Karnal Komix Presents What a World! Starring Two Cats and a Bird," in which two felines pursue a bird-woman for a meal; when they manage to finally decapitate her, her powerful body, headless, still runs rampant. On the last page they play baseball with her head (a nod to the famous 1953 EC horror comic "Foul Play!"). While both Crumb and Spiegelman's comics deal with violence through animals, the direct historical origins of Spiegelman's take on the funny animal genre is especially clear when seen after Crumb's.

Overleaf, where the solemn "Maus" begins, readers encounter violence in a landscape of cats and mice that appears no less brutal. This violence, however, emerges in a distinctly separate historical key. From the outset "Maus" flags itself as testimony and history, despite—and actually copacetic with—its iteration in the funny animal genre: a genre of comics and animated cartoons that was popular since both forms' earliest days and evolved in the 1920s and 1930s. Part of the pleasure this genre produces is in the seamless toggle from human to animal; the "animalness" of the characters often "becomes vestigial or drops away entirely," as Joseph Witek points out, so that, for example, Donald Duck serves turkey for Thanksgiving dinner.[9] In his comics memoir *Portrait of the Artist as a Young %@&*!* Spiegelman relates that after seeing old animated cartoons equating blacks and animals in a cinema class, he thought to create his strip for *Funny Aminals* based on race relations in America, with "Ku Klux Kats" and lynched mice, before "Hitler's notion of Jews as vermin offered a metaphor closer to home."[10] Like many cartoonists, Spiegelman is attracted the surreal political imagination of Kafka (*The Metamorphosis* is a funny animal story in its own fashion, as is Spiegelman's 2014 cartoon "The MetaMetamorphosis," which depicts Gregor Samsa waking up in bed as a human surrounded by a shocked cockroach family).[11] Kafka's character Josephine the Singer, he has said, referring to Kafka's last story, "Josephine the Singer, or the Mouse Folk" (1924), which has been interpreted in the context of Jewish identity, "began humming to me and told me there was something closer to deal with."[12] The documentary history of comics derives in part from the animal fable and evolves it, as Kafka did, to represent a concern with human history.

"Maus": Comics, War, Witness

"Maus" is the first iteration of Spiegelman's (re)invention of comics nonfiction and the invention of American comics as an expression of witness. Comics established nonfiction as a primary concern during the underground comix revolution of the late 1960s and 1970s. The form explored antinarrative aesthetics, which produced a spatial ethic of articulation apposite to the work of historical documentation and the expression of trauma. The grammar of comics, across all of its formats, shapes time and space; it suggests that one encounter the panel as an event, and it presents a nonlinear experience of time. Spiegelman demonstrated the possibilities of comics language by showing how its most basic formal elements could forcefully portray complicated historical realities. In this underground moment, comics became legibly equipped to challenge dominant modes of storytelling and history writing through expressing simultaneity, multiple perspectives, shifting temporalities, and paradoxical spaces. The central proposition of "Maus," like the later *Maus*, is the imbrication of the past with the present.

"Maus" adopts the abstraction of an animal metaphor and the flourishes of cartoon language (splash panels, sound effects, and paratextual notes and arrows) while verbally and visually bearing witness to both public and private traumas of the Holocaust.[13] It uses comics language to assess events typically considered the domain of journalism and prose nonfiction. The marks that begin the story are large bleeding black letters, two inches high, spelling out "MAUS." A violent slash across the horizontal of the page, the title appears urgently splashed on; ink even splatters upward from the left stem of the M into the page's blank corner and drips down into the space of the first frame. In this first panel, as Marianne Hirsch points out, Spiegelman filters his father's experience through the famous Margaret Bourke-White photograph of the liberation of prisoners at Buchenwald in April 1945.[14]

Despite the animal overlay, in "Maus" the opening salvo of translating (or, rather, transvaluing) a widely circulated journalistic photograph into comics establishes the story from the outset as about evidence, nonfiction, and transmission (Figure 4.2). The half-page opening frame—with black photo corners covering its edges—is a clear (re)creation of Bourke-White's image of seventeen male prisoners clustered behind a fence, some gripping its wire, "staring out at their Allied rescuers," as *Life* magazine put it, "like so many living corpses." In approximately the same posture, seventeen men drawn with the faces of mice gaze outward from Spiegelman's frame; a small arrow points to one, with the hand-drawn designation "Poppa." This paratextual note within the space of the frame, along with the photo corners, underlines that the drawing of the photograph appears to us as a handled artifact, not a window onto the reality of the past. The voice of the son, generically named Mickey, frames the narrative only once, on this first page below the "photograph," before the survivor father's speech and his experiences take over: "When I was a young mouse in Rego Park, New York, my poppa used to tell me bedtime stories about life in the old country during the war . . ." The ellipses lead into the two square juxtaposed frames that conclude the page: a mouse father tucking his mouse son into bed, hand on his shoulder, followed by a military-accoutred cat ramming a pistol into the mouth of a terrified mouse, hand on his neck. While "Maus" does not specify Jews and Nazis, or the full names of the family at its center, it clearly bears witness to a survivor's experience of World War II in comics form: the testimony is particular, while the characters remain generic.

The arrangement of another's voice as framed by its listener—in this case, in the context of the primary and secondary witness—is the formal element that distinguishes "Maus" from Spiegelman's earlier work. "Maus" immediately establishes itself as a narrative concerned with the communication of testimony, however confusing it may be for the son, who becomes the interlocutor to the survivor-witness: trying to visualize his father's experience as the opening narrative act of the story, he comes up against the dominance

Figure 4.2 Art Spiegelman, first page of "Maus," *Funny Aminals*, 1972. (From *Breakdowns: Portrait of the Artist as a Young %@&*!* by Art Spiegelman, copyright © 1972, 1973, 1974, 1975, 1976, 1977, 2005, 2006, 2007, and 2008 by Art Spiegelman. Used by permission of the Wylie Agency LLC and Pantheon Books, an imprint of the Knopf Doubleday Publishing Group, a division of Penguin Random House LLC. All rights reserved.)

of the photographic public archive. For "Maus," Spiegelman interviewed and tape-recorded his father, Vladek Spiegelman, a survivor of Auschwitz and Dachau, among other camps, soliciting his testimony at length, and he carefully researched available Holocaust history (there was substantially less in English in the early 1970s, of course, than there is now).[15] His work prior to "Maus," Spiegelman says, was "me trying to get myself born as a cartoonist. [The three-page] *Maus* represented . . . a voice I could recognize . . . it was the moment I was able to establish a sense of self."[16] Yet the driving voice of "Maus" is the voice of Spiegelman's father. Spiegelman gets born as a cartoonist through his father's voice, through developing comics as a form to document and bear witness. "Maus" is also a certain kind of comics getting born in the United States, a significant opening up of a tradition of "drawing to tell" in the modern era.

Spiegelman continued to experiment with the reach of nonfiction after "Maus," producing one of the earliest comics essays, the dense, intellectual four-page "Cracking Jokes: A Brief Inquiry into Various Aspects of Humor" (1975), which features Freud as a recurring character. "Cracking Jokes" went on to inspire Scott McCloud's classic 1993 work of comics theory in the form of comics, *Understanding Comics*, now a media theory staple. In "Cracking Jokes," McCloud recognized the "show-and-tell" potential of presenting arguments in comics form. Spiegelman, in his view, "was speaking directly to the reader half the time, and every point he wanted to make he demonstrated as he went. And that's what I've tried to do with *Understanding Comics*."[17] In January 1976 Spiegelman contributed the first sequential comics art to the *New York Times*'s op-ed page—an occurrence now much more typical, flying under the banner of "Op-Art."[18] It is a four-panel comic strip with a cat, a mouse, and a "building a better mousetrap" theme that accompanied a column on the politics of economic planning.[19] In this period underground comics and non-narrative film were both pushing at the boundaries of narrative and experimenting with formal vocabularies. The link between the two forms is explicit in the figure of Spiegelman, who moved in both self-consciously avant-garde worlds.[20] His sense of narrative experiment, especially in slowing down or speeding up time and in proposing the recursivity of the comics page, was honed in conversation with filmmakers such as Stan Brakhage, Ken Jacobs, and Ernie Gehr. Yet even as these media dialogues inspired Spiegelman to deconstruct comics form, he was also creating new idioms of expression for comics nonfiction.

Spiegelman's work after "Maus" is also haunted by the Holocaust and grapples with Jewish identity, sometimes in surprising ways. We see this in pieces such as "Prisoner on the Hell Planet," completed (as was Green's *Binky Brown*) in 1972, which is about the suicide of Spiegelman's survivor mother, and in several installments of his underrated "Real Dream" series from 1975. In the surreal "Real Dream: 'A Hand Job,'" the nontransparency that the handwritten medium of comics offers suddenly seems uncomfortable: Spiegelman's hands betray his Jewishness when the fingers of his right hand each turn into a small person who insults him, including a bespectacled man who screams, "**Jew!**"[21] These formal and personal preoccupations come together in *Maus: A Survivor's Tale*, the long-form narrative that Spiegelman began in 1978. *Maus* definitively changed comics from the inside and the outside; to even speak of a "comics field," as one does now, was not possible before its publication and what it presented internally and galvanized externally. As Jared Gardner states in an essay on the importance of the year 1972 for comics, "It would be the response of Art Spiegelman to the possibility of autobiographical comics, and his own unique approach to collective autobiography, that would be most influential in shaping the reception of the form in the decades to come."[22] *Maus* has done more, as Gardner indicates, than any other work to establish comics as a sophisticated, complex art form. It created widespread attention to the category of the "graphic novel" (a term Spiegelman has come to dislike) in the 1980s and beyond, creating the viability of the American comics publishing field that is so vibrant today. Yet I want to push farther than Gardner's invocation of "collective autobiography": the work that founded the field is about witnessing world-historical disaster. Comics is a form *disposed* to witness; in Spiegelman's hands, the profound reverberations of war display the link. *Maus* demonstrates the motivated connection between comics form and visual witness; it reveals witnessing as the modality of contemporary comics.

As critics and Spiegelman himself have pointed out, there would be no "Maus," or *Maus*, without Green's *Binky Brown Meets the Holy Virgin Mary*.[23] However, as I suggest in the Introduction, there also would be no *Maus* without Paladij Osynka's 1946 hand-drawn pamphlet *Auschwitz: Album of a Political Prisoner*, which I discuss below, and which Spiegelman's mother, Anja Spiegelman, a survivor of Auschwitz and Ravensbrück, among other camps, brought from Poland to Sweden to the United States after the war. Nakazawa and Spiegelman's innovation in the early 1970s—independently executed in terms of actual creation but both spurred by the traumatic inheritance of World War II—shows how the exigencies of war inspired the popular form of comics to reinvent itself globally, to intensify its intrinsic concern with the nature of words and images in order to bear witness to war. World War II created the conditions for the emergence of adult, contemporary comics out of legacies of urgent visual witness.

Picturing the Oxymoron of Life in a Death Camp

The relevance of wartime archives to the aesthetic and political shape of *Maus* gained focus for me when I collaborated with Spiegelman as associate editor of *MetaMaus* (2011), his book about the thirteen-year process of making *Maus*.[24] *MetaMaus* is at every level about questions of form and bearing witness, and it draws on Spiegelman's extensive archive of notes, sketches, and World War II research, documents, and artifacts. This archive revealed hand-drawn traditions of witness stemming from the war that, I argue, led to the opening out of the comics culture that sprouted in the late 1960s and early 1970s—and which is responsible for the existence of the adult comics field we have today.

Extensive documentation of a range of visual and other cultural production by both artistically trained and untrained inmates incarcerated in the Nazi concentration and extermination camps includes well-known paintings and drawings by Leo Haas, Bedřich Fritta, Yehuda Bacon, and Dina Babbitt, among others.[25] Some works were commissioned by the SS; some were secretly created and stored at great risk, as in the case of a group of Theresienstadt prisoners who concealed hundreds of documentary images under the guise of a work detail.[26] Nazis forbade inmates at Auschwitz-Birkenau and most camps to make or keep their own art or written texts.[27] Yet prisoners covertly created sketches, portraits, diaries, maps, birthday cards, game boards, stamp sets, playing and tarot cards, illustrated fables, tiny books, and decorated letters, among many other forms and genres.[28] "Most of the art produced during the Holocaust," however, "falls into the categories of documentation of the events that the camera did not see," as Stephen Feinstein suggests.[29] Drawings of life in the camps produced both by survivors—in some cases after the war—and by those who did not survive inspired Spiegelman, aesthetically and politically, to conceptualize the comics field as connected to a history of drawing to tell and to recognize the witnessing power of drawing in the age of the camera.

Spiegelman grew up with survivor parents, who, in keeping with what was for many a tacit mandate of postwar American Jewish immigrant culture, did not address with him in any explicit way what their experiences in Poland had been. As a child, he knew there was something called "the war," but his encounters of learning about it were a series of jarringly disconnected moments, mostly aural. This disconnect is the subject of a pivotal scene from Spiegelman's *Portrait of the Artist as a Young %@&*!* in which the six-year-old Artie overhears bits and pieces of his parents speaking Polish to each other about a former Auschwitz *Sonderkommando,* a member of a special unit forced to work in gas chambers and crematoria, who attended the fancy party from which the family is returning in a chauffeured car. The child inquires about his parents' conversation. After his father explains to his son, "It's rumors he put to the ovens his wife and son, so nobody wants to sit!" Spiegelman's mother pats him on the head: "Take a nap again, cookie! It's still a long drive, and we're just having grown-up talk!" (Figure 4.3).

Here, the confusion of "put to the ovens" and the invocation from his own father, sitting with his wife and son, of something that sounds like uxoricide and filicide—Spiegelman as an adult in *Maus* famously accuses both of his parents of being "murderers"—resonates deeply, and Spiegelman draws his child self looking shocked and perplexed, with a row of spiky emanata emerging from his head. This perplexity was typical. However, during the widely televised Adolf Eichmann trial in 1961, when he was thirteen, Spiegelman went searching through his parents' private—"forbidden"—bookshelf. There are many accounts, widely circulating, of encountering images of atrocity for the first time and experiencing the subsequent loss of innocence, such as Susan Sontag's famous description in *On Photography* of finding concentration camp photographs when she was twelve: "Nothing I have ever seen—in photographs or in real life—ever cut me as sharply, deeply, instantaneously. Indeed, it seems plausible to me to divide my life into two parts."[30] Unlike in most such accounts, however, the most significant object that Spiegelman found was not photographic: it was drawn.

It is hard to overstate the centrality of Spiegelman's encounter with the stuff of the "forbidden bookshelf" to his later creation of a mainstream adult comics field in the United States (and elsewhere) through *Maus.* *Meta-Maus,* which consists, excluding appendices, of a long interview between me and Spiegelman, virtually begins with a discussion of this discovery on its fourth page (approximately 230 pages of interview follow). Spiegelman

Figure 4.3 Art Spiegelman, panels from *Portrait of the Artist as a Young %@&*!*, 2008. (From *Breakdowns: Portrait of the Artist as a Young %@&*!* by Art Spiegelman, copyright © 1972, 1973, 1974, 1975, 1976, 1977, 2005, 2006, 2007, and 2008 by Art Spiegelman. Used by permission of the Wylie Agency LLC and Pantheon Books, an imprint of the Knopf Doubleday Publishing Group, a division of Penguin Random House LLC. All rights reserved.)

discovered mostly Polish, Yiddish, and Ukrainian small-press pamphlets by survivors that bore witness to experiences of regular people in the war. Funded by Jewish organizations, most of these were published in 1946, in the immediate postwar period.[31] (One can understand the pamphlets as connected at least in part to the tradition of *yizkor* books, a type of memorial book with roots in ancient Jewish culture that after World War II took on a new form as a book of testimony and demographic record.) Several of these pamphlets, significantly, feature drawings of everyday life in the camps—handmade images of witness. Four years later, in 1965, Spiegelman would also discover the influential Bernard Krigstein comic-book story "Master Race" (1955), a formally sophisticated fictional account of a Nazi commandant on the run after the war; in that it addressed genocide in serious tones, "Master Race" was a rare cultural product.[32]

Although he could not read the text of the pamphlets because he did not know the languages (his small amount of "passive Polish" was verbal), their images—with their amateur graphic design and the humble small-press printing—constituted Spiegelman's first recognition of his parents' circumstance and life during the war. This encounter was necessarily a visual one; more specifically, it was an encounter with the drawn line. Some of these pamphlets were cartoony—one was a booklet by a Ukrainian inmate, Osynka, with gag cartoons and jokes, often at the expense of a naive prisoner ("A new-beginner is amazed: is it true that this big stick is for him?"). The work Spiegelman found on "Anja's bookshelf," as he went on to designate it, is diverse: some of the postwar pamphlets and books are largely prose, like the Polish booklet *Destruction of the Jews of Sosnowiec* (about the Polish city where his parents lived before the war), which became a key reference for *Maus* and which Spiegelman's stepmother, Mala Spiegelman, also a survivor, translated into English for his research.[33] Some are lengthy, like Seweryna Szmaglewska's *Smoke over Birkenau* (1946), which is said to be the first eyewitness account of Birkenau (and is currently in its eighteenth printing), and some are short and remain obscure. Two pamphlets in particular, which are predominantly visual, both titled with simple place names of camps, had a profound effect on the would-be documentary cartoonist: *Ravensbrück* and *Auschwitz*. Anja Spiegelman had come through both camps.[34]

Ravensbrück, likely from 1946, is a small bound booklet featuring ten colored images inside, with captions in Ukrainian. *Ravensbrück* is not attributed to a single author—the artist is unknown—but its images, drawing and watercolor, are clearly done by the same hand. These images, which Spiegelman describes as "delicate" and yet in some cases "printed very badly out of register," reveal in detail daily life in the camp from a prisoner's point of view: the carrying of heavy canisters of soup, prisoner selections, guards with dogs menacing prisoners, eating, marching, beatings, shivering, cramming into bunks (see Figure 4.4). Their tone and composition suggest neither detachment nor sensationalism but rather straightforward observation, snatches of the everyday. The small booklet *Auschwitz*—subtitled *Album of a Political Prisoner*—by Paladij Osynka, dated 1946, features fifteen images with captions that appear in both Ukrainian and (loosely translated) English (see Figure 4.5). *Auschwitz*'s images are identified both as a "document" and as "cartoons" in the lengthy author's note that precedes them.

Праця під доглядом СС-манок і тічні великих собак-вов-
кодавів жахала більше, як смерть.

Figure 4.4   Artist unknown, page from *Ravensbrück*, c. 1946 ("Work under the gaze of the SS and large wolflike dogs, which terrified them more than death").

In *Auschwitz*—also, like *Ravensbrück*, a work of visual reporting—the images carry no less information, but they are edged with a dark irony. The captions can be substantial and literary; they are aware of the space between word and image, as with Goya's *Disasters of War*. Only the first image, in which chimney smoke wafts out the word "Auschwitz," has no caption sitting below it. When one opens the pamphlet, the visual indicates what Auschwitz is, with no further explanation needed: a prisoner hangs on the electrified fence, the chimney pumps, and a guard shoots. Auschwitz is simply, redundantly, death. Executed in what Spiegelman calls a "clumsy" style—people often appear with disproportionately large heads—*Auschwitz* mixes jokey images with desperately serious ones: two, which work sequentially, are of the gas chamber and have the simple titles

Figure 4.5   Paladij Osynka, cover to *Auschwitz*, 1946.

"Selection for gas chamber" followed by "In the gas chamber." One wonders if (and how) Osynka was in the gas chamber to see what he drew—his image, which depicts six men dying, has the simple clarity of authority (he could have been, perhaps, a *Sonderkommando*).[35]

That Spiegelman's comprehension of these pamphlets was, at the time, visual and *necessarily* not verbal allowed him to encounter the discourse of the visual in a heightened way, even as the visuals shared space on the page with captions. Further, the urgency of the small-press documents, revealing the texture of what he calls "the oxymoron of life in a death camp," their lack of pretension and their exigency, "struck [him] hard." The pamphlets "were so clearly not part of mass-cultural production, that they had a kind of fanzine-like magic to me," he explains. The drawings and their delivery are examples of the necessity of witness that requires only the most basic of platforms. The pamphlets' unpretentiousness, their transmission of both basic and detailed information, and their visual style—their (re)creation of a world through line—fascinated him. "Anything at all with cartoon-like drawings had an immense pull on me," Spiegelman continues of the pamphlets, "especially those from before my own childhood."[36]

When I started thinking about *Maus*, I was suspicious of the term *magical* as a descriptor, as in a blurb from Umberto Eco that graces many editions of the book describing the reading of *Maus* as entering a "magical world." To me it indicated something incorrect: namely, that *Maus*, as drawing, creates comfortable distance from the reality of the war; that it sugarcoats terror. I no longer think of "magical" as a backhanded compliment for a nonfiction text, especially in light of how Spiegelman describes his fascination with the often horrifying pamphlets. What it now indicates to me is the force, or force field, of the mark and line to impart information both external to the maker and also personal to the maker. The distilled register of the cartoon and the drawn line creates an enveloping, idiosyncratic world of expression that can be powerful for witness. This is how J. Hillis Miller repeatedly uses "magical" when analyzing *Maus* in *The Conflagration of Community*.[37] One person's line can create what feels like a secret world of experience—even as this person is testifying, as in the pamphlets, to the world at large. The primal interest in the world before he, a child of survivors, was improbably in it inspires many features of *Maus*, both foundational and complex; historical, aesthetic, and psychic. The pamphlets, most of which were completed quickly after the war, just make this cutoff: Spiegelman was born in 1948.

I would warrant that just as Sontag was preoccupied by photography in the long "second part" of her life after she saw the atrocity photos, Spiegelman's path to becoming the cartoonist he became—one who made hand-drawn witnessing, as well as nonfiction comics, reemerge for the postmodern American era—is connected to his early fascination with these word-and-image documents and their aesthetico-historical possibilities. The pamphlets inspired Spiegelman's "Maus" and his field-defining *Maus*. *Maus* first appeared, chapter by chapter, in similarly designed and printed serial booklets in *RAW* magazine starting in 1980.

The postwar booklets are the model for the format of Spiegelman's telling of his own parents' war story (see Figure 4.6). While few critics have noted the serialization of *Maus* prior to its publication in book volumes by Pantheon (1986, 1991), even fewer have actually analyzed the context of its appearance within *RAW*, the biannual "avant-garde comix and graphix" anthology magazine (1980–1991) founded and edited by Spiegelman and Françoise Mouly, his wife (the art editor of the *New Yorker* since 1993). Spiegelman and Mouly self-published the first eight issues of *RAW*, a large-format magazine boasting an international roster of artists, on a second-hand multilith printing press in their Soho loft; the first print run was about 3,500 copies, just a bit smaller than the likely print run of the postwar booklets.[38] *RAW*'s second issue, 1980's *The Graphix Magazine for Damned Intellectuals*—each issue carried a different subtitle—contained the first chapter of *Maus* as a small, digest-sized booklet, printed on inexpensive paper, which sat as a separate insert within the magazine against its larger, glossier, eleven-by-fourteen-inch art folio stock. *Maus* continued to be published chapter by chapter as an insert in *RAW* through its penultimate chapter, in 1991. (Volume 1 appeared as a book in 1986, halfway through *Maus*'s serialization, only because of Spiegelman's fears that producer Steven Spielberg and director Don Bluth's animated feature *An American Tail* [1986], whose concept he believed was stolen from the three-page "Maus," would eclipse the reception of his work on its own terms.)[39]

Other hand-drawn work by survivors of the Nazi camps—and those who did not survive—inspired *Maus*. Charlotte Salomon (1917–1943) painted the experimental word-and-image autobiography *Life? Or Theatre?* during a short period of freedom after internment by the French at Gurs and before her death at Auschwitz.[40] In the colorful series of 800-plus gouaches structured like a play, the application of the materials suggests a poignant haste; her marks encode a fleeting sense of duration. Meaningful examples of the tradition of hand-drawn images of witness include less well-known works by a range of camp inmates, including Waldemar Nowakowski, Alfred Kantor, and Mieczysław Kościelniak. Nowakowski created simple, evocative drawings at Auschwitz that documented events such as beatings; for Spiegelman, the drawings' purposefulness was moving. They convey important basic information (beating was done with a stick in front of barracks, prisoners were made to squat, certain patches were on the

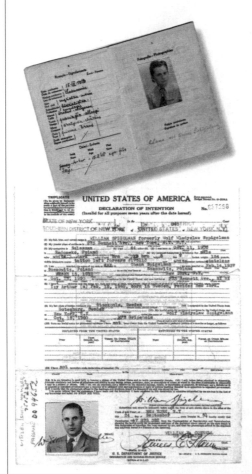

booklets included in *RAW* magazine when *Maus* was presented as a work in progress. Something about their humble graphic design and printing was important to me.

Let's clear something up which can be confusing. Can you clarify Anja, Anna, Vladek, Willie—can we set this straight?

Vladek was actually born Zev Spiegelman. His Hebrew name was Zev ben Abraham. He was brought up in a rather Yiddish household, but his Polish name was Wladislaw with a "W." Wladec was a diminutive of Wladislaw. When his part of Poland, Silesia, was controlled by Russia, it was Vladek with a "V." When the Germans took over—it was part of the Polish tug-of-war—he had a German name, Wilhelm, but was also called "Wolf." And then when he came on the boat to America he became William. I settled on the one people could pronounce, which is not W-l-a-d-e-c, but V-l-a-d-e-k. The Russian spelling is just easier to locate for American eyes. Anja was born "Andzia Zylberberg." Her Hebrew name was Hannah, though in her assimilated household that wasn't something she was called regularly. She became Anna Spiegelman when she moved to America.

TOP LEFT: Anja's Polish passport, 1946.
LEFT: Vladek's U.S. naturalization application, 1951.
BELOW AND FACING PAGE (counterclockwise): Booklets from Anja's bookshelf: *How I Survived the Nazi Hell; Auschwitz; Arsonists' World; Smoke Over Birkenau; We, the Ukrainians (Buchenwald); The Underground Movement in the Ghettos and Camps; Maus* insert booklets in *RAW.*
FACING PAGE, CENTER: Chapter 4 insert in *RAW,* vol. 1, no. 5.

Figure 4.6 *MetaMaus* double spread of Anja's postwar booklets alongside Spiegelman's *Maus* insert booklets in *RAW* (pages 16–17). (From *MetaMaus: A Look Inside a Modern Classic* by Art Spiegelman, copyright © 2011 by Art Spiegelman. Used by permission of the Wylie Agency LLC and Pantheon Books, an imprint of the Knopf Doubleday Publishing Group, a division of Penguin Random House LLC. All rights reserved.)

uniform, the shoes were wooden and not leather).[41] Kantor's watercolor work is looser than Nowakowski's but, significantly, it also contains hand-written captions (see Figure 4.7). He drew in pencil in Terezín and in Auschwitz, determined "to keep a continuous record" of his life in the camps, even though he destroyed his own sketches to avoid being caught.[42] Kantor, a Czech, reconstructed his drawings in a displaced-persons camp in Bavaria in 1945 as a visual diary, which was later published as *The Book of Alfred Kantor* (1971) and provided Spiegelman with an important clue to the daily grain of camp life, particularly in its word-and-image aspect.[43]

In Kantor's work Spiegelman found a "sophisticated notational system" and a matter-of-fact tone to which he could relate: "the pictures gave you information, but they weren't 'sexy.'" In contradistinction, Spiegelman—who has never been shy about critiquing the aesthetic value of any image—notes that celebrated survivor artist and former *Sonderkommando* David Olère's pictures are "kitschy . . . milking it for every bit of drama it's got."[44] Kościelniak's drawings appear more often than any other artist's in Spiegelman's archive of prisoner art; Kościelniak was a trained artist, and his highly detailed, precisely rendered drawings (those that were not SS commissions) present what Spiegelman calls "a clarity beyond most photography."[45] *Maus* incorporates (without citation) a detailed image of a louse that was a portion of a poster Kościelniak created at Auschwitz in German for the Nazis with the warning "One Louse Means Death." Kościelniak, then, becomes not only a reference for *Maus* but actually part of the stuff of its pages, one of the many pieces of history, a material history of the camps, on which it builds.

These works of surviving hand-drawn art from World War II—created in what we would certainly call the age of the camera—are exemplary occasions of drawing to constitute a record, to communicate exterior information. While the lines index the bodies of their makers, the images meditate less on the self, on subjectivity, than on observing history and experience. The drawings are "a return to drawing *not for its possibilities of imposing the self*, of finding a new role for art and drawing after the camera," Spiegelman says, in a comment also cited in my Introduction, "but rather a return to the earlier function that drawing served before the camera—a kind of commemorating, witnessing, and recording of information—what Goya referred to when he says, 'This I saw.'" He continues, "The artists . . . are giving urgent information in the pictures, information that could be transmitted no other way."[46] Prisoners in the camps, generally speaking,

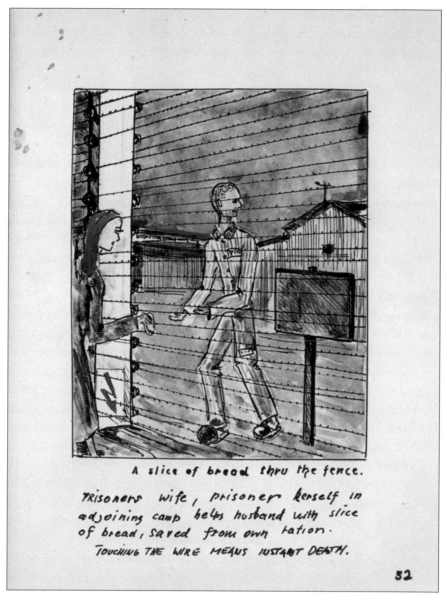

A slice of bread thru the fence.

Prisoners wife, prisoner herself in adjoining camp helps husband with slice of bread, saved from own ration.
Touching the wire means instant death.

52

Figure 4.7 Alfred Kantor, drawing of Auschwitz, from section "The Hell of Auschwitz: Pictures from Winter-Spring 1944" in *The Book of Alfred Kantor.* Kantor drew his visual diary while incarcerated, destroyed it, and redrew it in 1945 after the war. (Used by permission of Jerry Kantor.)

did not have access to cameras. (A very small number of photographs were smuggled out, including one that Spiegelman draws in *Maus*.)[47] These drawings, then, provide vital examples of the function of drawing as documentation.

This tradition of hand-drawn images of witness includes work inspired by the very specific comics language that informs *Maus*. When he saw the cartoon pamphlet *Mickey au Camp de Gurs* (*Mickey in Gurs*)—after his own work was finished—Spiegelman recognized it as a "validation that I'd stumbled onto a way of telling that had deep roots."[48] Horst Rosenthal's *Mickey in Gurs*, a poignant and amusing fifteen-panel bound booklet (designated by some sources simply a "comic book," and now owned by the Centre de Documentation Juive Contemporaine in Paris) was created in 1942 in the French internment camp Gurs, near the Pyrenees, where Charlotte Salomon had also been imprisoned (Figure 4.8).[49] The German-born Rosenthal died in Auschwitz that same year, at age twenty-seven. Mickey Mouse narrates *Mickey in Gurs*, and its graphically lovely red and black cover, dated 1942, states it is "published without the authorization of Walt Disney"—a joke that indicates not only the globalization of comic book culture, as Feinstein points out, but also, wryly, the constraints on actual "publication": only one booklet was made (unlike the postwar pamphlets, some quite similar, that Anja Spiegelman owned).[50] The black line art of Rosenthal's images, doodles, and handwritten text is confident and fluid; the booklet alternates between black-and-white and watercolor, a mix perhaps attributable to the availability of supplies over time. The booklet opens with Mickey's arrest and arrival at Gurs; he is the only mouse in *Mickey in Gurs*, interacting with human policemen, camp bureaucrats, guards, and fellow inmates. When asked who his father is, he replies, "Walt Disney"; he is subsequently asked if he is a Jew. ("Shamefully, I confessed my complete ignorance on that subject," the narrator-mouse reports.) One learns about camp life and policies from Mickey's parodically perplexed point of view as he describes meals, barracks, and censors. *Mickey in Gurs* is powerful in its concurrent delivery of information—even filtered through the abstraction of the nonmimetic mouse—and its alertness to its own ephemerality.

The visual-verbal testimony of *Mickey in Gurs* is a haunting precursor to *Maus* in several important aspects: the mouse (whose figuration as such is yet a cipher—Mickey is an evident stand-in for the human author) as the persecuted figure, engagement with the iconic nature of popular culture in the act of bearing witness, and the careful documentation of daily life's

Figure 4.8 Horst Rosenthal, cover of *Mickey au Camp de Gurs* booklet, 1942. (Used by permission of Mémorial de la Shoah, Paris, France.)

detail (such as exactly which seven-plus ingredients go into the "nauseating" soup served at Gurs), alongside a conspicuous awareness of the drawing medium. Mickey describes how a fellow prisoner offers "to rent me his bunk, just to . . ."—and then Rosenthal cuts off, since Mickey knows "this is a children's book."[51] Most movingly, in the last panel, Mickey simply erases himself from Gurs and indicates he will be instead in America, which in his critique of the French he mockingly describes as "the land of L . . . y, E . . . y, and F . . . y" (liberty, equality, fraternity). The booklet's last image, with a cheerful pink watercolor background, shows Mickey walking against the direction of reading (and the direction he draws himself entering Gurs) toward a cluster of skyscrapers enclosed in a fluffy thought balloon. This page is signed "Mickey" in lively script, below which sit the small, less effervescent letters spelling "Horst Rosenthal," and again, as on the cover, the location and date.

Rosenthal's medium allows him to erase himself before he can be erased in this fantasy of the elective—of the choice to disappear. One can understand Rosenthal's Mickey, as Lisa Naomi Mulman suggests, as a figure of Walter Benjamin's destructive and yet redemptive *Unmensch*, "the cannibal that devours his adversary in the savagery of his wit."[52] Rosenthal, she writes, making reference to Benjamin's language, "is the ultimate *Unmensch*. He 'steals' his body from himself, first detaching it from his own subjectivity, and then 'erasing' it entirely."[53] It codes as an aesthetically radical act. Through attention to the *immateriality* of drawing—its possibility of erasure and reconstitution elsewhere—Rosenthal in fact underlines the witnessing force behind the materiality of his lines that he does create before Mickey happily self-erases from Gurs.

Both the direct connections and the potent underlying formal connections between the postwar pamphlets and surviving art from the camps and Spiegelman's foundational *Maus* reveal how powerfully the earlier work shaped the possibilities of contemporary comics. It is exactly these traditions of drawn witnessing, seen in the postwar pamphlets and other survivor (and nonsurvivor) art that opened up the creation of today's comics field. Unearthing these archives and histories, we can trace the cross-continental movement of the booklets from Europe to the United States, where they helped instigate aesthetically and documentarily ambitious forms of graphic narrative in the taboo-shattering underground period. We should in turn understand the contemporary comics field, so deeply shaped and conditioned by the success of *Maus*, as inspired by, even founded on, these earlier acts of witness to war and disaster.

Maus: Creating a Testimonial Archive

The lines and marks of *Maus*, made with a fountain pen, are looser and thicker than those in the three-page "Maus" of 1972, also a black-and-white work. In the longer *Maus*, Spiegelman abandons the finely cross-hatched, tight rendering of the shorter work (which is highly attentive to textures, whether of a military coat or a mouse's fur), for shaggier, more open lines. *Maus* maintains the animal metaphor, but here the specified features of the animal characters are replaced by a more minimal notational style— a visual system in which the reader cannot "take comfort," as Spiegelman puts it, that "it ain't you."[54] The despecification, in other words, opens out to greater readerly identification.[55] Further, in order to reject the look and tone of visual mastery, Spiegelman created both the words and the images in *Maus* with the same Pelikan fountain pen, and used other common stationery-store materials, as well as a one-to-one ratio of drawing to print size.[56] *Maus*'s one-to-one ratio of creation to production, highly unusual in comics, produces a manuscript or diary-like effect (one sees the mark at the same size at which it was drawn) that echoes the urgent look and practice of drawings of witness made in the Nazi camps.

Almost 300 pages spread out over two book volumes—*Maus I: A Survivor's Tale: My Father Bleeds History* (1986) and *Maus II: A Survivor's Tale: And Here My Troubles Began* (1991)—the long-form *Maus* combines the formal experiment of Spiegelman's earlier underground work, particularly with narrative temporality and spatiality, with an account of survival that is gripping in its linear progression; *Maus* reads like the undertow and running river at once. In *On the Origin of Stories*, Brian Boyd even cites *Maus* as the inspiration for his book on "supremely successful" stories: his opening sentence announces, "My first debt is to Art Spiegelman."[57] In *Maus*, one knows that Vladek has survived the war, since he is testifying to his artist son, yet the situations the book presents are so harrowing as to make that conclusion feel remote.

While some of Vladek Spiegelman's testimony in the short "Maus" is repeated in the longer work—for instance, the incident in which he was discovered hiding in a bunker in the Środula ghetto and later buried the responsible party in Auschwitz—the arc of his life as presented in *Maus* is much deeper and begins much earlier, before the war.[58] Art Spiegelman's goal in *Maus* was to create a comic book that needed a bookmark.[59] Shuttling between 1930s and 1940s Poland and 1970s and 1980s New York, *Maus* is as much about the son's struggle to elicit testimony and visualize his father's history in comics form as it is about the father's extraordinary, terrifying narrative of survival during the war—and, as the artist-son takes pains to point out, after the war. "There is more to survival than bringing the body through its ordeal unscathed," Spiegelman muses about the premise of *Maus* in a 1985 entry in a notebook. "There is the building of a personality with depth and understanding—something difficult enough to achieve even without passing through the center of history's hell." And then on a separate line, by itself: "Survival is having children even if they hate you."[60] *Maus* intertwines the improbable story of its own making with Vladek Spiegelman's testimony of his life before, during, and after World War II (when his only surviving child often hates him).

It is not a coincidence that the hand-drawn word-and-image work that almost single-handedly created the contemporary adult American comics field—the one that licensed readers, publishers, cartoonists, and critics both in America and beyond to understand the potential of comics in a new light—is about war, witness, and documentation. If *Maus* marks the reemergence of a powerful tradition of drawing to tell, what does witnessing mean in *Maus*—the comics work about the war that created the postwar comics field as one inclined to document?

Comics is powerful precisely in how it intervenes against the trauma-driven discourse of the unrepresentable and the ineffable, as I suggest in *Graphic Women*, which explores the work of five contemporary cartoonists, each indebted to *Maus*.[61] The current prominence of comics, especially in our twenty-first-century age of global wars and endemic violence, indicates desire for forms of aesthetic expression that do face history and trauma, that even document it visually—as opposed to sacralizing absence and/or "staging . . . a refusal to stage," as Jean-Luc Nancy describes filmmaker Claude Lanzmann's landmark *Shoah*.[62] *Maus* demonstrates how the vocabulary of comics—the narrative shapes its grammar offers—along with its visual surface, the extrasemantic layer of its drawn lines, conveys information while at the same time accounting for the excess (or absence) of signification and reference. In the late 1970s, around the time he began work on *Maus*, Spiegelman wrote in a notebook: "Maybe vulgar, semi-literate, unsubtle comic books are an appropriate form for speaking the unspeakable." Almost forty years later, when I asked him about this in a public event, he quipped that today "the unspeakable gets spoken within ten minutes, by me if nobody else."[63] Despite his quip, it is important to understand how the previous half century has changed comics' ability to express what is routinely referred to as "unspeakable."

The mark is not merely mimetic but rather produces its own phenomenology. Nancy's articulation of the significance of the image, in the vein of artist William Kentridge's view of the mark, noted in Chapter 3, resonates with the visual presence produced by *Maus* and other comics works. In *The Ground of the Image*, Nancy describes how "the image is what takes the thing out of its simple presence and brings it to pres-ence, to *praes-entia*, to being out-in-front-of-itself, turned toward the outside. . . . This is not a presence 'for a subject' (it is not 'representation' in the ordinary, mimetic sense of the word). It is, on the contrary, if one can put it this way, 'presence as subject.' In the image, or as image, and only in this way, the thing—whether it is an inert image or a person—is posited as subject. The thing *presents itself*."[64] While Nancy here expresses the nature of any image, his language, with its reference to the turned-outward presence of the image, is strikingly relevant for comics, as if its form literalizes the figure of Nancy's description.[65]

With its febrile, nontransparent lines and its hand-drawn juxtaposed boxes that enclose, underline, and present a succession of moments, almost as in a series of windows, comics offers images replete with their own sense of turning toward the outside. Synthesizing old and yet pervasive debates about Holocaust representation, Nancy defines the significant aesthetic work that actually has high stakes as "exactly the opposite of the impoverishment of the sensory: not a thick and tautological presence before which one prostrates oneself but rather the presentation of an open absence within the work itself—within its sensory presentation."[66] This describes an important feature of *Maus*'s word-and-image witnessing: encountering it is a rich sensory experience of reading and looking, while at the same time one meets the open absence of its gutter spaces. This explanation of open absence built within the sensory resonates with Shoshana Felman's notion of the *textualization of the context* in works expressing trauma.[67] Nancy offers a similar proposition in terms strikingly evocative of comics grammar: "The criteria of a representation of Auschwitz can only be found in this demand: *that such an opening—interval or wound—not be shown as an object but rather that it be inscribed right at the level of representation, as its very texture.*"[68] Comics takes shape through intervals, including the gutter, its central, constitutive interval of absence. In *Maus*'s page depicting four hanged friends of Vladek's on a public street in 1941, for instance, the textualization inheres in the shaggy look of the lines—resisting Nazi tropes of mastery—and also in its compositional texture as a narrative unit stippled with gaps. A conspicuous horizontal gutter at the bottom of the page queers the movement of the narrative, halting causality or diachrony and instead marking traumatic repetition—in what become, through images and words, literal footnotes (Figure 4.9).[69] Spiegelman repeats and disarticulates the bodies of the hanged.

Maus portrays the spatial form comics can take, what Spiegelman calls "turning a narrative into geography"—a different aim, especially when visualizing testimony, than mimeticism, or even the verisimilitude associated with film.[70] Comics offers an "architectonics" that can bear witness forcefully in its ability to immerse readers within information in the space of the page. When testimony takes shape in drawing, it both expresses realities and "offers encapsulated sets of abstractions"—marks—"that trigger

Figure 4.9 Art Spiegelman, *The Complete Maus,* page 85. (From *The Complete Maus: A Survivor's Tale* by Art Spiegelman, *Maus*, Volume I copyright © 1973, 1980, 1981, 1982, 1983, 1984, 1985, 1986 by Art Spiegelman; *Maus*, Volume II copyright © 1986, 1989, 1990, 1991 by Art Spiegelman. Used by permission of the Wylie Agency LLC and Pantheon Books, an imprint of the Knopf Doubleday Publishing Group, a division of Penguin Random House LLC. All rights reserved.)

a response," as Spiegelman puts it. *Maus* is invested in "creating [the camps] as a mental zone," not just as a visual re-creation.[71] In *The Conflagration of Community: Fiction before and after Auschwitz*, J. Hillis Miller considers Holocaust literature through the "leitmotif," which for him is a "recurrent spatially deployed paradigm that corresponds to or expresses the imaginary inner space the novel generates in the reader." While he and I disagree about whether *Maus* is a novel, his description of its leitmotif, which he characterizes as the "ubiquitous matrix of a conventional comic book page that allows Spiegelman . . . to express so much in so little," highlights the power of how comics transmits information.[72] Miller writes of "the extreme temporal and spatial complexity" of comics.[73] And, joining many theorists of the image, Miller is not interested in the ineffable. Rather, he is interested in how *Maus* presents: "the 'nows' of the narration . . . made of discontinuous episodic blocks" and its punctuation "at irregular intervals, arhythmically, in periodic syncopes" by metanarrative.[74] As Nancy points out, representation is not just a copy of the thing but makes the thing observable; it exposes with insistence.[75]

Viewed as documentary, *Maus*'s comics form provides distinct layers of commentary and facets of Vladek's experience; its pages hold different kinds of information together through their visual surface. On a page in the chapter "Auschwitz (Time Flies)," for instance, different types of information come together in a visually heightened fashion (page 227; Figure 4.10).[76] As they stroll through the Catskills, Vladek tells Art, across the unbordered top tier of the page, about his time doing "black work" at the Auschwitz main camp. Art inquires, "Black work?" and the next tier, in defined boxes, opens by depicting the requirements of black work underneath Vladek's words: "Carrying back and forth big stones, digging out holes, each day different, but always the same." The shaded panel, whose background appears striated, shows a silhouetted worker in the left foreground with a shovel and the repeated figure of marching inmates with stones; it is a classic montage panel, as Spiegelman describes it, one that is emblematic.[77] Yet the page concludes, setting up a visual diagonal rhyme between same-size panels across the page, with highly specific information about a particular incident: Vladek hiding from a *Selektion* by sitting on a visually articulated toilet, with a hanging flush mechanism, in a detailed bathroom. In drawing his father's testimony, Spiegelman indicates duration and repetition in Eisensteinian gestures, and also by turns registers the concrete details, even minute ones, he was able to verify.[78]

Maus exploits the form of comics to do the work of documenting experience and information through diagramming both *experience*—locating bodies moving over time in space—and diagramming spaces and objects. By nature comics is a diagrammatic form: its fundamental narrative movement is to diagram time as space on the page. In the comics-format introduction to his 1978 *Breakdowns*, Spiegelman muses on his chosen form: "Better than the word CARTOONS is the word DRAWINGS; or better still . . . DIAGRAMS." In a 1978 essay, he explains, "All comic-strip drawings must function as diagrams . . . that indicate more than they show."[79] *Maus*, composed diagrammatically, also uses the form of the diagram meaningfully throughout, such as in the chapter "Mouse Holes," in which Vladek interrupts his own testimony, demanding of Art, "Show to me your pencil and I can *explain* to you"; drawing a diagram of a bunker, he reasons that "such things it's good to know exactly how was it—just in case" (page 112). Spiegelman draws Vladek drawing for Art, and then Spiegelman redraws Vladek's diagram—a side view of a bunker where the Spiegelman parents hid in the Środula ghetto—for readers as a panel of the page.[80]

Along with diagrams of bunkers and hiding places, *Maus* also features detailed diagrams of shoe repair (page 220) and other facets of camp life, such as currency in Auschwitz (page 224). Protesting its listing of *Maus II* on the fiction bestseller list in his 1991 letter to the *New York Times Book Review*, Spiegelman refers to the book's diagrams in order to underline its status as nonfiction, despite the visual abstraction of its mice: "It's not as though my passages on how to build a bunker and repair concentration camp boots got the book onto your 'Advice, How-to and Miscellaneous' list."[81] As the realm of Spiegelman's practical father transformed into the realm of the artist son through appropriation *and* through the formal dimension of comics itself, diagrams both carry emotional weight and exhibit comics' distinctive spatial grammar. And the diagram that carries the most weight is of the inside and outside of one of the four crematorium buildings in Auschwitz.

Maus is careful not to depict atrocity outside of Vladek's testimony (even when conveying "emblematic" information) without indicating its lack of corroboration. Thus Spiegelman visualizes *possibilities* for violent endings—and always partially covers images with balloons or boxes of speech—that accompany Vladek's unverified speech, such as when Nazis kill toddlers by smashing them against a wall on the way out of the Środula ghetto ("This I didn't see with my own eyes," Vladek says [page 110]), or when Vladek reports the death of his friend Mandelbaum ("He got killed. Or he died. I know they *finished* him" [page 195]). Vladek was an eyewitness and a participant in the dismantling of the crematoria toward the end of the war; he had worked in the tin shop at Auschwitz in the summer of 1944 and, as he explains in *Maus*, "when the Russians came near, the Germans made ready to run from Auschwitz. They needed tinmen to pull apart the machineries of the gas chambers." Vladek states clearly, "You *heard* about the gas. But I'm telling not rumors. But only what I really *saw*. For this I was an *eyewitness*" (page 229). In a perspective unusual to the book, Spiegelman draws his father's face cut off just below the mouth but with eyes gazing directly outward, meeting the reader's gaze, underscoring Vladek's optical apprehension. Turning the page, one encounters *Maus*'s most clinical and realistically precise set of drawings (page 230; Figure 4.11). This page, which opens "I came to one of the four cremo buildings. It looked so like a big bakery . . . ," is the only one of the entire book that does not picture a single person (or animal) within its frames.

For the "cremo building" Vladek saw, Spiegelman offers what comics does best, charting and detailing space. One sees the outside of the crematorium, with arrows identifying aboveground spaces (ovens) and belowground spaces (undressing rooms, gas chambers), along with a smaller diagram of the complete interior building—Crematorium II—lying vertically on the right across two views of the exterior. The diagram of the interior, a blueprint, shows the relation and scale of spaces like the toilet, coal storage, room for melting gold fillings, and "corpse lift," in addition to the incineration room and gas chamber. On the page's bottom tier, the panel depicts the ramp down to the so-called disinfection room from the perspective of someone walking down it. The final panel takes readers into the space of the undressing room with its signs designed to perpetuate the illusion of return: "Important—remember your hook number." On this page the crematorium chimney itself breaks the frame of reference, in its comics expression as in life: its stack bursts upward, jutting out of Spiegelman's topmost border, sitting conspicuously and ominously against white space. (On the previous page an Auschwitz chimney also breaks the top of the frame, its wafting smoke joining Spiegelman's cigarette smoke in the above tier; even as a second-generation witness, the book implies, Art breathes Auschwitz, perhaps as a habit and perhaps to his detriment).

Spiegelman notes that he initially assumed that he would draw Auschwitz in a deliberately sketchy mode—"seen through a fog of scribbled lines."[82]

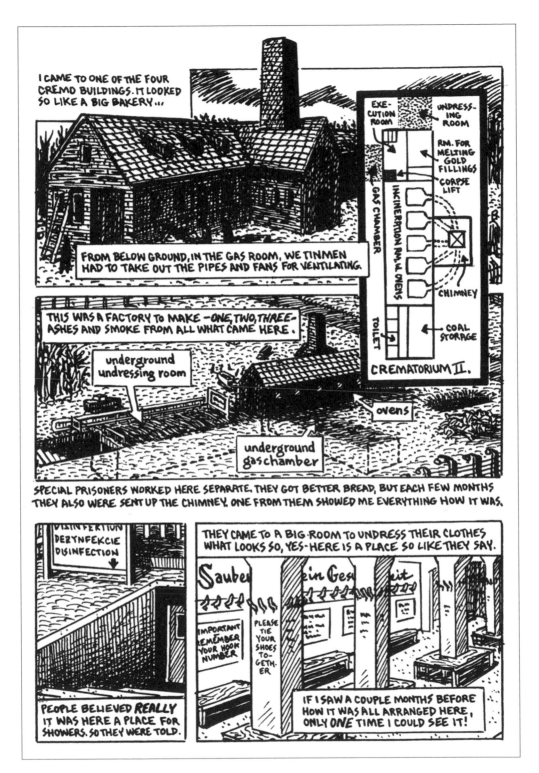

This style, which gestures to its own distance and provisionality, is akin to the one he had used earlier in *Maus* (page 63) to portray a group of Jews who were taken into the woods and shot, a scene he rendered, harking back to a significant tradition, to look like "a journalist illustrator's sketch."[83] The drawings of the mechanisms of the extermination camp, however, took shape as the most detailed in the book as Spiegelman documented the spaces of death that his father saw: "Maybe as a way of getting past my own aversion I tried to see Auschwitz as clearly as I could. It was a way of forcing myself and others to look at it."[84]

The second page of the double spread of the cremo building, a closer look at its gas chamber and ovens, produces a defamiliarizing recognition beyond what one might experience in a work with a consistent mode of verisimilitude (page 231; Figure 4.12). What is most jarring on the page is the interaction between the stylized, minimal mice to which we are accustomed and the detailed, realistically rendered machinery of Auschwitz. These images of Auschwitz's awful spaces carry the neutrality and chill of a dehumanized handbook; they are replete with cross-hatching, more technical, different in look and feel from other pages of *Maus*.

The deliberately unsynthesized collisions of style—the representational and the nonrepresentational, and the disjunctions between them—are the root of *Maus*'s expression of horror. Nancy argues the Nazi ethic is all about *representation*—this, he suggests, is the logic of the camp.[85] Spiegelman meticulously documents the history to which his father was an eyewitness, aiming for accuracy and "essential actuality" throughout, while making his own system conspicuously heterogeneous to itself.[86] In an interview with Harvey Blume, Spiegelman identifies a friction that inheres in his comics: "Whatever value I find in totally non-representational painting or in totally representational painting, the moment of collision is the one where I get the biggest charge."[87] The drawn animal metaphor, especially because it registers as an abstracted style interacting with other styles of documentation, destabilizes *Maus*'s own mode of expression; it is one of the book's inscriptions of collision and rupture, here in the very heart of the death mechanism of Auschwitz.

The movement of the page, its rhythm between open and closed, action and stillness, underlines this. Unsurprisingly, the mice—Vladek and a fellow prisoner, a *Sonderkommando*—make their only appearance on the page sandwiched in the center tier, blocked on both sides, it would seem, by the fact of death. A cutaway view of the gas chambers in the first

Figure 4.12 Art Spiegelman, *The Complete Maus,* page 231. (From *The Complete Maus: A Survivor's Tale* by Art Spiegelman, *Maus,* Volume I copyright © 1973, 1980, 1981, 1982, 1983, 1984, 1985, 1986 by Art Spiegelman; *Maus,* Volume II copyright © 1986, 1989, 1990, 1991 by Art Spiegelman. Used by permission of the Wylie Agency LLC and Pantheon Books, an imprint of the Knopf Doubleday Publishing Group, a division of Penguin Random House LLC. All rights reserved.)

panel—Vladek's testimony says it was closed "hermetic," but our view is open, going above its ceilings to the roof and outside—opens out our perspective, which is immediately shut down in the next panel: a drawing of the closed door to the chambers, punctuated by a window facing us directly (page 231). While Spiegelman does suggest that narrative generally, and comics specifically, is like a row of windows, here we do not get to look through the window of the tightly locked door (as the Nazis did to check the status of prisoners, who Vladek reports took three to thirty minutes to die).[88] In the middle row of frames, Vladek and his coworker move heavy piping, walking to the right, moving us forward through the page. But while they point forward, the bottom tier—a single, horizontal panel concluding the page, depicting a stretch of ovens—visually ends this movement swiftly, hauntingly. Vladek's testimony on the page ends without a period, as his words stretch into the dark space of the receding ovens ("to such a place finished my father, my sisters, my brothers, so many").

Spiegelman's inked lines materializing Vladek's "deposition," a performative, cross-discursive collaboration that goes inside the camps, portrays death in word and image. As a richly visual work, and one invested in its ability to show, *Maus* refutes on many levels the anti-imagism in discourse about the Holocaust, described recently in Georges Didi-Huberman's incisive *Images in Spite of All*. Didi-Huberman uses his discussion of four rare photographs smuggled out of Auschwitz by prisoners in 1944 to refute theorists and filmmakers attached to a thesis of the unimaginable, the aesthetics of "showing absence."[89] Among the four photographs Didi-Huberman analyzes, all secretly taken by the same inmate within the space of about ten minutes, is one that Spiegelman draws in *Maus*. It appears on the page directly after the double spread of the crematorium: an image of Hungarian Jews, outdoors, being dragged and thrown into burning pits in August 1944. The image appears with a jagged border, indicating its difference from the other framed images on the page; it sticks out slightly into the horizontal gutter, as if laid on the space of the grid instead of created within it. A *Sonderkommando* stands in a heap of dozens upon dozens of bodies laid out on the ground, grabbing the limbs of one and balancing his own body weight with an outstretched arm in order to throw it into an open-air incineration pit from which smoke thickly rises in front of him. "Train after train of Hungarians came," Vladek explains, and above the drawing, whose quavery border marks its status as a separate kind of frame,

"And those what finished in the gas chambers before they got pushed in these graves, it was the lucky ones" (page 232).

Maus is interested in documenting as the texture of visual articulation, however supposedly direct, mediated, or re-mediated. Spiegelman not only incorporates Kościelniak's camp-commissioned louse poster as a reference but reactivates it to perform the work of witnessing (of daily camp life) as part of the visual stuff of Maus. In much the same way, the clandestine photograph of the bodies being dragged into the pits—taken by a Greek Jew known only as Alex—becomes part of the book's testimonial visual surface (page 232; Figure 4.13). If Spiegelman was inspired by the postwar pamphlets and by inmate drawings for their urgent transmission of visual information, Maus also relies on hard-to-find photographic documentation—here, on the "chilling out-of-focus snapshot" that bears urgent witness.[90] But instead of *adding* the photograph to the book, as with the three family photographs that appear across Maus's pages (unlike anywhere in Naka-zawa or Sacco's work), Spiegelman makes a publicly circulating photograph part of the tradition of drawing to tell by re-mediating his own version.

In Maus, one recognizes the sheer overwhelming significance of any visual information in the framework of eyewitness testimony from the camps. Maus documents Vladek Spiegelman's experience, but its testimonial form includes the collective modality of witness the snapshot signifies. In August 1944, a civilian worker smuggled a camera into Auschwitz II–Birkenau. Damage was deliberately done to the roof of Crematorium V so that Sonderkommandos, supposedly repairing, would have an excuse to have a lookout perch from above. The camera was hidden in a bucket given to Alex, who slipped inside the gas chambers to quickly photograph four images without detection. The camera made it back into the bucket, and eventually the small piece of film was smuggled out in a tube of toothpaste by an employee of the SS canteen to reach the Polish Resistance in Krakow.[91] Across media and time periods, very few works offer a sustained visual and narrative materialization of Auschwitz, aside from fictionalized films and scattered photographs. Maus goes into the camps and stays there at length, re-creating a world meant to be studied and engaged at one's own pace.

Maus sidesteps what Didi-Huberman calls "the extreme engagement with the question of the figurable" in order to simply productively figure and refigure, to *make seen*. It draws on archives, including traditional archival material such as posters and photographs, to open and recirculate

Figure 4.13 Art Spiegelman, *The Complete Maus,* page 232. (From *The Complete Maus: A Survivor's Tale* by Art Spiegelman, *Maus*, Volume I copyright © 1973, 1980, 1981, 1982, 1983, 1984, 1985, 1986 by Art Spiegelman; *Maus*, Volume II copyright © 1986, 1989, 1990, 1991 by Art Spiegelman. Used by permission of the Wylie Agency LLC and Pantheon Books, an imprint of the Knopf Doubleday Publishing Group, a division of Penguin Random House LLC. All rights reserved.)

them in its comics form. *Maus* treats Alex's photograph as one among many documents, including drawings and Vladek's oral testimony; it enters into the surface of the page, but with no special authority. *Maus* treats Alex's photograph, too, as both a document and an aesthetic object able to be studied at the level of composition (*Maus* flips it). "The only ethical position, in this frightening trap of history, consisted in resisting *in spite of all* the forces of the *impossible*," Didi-Huberman writes, "to create *in spite of all* the *possibility* of a testimony."[92] These earlier acts of visual witnessing lay a theoretical—and literal—foundation for *Maus*, which is inspired by, and built on, the creation of archives.

Coffins/Archives

Describing a recent special issue of the politics and performance journal *e-misférica* on archives—to which I contributed an essay on *Maus* and *MetaMaus*—Marianne Hirsch and Diana Taylor suggest that the question raised by archives is "the politics of what is saved (remembered) and what is discarded (forgotten)."[93] *Maus* simultaneously does the work of archiving and is *about* archives. Centrally, we recognize its own archiving process in how it inscribes Vladek Spiegelman's voice, his private Holocaust testimony elicited by his son, and places it in print and into the public record. In this archiving of testimony *Maus* reveals how the comics medium is not only dialogic but cross-discursive as well. Thus Spiegelman, for instance, in an incident in which the two disagree about the existence of orchestras in Auschwitz, draws against his father's narration/testimony even while materializing Vladek's words on the page; both kinds of "voice" become archived (page 213). And *Maus* assimilates wartime archives, from the obscure to the famed, into its visual idiom of witness. (*Maus* is even motivated by a rich archive of Nazi propaganda in its animal metaphor; Spiegelman has called Hitler his "collaborator").[94] At a denotative level, one of its chief dramas is the cartoonist's desire to search out any archival material relating to his parents' lives before his own unlikely birth—both of his parents were in death camps, and their first son, Richieu, died in the war at age six.[95]

The issue of what was saved—what *could* be saved—by survivors from the war is paramount, as is the question of what happens in post-war life to what *does* get saved. Vladek burned his wife Anja's notebooks recounting her Holocaust experiences—which she re-created, like Alfred Kantor, after the war from what could not be saved during the war—after her suicide in

1968, along with other documents relating to the war, such as letters from a French friend incarcerated with him in Dachau. "Of *course* I saved," Vladek responds to his son when asked about the letters. "But all this I threw away together with Anja's notebooks. All such things of the war, I tried to put out from my mind once for all . . . [u]ntil you *rebuild* me all this from your questions" (page 258). *Maus* is a process of rebuilding—archiving or rearchiving the past—especially after the violence Art feels was committed to his mother's archive, and by extension to her very person. The last word of *Maus I: My Father Bleeds History* is "murderer": Art accuses his father of murdering his already dead mother by incinerating her notebooks after her death. (There is a parallel to the camps here: the incineration of her archive as the incineration of bodies in order to destroy any remnant.) And Art feels murdered by Anja, too: she left no note, no paper trail, when she died, and in its absence his own body—something she did generate—defaults to becoming a kind of document, an archive or index of failure, standing in for her own failure to want to live. He addresses her in "Prisoner on the Hell Planet": "You *murdered* me, Mommy, and you left me here to take the rap!!!"[96] Anja's evaporated archive, from her notebooks to her spectral, nonexistent suicide note, haunt *Maus* through and through. Which kinds of archives can survive the war and its aftermath—and exist from which parents?

As I have argued, comics—with its boxes that store and display information—and the idea of the archive are intimately linked.[97] Critics have identified an "archival turn" in the past twenty-five or so years: Jacques Derrida gave the lecture that became *Archive Fever* in 1994, and art historian Hal Foster identified an "archival impulse" in contemporary art in 2004.[98] The form of contemporary comics, so conspicuously riveted to exploring history and evidence, has amplified this archival turn and become one of its most popular and visible locations. Jared Gardner identifies "the archival turn in contemporary graphic narrative" in an essay in 2006—the same year that Alison Bechdel published *Fun Home*, the best-selling graphic memoir that makes the search for private, family paper archives its central action and aesthetic drive.[99] Yet it is Spiegelman's *Maus* that first and forcefully established the connection between comics and archives.

In *Maus*, so deeply steeped in the past and in the present tense of making sense of the past, one recognizes how comics form literalizes the work of archiving: selecting, sorting, and containing in boxes. Comics makes the process of assembling, ordering, and preserving intelligible in a way that few forms can. The juxtaposition of frames on the page calls overt attention to the basic grammar of comics as selection—to the rhythm of the displayed and the evacuated, and how they constitute each other. This is not only an evocative phenomenon in *Maus* but also its actual constant narrative process. In her essay "Archival Bodies," Anne Golomb Hoffman points out that the *OED* definition of *archive* indicates both the container for documents and the documents themselves.[100] Comics makes this important transfiguration legible. Comics frames, as Valerie Rohy suggests, can be understood as vitrines that focus our attention on the subject, and object, of research.[101] "The archive" is a process, as *Maus* makes clear, and not only a repository of evidence.

Maus is also about holding together the tension between the visual (which includes the photographic and the drawn), the written, and the oral in how it expresses the memory of the eyewitness and the secondary witness and in how it creates its own testimonial archive. What media, and what perceptions, determine the shape of this archive? *Maus* enfolds these concerns and distinct valences of expression into its testimonial form, its insistent, cross-discursive presentation that carries within itself Nancy's "open absence." One of the most famous philosophical meditations on testimony, Giorgio Agamben's *Remnants of Auschwitz: The Witness and the Archive*, posits the opposition of the archive and testimony. Agamben writes of testimony's "unarchivability, its exteriority with respect to the archive." Testimony, Agamben argues, because "its authority depends not on a factual truth . . . but rather on the immemorial relation between the unsayable and the sayable, between the outside and the inside of language," is not archivable.[102] *Maus*, which archives Vladek Spiegelman's testimony in comics form, suggests the reverse. Comics takes shape as documentary precisely on the contingent lines of the boundaries that Agamben identifies.

Maus expresses the existence of this "relation," as opposed to pinning down its meaning, through its syntax, which is an interplay of presence and absence. Comics, with its frames and gutters, is always about boundaries— inside, outside; containable, uncontainable; figurable, unfigurable; constituted, deconstituted—and acknowledging them while articulating chronotopes not riven by the dichotomies they imply. *Maus* presents and makes relevant if not choate, graphically and semantically, precisely those boundaries of the outside and the inside of language through its own word-and-image form. It shows how testimony, its central medium, and the archive, its central aesthetic, historical, and psychic foundation, are mutually inflected, each contradictory, fluid, and embodied. Elisabeth Friedman argues that *MetaMaus* proposes "a rethinking of what counts as an archive, and, by extension, what counts as history"—and this is also central to *Maus*.[103]

Spiegelman has likened comics panels to the tightly packed suitcases his father, always ready to expect the worst, insisted on teaching him to arrange ("It was the one thing he wanted to make sure I understood").[104] He has also figured comics panels as boxes of memory smashing up against each other, something we see forcefully in his memoir *Portrait of the Artist as a Young %@&*!*. And he has also repeatedly likened comics panels to coffins (see Figure 4.14). *Maus*, he told me, is about "choices being made, of finding what one can tell, and what can reveal, and what one can reveal beyond what one knows one is revealing. Those are the things that give real tensile strength to the work—putting the dead into little boxes."[105] The language of "putting the dead into little boxes" is especially resonant given that *Maus* literally buries Vladek Spiegelman, ending the book with his headstone.[106] Suitcases, boxes of memory, coffins: these are different figures for comics grammar as containment, for panels as archival spaces instantiating the drive to enclose and preserve—even if elements will not stay still, spilling out or breaking the frame; even if they are ridged by their own instability. The suitcase, a figure for transportation and escape, limns the figure of the coffin, implying a stillness and sealing.

And while *Maus* is inspired by the urgency of drawings such as Kantor's or Salomon's, its succession of "little boxes" of history—while motivated by its own desire to bear witness—is the result of careful, painstaking mapping of each page, tier, and panel. Once, asked if making *Maus* had been cathartic, Spiegelman mused: "With comics, you're cobbling together little things and carefully placing them. It would be like the catharsis of making a 100-faceted wooden jewel box. It's highly crafted work."[107] Spiegelman created roughly a dozen sketches—sometimes many more—for each panel, often by creating numerous studies of the panel in different colors to help him discern visual volume and weight in the space he was forming through line.

The son's concomitant identification and disidentification that shapes his attachment to his father is evident in *Maus*, and underscored in *MetaMaus*, which reveals the obsessive labor behind Spiegelman's comics. In a notebook entry that records a 1988 conversation with Paul Pavel, a survivor who was then his therapist, Spiegelman writes of Vladek, "The family legend was that he could fix anything. It seemed like MAGIC . . . until I got older

Figure 4.14 Art Spiegelman, sketchbook page, April 4, 2007 (from *Autophobia*, 2008). (From *Be a Nose!* Copyright © Art Spiegelman. Used by permission of the Wylie Agency.)

and realized Vladek was going through hell down in this garage workspace. . . . Proceeding by trial and error. Searching for tools—for the right screw among thousands he'd found and salvaged." *Maus*'s very first page features Vladek sawing wood in front of the garage—and Artie crying. Spiegelman muses, "I'm really *like* Vladek—agonizing over *MAUS* the way he agonized over his repair jobs. The words I used to describe *him* working are how I describe my labors."[108] In his career as a cartoonist (making a book about his father) he repeats the strenuously haptic work of searching and sorting that links him to his father.

In her reading of Derrida's *Archive Fever*, Friedman identifies two registers of archival documentation: one that locates historical truth in "manifest content" or documentary evidence that may be directly apprehended, and one that also locates historical truth in performative repetition, what Derrida calls the "virtual." Because repetition, or acting out, is also a form of preserving the past, it too creates an archive.[109] From this angle—packing his father's suitcases, and using his toolbox to commemorate and bury him—Spiegelman creates *Maus* through its very comics form as an archive, a register of recurrence that preserves. The form archives Vladek's testimony. But Vladek's affective posture—history's inscription on his person—also comes to form a comics archive.

| 5 |

HISTORY AND THE
VISIBLE IN JOE SACCO

*Comics in their relentless foregrounding . . . seemed to say what
otherwise couldn't be said, perhaps what wasn't permitted to be said
or imagined.*

—EDWARD SAID, "HOMAGE TO JOE SACCO," 2001

Maltese-born Joe Sacco, whose books report from the Middle East and
the Balkans, among other globally volatile locations, is the contemporary
force behind comics journalism, a term he devised.[1] Comics journalism is
a genre both old and new, a practice in which we recognize the forceful
reemergence of long traditions of "drawing to tell" alongside newer features that reflect the conventions of modern comics and an engagement
with what Mary Layoun calls "transnational circuits of seeing."[2] He funds
his own travels and works independently—a feature encouraged by the
auteur-driven form of comics, and the simplicity of its implements, pen and
paper.[3] Sacco established the terms for the field in the early 1990s with
the nine issues of his comic book series *Palestine* (1992–1995), which won the
American Book Award in 1996 and was issued as a single volume in 2001.

The field has thickened considerably since the early 1990s, but Sacco's work continues to define its possibilities and to demonstrate the reach of today's visual work of witness.

Sacco's major subsequent works—all created as original books after *Palestine*—are *Safe Area Goražde: The War in Eastern Bosnia 1992–1995* (2000), *The Fixer: A Story from Sarajevo* (2003), and *Footnotes in Gaza* (2009), an "anatomy of a massacre" that became the first comics work to win the Ridenhour Book Prize recognizing "investigative and reportorial distinction."[4] Sacco released two additional volumes in 2012: *Journalism*, a collection of his short reporting pieces, and *Days of Destruction*, *Days of Revolt*, a collaborative work about American poverty created with the prose reporter Chris Hedges.[5] In 2013, Sacco published *The Great War*, a wordless, twenty-four-foot accordion foldout "illustrated panorama" of the first day of the Battle of the Somme (the panorama, which cannot be seen from a single viewpoint, like comics, introduces "a dimension of temporality to the act of viewing," as Tom Gunning puts it in his essay comparing the two forms).[6] Sacco is one of the most innovative figures to come out of centuries of traditions of witness to violence. His works ask readers to confront key epistemological questions, using the word-and-image form of comics to provoke consideration of how history becomes legible as history.

Sacco's comics journalism is shaped by twin drives. On the one hand, in addition to the artifice innate to comics, his work is openly reflective about itself, actively acknowledging the instability of knowing—and the problem of transmitting knowledge. We see this in wry *Footnotes in Gaza* chapter titles such as "Memory and the Essential Truth" and "The Story Is Dead." On the other hand, the investigative drive for accuracy, the drive to create a record of unarchived voices, all in the service of compelling an acknowledgment of the specificity of the other, is paramount.

Because comics texts are conspicuously drawn by hand and thus inherently reject transparency, instead foregrounding their situatedness, nonfiction comics demand attention to history's discursivity. The question of the nature of the visual—the work that it does, and how—is critical to texts that claim historicity, and that operate within, and are expressive of, the landscape of the traumatic. The medium of comics is always already self-conscious as an interpretive, and never purely mimetic, medium. Yet this self-consciousness, crucially, exists together with the medium's confidence in its ability to traffic in expressing history. Taking for granted that "pure" historical representation is never possible, comics calls into question the status of any "objective" or "realistic" account, including historiographies—especially those that bank on the seeming transparency of words. Both Spiegelman and Sacco contrast their charged realism with what Gary Groth calls "that interpretive power I see as cartooning," what one could think of as a stylized anti-realism.[7] While Nancy K. Miller writes that comics is "a medium in which accuracy is *an effect of exaggeration*," I suggest further that all nonfiction comics call crucial attention to the fact that in any medium or genre, "accuracy" is always an effect.[8]

Sacco, like Spiegelman, was absorbed in the realities of war from childhood; his southern European parents survived terrifying German and Italian air raids on British-controlled Malta during World War II. "War is a fact of life," he claims, and this preoccupation consistently motivates his innovation with word-and-image narrative.[9] Sacco lampooned his interest in war with early comics titles such as *War Junkie*. Born in 1960 to a Catholic family in Kirkop, population 800, Sacco currently lives in the United States.[10] His status as neither Jewish nor Muslim helped him socially to navigate Israel, Palestine, and Bosnia as a reporter, and although he is often taken as a representative American in the countries from which he reports, his Maltese passport has enabled mobility in the Middle East and elsewhere.[11] "More Women, More Children, More Quickly: Malta 1935–43 as Recollected by Carmen M. Sacco" (1990), in which he interviews his mother about her experiences during the raids, which injured or killed her friends and family, is one of Sacco's first pieces of mature comics work. Here one sees for the first time his visual re-creation of testimony by witnesses to historical trauma, the feature that anchors and structures all of his subsequent work.[12]

Sacco was trained as and identifies as a journalist, as the almost polemical title of his 2012 *Journalism* indicates. Specifically, he understands his comics as operating within the rubric of the New Journalism that began in the 1960s—a genre one of its central innovators, Tom Wolfe, in a description apposite to Sacco's comics, calls "saturation reporting."[13] New Journalism—which also crucially eschewed the notion that nonfiction as a genre had to be didactic—shifted away from the common view of reporting as an objective act of uncovering raw data. As Wolfe explains, the basic reporting unit ceased to be "the datum," but rather became the scene.[14] Sacco makes clear that he does not "believe in the idea of objective journalism," but as with the genre of New Journalism, "my professional standards are every bit as good as those of other journalists."[15]

Other journalists seem to agree. In the *New York Times*, David Rieff (who happens to be Susan Sontag's son) called *Safe Area Goražde* "the best dramatic evocation of the Bosnia catastrophe," noting Sacco's ability "to evoke reality in lived details" and explaining that "Sacco's Bosnia is the one that those of us who covered the fighting actually experienced day by day, rather than the one we mostly reported on."[16] Sacco uses comics to expand the range of journalism's objects, capturing stories that might otherwise go unnoticed and describing individuals who might be overlooked. As a journalist who mobilizes visual and verbal registers together—forcing an interaction between their styles, capabilities, and ontologies—Sacco focuses on the lives that get left out, obviated, or ignored by mainstream and institutional narrativizations of history across (and enforced by) conventional genres and disciplines. Layoun correctly points out that Sacco takes pains to figure structural relations in addition to stories. She calls this a "relational reading ability" that is widely missing in the transnational circuit of images.[17] Sacco's work bridges what one might think of as the methods of microhistory, "the symbolic register of particular people" through close and local views, and macro, larger-scale externalist inquiry.[18]

Sacco is influenced in equal measure by Goya and Michael Herr, Pieter Bruegel the Elder and Hunter S. Thompson.[19] He is interested in the shape of world-historical conflict—and how it intersects with the individual body in pain. Sacco's comics evoke this combination by featuring diverse styles of linework that suggest different kinds of information in order to make them brush up against each other. In the early part of his career, inspired by trailblazing Vietnam journalism, Sacco created a lengthy comics story on the Vietnam War (which failed to find a publisher), and he considered illustrating a watchdog report, a legalistic book collecting case studies of human rights abuses. These two early projects demonstrate his fascination with what Fredric Jameson calls the "untranscendable horizon" of history, but they are missing the feature that makes "More Women" and his subsequent books powerful: Sacco's firsthand eliciting of testimony.[20]

Sacco is the cartoonist whose work most clearly follows Spiegelman's precedent. If Spiegelman's subject, as we saw in Chapter 4, is the "faultline where World History and Personal History collide," so too is it Sacco's, although in a different key.[21] And as with Spiegelman, who says "disaster, war, horror seems to be the muse that comes and visits me," Sacco's comics invariably engage traumatic history.[22] In contradistinction to works centered on the essential unrepresentability of trauma—its unspeakability, inaudibility, and invisibility—Spiegelman and Sacco's works present the complex and ethical plentitude of the visual.

Comics and Ethics

But while both Spiegelman and Sacco demonstrate the efficacy of the visual for materializing history and testimony, each registers a separate kind of concern with the political project of representation. In *Maus*, Spiegelman employs loose, sketchy lines in order to signal his abdication of aesthetic mastery as appropriate to representing the Holocaust. Sacco's style, on the other hand, is dense, virtuosic, and often photorealistic, an ethical attempt to represent intimately those ignored in the world arena. The places from which Sacco reports—the Middle East and the Balkans—are linked in Sacco's project of representing those whom history devastates and ignores, in this case largely Muslim populations: "You see extremes of humanity in places like Palestine and Bosnia. . . . Mostly what you see is innocent people being crushed beneath the wheels of history," he says.[23] Sacco works outside of newsroom (and Internet-instantaneous) deadline culture. In his investigation of brutal and often genocidal systematic political oppression, Sacco is riveted by the complexities of particular, war-torn ordinary people, examining and presenting details of their lives that are elided in mainstream media and journalistic enterprises. For this reason, he calls his work "slow journalism."[24]

Sacco's comics are resolute in their slowness—for the creator, in terms of his production time, and for the reader, in terms of navigating dense narrative surfaces. *Palestine* took two months to research and three years to draw; *Footnotes* was almost seven years in the making—four of which were spent drawing. This pits Sacco's style of journalism against much (spectacular) media and specifically against what Nicholas Mirzoeff calls today's quick-cut "present tense only" mode of watching.[25] Indeed, especially in the context of war reporting—and the circulation of what Mirzoeff calls "weaponized images" that accompany and play a role in justifying war— the slowness of Sacco's comics is both a mode of ethical awareness and an implicit critique of superficial news coverage. The thicket of words and images on any given page of Sacco's work presents what can often feel like a surfeit of information, and his pages demand substantial cognitive engagement—especially in how a reader figures the connection of words and images, since Sacco's irregular text boxes, which often split sentences, float all over the page at different angles. Even fans of Sacco's work acknowledge what can be its exhausting aspect.

The very first page of *Palestine* is an example. It features boxed text in slanted, itchy handwriting—clauses or phrases, sometimes full sentences, most punctuated with exclamation points—spiraling down from the top left-hand corner of the page, producing a disorienting zigzag effect (Figure 5.1). This crumbling stairway of words is eventually interrupted by a speech balloon, all in capital letters: "THERE ARE MUSLIMS AND THERE ARE MUSLIMS." Sacco is distinct among cartoonists in how he incorporates word and image on a page, especially with what one interviewer names the "Sacco-patented technique of floating [and fragmented] captions that run throughout panels or over panels"—an elliptic aesthetic mode that Sacco borrows from Louis-Ferdinand Céline, whose 1932 *Journey to the End of the Night* provides a formal inspiration.[26] Sacco's translation of Céline's elliptical prose style for comics encourages the eye to slow down, to tangle with the verbal and visual detail of the palimpsestic page. As Said writes, there is no attempt to "smooth out" in Sacco's work (his language recalls Jameson's cautions about flattening history).[27] Sacco renders a detailed cityscape at the top of the page. In the terrain of the city we note a teeming bus in traffic, a police officer blowing his whistle, a one-eyed and gap-toothed man. Sacco draws almost thirty people with distinct, individuated faces. Below the word "CAIRO" the city space melts into the foreground café scene of three men teasing each other about the funny and unfunny situation of blown wages.[28]

Sacco's investment in slowing readers down and asking them to grapple with producing meaning is a deliberate technique positioned both against the global news media's propensity to offer quickly consumed visual spectacles and against the restless acceleration of information that is characteristic of so many of today's reporting outlets.[29] In his introduction to the *Palestine* book, Edward Said praises this, citing "the unhurried pace and absence of a goal in [Sacco's] wanderings"—what he has also called the power of non-narrativity in Sacco's work. In its detailed density, Sacco's comics calls attention to the issue of pace—a formal aspect Said suggests "is perhaps the greatest of [Sacco's] achievements."[30] Sacco's work brings new information to the histories of the regions he covers—as in *The Fixer*'s little-known history of Sarajevo's Bosnian paramilitary warlords—and it is about an ethics of attention, not about producing the news.

Figure 5.1   Joe Sacco, *Palestine*, page 1, first published 1992. (Used by permission of Joe Sacco.)

More than any other work in the field, Sacco's closely packed pages, which obstruct a quick purchase on meaning, require an awareness of pace. Naseer Aruri even writes of *Palestine* that "each page is equivalent to an essay"—an appraisal of density that is not restricted to the text's prose but rather indicates how the thickness of the visual-verbal form in Sacco's hands transmits what can even feel like surplus information.[31] There are few graphic narrative texts that resist or work against easy consumption more effectively than Sacco's; the very formalism of his pages presents a thicket that requires a labor-intensive "decoding"—to employ a term, connoting difficulty, that both Spiegelman and Said use to discuss reading comics.[32]

Sacco's works push on the disjunctive back-and-forth between looking and reading. It is this rhythm—often awkward and time-consuming—that is part of Sacco's "power to detain," to use Said's formulation: with a subject as highly politicized and ethically complex as the Israel-Palestine conflict, what Said praises in Sacco's bizarre formal matching of acceleration (the pages jump and move with urgency) and deceleration (the wading through that each page requires) is that the effect is to "furnish readers with a long enough sojourn among a people" for whom complex and thorough representation is rarely at play.[33] It is this contradictory flow of movement that a comics page, unlike film or traditional prose narrative, is able to hold in tension, as narrative development is delayed, retracked, or rendered recursive by the depth and volume of graphic texture.

Sacco travels to war-torn locations and interviews people about their experiences of traumatic conflict or war on the ground. Those who speak with him do so electively and are not compensated. Working independently of organizations, Sacco is answerable only to his own "journalistic ethic," which in part developed out of his outrage at the lopsided Western coverage of the Middle East in the 1970s and 1980s.[34] Although he correctly recognized that it would be "commercial suicide to do a comic book about the Palestinians," Sacco spent two months in Israel and Palestine in late 1992 and early 1993, interviewing about a hundred people on both sides of the conflict.[35] *Palestine* takes place toward the end of the First Intifada (1987–1993), and its forthright title reflects the elided perspective Sacco sought to grasp. The heart of the narrative takes place in the Jabalia refugee camp, where Sacco often stayed with a camp resident and translator named Sameh. Portraying the First Intifada, the uprising that began in the Jabalia camp and became known for its stone-throwing, *Palestine* ends presciently, with a gesture toward what would later become the signal act of the Second

Intifada (2000–2005): suicide bombing. *Palestine*'s last chapter, titled "A Boy in the Rain," ends by cutting to a wide view of a bus, a vehicle that has become the site of many suicide bombings, lost on its way out of Israel.

This chapter focuses on the concatenation of drawing, history, and ethics that Sacco's word-and-image texts ask us to encounter. Sacco's relationship to the histories he enters and painstakingly visualizes is distinct from Spiegelman and Nakazawa's relationship to World War II, which is filtered—however much as a negative proposition, and however provisionally—through genealogy and inheritance. Sacco has no direct autobiographical or familial connection to the histories he documents in his books. His work is not primarily about his identity or identitarian attachment to the communities he covers as a journalist. He creates, in comics, visual and verbal counterarchives to official histories, but his work is not about figuring out how the past has shaped his own present, nor is it about making injury the site of his own politicized identity (as Wendy Brown, among others, describes).[36] Rather, that Sacco "draws to tell" others' memories and testimonies without rerouting these stories into narratives of his own self-understanding, and without assimilating them into narratives of easy consumption, makes clear his desire to remain responsible to "others" *as* others. Sacco's attention to detail and focus on the situation of testimonial address, among other formal features this chapter considers, serves to acknowledge the particularity of the other. Sacco's work proposes a conception of self-other relations that Seyla Benhabib identifies as the standpoint of the "concrete other" in the context of moral philosophy; this standpoint centers on particularity, allowing for the "otherness of the other" to emerge, as against a substitutionalist universalism that disembeds and disembodies selves behind the façade of a definitional—rather than specific—identity.[37]

Drawing is a mode of description in Sacco's work through which readers are forced to encounter a specified person. In the recent book *The Right to Look*, Mirzoeff discusses the history of the term "visuality" as essentially a nineteenth-century battle term, denoting a top-down authoritarian gaze and practice. In distinction, what "the right to look" would generate is a mutual gaze—something we see literalized here in the exchange of gazes with reader and witness proposed by Sacco.[38] Sacco's treatment of oral testimony is crucial to understanding how his comics acknowledge the particularity of the witness. He does not merely quote testimony in his works but further gives it form in drawing. Sacco's basic comics method-ology becomes a condition of mutual address. Through his research he is an interlocutor for testifying witnesses; he then joins his own "visual voice" to the expression of spoken testimony on the page, working responsively with the substance of language to also produce visual, pictorial substance. Speech in comics, and in Sacco's work in particular, has material weight on the page—a feature that highlights the performative force of testimony as an encounter. With its dual investigative and imaginative capacity, Sacco's work functions as its own second-order event of witnessing to the act of bearing witness.

Sacco's interlocutory role, which produces the scene of testimony, opens out into the material act of visually incarnating the oral testimonies of wit-nesses to trauma. Sacco, then, is present in his journalism not only because he is a protagonist in all of his reportage, in New Journalistic mode, but also by virtue of his hand creating the page, his haptic presence throughout. The attention to the other is not simply thematized or described in Sacco's work.[39] Rather, this attention is further instantiated in form, in the ethical engagement proposed by Sacco's drawing (researching, imagining, visual-izing, materializing) of other people's experiences—along with their acts of testifying. It is an act of inhabiting their memories and pasts in order to acknowledge and particularize them.

Comics grammar exhibits the legibility of double narration—and stages disjuncts between presence and absence and between word and image—in order to pressure linearity, causality, and sequence: to express the simul-taneity of traumatic temporality, and the doubled view of the witness as inhabiting the present and the past. Comics journalism's aesthetics ask us to consider how modes of knowledge are formed and transmitted. These aesthetics produce its ethical engagement in the arena of knowing history, and articulating the complexity of observed experience in words and images. In accretive readings, I consider form and perspective in *Palestine*; realism and the role of detail in *Safe Area Goražde*; knowledge, trauma, and testimony in *The Fixer*; and, finally, how documents and archives are created—and how the embodied form of comics expands on official histories—in *Footnotes in Gaza*. Across these works, each of which proposes a different kind of relationship to its subject and has a different inflection, the spatiotemporal form of comics generates its ability to approach history. The uniqueness of comics is the way that it portrays and interacts with history (the temporal) in terms of space on the page, so that space—how events and details are sequenced—becomes a way to rethink or refigure the temporal.

Decoding, Density, and "Double-Vision"

The appearance of *Palestine* as individual twenty-four- and thirty-two-page comic books, with their full-color covers depicting protests, gravesites, and torture, marks a major shift in late twentieth-century aesthetic and political culture. Issued by independent comics publisher Fantagraphics and sold for $2.95, the *Palestine* comic books reflect not only the fragmented, episodic nature of daily life in Palestine but also the commensurability of discourses that might have seemed disparate: the energy and immediacy of the cheap, accessible, comic book form combined with the seriousness and meticulousness demanded by an investigation into world-historical conflict and its effects on the ground. *Palestine* does not eschew comic book conventions but works within them, owning them for a new context. Sacco displays the apparent incongruity of format and content, as large, hand-drawn block letters, in outline with shading, colorfully spell out PALESTINE across the top of each issue—for example, over an image of a hooded prisoner tied to a chair (see Figure I.1).[40]

When *Palestine* appeared, no other Western work had captured the everyday life of Palestinians in such detail; it also revealed information that had not been covered in the media before, such as the factional organization of Palestinian prisoners in Israeli captivity at prisons such as Ansar III. Acknowledged as groundbreaking, *Palestine* was reviewed in mainstream venues such as *Publishers Weekly* and the *New York Review of Books*. Although Sacco works within recognizable traditions, such as the practice of "drawing to tell" in the work of Goya and the nineteenth-century Special Artist reporters, he re-created this tradition within the idiomatic specificity of modern comics, creating a new cultural and aesthetic space. Sacco made this tradition blossom within the language of comics; he made comics accommodate the complexity of witnessing in contemporary times.

Palestine is a pioneering work in how it details the space and rhythms of everyday life for Palestinians living under the occupation. This is a quality Edward Said and Jean Mohr's 1986 visual-verbal collaboration *After the Last Sky* also exhibits, and the language of fragmentation, "double-vision," and hybridity that Said calls for in the introduction to that book could be a description of the formal capacities of comics.[41] Significantly, *Palestine* is also distinguished by its focus on the situation of journalism itself—and especially the journalist's interactions with Palestinians, who respond to him as such. Here, as elsewhere in his reportage, Sacco addresses the distinctive abilities of comics journalism, calling our attention to how it is like and unlike other journalistic forms, including other visual forms. Across his graphic narratives, other visual media such as photography and video make a significant contrastive appearance, particularly in how they produce or replicate spectacles of violence.

The inclination of comics to document, to be journalistic, resides in part in the expansion of perspective enabled by drawing. Comics brings first- and third-person perspectives to the surface of the reported narrative simultaneously. Much has been written about the duality of the figure of the journalist, as well as the mediating role that is the situation of the journalist but is so often dropped from the official published artifact (as has been dramatized in works such as Janet Malcolm's 1990 *The Journalist and the Murderer*). Comics journalism embodies and performs that duality by enabling the journalist both to inhabit a point of view and to show himself inhabiting it. The form is able to picture the *scene of perspective*—to picture the journalist's optical perspective and to picture his body. This proliferation of perspective is part of the most basic grammar of comics, and occurs on at least two different levels: the interaction of the narrative's prose and visual dimensions, which are never precisely unified, and the ability of comics on a purely visual plane to make possible simultaneous views, even in the space of a given moment. The simultaneity that is a constitutive feature of comics allows us to recognize, unobtrusively, the duality of the journalist, and it captures the production of journalism as journalism broadly.[42] Sacco's work highlights scenes of enunciation and exchange in addition to the hard information revealed in those exchanges. Self-reflexivity is not only thematized in comics journalism but also constantly enacted through the point of view of its most basic syntactical element, drawn frames.[43] In its most fundamental procedures, comics calls attention to itself as a medium that is engaged in the work of literally framing events and experiences, and as such is a figure for the mediating work of journalism itself.[44]

The subtle and virtuosic "A Thousand Words," one of *Palestine's* forty-eight episodes, stages an ur-moment about the capabilities of drawing as journalistic practice. As its title indicates, the episode is about producing images; it enacts the phenomenon of comics journalism in comparison with other forms such as photojournalism. Strolling through East Jerusalem with his Japanese photographer friend Saburo, Sacco encounters a group of Palestinian women and children marching down Nablus Road through traffic, loudly protesting expulsion orders. Israeli police and border police converge on the scene, whacking protestors with truncheons and herding them into the backs of jeeps. Sacco, who carries a camera in order to produce reference shots for his drawing, thinks he has "got a coupla good shots" of the beatings; he and Saburo later run into a Palestinian photographer for an international wire service, who encourages Sacco to bring his film in and have his office develop it (page 57). Energized by the pace of the newsroom, Sacco fantasizes about his photo making the news.

At the end of the six-page episode, we wonder to which documentary medium the designation "a thousand words" belongs. In the page's last tier, bending over the negatives with a loupe on the office light table, the editor declares, "There's nothing here." Sacco, confused, listens in the next panel as another photographer, whose pencil we see mark a location in a frame on the visible strip of negatives, explains to Sacco: "See, if you'd been standing where this guy is standing, you would have got faces." The last panel focuses more closely on the two conversing men. "The idea was good," says the photographer, his speech balloon hovering above their heads. The episode ends with the narrator's refrain in a small rectangular box that floats over Sacco's chest: "The idea?" (page 58).

This exchange about perspective, placement, and images is a figure for comics journalism itself. In this comparison of media aesthetics and procedure, "where you stand" is definitional. With photojournalism, one needs to be standing in a certain place to capture the moment, to "get faces." With comics journalism, one can place oneself literarily in any position, inhabit any point of view. "There are very few photographs—and we know them well—that capture an exact moment," Sacco says in *The Believer*, "and that image is always with us. . . . Now, when you draw, you can always capture that moment. You can always have that exact, precise moment when someone's got the club raised."[45] Comics makes possible the simultaneity of view, of perspective. When one opens the book to the middle of "A Thousand Words," the left-hand page, an unpanelized bleed, presents an optical and otherwise sensory immersion in the viewpoint of the journalist, expressing what the protest looked like and felt like for the observer: clumps of bodies and noise coming and going, heaped together, swirling across the space of the page. The right-hand page begins with a panel, uncluttered and clearly bordered, that pictures Sacco from behind, in conversation. In his comics, we both see *from* Sacco's perspective and see Sacco himself pictured *for* us (it is his weary face that appears in the frame when he is advised that he ought to "get faces"). Further, in several pages in this episode Sacco inks his text in conspicuous diagonal swaths that cut across the page at an awkward angle from right to left, against the conventional direction of reading, compelling readers to crane their necks or switch the position of the page in front of them, to consider the question of their own embodied perspective.

Activating this tension, switching back and forth, comics enables artists to step outside of what they see in front of them to also picture themselves, reminding us that all journalism is limited (literally about perspective), but also reminding us of the limits of one visual form, photojournalism, in contradistinction to a form that allows one to be simultaneously visually working in the register of the first and third person, the filter and the subject. "The idea was good," says the newsroom photographer. The bewildered response "The idea?" is, in a sense, a figure for the book itself. Sacco's comics are invested in the ethics of attention to the face, as I will discuss further, and he will "get" many faces, although not always because he happened to be standing in the right place at the right time.

The comics journalist can be both inside and outside the frame, dramatizing the question of perspective and inhabiting the view of the other. Comics is about animating layers and kinds of information—syntagmatic and synchronic—to interact and work with each other. "One benefit of comics and journalism together," for instance, as Sacco understands it, because the form is not always about capturing the present, "is the ability to take readers back in time."[46] And Sacco's work materializes histories from places where photography cannot travel, such as the solitary cell where Ghassan, who gives his testimony to Sacco, was tortured in the chapter "'Moderate Pressure' Part 2"—a scene a *Journal of Palestine Studies* reviewer, praising the absence of a camera, called "the most realistic account of imprisonment and torture I have ever read."[47] Sacco's drawing of another's testimony is both meticulously researched, in collaboration with the witness, and necessarily imagined. In Baudelaire's famous terms, his line aspires to be both "the secretary and the record-keeper" to whom Baudelaire assigns photographic function, while it also sustains the art of the imaginary, the nonobserved, that Baudelaire assigns to painting.[48]

In Palestine, there was already a context in which Sacco's project of drawing history and the present could be understood. The cartoonist Naji al-Ali (1936–1987) was and remains a potent figure in Palestinian culture and society. A recent scholarly study of al-Ali opens by arguing that cartoons have surpassed poetry as the preferred medium for political resistance in Palestine: "Whereas poetry continues to be important, political speech has migrated to cartoons."[49] We can see this emergence across the Arab world in the many communities of cartooning and visual art practice that have sprung up around the Arab Spring and other revolutionary movements.[50] When Sacco explained the nature of his project to Palestinians, he told me, "they would say, 'Oh, well, we have this cartoonist, he's a big hero.'" Palestinians he encountered hung pendants of al-Ali's main character, as well as of the cartoonist himself, on their walls.[51]

Al-Ali was a refugee; around age ten he settled in the Ain al-Helweh camp in southern Lebanon, a camp with some of the poorest conditions in the world. Originally a student of painting (he spent one year at the Lebanese Art Academy), al-Ali quickly moved to a form of expression more direct and more invested in the everyday: he published cartoons for thirty years before his assassination in London. (While "paintings are only for special occasions," he once said, describing his populist view of the work of the line, "every drawing is like a drop of water that makes its way to the minds of the people.")[52] Exhibits of his cartoons are mounted in camps today, and contemporary posters and political pamphlets often feature his signature character, a child witness named Hanthala.[53]

Al-Ali was an important, revered political voice; his cartoons are based in strong class analysis and condemn greed in Israel, the United States., and the Palestine Liberation Organization (PLO). The *New York Times* article reporting on his assassination—al-Ali was shot in the head while walking down the street—named him "one of the most controversial journalists in the Middle East."[54] His simple line drawings circulated widely throughout the Arab world, as well as in London, and were treated seriously as commentary and depiction. Arafat even negotiated a meeting with him, a situation that underscores the cartoonist's political power.[55] Arafat was displeased enough about al-Ali's portrayal of him to try to disperse tensions face-to-face (many believe al-Ali was killed by the PLO, if not the Mossad; he had been underground in the Middle East while publishing his cartoons there in the later part of his life). On the artistic side, Orayb Aref Najjar explains that "all Palestinian cartoonists" currently featured on the Arabic Media Internet Network have been influenced by al-Ali's "style and choice of characters" and have even created "The Naji al-Ali Plastic Arts Society."[56] *Baddawi*, a new graphic memoir by Chicago-based Palestinian cartoonist Leila Abdelrazaq, opens with a description of Naji al-Ali's most famous character, a child, who is also evoked by the book's cover.[57] Many consider al-Ali the most popular artist in the Arab world.

Al-Ali's work differs from Sacco's in significant ways; the most evident is that al-Ali's work usually appeared in newspapers as one-panel cartoons.[58] But both cartoonists' work, significantly, is about the scene of witness. Al-Ali's cartoons all feature Hanthala, perpetually ten years old, barefoot, and in patched clothes; in most images, his back is turned to the audience, as he watches the scene also in front of us.[59] We infrequently see his face. What we see, instead, is Hanthala seeing (see Figure 5.2). The doubled act of looking staged by cartoons makes us join Hanthala in a mutual act of apprehending. The character that became an icon—emblazoned on T-shirts and graffitied all over the Occupied Territories—generally stands with his hands behind his back, simply looking.[60] He is a figure for witness. It is through his eyes, as with many witnessing interlocutors in Sacco's work, that we are meant to understand the impact of the political situation shaping Palestinian lives. As Sacco points out in an English-language collection of al-Ali's cartoons, *A Child in Palestine*, Hanthala's appeal comes from his witness status: "He was *knowing*. . . . Hanthala's stance says, *Don't mind me. I'm off to the side. Watching. Recording.*"[61] (Graphically, however, Hanthala is not always off to the side; often al-Ali eschews perspective and the character's small body overlays another figure in the frame, creating bodily overlap that proliferates temporalities, a technique we also see in Sacco's later work.) The child's gaze records the scene. Here it is worth noting that the Arabic word for martyr, *shaheed*, originates from the Qur'anic word for "witness."[62] "Martyr," in English, is a variant of the ancient Greek word that means literally "witness"; in the classical period, it had the full legal meaning of the English "witness," which is to say a witness in a juridical proceeding.[63] Hand-drawn work centering on witnessing constitutes a key part of Palestinian political and visual culture. (Palestinian visual culture includes another widespread visual genre that deals with the will to record, as Lori Allen and Laleh Khalili have recently analyzed: martyr posters, which adorn both public and private walls).[64] Naji al-Ali exemplifies a popular tradition—of drawing as a sophisticated yet accessible circulating form that brings attention to the witness; this tradition is

Figure 5.2   Naji al-Ali, "The Last Supper," April 1980, from *A Child in Palestine*. (Verso Books.)

a global one that Sacco's comics join. In both cartoonists' projects, one recognizes the efficacy—the directness, the immediacy—of manifesting the will to record through the work of the line.

Comics has the ability to show the powerful interpenetration of private and public histories through the spatial juxtaposition of the frames on which its grammar is built. From the outset *Palestine* zooms back and forth across world history and personal history. It weaves them swiftly; the book's opening presents itself as about the production of discourse.[65] The first handful of pages picture publicly circulating images of infamous Palestinian violence (the famous airport explosion engineered by Palestinian hijackers in Jordan at Dawson's Field in 1970; the 1985 murder of tourist Leon Klinghoffer on the Mediterranean Sea), as well as the everyday concerns of Sacco's Palestinian street interviewees, which are displayed along with Sacco's personal memories of a would-be romance soured by political debate. As with the form's ability to traverse spaces of the past and the present (in a sequence or even, sometimes, in an individual panel), this can indicate suture or contrast, proximity and continuity or the opposite.

Further, as we see in the opening page of *Palestine*, Sacco's rendering in his comics, as with Spiegelman's, holds in tension "realism" and what would seem to be its other: "cartooning." Historical graphic narratives are openly interpretive in terms of style: while they represent real lives, they neither aspire to nor perform the (putative) transparency of photography or film (as, indeed, they could not).[66] Sacco, like Spiegelman, prizes representational collision—the refusal of synthesis that we see in *Maus*, where cartoon cats brandish snarling "realistic" dogs on leashes. Sacco's style is by turns meticulously photorealistic and brilliantly caricatural, and even, as we will see, in some portions abstract. The caricatural aspect of Sacco's work is a by-product of his attention to a tradition of political satire in comics stretching back to *Mad*, as well as the influence of underground comics storytellers such as Robert Crumb, whose rubbery, "bigfoot" style of cartooning became a cultural flashpoint of the late 1960s. Style in Sacco's work represents a multivalent textual practice that flags its own contingency and is a register of competing desires that come to the surface in the work of the hand.

Style and Suffering

In *Safe Area Goražde*, for which Sacco visited the Bosnian municipality of Goražde four times in late 1995 and early 1996, his interest in documenting life for Goraždans is about their stark medialessness while they were isolated during the Bosnian War. *Goražde* takes place at the end of the war, focusing on the residents of a largely Muslim enclave in Bosnian Serb territory that the UN had designated a so-called safe area. Access, even for international journalists, was hindered both by French peacekeeping bureaucracy and by Serb roadblocks. "Goražde," Sacco writes above an image of a dismembered man in the street, one leg sitting solitary near his blasted torso, and correcting this phenomenon visually even as he attests to it verbally, "had been cut off from cameras. Its suffering was the sole property of those who experienced it" (Figure 5.3).[67] Four text boxes unfurl vertically, evoking a shell dropping to the ground, and the body lies in the space between the last two bars of text, another leg lying underneath the final box of text and pointing out of the frame. Sacco's voice enters the frame *with* the body, surrounding it, joining it in space.

Within the panel:

Many towns got pasted in the Balkan wars of the early and mid '90's.

Dubrovnik and Sarajevo endured their maulings in the living rooms of all those with a T.V. set.

But Goražde had been cut off from cameras.

Its suffering was the sole property of those who had experienced it.

Figure 5.3 Joe Sacco, *Safe Area Goražde*, panel from page 126. (Used by permission of Joe Sacco.)

Sacco ramps up attention to the testifying face in *Goražde*, anchoring testimony at its outset in highly detailed portraits of witnesses, in the act of speaking, directly facing readers. In the book, Sacco explains that by spring 1995, with unrelenting Serb attacks and a growing death toll, Goražde, one of six enclaves including Srebrenica deemed "safe" by the UN in 1993, had become "a symbol of the meaninglessness of the safe area concept specifically and the impotence of the international community generally" (page 184). As his work develops forward from *Palestine*, it is more consistently invested in a style of drawing one can consider photorealistic (Sacco reserves a more exaggerated line for all depictions of himself in his work; his eyes, for instance, are never visible behind the blank circles of his eyeglasses).[68] In *Goražde*, his style shifts even further to highlight the role of the detail. His focus on the detailed visual work of documentation is such that for a scene described by his translator Edin, in which Edin and others identify the bodies of months-dead friends who had been disinterred from a mass grave, Sacco consulted a forensics expert in order to draw the corpses (page 93).[69]

Among cartoonists, even those working in nonfiction, Sacco's style is distinct in its quality of realism. Sacco's images are shaped by what we might think of as an ethnographic aesthetics of precision and accuracy. In *Goražde*, which takes on genocide in the context of war and is an often brutally violent book, Sacco's work frames itself around producing a concrete picture of the other through capturing the rhythms and details of both ordinary and extraordinary experience. Sacco's drawing involves painstaking attention to detail, dramatically evident in crowd scenes in which he draws upward of fifty individuated faces, or in striking panoramic views in which he thoroughly, meticulously draws buildings, streets, and fields of a specific location. This is the work of mapping lives and landscapes. Sacco locates people in time and, importantly, space; the topography and architecture are precise.[70]

While Christopher Hitchens inserts "medieval paintings of breakdown and panic and mania" into his assessment of Sacco, many of Sacco's panoramic images evoke Bruegel in their saturation in detail and their desire to record everyday life—as well as in their composition, a wide view in which there is often no central object.[71] As with Bruegel, his principal influence in the fine arts, Sacco is drawn to what critic Thierry Smolderen calls "swarming" images—a feature we also see in the fifteenth-century painter Hieronymous Bosch and in William Hogarth, whose description of the eye's enjoyment in "winding walks and serpentine rivers" in his *Analysis of Beauty* is Smolderen's inspiration for analyzing swarming images.[72] (Cartoonists have historically been attracted to the artists noted above, whose swarming images, like sequential art, "generate a creative space-time."[73] Bruegel's work appeals to Sacco, as he puts it, because it "provides a window into daily life in Flanders"—he understands Bruegel to be a model in creating "the whole aesthetic of 'this is how we lived.' "[74] *Goražde*, as with all of Sacco's works, reflects this influence, as an ethic of attention and an aesthetic art practice. It is even a filter for Sacco's apperception of setting: "In Goražde I felt I'd stepped into a painting by Brueghel."[75] In *Goražde* we see Sacco's teeming panoramas, steeped in realistic detail, where the landscape itself is as much a focus as the many bodies that move through it.

At every level of his work, Sacco is driven to convey particularity. This is strikingly apparent in a double spread of a busy Goražde street, an image that makes legible, as Sacco noted recently, how comics journalism can propose that "landscape is a character" (Figure 5.4).[76] At the outset of *Goražde*, Sacco answers a question posed to him by a schoolgirl: "Why did you come to Goražde?" (page 13). "Why?" he responds, drawing the word sitting alone in a single text box at the top of the double-page spread that follows. While the visual promiscuity of the page alone appears as an answer, registering his evident fascination with a regular day on an ordinary street in besieged Bosnia, text stamps itself in five, small, diagonally descending boxes, over a swarming, Bruegel-like scene of men and women chopping and carrying wood, children playing soccer, a girl with a backpack, laundry strewn over balconies, a three-legged dog.

Sacco performs a counteraddress, movingly adopting the "you" and making it collective: "Because you are still here . . . not raped and scattered . . . not entangled in the limbs of thousands of others at the bottom of a pit. Because Goražde had lived and—how?" (pages 14–15). The fragmented text boxes, which start in the sky (indicating a distant view), move in a downward arc, joining the road with the pedestrians, as if traveling through space and winding up with the people on the ground among them. The image is a bleed, spilling off each page. Tree branches growing upward into the sky overflow out of the left-hand edge of the page; on the right we observe stacks of wood, organized in rows below a pockmarked apartment building.[77] Thirty-two people roam through the space; while a still image, it captures the movement of bodies in the collection of small incidents that constitute the scene (an axe is raised; a soccer ball is elevated off the ground). The intricate grain of the wood is everywhere visible. We can count the tiny socks on hanging clotheslines, notice the faint UNHCR plastic sheeting in the windows.[78] We observe the texture of clothing, detect the triangle pattern of an elderly woman's skirt. Approximately fifty

Figure 5.4 Joe Sacco, *Safe Area Goražde*, double spread, pages 14–15. (Used by permission of Joe Sacco.)

homes, some wrecked, populate the background; a line of trees is visible on the hills above the action. This image conveys the attention to detail that we also see in Bruegel, and the observational perspective his paintings offer—in which, as Joseph Koerner writes in an essay on Bruegel's ethnography, "history itself . . . is the shaping force of nature."[79] This double spread is evocative of Bruegel's *The Triumph of Death* (1562), whose swarming composition—from the hills right down to the dog in the center right foreground—is similar. But its view of a wrecked landscape is a countervisual to *Triumph*. It is one in which beset people, in the presence of death, are not devoured by it but maintain daily life.[80]

Sacco's style, the force of his realism and detail, works in another specific register, one that makes up an enormous aspect of his journalism: picturing atrocity. While Spiegelman and Sacco are united in their endeavor to "depict things graphically that are very uncomfortable to look at," as Sacco puts it, their styles diverge.[81] While Spiegelman's line is loose, Sacco's is not; while Spiegelman eschews virtuosity with his expressive linework, Sacco has been praised for his. (Said, among others, notes his "almost careless virtuosity.")[82] Spiegelman comments on the vicissitudes of narrating a Holocaust testimony: "I thought of [*Maus*] as trying to structure and visualize something that was not for me visualizable. And the only way to do that was to move toward a sort of abstraction."[83] In contrast, Sacco's investment in realism, which includes a detailed quality of line, stems from his belief in the ethical efficacy of "showing what it was like." Of *Goražde*, Sacco says, "[The Serbian nationalists] were killing kids. . . . I decided to make this a realistic comic, and once I made that decision I just thought . . . 'I'm not going to try to make it abstract. I mean, killing a kid is killing a kid.'"[84] Spiegelman's decision to reject drawing human faces in the main narrative body of *Maus* fits his work within the category of "allusive realism" that Saul Friedlander, among many others, suggests for Holocaust representation. Writing on *Maus*, Andreas Huyssen praises its "affective mimesis"; Joseph Witek, in a similar observation, commends the text's "paradoxical narrative realism."[85] Sacco's work, on the other hand, is less "allusive," less "distanced": he draws faces, homes, topography, and murders as accurately and as intricately as he can. Scott McCloud's well-known argument proposes that simpler, iconic rendering of faces allows one to project oneself into the image and promotes identification. With Sacco's detailed images, the aesthetic effect on the reader may differ from the projective "filling up" McCloud describes. While Sacco's work, in some regards, does endeavor for one to be able to "see yourself," as McCloud puts it, his emphasis is on producing recognition of the visually elaborated other.[86]

One only needs to compare Spiegelman's depiction of mass graves with Sacco's to understand these differing investments in the aesthetics of documenting war and suffering. Spiegelman's version, based on the eyewitness testimony of his father, Vladek, is located in Auschwitz (see Figure 4.13). One single horizontal panel punctuates the page, showing only the faces of six stylized mice screaming, with their heads thrown back, as thick, expressionistic flames lick upward (Vladek's comment, overlaying the panel, is chilling: "The fat from the burning bodies they scooped and poured again so everyone would burn better") (*Complete Maus*, page 232). This panel, while it spans the page horizontally, is small, and intentionally so.

Sacco's drawing of mass graves at Srebrenica, in contrast, is fully representational in its drive and desire—it is one of his most clinical drawings in the book, and the largest that exists within a frame. It looks as realistic as one could imagine comics to be: in a large panel set against a black background, Sacco draws roughly twenty human bodies in a winding ditch, with details such as shirt fabrics and the pattern of sneaker soles fully evident in the crowded, serpentine pile (*Goražde*, page 203; Figure 5.5). Six gunmen, standing behind their victims, shoot ten more bodies into the grave, pictured here in the moment they are penetrated by bullets, while a further gunman, taking no chances, shoots upon the pile; a bulldozer with an operator, a truckload of waiting Muslim men, and a car—against which a Serb soldier leans—are depicted in the background, as are thickets of forest, tree-lined hills, and ominous stretches of detailed rocky soil. Three text boxes linger in the corners of the panel: failing to anchor the panel at all points with symmetrical placement of text, Sacco allows the panel a gap, and it is in this direction that the blindfolded men, dead and grimacing, face.

In this materialization of one moment of July 1995's Srebrenica massacre, the largest mass killing in Europe since World War II, the detail emerges in a new role from the studious texture of haystacks and cords of wood that earlier establish Sacco's documentary aesthetic. Here we see that Sacco's images also contain the detail as a puncturing element. A single cane, in the mass, left of center and falling over two bodies, a slim backward J, perfectly vertical, is the wounding detail—the *punctum*, to use Barthes's term from *Camera Lucida*. Barthes, writing on photography, analyzes news

Figure 5.5 Joe Sacco, *Safe Area Goražde*, top panel of page 203. (Used by permission of Joe Sacco.)

photographs' ability to "shout" rather than wound: "A certain shock—the literal can traumatize—but no disturbance. . . . I glance through them, I don't recall them; no detail (in some corner) ever interrupts my reading." Sacco's drawings, on the other hand, are, to use Barthes's language, "lashed, striped by a detail."[87] While the question of style and code offers a way to read the difference between Spiegelman and Sacco, both projects hinge on the plenitude of the visual, the ability to present an uncategorizable excess that is outside of the logic of the denotative.

Their texts' most forceful intervention in contemporary popular culture (comic books about *genocide*) and in the extant discourse of trauma (*comic books* about genocide) is this visual register, which rejects the absence that trauma theory has for so long demanded.[88] In comics, absence and excess brush up against each other. Spiegelman and Sacco share a common project, the transmission of testimony, and their works are underwritten by a belief in the efficacy of form: the ability of the textual and aesthetic practices of comics to articulate visual presence as informative and affective, situated and ethical—and, as Barthes puts it, "pricking" in a way that moves beyond the literal. Their work suggests and "foregrounds," to cite Said's language from this chapter's epigraph, the enormous narrative and affective faculty of the visual expressed in comics form. We might understand what comics offers as the radical visible—a capacious, expansive, and self-conscious mode of representation that refuses to shy away from the power of presence and visual plenitude. Despite and across its differences, both authors' work is anchored by visual plenitude, which is evident in a shared, meticulous attention to form: how the texts uncover, frame, harness, segment, and stress the visual in their hybrid narratives. Creating this kind of surfeit, this overfull register that points to the extrasemantic, comics exceeds the mimetic.

Comics enacts the rethinking of reference that is aimed at resituating history. Sacco's *The Fixer: A Story from Sarajevo* (2003), another exploration of the Bosnian War, suggests what Cathy Caruth also proposes when she writes of "[beginning] to recognize the possibility of a history that is no longer straightforwardly referential (that is, no longer based on simple models of experience and reference)."[89] *The Fixer* takes the contingency that Sacco makes a part of the surface of his work (in which the seams always show), which is part of the journalistic enterprise itself, and brings it to the center as a subject, revealing also how comics is inclined to call "simple models of experience and reference)" into question through form. One sees this in the amplified focus on the situation of journalism, particularly the doubled mediation that attending to "fixers," paid local professionals who guide journalists, makes evident for the already intermediate figure of the journalist. One also sees this in the dramatic collisions or ruptures in style the book stages, and in the book's persistent focus on the problematic of knowing and not knowing that is so essential to the transmission of traumatic history.

Comics and the Rhythm of Knowing

The Fixer is guided by the dialectical movement of what it delivers and what it withholds. In its staccato flashbacks and temporal weave, it investigates "the murky depths beneath the flashy brutality of Sarajevo's war."[90] It is also one of the first, and still only very few, published books or essays examining the journalistic practice of employing fixers.[91] A fixer, as Sacco defines the professional term, "is someone who's with me eight hours a day. He drives me here. He drives me there, knows who to speak to and he'll translate."[92] A book thoroughly about instability, *The Fixer* focuses on subjects that converge in the figure of the fixer Neven: the shady history of the rogue war icons who defended Sarajevo in the Bosnian War; the reliance of journalists, Sacco included, on "fixing," an often exploitative profession that reveals how unstable the idea of "objective" journalism is; and the parameters of trauma itself, in a city and with an individual who has experienced death around him and who has caused it.

Neven, ethnically mixed, is a "loyal Serb"—loyal to the Bosnian government.[93] He fought on the front lines with a unit that was almost entirely Muslim; such rogue army cells often terrorized loyal Serbian civilians with extrajudicial, racist action, including kidnapping, forced labor, and the murder of civilians. Sacco provides a thorough history, for which there is no precedent in English, of Bosnia's warlord paramilitary defenders, including the careers of Neven's boss, Ismet Bajramovic (nom de guerre "Celo"); Jusuf Prazina ("Juka"); Musan Topalovic ("Caco"); and Ramiz Delalic (also "Celo"), among others. Devoting time and space to these morally complicated figures, to their personal lives and military careers—as well as flipping focus from *Goražde* to Serb victims of violence in the same war—*The Fixer* demonstrates that documentary comics do not only focus on what one might think of as the position of victims, but rather that this genre can lend itself to elaborating conditions and contexts on multiple sides of a conflict or moral spectrum. Sacco's work is not about advocacy; it is about history.

The rethinking of reference is something we see in the book's quality of abstraction. The complication of realism and reference that we see in comics journalism is clear in Sacco's mobilization of different aesthetic registers, different styles of rendering that inhabit the same space. Sacco's work signals its multivalent aesthetics in images in which the precise and representational interacts with the expressive and abstract line. The shortest of his books, at 105 pages, *The Fixer* offers eighteen nonlinear chapters, all of which are temporal markers—years, or dates, or durations (say, "1992–1993"; eight chapters are simply named "1995"). The most jagged and fragmented of Sacco's books, *The Fixer* is also in a sense the most emblematic for this very reason. Full of dense, tight crosshatching and dominated by black, *The Fixer* initially looks darker than Sacco's other works. While the gutter of a comics page is traditionally white, more than one-third of *The Fixer*'s chapters are composed with black gutters and an entirely black background. At the beginning of the book, after twinned prologues ("Prologue 2001" followed by "Prologue 1995"), one sees Sacco arrive in Bosnia for the first time in 1995, during the war. Following seven pages of dark interior spaces, the book opens out to offer readers a silent double spread of Sacco moving through the cityscape of Sarajevo (Figure 5.6). "Put yourself in my shoes," the narrator implores. "Your teeth are still chattering from the APC ride over Mt. Igman . . . and someone has just pointed you down a road into an awful silence" (page 11).

Overleaf, we plunge with Sacco into the silence via the book's largest image, a bleed of bombed-out urban space, unmarked by dialogue or verbal narration. A tiny figure with a duffel bag, Sacco is the only human in the scene, walking determinedly across the page from the left, eyes to the ground, on a road in front of two modern, bombed-out skyscrapers, the attacked and abandoned Bosnian parliamentary buildings. Their substantially defenestrated facades loom over the scene. With their neat rows and gaping holes, the skyscrapers are drawn with eerie precision (we can count the floors—forty-five). The composition emphasizes their height and stature. The left of the twin skyscrapers bleeds off the page; they are relics of modernity and also, abandoned, artifacts of violence.[94]

Like the *Goražde* panorama, this image has remarkable volume and depth: Sacco draws homes, downtown and up in the rising hills, in various degrees of ruin. On the right is the shell-pocked Holiday Inn hotel, a fortresslike structure with its incongruously cheerful, recognizably American 1950s logo, a script font in reverse italics, in front of which sits an abandoned, doorless car and litter-strewn paths. In minute detail, Sacco offers shrubs, grass, dirt, rocks, and ambiguous debris: bags bursting with garbage, discarded packaging labeled "USA." The chock-full scene is also, perhaps most conspicuously, brimming with clouds. No space fails to be marked and demarcated. The clouds, which completely fill the broad expanse of Sarajevo's sky, invade every corner. Puffy, like pieces of popcorn falling out

Figure 5.6 Joe Sacco, *The Fixer*, double spread, pages 12–13. (Used by permission of Joe Sacco.)

of the sky, they are cartoon clouds, their outlines are composed of aggregations of little half circles. The clouds are angled in the same direction; their protuberances point down diagonally toward Sacco (against his advance and against the direction of reading), bearing down on him as he walks past the sniper's wall to get to the Holiday Inn. In their own rows, with a kind of beating pulse of downward movement, the clouds are a natural and ominous counterforce to the tight tiers of the still parliament skyscrapers.

"That picture, what is that stuff in the sky?" Sacco explains he has been asked. With their bubbly contours, the clouds collide with the precision drawing and the desire to document that it codes so strongly, which is on display in this haunting image with its densely rendered buildings. This friction makes the image uneasy; the code-switching produces a tension, a sense of strafed repletion. (In this sense, the drawing seeks to create the mood in the reader that Sacco the character is also experiencing.)[95] The image is full of its own emptiness (or empty in its fullness). The collision, or rupture of the narrative surface the image engenders for itself, calls our attention to what is being documented, recorded: not only the battering of the urban landscape but also the feeling of dread and solitude produced by being inside a space so emptied out and yet so overlaid with history. The abstraction of the clouds meets the details of architecture to evoke the unknowable—and the unknowingness that Sacco felt as he entered the location of the Great Siege.

Sacco is selective about what information matters in what medium, word or image, and in what "hand," as cartoonists call style. As one sees, while his lines often document intricate data, he is not trying to replicate a photograph. What matters here is the urge to articulate the physical parameters of space and the affective, immersive parameters of mood by harnessing the expressivity of drawing.[96] He is dwarfed by the buildings, but also by the clouds and (synecdochically) the war itself—by the whole atmosphere he materializes. In composition and style, Sacco emphasizes his lostness, a feature that cuts against the traditional image of the journalist. While Sacco's work is invested in realism and, one might say, a virtuosic command— evident in his sharp, detailed, cross-hatched images—he undercuts his own mastery throughout *The Fixer*: he makes the instability of knowledge, "truth," and especially memory a self-conscious methodology. *The Fixer* instantiates comics journalism's conflictual drives. That the ethical drive to record manifests itself as realism is a conventional view of representation. But this ethical impulse toward realism evident here works in con-tradistinction to a feature the book also presents that one can mark in its registers of style: a conspicuous abdication of transmitting information, a visual and verbal inhabitation of aporia. This active tension steams from the book's pages.

Sacco ends his book with the chapter "Epilogue 2001," a portrait of a trau-matized person, the book's namesake. It is here, in its conclusion, that trauma itself emerges as the subject of *The Fixer*. In Sacco's book, trauma is the framework for textual and aesthetic practice; it is the context of *The Fixer*'s "textualization of the context," which we see in the text's constant counterpoint of presence and absence, the fullness of images sized against the space of gutters, the collisions of style, the enclosures that yet refuse closure.[97] In this concluding episode, furthermore, trauma also becomes the theoretical and denotative subject of Sacco's book: the pages of the epi-logue are crucial to a reading of Sacco's approach to the project of nonfic-tion comics, their presentation of the political work of public memory.

The Fixer opens in 2001 with a prologue: Sacco is back in Sarajevo, and he's looking for Neven. In the 2001 epilogue, Sacco finds his fixer, and, it seems, readers find him too: with Neven's glasses off, we essentially see his eyes for the first time.[98] Yet *The Fixer*, at its midpoint, staged a crisis of au-thentication of its own project: Sacco, addressing readers, detailed his cu-riosity about Neven's testimony, which he puts into form on the page. While he was inclined to believe Neven, others had questioned Neven's credibility. Freely allowing this crisis to become a subject, Sacco involves readers in the situation of enunciation of his own book: "Dear Reader, put yourself in my shoes . . . You recall how salty warriors greeted Neven in the street. You recall, too, what those around you have been saying: 'He's a little crazy but a nice guy'" (page 62). This crisis, which occupies an important and conspicuous plotline of *The Fixer*, reveals how Sacco, like Spiegelman, ren-ders the instability of historical emplotment, and testimony, part of the very project of ethical narrativization. Further, what *The Fixer* finally sug-gests is that whether or not the testimony from Neven is verifiable, this ques-tion ultimately does not matter.

The epilogue is set against an open white background. Its pages are the least cluttered in the book. In the panel in which Joe and Neven reunite, Sacco even drops the borders and the street background entirely. Over lunch—for Sacco has hired Neven to be his fixer yet again—Neven ad-dresses the subject of the war. Explaining his decision to quit drinking,

Neven says, "I wasn't feeling very good about some things I did during the war. I told you I was a sniper . . . [i]t's very strange when a man gets to play God" (page 99). Up until this moment in the text, regardless of the skepticism that Sacco the character introduces in the narrative, the text itself allowed Neven to be a "tower of information." It had given Neven the space to provide intricate and grim details of the war and his own violent participation—which Sacco painstakingly visualizes—with an affected, world-weary enthusiasm.

Here, however, the discourse shifts. Neven, who Sacco frequently notes appears unwell, keeps talking: "Time has passed. But still I have some sort of anxiety attacks during the night. Sometimes I am nervous without any reason. Sometimes those things simply bounce back into my memory although I'm doing my best to stash them deep. We all pay the price for actions taken during life" (page 100).[99] As he had done six years previously, Neven produces a photograph of himself with ten comrades of Celo's unit. In the earlier episode Neven produces the photograph as evidence and to instigate narrative—"Of these men, only four of us are still alive. It was taken shortly before we went into action against the 43 tanks" (page 34). In the epilogue, however, he produces the photograph as evidence of absence: he confesses to Sacco, who illustrates the photograph in both instances: "The worst thing is now I can't remember the names of most of those guys. . . . Most of them I somehow forgot. I can't remember the names of my friends who were killed" (page 100). *The Fixer*, like *Maus*, suggests the problematic of memory as evidence; it foregrounds its instability, constructing and valuing memory as a continuing process, rather than the insuperable, the limit created by trauma.[100]

As Neven and Joe depart after lunch, Neven calls Sacco "a godsend" for bringing him well-paid work. The text then shifts dialogically, as if tired with its own previous trajectory, its detailed presentation of hard-won information. "Neven is a godsend to me, too," Sacco declares, in a box of prose that vertically overextends the last frame of the page, its slightly shakier lines overlaying the straight panel borders. "Finally someone is telling me how it was—or how it almost was, or how it could have been—but finally someone in this town is telling me *something*" (page 100). This striking comment comes after Neven's statements that "I can't remember. . . . I somehow forgot . . . I can't remember"—and after Sacco, in the course of the book, has interviewed well-informed inhabitants of Sarajevo, including Bosnia's former intelligence chief and head army colonel. The *something* to which Sacco refers is a quality of truth not necessarily directly attached to actual veracity. Neven is a traumatized person who can no longer remember relevant factual details, yet Sacco posits that what he offers now, what he, in fact, testifies to—his inability to "stash" memories and his concomitant lack of memory—is a vital transmission of knowledge.

Neven has the last word of dialogue in the book: "possible." In the epilogue, once they start conversing, Sacco does not give himself a single line of dialogue; while Neven's speech is ballooned, Sacco addresses readers directly in text boxes. As Neven starts to walk away—they have shaken hands, exchanged goodbye wishes—Sacco, in the last panel of the book's penultimate page, draws himself staring at Neven's receding back: "He walks back to where his pals are playing cards. And I go to see someone who knew Neven well, someone whose opinion I trust" (page 104).

The last, graphically spare page of *The Fixer*, which allows for the most white space of any in Sacco's books, tracks a movement of opening up and out (Figure 5.7). In the first panel, Neven walks toward us. Sacco presents him unencumbered by detail: he is a man walking alone against a background of white. The second panel stretches a little wider; Neven, smaller now as the view moves upward, is the only full figure depicted, while the leaves of a tree dot the right-hand corner, and we notice Sacco's retreating legs and a sliver of his torso in the act of turning away. The third panel, ending the book, is not panelized at all: it is borderless, an aerial, wide-open view of a tree-lined street. Neven, tiny now, one among others in the city scene, walks toward a café lodged below a high-rise apartment building, with its many little windows and balconies. The text scrolls down toward us, flowing in the direction of reading—while Neven walks in the opposite direction. Neven faces readers in the first two panels of this last page, but in the third, his back is turned as he strides away from Sacco and away from our gaze. The twelve boxes of fragmented text, spiraling downward, loosely form the shape of a question mark, which is where Sacco leaves us: the "truth" about Neven remains withheld from us through the very end of the book. Sacco chooses to end a book that is about the power of visual and verbal information—that offers a wealth of historically valuable and previously unavailable information, and which is about the process of uncovering and gathering this information—with an ethical act of withholding appropriate to the texture and work of memory itself. "I ask him about Neven," Sacco starts, across three slightly jagged text boxes. "He smiles. He remembers Neven as a bit of a blowhard" (page 105).

Figure 5.7 Joe Sacco, *The Fixer*, page 105. (Used by permission of Joe Sacco.)

In a tilted box, overhanging the gutter of the two panels that make up the top tier of the page, the text continues: "He tells me one or two stories about Neven that take me aback . . ." This box stamps itself symmetrically over the top of the gutter, suggesting the momentary elimination of time, a kind of backward movement, a stoppage.[101] The subsequent boxes then descend downward, the text falling vertically, as Sacco continues, "That make me feel like I didn't know the half of what Neven was about . . . that I'd barely traced the edges of his secrets." Neven—his war stories, the outlines of his life, and questions about the veracity of his claims—propels *The Fixer*. Here, Sacco suggests that he may finally know an answer to the open question the text submits, and yet he withholds that information, engaging it as part of the horizon of the unfinished, of the book's own ethical provisionality.

In a book all about the question of knowledge—knowing, not knowing—Sacco lets Neven remain oblique, ambiguous; retains the unknowability of both of his actions and his trauma. "But, I ask my acquaintance," he writes, "what about Neven's wartime heroics? What about—?" The answer, while it confirms an aspect of Neven's integrity, is yet framed explicitly by the problem of *not knowing*. Sacco's source responds, "Everyone was surprised when he turned out to be a fighter for Celo . . . I heard from very good sources that he was unbelievably courageous. From the very beginning he was throwing himself into action as if he wasn't aware what could happen to him. He passed through many bad times." And then, the last words of the text: "I didn't even know he was around any more." The spatial gap between the penultimate and the last box of text is the largest on the page; the last box gravitates toward the edge of the page, for there are no margins. While Sacco writes with splintered captions, so that "the words will just be all over the page, leading the eye down to something," here he sets up the fragmented train of words on the page to lead to nothing: white space, the end (or not) of narrative.[102]

Sacco's work, like Spiegelman's, demonstrates how literature can be what Felman calls "the alignment between witnesses," for the witness is not only "the one who (in fact) *witnesses*, but also, the one who *begets* . . . through the speech process of the testimony."[103] These texts, then, double the act of witness (as Felman points out, testimony can function as signature; as Sacco points out, drawings too function as a signature).[104] They do not conceal or cloak trauma, but rather put its elements on view: graphic narratives make the roiling lines of history readable.

This building of collectivity through the literary act is clear in Sacco's use of address throughout his work. In *The Fixer*, Sacco often aligns the "you" with Neven: he narrates several entire chapters in this mode of address ("You've done your stint in the Yugoslav People's Army"), hailing the reader, with the intimate second person, *as* Neven. (This also puts the reader in Sacco's own place, as the researcher addressing Neven and attempting to understand his subjectivity.) The phrase "Put yourself in Neven's shoes" occurs at regular intervals over the course of the book, along with Neven's first-person testimony: in fact, it is our introduction to Neven. Sacco interpellates, in a self-consciously ethical maneuver, the "ordinary" reader, who is just as "ordinary" as the testifying Neven—despite Neven's putative status as other: sniper, rogue soldier, criminal, war-traumatized fixer, thug. Felman writes of the dire importance of "*creating* (recreating) *an address*, specifically, for a historical experience which annihilated the very possibility of address."[105] Sacco's mode of narration powerfully underscores Felman's assertion that a literature of witness works to create an address—what she calls a "listening community"—for regular people with testimonies.[106]

"Events Are Continuous": *Footnotes in Gaza* and the Counterarchive of Comics

The figure of the witness is most fully elaborated in *Footnotes in Gaza*, at 418 pages Sacco's longest work. *Footnotes in Gaza* investigates two little-documented massacres of Palestinians by Israeli soldiers that took place on Palestinian soil in 1956 in the wake of the Suez Canal crisis. Sacco amplifies the grammar of comics to express temporal diachronic connection, and the simultaneity of traumatic temporality. Comics conveys simultaneity the way other forms cannot—both in expressing trauma's nonlinear temporal effects for terrorized witnesses and also in expressing the ongoing presence of the past. *Footnotes* toggles back and forth between the present and the past over its fifty-eight chapters, and diagrams their connection, using the space of the page both to collapse temporalities and to arrive at dramatic juxtaposition.

Sacco lived in the Gaza Strip in 2002 and 2003 and tracked down as many survivors of each event as he could find. In the first massacre, in Khan Younis on November 3, in which unarmed men were lined up against a wall and shot, a presumed 275 people were killed; in the second, on November 12 in the neighboring town of Rafah, a presumed 111 men, also unarmed, were shot and beaten to death during a daylong screening operation that forced people en masse out of their homes and into a schoolyard. Perhaps the most brutal work in a substantially brutal oeuvre—the sheer number of bodies is staggering—*Footnotes* is on every level about picturing atrocity: for Sacco, and for the witnesses to whom he speaks.

Footnotes is an intensification, both formally and philosophically, of the preoccupations of Sacco's earlier works with the nature of documentation, the shape of history, and concretizing the experience of the other.[107] Sacco undertook thorough archival research with United Nations and Israeli documents, some of which appear here translated in English for the first time. Intensely archival in a way his earlier books are not, *Footnotes* presents itself as a counter to official documentation, visualizing history based on oral testimony, and meticulously archiving previously unarchived voices. The movement of history is the tacit subject of all of Sacco's work, but here "history" is explicit, referred to throughout as a discourse ("History chokes on fresh episodes").[108] While in his earlier comics the past and present produce a spiky rhythm (in which the past constantly surges forward but is often marked, say, by black backgrounds), in *Footnotes* there is a greater focus on the intermingling of past and present, a notion Sacco makes graphically legible.

"As someone in Gaza told me," Sacco writes in his foreword, "'Events are continuous.' Palestinians never seem to have the luxury of digesting one tragedy before the next one is upon them. When I was in Gaza, the younger people often viewed my research into the events of 1956 with bemusement. What good would tending to history do them when they were under attack and their homes were being demolished *now?* But the past and present cannot be so easily disentangled. They are part of a remorseless continuum, a historical blur" (page xi). One reason comics can address itself powerfully to historical narrative is because of its ability to use the space of the page to interlace or overlay different temporalities, to place pressure on linearity and conventional notions of sequence, causality, and progression. "Every day here is '56!" a disgruntled son of a survivor of the Rafah massacre chides Sacco (page 253). Sacco not only states his view of history in his book but also displays it.[109] This is what the form of comics always does best: enacting, rather than only thematizing, the relationship of past and present.

Throughout *Footnotes*, Sacco overlays past and present to demonstrate on the page how events and experiences resist isolation. *Footnotes* often merges—within a panelized space traditionally meant to chart one temporal moment—a younger self with an older self who is testifying in the present tense of the book: it graphically places the witnessing self in the past with his or her own younger body. (This shows us both how vivid the past is and also how, even if readers enter the story through following a body in the past, the telling is marked by the situation of testimony in the present.) We see this prominently, for example, with an unnamed *fedayee*, a stubborn, elderly guerrilla fighter Sacco visits on multiple occasions. In the drawing, his present self and his past self are often contiguous, literally touching each other (see, for instance, pages 43 and 45). *Footnotes* makes legible the continuousness of past and present, however, not only in overlaying temporalities, but also by directly juxtaposing them on the page.

A stunning example appears in the chapter "Nov. 3, 1956 Pt. 1: Khan Younis Town Center." Faris Barbakh was fourteen at the time of the shooting in his town. Thirty to forty-five minutes after Israeli soldiers burst into his home and took its adult men away, he was sent out with a jug to fetch water. Sacco draws Faris creeping out into the silent street by the fourteenth-century Mamluk castle near his house in Khan Younis. In the last of three same-size panels occupying the bottom tier of a page, the detailed background suddenly disappears, replaced by black; time freezes. Faris's head is turned in the opposite direction from the first two panels. "'I saw all the bodies," a text box reads—open quote—angling out of the panel's right-hand vertical border and pointing on its side like an arrow into the white space of the gutter, pushing one overleaf (page 97). When one turns the page, one is confronted by a double spread of two images, each absorbing an entire page: the wall of the castle on November 3, 1956, cutting diagonally across the page, bodies heaped along the wall from its beginning to end—and, on the following page, the wall in 2003, cars parked casually along its perimeter (pages 98–99; Figure 5.8). We can count fifty individuated bodies in the drawing (of the more than 100 Faris saw, including twelve of his relatives), as we can count eleven cars parked at the wall, with a truck and taxi moving toward the reader, along with passersby ambling through the space.

Drawn with minute precision at the exact same angle where a difference of forty-seven years passes in the nonexistent gutter between the two bleeding pages, the before-and-after juxtaposition of the Mamluk castle wall feels shocking. The terrifying aspect of the 1956 image, in addition to the sudden reveal of the felled, silent bodies, is Faris's position in space, alone in the lower right foreground of the frame. His body is the only one moving; his back is to us. Four text boxes, disconnected, each a small, floating, irregular square, continue the testimony. "I put down the jug," the last one reads—full stop. Faris's jug is behind him on the ground. He walks (calmly, it seems, from our elevated view behind him) off into the rows of bodies. The ground is white, unmarked; the wall is tightly rendered, dense with slumped, bloody men, their feet and scattered shoes pointing outward. We are looking at Faris looking; it is a doubled scene of witness, and he walks away from us, it appears, into the death. In the contiguous 2003 image, Faris, sixty-one, appears in the same location in space, walking from the lower right foreground toward the wall—this time accompanied by Sacco and his translator Abed.[110] We are looking at him perhaps looking at, or through the eyes of, his own younger self, from the exact same angle, facing the wall; when Sacco asks him two pages later how he feels, he says, this time facing readers: "I feel like I am that child again" (page 101). The present-day wall is built up; a floodlight overhangs its arched passageway; graffiti marks its lower expanse; new residences and trees dot the background. And, crucially, looking hard at the faint lines among the stones, one notices upward of a dozen discrete martyr posters—most in multiples, flocked in groups all over the wall. Indexing absent bodies, these posters mirror, and in a sense actually reflect, the murdered men of 1956.[111] Where once there were bodies of the murdered, now there are icons of martyrdom.

Footnotes also presents dense multivalent pages in which Sacco both visualizes the substance of oral testimony, materializing the past, and visualizes the situation of testimonial exchange in the present. In the same chapter Sacco solicits the testimony of Misbah Ashour Abu Sa'doni, a married handyman who lived in the center of town in 1956. Israeli soldiers with heavy machine guns had fired directly on lines of men; Misbah was among them. Sacco begins Misbah's testimony by drawing the two talking in his home; Misbah's first speech balloon sits in the domestic space of 2003. His second, part of the same sentence, divided by ellipses, bridges the next gutter, lying over it, to place readers with him in 1956 (page 87).

The most moving page of Misbah's testimony opens with a direct quotation from him, in a floating text box that lingers just above gunfire shooting against the direction of reading. Four machine guns fitted on

Figure 5.8   Joe Sacco, *Footnotes in Gaza*, double spread, pages 98–99. (Used by permission of Joe Sacco.)

bipods fire, in a confrontational and deliberately awkward panelization, across the page. The composition of multiple guns pointing left, occupying horizontal space across the image, is evocative of Goya's famous history painting of execution, *The Third of May 1808*, whose composition is also present in numerous of his *Disasters of War* etchings. (Goya's *The Third of May 1808*, as I note in Chapter 1, inspired Manet's similar *The Execution of the Emperor Maximilian* paintings.)[112] The gun in the foreground of the panel stretches across the entire unbordered space; there is no gutter after we enter the page by moving into the muzzle. Surrounded by gunsmoke, the small box, hovering above the gunfire on the left, cites Misbah: "They fired four different times" (page 90; Figure 5.9). Directly below, Sacco draws Misbah as he is testifying. This inch-high panel, which also spans the page, is entirely black except for a detailed close-up of Misbah's face and his speech. Cutting him off above the eyebrows and just below his moustache, the panel most prominently displays his eyes. Misbah is looking out not at readers but presumably at Sacco, calling attention to the context of transmission of testimony; on either side of his face his testimony continues in speech balloons. (From a visual perspective, in which one looks directly at the speaking witness, Sacco, absenting his own body from the frame, suggests the reader as the testimonial interlocutor.) The page is multivalent, switching from direct quotation, in the scene in which Sacco imagines and visually reconstructs the firing squad, to speech balloon, in the immediately following horizontal panel of Misbah's face.

While one perspective, then—a literally central perspective—pictures the witness speaking, the following four panels take us into the past and even assume the optical perspective of Misbah himself. In the space of the thin horizontal gutter we move back into 1956 and directly into a panel clotted with bodies. Sacco next stretches Misbah's text, again in quotation marks, in irregular boxes over and across the images of the shot men. "I was reciting the Koran . . . ," Misbah says in a text box that floats next to a row of bodies, including his own, and then when he says, "And my spirit went all the way up to the sky," the following panel takes this point of view, looking down at the complete row of crumpled, dying men from above, before in the next panel picturing Misbah's face, on the ground, in a pool of blood. Misbah's spoken and now written testimony appears in text boxes that stamp over gutters, implying the simultaneous frozenness of the moment (the passage of time is blocked for the victim) and its movement (his soaring spirit). The text boxes float across the page and over gutters in an upward

Figure 5.9 Joe Sacco, *Footnotes in Gaza*, page 90. (Used by permission of Joe Sacco.)

diagonal, evoking Misbah's skyward-moving perspective. In the last panel, Sacco's narration, unboxed, also appears, describing where the bullets entered Misbah's body. In this page, as in others, one recognizes how comics, a form for which there is always the legibility of double narration, pictures the scene of address of testimony, and also captures the layered view of the witness, who sees his own body ("my spirit went all the way up") as well as seeing *from* his body. It expresses the synchronic temporality of witnessing. The page moves from Sacco's perspective to the witness's perspective, switching in and out from citation to dialogue to authorial narration; one sees the dexterity with which comics documents the always frame-breaking modality of testimony.[113]

Footnotes in Gaza opens with the 116-page section "Khan Younis," offers the short, twenty-seven-page interlude "Feast" (set mostly in the present tense, particularly around the annual feast Eid al-Adha), and ends with the 236 pages of "Rafah" before moving into its four appendices and bibliography.[114] Its multiple appendices render *Footnotes* structurally unusual, even among documentary comics, marking out portions of research that suggest its own scholarship, its archaeology. The end of the book's first major section, "Khan Younis," reflects on the procedure of the book itself. "Khan Younis" closes with the chapters "Memory and the Essential Truth" and "Document."

At the outset of the former, Sacco notes that we "have just finished reading a string of personal recollections that tell the story of the widespread killings"—before he demonstrates a conflict across testimonies (page 112). Sacco mulls over this problem for a handful of characteristically dense pages. (As he does elsewhere when factual conflicts arise, including later with Golda Meir's account of the November 1956 killings, Sacco draws, if briefly, the scenes that portray conflicting accounts, materializing and juxtaposing plausible options on the page.)[115] In the chapter's last panel, he writes, "I only want to acknowledge the problems that go along with relying on eyewitness testimony in telling our story" (page 116). The panel, visually arresting, is largest on the page, occupying an entire tier. Four corpses float in what is otherwise black space; one is a shot toddler. The "essential truth" is bodies, is death. The pictured men—whether or not their surviving brother watched them die, as is in question—"were among what a U.N. report alleges were 275 Palestinians killed in Khan Younis town and camp that day." The book then immediately segues from the bodies on the bottom of one page to a document at the top of the next; the transition is deliberately stark.

This opening page of the chapter "Document" makes legible the project of *Footnotes* (Figure 5.10). The entire book is a counterdocument, a countermodality to the kind of archive Sacco encountered in the official records of the United Nations and the Israel Defense Forces. The page—what a reader runs right into coming off dead bodies in black space—also shows the ability of comics form to actually *incorporate* visual archives into the frames of its panels and pages (ones sees this more typically with photographs, a practice Sacco has never touched, although he embeds a newspaper article in *Palestine*). The page opens with a horizontal, unbordered panel and the truncated typeset words of the text of a photocopy of an actual archival UN document; the left edge of the page slices down through the column of text.[116] The document's next column of text is incomplete too, sliced by the right edge of the page, yet in this opening bleed we recognize plenty of words and fragments: "Gaza Strip," "civilian casualties," "resistance to their occupation," "140 were refugees and 135 local residents" (page 117). Stamping over the official typeset text—which contains its own gutter, graphically, in the space between double columns—are two of Sacco's own hand-drawn text boxes with their quavery lines. They appear on either side of the chapter title, "Document," which is drawn in large black block letters and appears uncentered (just as the document itself, Sacco implies, is off-kilter). Sacco creates a palimpsest: he lays his writing on top of the official writing, covering it, contrasting his handwritten words with the status of the typed and filed.

"You can read that report for yourself," the narrator states, "at the U.N. archives on East 43rd St. in New York City." And then Sacco names the 1957 document: it is the "'Special Report of the Director of the United Nations Relief and Works Agency for Palestine Refugees in the Near East Covering the period 1 November 1956 to mid-December 1956' to the General Assembly." Below, the following smaller tier offers two frames unusually separated in their middle not by a blank gutter but rather by Sacco's commentary, which fills the space. The panelization focuses our attention on what is graphically central, the handwritten—which is to say, on the *type* of researched document that Sacco's book itself is: one that creates an archive, inscribed by hand, from unofficial, previously unarchived voices. In the first panel, an archivist approaches, wheeling a cart of documents; the

Figure 5.10 Joe Sacco, *Footnotes in Gaza*, page 117. (Used by permission of Joe Sacco.)

second focuses on hands. This panel depicts the cover of the document, with its title and official U.N. seal, and Sacco's hands gripping it on either side: readers are placed with the viewpoint of the cartoonist, looking down at the only certified document to detail the incidents under investigation. The document is held so that below the conspicuous hands that clasp it, one notes further evidence of manual activity: a notepad on a desk, full of lines of writing, and a pencil pointing out of the frame.

Sacco portrays his own research, which here is part of an ethic of demystification as well as an act that highlights (literally, if one considers highlighting to be marking out important lines of a text) exactly how sparse the official record is that accounts for so many deaths: one can call it up in a single afternoon in Manhattan. Significantly, Sacco presents the research ritual as part of bearing witness (in the doubled act of witnessing comics brings to the reader). And, crucially, Sacco calls attention to oral testimony and to the drawn, the handwritten, as counter to what he identifies on the next page as "history-by-document"—which is to say, disembodied history; his own document engages with archives, but further refigures what counts as archival, as documentary, by bringing the bodies and voice of witnesses forward (page 118). Sacco notes in his foreword, "Documentary evidence is usually considered more reliable than oral testimony by historians" (page x)—but in the book, he treats oral testimony, when he can corroborate it, as just as "documentary" as other forms of information. In making a place for oral testimony as evidence, *Footnotes* along with all of Sacco's other work is evocative of Lanzmann's 1985 documentary *Shoah*. However, unlike *Shoah*, whose shots of expanses of now-empty fields and rustling trees stand in the place of the violence that comics in many ways delivers, Sacco does bank on the power of images in presenting others' experience of the past; *Footnotes*'s replete images function in contradistinction to *Shoah*'s chilling, roaming images of landscapes of serene depletion.

In the key opening page of this chapter—as on only one other page, in the last chapter of the book—Sacco refers to himself as a historian, albeit in the third person: "To the historian . . . a contemporary document like this can represent a more definitive version of events than decades-old memories" (page 117).[117] The third-person construction is a wry take on the figure of the disembodied historian; the page where he names himself a historian is the *only* page in the whole book in which Sacco diegetically locates his own body outside of Gaza and its environs. However, even if the tone is wry, it is significant that Sacco identifies himself as a historian—a self-description absent from his previous works—when he shows himself researching in a certified archive (his earlier works do not feature similar scenes). Sacco's work functions to help create the historical record, as Patrick Cockburn's review of *Footnotes* in the *New York Times* makes clear (Cockburn, a seasoned Middle East correspondent, even frames *Footnotes* as counteracting an "editorial bias against history").[118] Yet *Footnotes* raises the question of what constitutes the production of history; when "history" appears throughout the book, it is almost always aligned with official, hegemonic discourse, in lines like "That's the big picture, what gets remembered in history books, and we can skip it for now" (page 48).

But if the historian is seeking "a more definitive version," the official document, of course, does not yield definitive answers (and, as the book's appendix that reprints it reports, the agency's own sources of information "included eye-witness accounts by UNRWA employees" [page 399]).[119] The report—which was never followed up on—indicates "there is some conflict in the accounts given as to the causes of the casualties." Sacco ends the page continuing to quote the UN Relief and Works Agency report, drawing, in juxtaposition, two versions of the precipitating factor of the Khan Younis killings: Palestinians as resistance fighters, and Palestinians as unarmed civilian men. The same document resurfaces on page 376 in connection with the Rafah incident, just as inconclusively stating the reason for the killings.[120]

Here we recognize the triple valence of the book's title, a play on bodies and documentation. The "footnotes" of the title refer to conventional footnotes: the small stuff—the details—in the historical and official documents that focus on "big man" history.[121] (As Sacco's book itself, a counter-document, is full of footnotes, *Footnotes in Gaza* can also be read purely descriptively as what is between its own covers.) "Footnotes" here is also a reference to dispossessed people; in the chapter titled as such, below a text box that reads "And the footnotes—" Sacco draws a panel of men with their hands in the air, as if they are hanging on and are about to be dropped from the historical record (the cover figures captive men as literally trying to hang on to the letters of word *Gaza*). Further, Sacco explicitly figures the multipart incidents themselves in Khan Younis and Rafah as footnotes; when the Khan Younis section concludes, he states we have "one more footnote to go" (page 119). Discourse, bodies, events: *Footnotes in Gaza* intertwines embodiment with citation, underscoring the relation between bodies and archives.

If Sacco's relationship to the archival is about reconstructing the bodies of others, bodies that have been ignored by official discourse, it is also specifically about making the concrete other legible—not only the generalized other. The drive behind his "slow" comics journalism, his "sojourns" created with pen and paper, is the ethical project of concretizing the other. In the section on Rafah, Sacco heightens attention to his own procedure of soliciting testimony, including from reluctant witnesses, in the cleverly titled chapter "Time Management" (any historian's project). This chapter reveals a thoroughgoing procedure: Sacco and Abed number each witness, compare accounts and notes with each other after each visit with a survivor, and log plausible information (linked to each witness) onto a huge chart that breaks down what people in Rafah call "The Day of the School" into its component parts. (Comics itself is a kind of charting; the chart full of ordered boxes Sacco draws in the background of "Time Management" could be one enormous comics page.)[122] And it is with this focus on the hard-won collection of evidence that Sacco turns from the generalized other to the concrete other in the chapter "Announcement."

On November 12, 1956, an announcement was made in Rafah over the loudspeaker of an Israeli military vehicle; "Time Management" leaves us there. In *The Body in Pain* Elaine Scarry points out that a torturer's voice is the locus of power; he or she is exempt from the radical embodiment (the awareness of woundability) that is the condition of the tortured. Sacco moves immediately in "Announcement," following a depiction of the vehicle and loudspeaker that ends the previous chapter, to bodies—specifically, the faces of six particularized witnesses, which fill the page (Figure 5.11). Countering the disembodied voice of authority are *embodied* witnesses and a presentation of their bodily specificity—but also their own voices. They look at the reader with their diverse features and clothing—Khalil Ahmed Mohammed Ibrahim, an older man with deep-set eyes, a lined face, and a short white beard, who is wearing a blazer and has a keffiyeh on his head, while Mohi Eldin Ibrahim Lafi, who has a sparse dark moustache and is missing two bottom front teeth, wears a tall cap and a sweater under a zip-up vest—and their speech. As Scarry writes, "acts that restore the voice are a partial reversal of the process of torture itself."[123] Sacco offers a page—called a democratic page in comics because of its same-size frames—that locates us precisely with the names and physical facial details of survivors whose slightly different accounts of the announcement are juxtaposed

Figure 5.11 Joe Sacco, *Footnotes in Gaza*, page 205. (Used by permission of Joe Sacco.)

across the page and whose eyes meet our gaze, to recall Mirzoeff's emphasis on the significance of the reciprocal gaze.

The rigorous identification of witnesses by full name in *Footnotes* is intensified from Sacco's previous works; complete names are almost always given, in small text boxes that appear with the person's face.[124] Across Sacco's work, and especially apparent in a page like the one opening "Announcement," comics manifests an ethics of attention to the individual face ("faces are what it's all about," Sacco declares in *Palestine* [71]). Emmanuel Levinas's definition of the ethical as an encounter with the face of the other, then, feels relevant for understanding the import of Sacco's work. Levinas, whose philosophy is built around this ethical encounter, writes of "the verb in the human face" that "calls upon" one, "ordering responsibility for the other."[125] As Judith Butler points out in her discussion of Levinas, "it would seem that the norms that would allocate who is and is not human arrive in visual form. These norms work to *give face* and to *efface.*" There are, as Butler puts it, "frames that foreclose responsiveness," and also, on the other hand, "ways of framing that will bring the human into view in its frailty and precariousness."[126] Butler's discussion of the frames that "determine what will and will not be a grievable life" appears in a discussion of photography; Sacco's work suggests an alternative practice of framing here explicitly aimed at acknowledging the particularity of the other, at *giving face* through drawing—making a picture as opposed to "taking" it.

Sacco, as with Spiegelman, often uses the verb *inhabit* to describe his experience of drawing. Drawing someone carefully is a form of dwelling (to evoke *inhabit*'s Latin root) in the space of that person's body, taking on their range of postures that themselves reflect experience. The concept of habitus, from the field of sociology and specifically Pierre Bourdieu, is relevant here. Habitus, which can be defined as "an embodied, as well as cognitive, sense of place," refers to the particular, and bodily, inhabitation of social forms—features that can be expressed in posture, gait, the animation of limbs: the aspects of a person a cartoonist needs to study to express visual essence.[127] Cartoonists, who distill essence with their drawn lines, study habitus—and themselves, it seems, inhabit these bodily attitudes in order to materialize specified persons. "When you're drawing something, you kind of have to inhabit it," Sacco explains. "Drawing people running with their arms up, you have to think of how the shoulders raise, how the cloth goes, how the hands would spread out or not spread out, how people have their hands in a different way."[128] This is also the case with drawing the dead. Sacco told me, "You kind of have to feel weight, you have to sort of imagine what it would be like, you kind of inhabit it."[129] And, significantly, in visualizing bodies on the page, as Sacco put it to W. J. T. Mitchell: "You have to inhabit other peoples' pain or other peoples' aggression."[130]

If drawing suggests inhabiting the social, physical, and emotional perspective of the other, what *Footnotes* also shows is how traumatized people, in their acts of memory, inhabit their own past selves. *Footnotes*, as I have noted, is about the *situation* of testimony as much as it is about creating a record of experience—which is to say, it is a book about address, memory, and the transmission of trauma. Locating bodies in space on the page, *Footnotes* focuses not only on the factual substance of the testimonies it gathers but also on what the procedure of memory feels like for the witnesses—it demonstrates the embodiedness of memory, in which accessing a certain time also means accessing a certain location in space.[131] A form that turns "time into space" through frames on the page, comics inclines itself to the layered, complex, and fragmented speech acts that constitute testimony. *Footnotes* presents a doubled inhabitation: Sacco's subjects are inhabiting their pasts as Sacco attempts to inhabit them in order to draw their experiences.

Both Sacco as an artist (a secondary witness) and those he interviews (as primary witnesses) struggle to describe, verbally or visually, intense physical pain. In so many ways, *Footnotes in Gaza* is about sentience, expressing sensation. It is much less a book about rights and injustice—the injustice sits on the surface—than it is about pain, and exploring how one might open access to the subjectivity of another. "Sea Street," the last chapter, is named for a bustling Rafah street that is also the site where in 1956 the town's men were herded to a schoolyard. Some were murdered along the way; those who arrived were forced to jump over a ditch to gain access, where they were met on the other side by Israeli soldiers who bashed them on the head with heavy sticks as they entered. These beatings—a consistent reference point in testimony about the Rafah massacre—are detailed in the chapter "The School Gate." In the last chapter, leaving Rafah, Sacco muses in part on the traumatic reenactments he provoked: "How often we forced the old men of Rafah back down this road lined with soldiers and strewn with shoes. . . . How often we made them sit with their heads down and piss themselves" (page 383). Sacco then recalls a specific witness,

Abu Juhish, the grandfather of one of Abed's friends. He draws him from the chest up, rising from the bottom of the page, an old man in a cardigan and cap, with a heavy brow and what looks like a frown.

Abu Juhish shares space, shoulder to shoulder in Sacco's rendering, with his younger self in 1956's schoolyard after having been clubbed in the head. (His friends tried to stanch the bleeding with sand; one sees a pile of sand sitting saturated in his wound.) On the following page, in Sacco's visit with him, Abu Juhish, who strained to tell his story, starts crying. His grandson Belal, present at the interview, asks his grandfather, "What was the worst thing you remember from that day?" "Fear," he says. "Fear" (page 384). This is the last word of dialogue spoken in the book. The next panel, spanning the bottom of the page, depicts Abu Juhish and Sacco in profile, facing each other, divided by a shaft of words in the middle—a full space of words, Sacco's words, that represents a gulf separating them. Here, significantly, for the first time in his journalistic works, Sacco's eye is partially visible behind the arm of his glasses. The next page, as at the beginning of the chapter, shows Sacco in the back of a taxicab driving out of Rafah, reflecting on different types of knowledge: he states he remembers of witnesses "how often I sighed and mentally rolled my eyes because I knew more about that day than they did" (page 385). These are the last words in the book. Uncharacteristically harsh even for Sacco's often ironic narration, the starkness of this closing line points to the cross-discursivity of comics form, for the statement is immediately counteracted by drawing.

Sacco does not know more than they did, as the effort to understand sensation that concludes the book makes clear; he does not know what cannot be communicated by fact. He does not know, and cannot know, the fear of which Abu Juhish speaks. The top panel of the page, his exit, dissolves into a grid: one sees the taxi move out of the first frame rightward, and in the second frame an Israeli jeep drives in from the left. We are back in 1956. The rest of the page, like the next four pages, are wordless. When one turns the page, the gutters and margins are all black, as will remain the case to the end; no numbers appear to chart these pages. In the first panel—the frames unfold at the same size, indicating equal beats, a quick movement—three stricken people, two women and a man, stare directly at the reader, mouths open, worried. The look that hails the reader is troubling; one feels thrust into a space of panic. The panels become increasingly cluttered and confusing. By the fourth—there are two to a tier, six per page—it is possible to realize that Sacco is drawing the frames from one person's—Abu

Juhish's?—continuing optical point of view, drawing what he sees. The reader is in this person's visual position. His hands, which emerge in the fourth panel, are figured as the hands out in front of the reader, who is dropped into the perspectival space of his body and vision. One stays stable in this view through the hands, up and out in front in surrender, guiding one in the panel as people fall to the ground, as sticks and guns are raised. Three pages in, the wall of the school appears, and the panels picture swirls of panicked bodies; the hands figured as the hands of the reader are jostled close (Figure 5.12). Then suddenly the stick appears, surging across the panel like a wave, appearing as though it will fly out of the page, and black space takes over; the book ends.

Sacco's work endeavors to capture the experience of pain, of suffering, of radical embodiment without, here, the authority of his own speech, his own written language—but with his attentive drawing, which operates as an ethical counter-address. The silence of these pages focuses our attention on the experience of Abu Juhish's spatial coordinates as he tries to navigate his confusion and awareness of his vulnerability. It is Sacco's attempt to picture the other by inhabiting his point of view, by inhabiting, in a sense, and asking readers to inhabit, the space of the other's body (the "put yourself in Neven's shoes" injunction made literal through the discursive capacities of comics). And if Sacco's work is about the embodiment of others, Sacco's own body, too, is a part of every page of his work—a fact made legible by the fact that he signs and dates each page (even pages, like the ones concluding the book, that themselves defy the logic of pagination). The hands, featured so movingly and so prominently here—hands shaped in captive surrender, but which yet enter each side of the frame to stabilize our view—are the hands of the prisoner the reader optically occupies, but they also rhyme with the focus on the hands of the artist-reporter that one sees throughout. The only other time that a panel adopts this perspective is when Sacco's own hands are featured as he grasps the report at the UN archives and the reader is put in his optical position. Embodiment in comics—*on* the page and *in* the mark, an index of the body—is a kind of compensation for lost bodies, for lost histories.

Across languages, iconographic traditions, and countries, Sacco's comics journalism has been significant in instigating a renewed attention to—and practice of—the power of *drawing to tell*, an old documentary and aesthetic

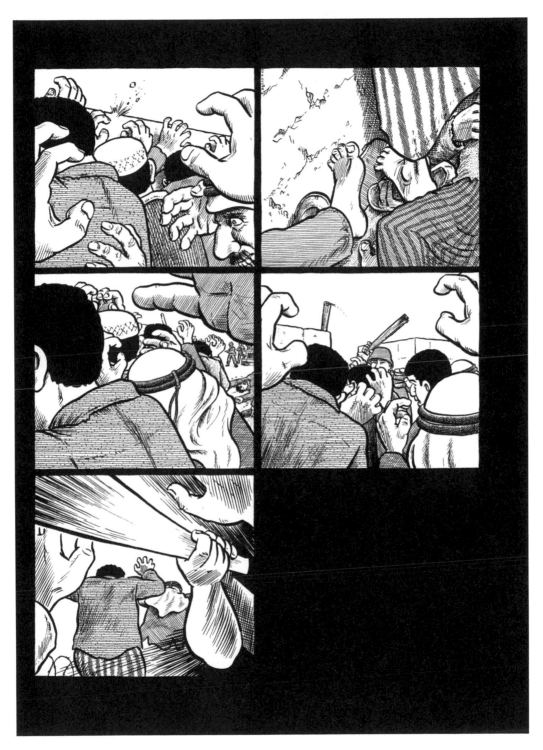

Figure 5.12 Joe Sacco, *Footnotes in Gaza*, unpaginated. (Used by permission of Joe Sacco.)

practice that has reemerged to exemplify "the simultaneity of making and seeing" that characterizes contemporary image creation.[132] In the years since Sacco started both writing and drawing from the Middle East, there has been a steady growth of comics about the region in Arabic, Hebrew, French, and English; Beirut, to name just one of many locations, has a thriving comics scene. Enacting emplacement and situated perspective, Sacco's comics work against placelessness, what geographer Edward Holland, making a reference to the Apollo space photographs, suggests is the distant "geopolitical eye" that offers vision as "Cartesian in its dualism of subject and object, viewer and viewed, and Apollonian . . . in its ubiquity."[133] Sacco's comics rethink and rework absence and silence in presenting witness on the page. The abundance of visual information can be ambiguous, even, in its very amplitude. But Sacco's work rebukes the antivisual bias that demands inaudibility, the invisible, the unspeakable. He visualizes on the page the processes and effects of history, however steeped in trauma and alterity, bringing memory forcefully into public discourse—even if it creates, to use a phrase of Lawrence Weschler's, "crystalline ambiguity."[134] The most powerful suggestion that Sacco's texts make is that witnessing and memory can be treated as a creative interlocutionary process, rather than something anchored in the unfaceable.

CODA
NEW LOCATIONS, NEW FORMS

Right now is a confusing and fascinating time for what W. J. T. Mitchell has called "the lives and loves of images," and this inflects how we can think about the contemporary emergence—popular, critical, and practical—of the visual-verbal form of comics to communicate war and trauma. It seems as though, in the present moment, images have never been more important, or more under siege. There exists a tension between the revelatory strength of the image that operates with evidentiary force, on the one hand, and its potency to trigger an affective response, on the other.

One sees this clearly with photographs. Famously, Donald Rumsfeld, detailing the trajectory of his own response to prisoner abuse at the Abu Ghraib prison, claimed, "Words don't do it." Rumsfeld went on: "You read it and it's one thing. You see the photos and you cannot help but be outraged."[1] Perhaps this is why news photographs of returning fallen American soldiers, even at funerals and ceremonials in their honor, were prohibited from 1991 until 2009, when the ban was lifted by the Obama administration. Photography in particular has been an embattled medium in the wake of recent disasters in the United States: after 9/11, the "falling man" photograph by the AP's Richard Drew, which showed a man who had jumped from the North Tower falling headfirst before the building collapsed, was censored.

Recently, cartoons have been at the center of major international controversies over images. In the 2005 Danish "cartoon war," the conservative Danish newspaper *Jyllands-Posten* ran twelve cartoons of the Prophet Muhammad in a feature titled "The Face of Muhammad," scornfully violating the hadith prohibition on images of the Prophet, and outraging Muslims worldwide. The Danish cartoons prompted violent protest in January and February 2006 that led to more than 200 deaths in Nigeria, Libya, Pakistan, and Afghanistan. And in the Paris attacks of January 7, 2015, two terrorists stormed the offices of the French satirical weekly *Charlie Hebdo* with assault rifles, killing twelve people (including the magazine's editor in chief) and injuring many others; the attackers were allegedly inspired to take revenge after *Charlie Hebdo*'s publication of mocking cartoons of Muhammad. The magazine had republished the original *Jyllands-Posten* cartoons in 2006 and drawn Muhammad for a 2011 cover dubbed "Charia Hebdo." These were only some of the satirical depictions of the Prophet that were published in the magazine over the years.

In a *New York Times* article titled "A Startling New Lesson in the Power of Imagery," critic Michael Kimmelman reflected on the crisis instigated by the Danish cartoons: "Over art? These are made-up pictures. The photographs from Abu Ghraib were documents of real events, but they didn't provoke such widespread violence. What's going on?"[2] As Judith Butler points out, we are, after the commencement of wars in Iraq and Afghanistan, in the midst of a "political battle that is taking place in part through the medium of the visual image."[3] Indeed, the issues attached to the Danish and Parisian cartoon controversies are complex, delicate, and thorny, and their stakes high. They concern the very parameters of free speech, the force of religious proscription, and the fraught current global political context.

What I would like to underline is the current power, for good or for ill, of hand-drawn images, which is undiminished even in our current age of the camera and digital media. The 2006 Danish cartoon crisis and the 2015 Paris attacks show that today the political and aesthetic issues that attend the act of picturing through cartoons—materializing in marks on the page—are central and inescapable. Jytte Klausen, a political scientist, affirms in *The Cartoons That Shook the World* that "cartoons are a form of political speech."[4] As Art Spiegelman writes in "Drawing Blood," an essay about the Danish cartoons, "the compression of ideas into memorable icons gives cartoons their ability to burrow deep into the brain."[5] The "right to picture" in cartoon language—in marks and lines that aim to distill and condense essence—has now become again, with amplified force, the subject of countless current debates.

In the days after the *Charlie Hebdo* attacks, cartoonists and the practice of cartooning came suddenly into focus all over the globe. On January 8, Palestinian cartoonist Naji al-Ali's name cropped up in the *New York Times* for the first time in years—grouped with the *Charlie* cartoonists as an artist assassinated, presumably, because of the substance of his work. The simple figure of the old-fashioned pen was thrust into the spotlight as a symbol of free speech. Support rallies for the *Charlie Hebdo* victims saw huge masses of people holding pens in the air above their heads. "Cartoonists' tools of the trade were waved in the air and made into impromptu altars," NBC reported, with the headline "Charlie Hebdo Attack: Pen Becomes Defiant Symbol of Freedom."[6]

Public appetite in the days after the attack revealed a need to hear from cartoonists central to this book and versed in the politics of image making: Art Spiegelman and Joe Sacco. Their comics, which circulate globally, are widely known to be about difficult acts of witness (what we might consider a kind of "speaking truth to power," evident even in work that eschews the didactic). Further, they are known for picturing historical violence—and for balancing the violence that can be inherent in images themselves with intellectual probity, creating searing and yet nonexploitative word-and-image narratives. The day after the attacks, Spiegelman defended cartooning and free speech on the news program *Democracy Now*; two days after the attacks, Sacco responded with a one-page comic strip, "On Satire."[7] And the two cartoonists' views diverged—as they had previously around the *Jyllands-Posten* cartoons.

In 2006, the *Nation* ran an interview feature titled "Only Pictures?" in which Spiegelman and Sacco disagreed on the republication of the Danish cartoons. Both cartoonists articulated the affective power of images, but while Spiegelman stood behind the idea of the "right to insult" as part and parcel of drawing images, Sacco edged away from it, invoking a "bigger context" in which "segments of the Muslim population around the world . . . have been pummeled with other images, like Abu Ghraib." ("I think maybe the idiot cartoonist should feel a need to be a little more self-censoring," he added.)[8] They also prominently disagreed on the decision by American newspapers to not reprint the cartoons, even in stories reporting on them. Spiegelman pointed out that the "picture/word divide" is "as big a divide as the secular/religious divide" and that descriptions of the images would not substitute for showing the images themselves, as many news outlets had suggested ("The banal quality of the cartoons that gave insult is hard to believe until they are seen").

A few months later, Spiegelman published a cover story in *Harper's* in which the magazine reprinted each of the twelve Danish cartoons—something most mainstream venues, including the *New York Times*, refused to do. "Repressing images gives them too much power," Spiegelman writes in the essay.[9] "Drawing Blood: Outrageous Cartoons and the Art of Outrage" offers an incisive history of insult and satire in cartooning, from Honoré Daumier and Thomas Nast forward. Further, Spiegelman slows down enough, crucially, to actually consider the cartoons aesthetically as images: he rates each one on its aesthetic merits, using a "Fatwa Bomb Meter" system in which he assigns a high or low number of lit bomb icons to each image based on its success as a cartoon. Spiegelman concludes the essay by reprinting his own entry for an Iranian anti-Semitic cartoon contest, a reaction to the Danish cartoons, and several entries from Israel's own anti-Semitic cartoon contest.

The June 2006 issue of *Harper's* was censored by Canada's Chapters-Indigo bookstore chain—placing Spiegelman in the company of Adolf Hitler as one of very few authors censored by the chain, as one commentator pointed out.[10] Even more surprisingly, however, an academic institution, Yale University, decided to yank the *Jyllands-Posten* images from Jytte Klausen's then in-progress book *The Cartoons That Shook the World*, published by Yale University Press. Klausen, a professor at Brandeis, reluctantly agreed to go ahead with publication without images, but she refused to sign a confidentiality agreement that forbade her from discussing a document revealing the decision making behind Yale's choice.[11] The *New York Times* broke the story, which became a widely circulating news item; Yale drew ire from organizations such as the Foundation for Individual Rights in

Education, which published an angry open letter to President Richard C. Levin. The former commissioning editor of the book at Yale University Press, now the director of the YIVO Institute for Jewish Research, recently noted that the Press had faced pressure from the administration; in December 2014 media figure Fareed Zakaria wrote that he "deeply regretted" writing a statement at the time in favor of the redaction.[12]

In the wake of the *Charlie Hebdo* attacks, one again found Sacco and Spiegelman, two major voices in matters of the circulation of images and picturing history, to be divided. Sacco's most recent book, from the fall of 2014, is *Bumf*, an exceptionally dark work of surreal satire that takes stock of the seemingly unending Vietnam-to-Iraq cycle of American deception and violent power-mongering. The cover spotlights a drawing of Richard Nixon, with a long phallic nose à la Guston's *Poor Richard*, and two speech balloons announcing, "My name is Barack Obama . . . [a]nd I approve this message." A hooded figure in a suit and tie walks toward the foreground, clutching a headstone in either hand each inscribed with a series of numbers and the status "classified." Buildings resembling the World Trade Center explode in the background. In *Bumf*, heavily inspired by Vietnam, Sacco draws his satirical characters within the panels of his own drawings of famous Vietnam war photos, such as Eddie Adams's "General Nguyen Ngoc Loan Executing a Viet Cong Prisoner in Saigon" (1968) and Nick Ut's "Napalm Girl" (1972). His comics response to the *Charlie Hebdo* attacks, "On Satire," also remediates a notorious image from a more recent war, that of a hooded and wired prisoner forced to balance on top of a box—a photograph that became symbolic of American torture.

Noah Feldman has suggested that al-Qaeda, in organizing an "old-school" international-headline attack (unlike the sovereignty-creating jihadism enacted by the Islamic State in Syria and Iraq), was likely "simply looking for a media target in a Western capital," and Paris's satirical, eager-to-offend *Charlie Hebdo* offered a convenient reason on top of the fact that "the rest of the media can be counted upon to comment on the attack on one of their own."[13] Regardless of the particular motivation of the attackers and the organization that funded them, the presumptive attack on the freedom to circulate images, in particular, gave rise to impassioned responses about hand-drawn imagery from its makers. "On Satire," a dense one-pager that also offers Sacco's own self-consciously "offensive" drawings of a black man eating a banana and a Jewish man counting money, opens with a panel in which Sacco states that his first reaction was not a defiant reaffirmation of the principles of free speech but simply sadness. He expresses a concern about the kinds of images *Charlie Hebdo*—which began as a magazine called *Hara Kiri* in 1960—publishes, especially of Muslims. "When we draw a line we are often crossing one, because lines on paper are a weapon," he writes, in a panel in which he draws himself directly addressing readers. Spiegelman, on the other hand, while not an admirer of each and every *Charlie Hebdo* cartoon, has again come out strongly as a defender of the right to insult and has been a vociferous critic of the decision of American news outlets to not reprint *Charlie Hebdo* images. He rejects as both philosophically incorrect and cowardly newspapers' suggestions that verbal descriptions can be satisfactory substitutes for the images themselves. (Furthermore, as Spiegelman points out, newspapers asking readers to go to the Internet for the images are sounding their own obsolescence.) Images deliver us something words do not, however uncomfortable; that is part of their allure and danger.

The different positions of Sacco and Spiegelman, two of the most prominent voices in this field, demonstrate the trickiness—and importance—of issues around what can be said and shown. Yet it is indisputable that comics- and cartoon-making is on the rise, especially in the service of observation, documentation, and witness. The American digital magazine *Symbolia* was created in 2013 specifically as a venue for comics journalism; it joins the online Cartoon Movement, a global collaborative publishing platform for comics journalism and political cartoons, and other ventures.[14] In fall 2014, Al Jazeera America published its first graphic novella, a collaboration between reporter Michael Keller and Josh Neufeld, a cartoonist who in 2009 published a documentary graphic narrative about Hurricane Katrina. A sign of the actual strength of the field, its tooth, is its diversity of quality. Among the range, for example, of comics about 9/11, there is trenchant and transformative work, including rapid pen drawings by Gary Panter that he sketched in real time from his New York City rooftop on September 11, published interspersed with other daily sketches in his *Satiro-Plastic*, along with Spiegelman's dense and biting *In the Shadow of No Towers*.[15] And then there is also sentimentalizing work. *Maus* is no longer the only comics text about the Holocaust. It is now joined by a dozen or so other titles, from all over the world, but its ability to be abstract and precise, universal and particular through its visual animal metaphor lends the work a porous and controlled surface that saves it from what Spiegelman terms "Holokitsch"—a fate that belongs, for example, to the growing body of comics work about Anne Frank.[16]

The possibilities that word-and-image documentary opens up are today seized all over the globe. (Criticism has been attentive to this fact: the important twice-yearly *International Journal of Comic Art* was founded in 1999; recent comics studies titles include books such as *Transnational Perspectives on Graphic Narratives*.)[17] There are now many, many genres of nonfiction comics, including comics of witness. Drawing caught attention, among a range of available media technologies, for reporting during the Iraq War. The War brought artist-reporters conscious of the tradition into the public fold—including, among others, Sacco, for *Harper's*; Steve Mumford, whose *Baghdad Journal: An Artist in Occupied Iraq* is a richly colorful and detailed book of watercolor and drawings; and Dan Archer, a comics journalist who published the interactive webcomic "The Nisoor Square Shootings."[18] The *New York Times* published drawings made by Michael D. Fay, who had traveled to Afghanistan as an official Marine Corps artist and made drawings there from 2002 to 2005.

And Sacco is far from the only prominent comics voice publishing on the Middle East. Arabic-language comics are flourishing across a range of formats in many countries, chronicling contemporary lives. One sees this in Egypt's *TokTok* magazine and Lebanon's *Samandal* magazine, as well as in the work of Tunisian cartoonists Jorj Abu Mhayya, Z, and Nadia Khiari; Algerian cartoonist Ali Dilem; and Syrian cartoonist Ali Ferzat, whose hands were broken by Bashar al-Assad's militia.[19] Several important works by Middle Eastern cartoonists have now been translated into English, including Iranian Marjane Satrapi's international best seller *Persepolis*, first published in French in 2000, chronicling her childhood during the Iran-Iraq War. Encoding fascinating circuits of influence, *Persepolis* is as inspired by Persian miniatures as it is by German Expressionist film and Sacco's own comics. It is joined by Magdy El Shafee's *Metro: A Story of Cairo*; and Lamia Ziadé's *Bye Bye Babylon: Beirut 1975–1979*, a hybrid memoir of watercolor and text, among others. Afghanistan is the subject of two important graphic works, Emmanuel Guibert's *The Photographer: Into War-Torn Afghanistan with Doctors without Borders* and Ted Rall's *To Afghanistan and Back: A Graphic Travelogue*. In Israel, comics has grown exponentially in recent years with Actus, a comics collective founded in the mid-1990s with the explicit goal of international circulation—its most famous member, Rutu Modan, won acclaim for her graphic novels *Exit Wounds* and *The Property*. And Ari Folman's animated documentary film *Waltz with Bashir* (2008) was later published as graphic narrative, in an unusual film-to-comics adaptation.

Waltz with Bashir, delving into history and memory as they connect to the experiences of a young Israeli solider during the 1982 Lebanon War, including the Sabra and Shatila massacre, brought international attention to drawing as a documentary form. It inspired a timely special issue of the journal *Animation* on documentary—a genre the medium of comics has been steadily innovating for decades. Guest editor Jeffrey Skoller, introducing an essay on *Waltz with Bashir*, writes of how "the use of animation in the context of an historical event creates a Benjaminian dialectical image between 'mental ideas and optical representations'"—something Sacco's work creates throughout.[20] *Bashir*'s Folman is indeed indebted to Sacco: "Whenever I'm asked about animation that influences me," he told the *Associated Press*, "I would say it's more graphic novels. A tremendous influence on me has been Sacco's 'Palestine.' . . . His work quite simply reflects reality."[21] Folman's comment points to the motivating desire of much comics journalism, which highlights its own mediation, contradiction, and artifice in order to document and record. This is work that one can consider, perhaps, a frictive "'realism' of countervisuality," to use Mirzoeff's formulation, in which the observed and the abstract inhabit the page in order to produce new expressions of embodiment and location in the psychic or physical space of history.[22]

The form of comics is traveling so fast across the globe, including springing up in countries where long traditions have not been active, because of its connection to expressing conflict and trauma; several powerful works now exist, for instance, about the Rwandan genocide.[23] The immediacy of the drawn line, both for the maker and the viewer, communicates urgency, and suggests the intimacy—the embodiedness and the subjectivity—that the act of bearing witness to trauma unfurls. Lines on the page, in how they juxtapose time and space, convey the simultaneity of experience—the different competing registers—so often a feature of traumatic experience, such as the concomitant presence and absence of memory, consciousness, agency, and affect.

To conclude, I will very briefly discuss emblematic work in as yet uncharted formats. Phoebe Gloeckner's in-progress visual-verbal work about the hundreds (in some reports, thousands) of ongoing murders of young women in Ciudad Juárez, Mexico is one of the most compelling current works of experimental reportage. Gloeckner's project, *The Return of Maldoror*, involves a three-dimensional sculpting and modeling technique. The published form will be a combination of traditional print reading, and limited animation in an electronic book format (Gloeckner is interested in making bodies move—or in making it ambiguous whether a body might move, whether a person is alive or dead; a reader may be able to "animate" that person).

A trained medical illustrator, cartoonist, and art professor, Gloeckner first investigated Juárez with "La Tristeza," a contribution to the 2008 volume *I Live Here*, for Amnesty International. She is now completing a long work about the particular case of one murdered girl—for which she has visited Juárez upward of twenty times—that integrates drawing, photography, text, sculpture, and animation, mixing narrative forms and genres, such as traditional reporting with the photonovella. *The Return of Maldoror*, despite its code and genre mixing, especially around images, is a fully investigated work. "Although my research methods are not conventional . . . much of my [working] process is focused on pursuing fact and 'truth,' the fundament of my work," Gloeckner told me. In addition to on-the-ground investigation in Mexico, Gloeckner builds quarter-scale physical sets of Juárez in her Michigan studio that feature felted wool dolls with wire armatures that she poses for scenes to which she had no access when they unfolded— such as the actual murders. She builds the dolls so precisely that they have genitals, so that she can accurately pose scenes of rape.

"Inhabitation" is a key concept for the works this book treats. It focuses our attention on how people remember and reenact their own histories through drawing, and on how cartoonists endeavor to enter ethically into others' histories by materializing them on the page. It also describes graphic narrative's connection to worldmaking—its ability to create worlds on the page for its readers to inhabit. Visually representing space, and evoking and rendering space aesthetically though a series of stylized marks that constitute a narrative universe, graphic narrative produces worlds to be inhabited by the reader—it has a purchase on the formal constructions, especially spatiotemporal ones, that make up what Eric Hayot calls "the 'physics' of aesthetic worldedness."[24]

For Gloeckner, (re)building scenes from Juárez, creating them visually and three-dimensionally, allows her to inhabit the worlds about which she writes and draws ("Any world that you're making in a story, you kind of have to live in it," she says).[25] Her mix of media, styles, and codes, so much a part of the language of comics, here informs a new kind of word-and-image document: a testimony to the physicality and materiality of death, an attempt to re-create/resurrect bodies and subjectivities, even and especially expiring ones. A substantial part of her project is reporting, but she also imagines—and actually creates—scenes of death and murder, scenes for which no witnesses have testified, for which she (and we) then become witness to the specificity of another's death. In this form of documentary, Gloeckner seeks to picture the most private kinds of moments—murder—and make them public as an ethical proposition.

Comics of witness also circulate now more than ever online, often as a response to war or disaster. Comics has become a form of almost instantaneous dissemination and accessibility in addition to one serving long-term book projects such as Gloeckner's. Belal Khaled, a photojournalist and painter in Khan Younis, creates artwork he posts online that features drawings overlaid onto pictures of explosions from Israeli bombs; he began this practice in the summer of 2014, from the inside of the war, when art supplies were scarce, as did other artists with few other means to express what was happening.[26] Another recent example of comics's ability to depict history in close to real time is in Chinese cartoonist Coco Wang's drawn documentary webcomics that she calls, simply, "earthquake strips"—dispatches from China's May 12, 2008, Sichuan earthquake, in which almost 70,000 people were recorded dead, with thousands upon thousands of others missing or injured. Unlike a long-term reporting project, the very quickness of these drawn accounts sparked attention and reveals drawing's immediacy.

Wang posted twelve earthquake strips on her blog, one a day starting on May 17. They instantly became an Internet phenomenon, as people followed each day's reporting installment. There is an urgency to Wang's witnessing of China's devastating earthquake: anecdotes, sensibilities, images seared into the brain. The strips, in a spare graphic style, use only red, white, and black; they tell stories of ordinary people—some in very grave circumstances—covering details of daily life, including survival and death. Wang participated in the 2008 exhibition "Manhua! China Comics Now" in London, which was part of Britain's China Now festival and the first of its kind in the country. As comics scholar Paul Gravett reports, she is "an ambassador for her upcoming generation of experimental, underground Chinese comics creators," publishing in collectives like *Special Comics* and

Cult Youth. Wang, as Gravett notes, also edited, translated, published, and contributed to an impressive anthology of these cutting-edge innovators' stories entitled *Freedom.*[27]

The comics medium has evolved as an instrument for commenting on and re-visioning experience and history. Drawing today still enters the public sphere as a form of witness that takes shape as marks and lines because no other technology could record what it depicts. In February 2014 the United Nations released its report on human rights in North Korea that contained drawings documenting the brutal experiences of an escaped political prisoner, Kim Gwang-Il; these became a subject of much debate and commentary. That Wang's strips circulated so quickly and widely is a testament not only to the Internet but also to the undimmed force of the hand-drawn image.

NOTES

INTRODUCTION

Epigraph: From Norman Mailer, *Cannibals and Christians* (New York: Dial Press, 1966). By permission of the Estate of Norman Mailer. All rights reserved.

1. Reprinted in Art Spiegelman, *MetaMaus* (New York: Pantheon, 2011), 150.

2. The 1986 nomination of *Maus I* for a National Book Critics Circle Award in the category of biography was a field-shifting moment for two reasons: first, the seriousness that was accorded a graphic narrative; second, its inclusion in a nonfiction category. Elizabeth Hardwick, one of the jurors, famously was contemptuous. In a remembrance of her written by her fellow juror Mark Feeney, he recalls her negative vote: "'You mean we're going to give this award to a book about a . . . mouse?" See Mark Feeney, "The Honey and the Chisel," *Boston Globe*, December 5, 2007.

3. Lynne Huffer, "'There Is No Gomorrah': Narrative Ethics in Feminist and Queer Theory," *differences: A Journal of Feminist Cultural Studies* 12, no. 3 (2001): 4.

4. See Rosalind Krauss, *Perpetual Inventory* (Cambridge, MA: MIT Press, 2010), and Krauss, *"A Voyage on the North Sea": Art in the Age of the Post-Medium Condition* (London: Thames and Hudson, 1999).

5. See Martin Randall, *9/11 and the Literature of Terror* (Edinburgh: Edinburgh University Press, 2011). Randall specifically attributes this to a word-and-image problem: documentary images versus fictional prose.

6. The Op-Doc series, featuring short-form films by Errol Morris, Jessica Yu, and others, began running in the *New York Times* in 2011. See www.nytimes .com/ref/opinion/about-op-docs.html. Another genre, documentary theater, a fact-based theatrical genre, has developed over the course of the twentieth century, and has been popularized by plays such as Jessica Blank and Erik Jensen's *The Exonerated* (2002). See Alison Forsyth and Chris Megson, eds., *Get Real: Documentary Theatre Past and Present* (New York: Palgrave Macmillan, 2009); Jacqueline O'Connor, *Documentary Trial Plays in Contemporary American Theater* (Carbondale: Southern Illinois University Press, 2013).

7. By "sustained" I mean both assessing contemporary work and placing its practices within a meaningful tradition, or revision, of documentary practice. There are two proximate studies: Joseph Witek's pioneering *Comic Books as History: The Narrative Art of Jack Jackson, Art Spiegelman, and Harvey Pekar* (Jackson: University Press of Mississippi, 1989), a classic in the field of comics studies, and Jeff Adams's *Documentary Graphic Novels and Social Realism* (New York: Peter Lang, 2008). Although both works treat some of the same cartoonists I do, neither specifically treats the connection of witnessing and documentary form in comics, or the histories of witnessing in words and images that I do here.

8. Invisibility can be enforced in two different ways: a culture of censorship, and trauma theory's focus on the unrepresentable. We have seen an increase in the culture of censorship in the United States since 9/11 and the Iraq War. For "risk of representation," see Hillary L. Chute, *Graphic Women: Life Narrative and Contemporary Comics* (New York: Columbia University Press, 2010), 3.

9. Despite the numerous studies on trauma and visuality, there has been no book-length work focusing on comics in this context—though there are numerous books on, say, trauma and photography. See, for example, Ariella Azoulay, *Death's Showcase: The Power of the Image in Contemporary Democracy* (Cambridge, MA: MIT Press, 2001); Ulrich Baer, *Spectral Evidence: The Photography of Trauma* (Cambridge, MA: MIT Press, 2002); Susie Linfield, *The Cruel Radiance* (Chicago: University of Chicago Press, 2010), titled after a phrase from *Let Us Now Praise Famous Men*; Nancy K. Miller, Geoffrey Batchen, Jay Prosser, and Mark Gidley, *Picturing Atrocity* (London:

Reaktion, 2012); and Mark Reinhardt, Holly Edwards, and Erina Duganne, *Beautiful Suffering: Photography and the Traffic in Pain* (Williamstown, MA: Williams College Museum of Art, 2007).

10. While this book is interested in tracking circuits of influence, especially those motivated by war, as in the case of the American occupation of Japan and the resultant comics culture, I am not proposing comics as a form parallel to what has come to be known, contestedly, as "world literature." For more on "world literature" debates, see Emily Apter, *Against World Literature: On the Politics of Untranslatability* (New York: Verso, 2003); David Damrosch, *What Is World Literature?* (Princeton: Princeton University Press, 2003).

11. Keiji Nakazawa, *I Saw It: The Atomic Bombing of Hiroshima: A Survivor's True Story* (San Francisco: EduComics, 1982); Art Spiegelman, "Maus," in *Funny Aminals*, ed. Justin Green (San Francisco: Apex Novelties, 1972). For an account of Japan's involvement in the Vietnam War, see Thomas R. H. Havens, *Fire across the Sea: The Vietnam War and Japan 1965–1975* (Princeton: Princeton University Press, 1987).

12. Michael Herr, *Dispatches* (New York: Knopf, 1977), 61, 214.

13. Michael Silverblatt, "The Cultural Relief of Art Spiegelman," *Tampa Review* 5 (Fall 1992): 36.

14. Lorraine Daston, "Marvelous Facts and Miraculous Evidence in Early Modern Europe," in *Questions of Evidence: Proof, Practice, and Persuasion across the Disciplines*, ed. James Chandler, Arnold I. Davidson, and Harry Harootunian (Chicago: University of Chicago Press, 1994), 243. Across fields in the twentieth century, the meaning of evidence has been shaped by critiques of the positivist tradition in the philosophy of science. See *Questions of Evidence*, particularly Daston's historicization of the "neutral facts" versus "enlisted evidence" schema, and her discussion of historical epistemology. Carlo Ginzburg, in "Checking the Evidence: The Judge and the Historian" in that volume, warns of the oversimplification of the relationship between evidence and reality—but also of the extreme antipositivism that is itself simplistic and turns out to be a sort of inverted positivism (294).

15. Lisa Gitelman, *Paper Knowledge: Toward a Media History of Documents* (Durham, NC: Duke University Press, 2014).

16. Stella Bruzzi, *New Documentary*, 2nd ed. (New York: Routledge, 2006); Michael Renov, *The Subject of Documentary* (Minneapolis: University of Minnesota Press, 2004); John Ellis, *Documentary: Witness and Self-Revelation*

(New York: Routledge, 2012). These books extend forward from a host of studies on documentary film, including Paul Rotha, *Documentary Film*, 3rd ed. (London: Faber and Faber, 1968); the oft-cited Bill Nichols, *Representing Reality* (Bloomington: Indiana University Press, 1991); Eric Barnouw, *Documentary: A History of the Non-Fiction Film*, 2nd ed. (New York: Oxford University Press, 1993); and Charles Warren, ed., *Beyond Document: Essays on Nonfiction Film* (Hanover, NH: University Press of New England, 1996), the last a volume based on a conference organized by Robert Gardner and Stanley Cavell.

17. William Stott, *Documentary Expression and Thirties America* (Chicago: University of Chicago Press, 1993).

18. More typical might be the breadth of two recent additions to the University of Minnesota Press's Visible Evidence series. Jane Blocker's *Seeing Witness: Visuality and the Ethics of Testimony* (Minneapolis: University of Minnesota Press, 2009), despite the framework implied by its broad title, is entirely about the fine art world (Ulay and Abramovic, Alfredo Jaar, and Eduardo Kac, among others); Leshu Torchin's *Creating the Witness: Documenting Genocide on Film, Video, and the Internet* (Minneapolis: University of Minnesota Press, 2012) is entirely about "screen media." The excellent special issue of *Animation* on documentary animation includes some minor attention to drawing. See *Animation* 6, no. 3 (2011), guest ed. Jeffrey Skoller.

19. Bruno Latour and Peter Weibel, eds., *Iconoclash: Beyond the Image Wars in Science, Religion, and Art* (Cambridge, MA: MIT Press, 2002), 7.

20. The debates about trauma and visuality over the past few decades—profuse even before the trauma of the highly spectacular 9/11 attacks—have largely ignored comics (notable exceptions include the work of Marianne Hirsch, Nancy K. Miller, and Michael Levine). Scholarship on this subject focuses primarily on the fine art world—or on popular photography and film, as in Shoshana Felman's focus on Lanzmann's *Shoah* and Cathy Caruth's focus on Duras and Resnais's *Hiroshima Mon Amour* in their well-known respective works: Shoshana Felman and Dori Laub, *Testimony: Crises of Witnessing in Literature, Psychoanalysis, and History* (New York: Routledge, 1992), and Cathy Caruth, *Unclaimed Experience: Trauma, Narrative, and History* (Baltimore: Johns Hopkins University Press, 1996). See Jill Bennett, *Empathic Vision: Affect, Trauma, and Contemporary Art* (Stanford, CA: Stanford University Press, 2005); Lisa Saltzman and Eric Rosenberg, *Trauma and Visuality in Modernity* (Lebanon, NH: Dartmouth College Press, 2006);

and Jane Blocker, *Seeing Witness: Visuality and the Ethics of Testimony* (Minneapolis: University of Minnesota Press, 2009).

21. For instance, Kate McLoughlin, in *Authoring War: The Literary Representation of War from the Iliad to Iraq* (Cambridge: Cambridge University Press, 2011), with a noncirculating context in mind, frames its history as such: "War representation is 12,000 years old, dating from at least the Mesolithic period (10,000–5,000 BCE) in the form of rock-paintings of battle scenes found in the Spanish Levant" (7).

22. William M. Ivins Jr., *Prints and Visual Communication* (Cambridge, MA: Harvard University Press, 1953), 31–32.

23. See Ulrich Keller, *The Ultimate Spectacle: A Visual History of the Crimean War* (Amsterdam: Gordon and Breach/Overseas Publishing Association, 2001), and John Stauffer, "The 'Terrible Reality' of the First Living Room Wars," in *War/Photography: Images of Armed Conflict and Its Aftermath*, ed. Anne Wilkes Tucker and Will Michels (New Haven, CT: Yale University Press, 2012), 80–91, the latter a thoroughly documented survey essay on visual representation of the Crimean and American Civil Wars.

24. Paul Hogarth, *The Artist as Reporter* (London: Studio Vista, 1967), 12.

25. In the early 1900s, cartoonists also did comics reporting on sports and politics—including George Herriman, who went on to win acclaim for his existentially inflected modernist comic strip *Krazy Kat* (1913–1944).

26. Joseph Campbell, *Getting It Wrong: Ten of the Greatest Misreported Stories in American Journalism* (Berkeley: University of California Press, 2012).

27. Collections include Michael Uslan, *America at War: The Best of DC War Comics* (New York: DC Comics, 1979), and, more recently, David Kendall, ed., *The Mammoth Book of Best War Comics* (New York: Carroll and Graf, 2007).

28. Ferenc Morton Szasz, *Atomic Comics: Cartoonists Confront the Nuclear World* (Reno: University of Nevada Press, 2012), 21, 38.

29. This is something we also see in prominent stories such as Harvey Kurtzman's dark 1952 "Corpse on the Imjin," about the Korean War, part of the EC war stories series *Two-Fisted Tales* (it also published *Frontline Combat*).

30. Miné Okubo, *Citizen 13660* (1946; repr., Seattle: University of Washington Press, 1983); Justin Green, *Binky Brown Meets the Holy Virgin Mary* (San

Francisco: Last Gasp, 1972); Paladij Osynka, *Auschwitz: Album of a Political Prisoner* (Munich: Osiris, 1946; also reprinted in Spiegelman, *MetaMaus*).

31. Marshall McLuhan, *Understanding Media* (Cambridge, MA: MIT Press, 1994), 161; Seymour Chatman, *Story and Discourse: Narrative Structure in Fiction and Film* (Ithaca, NY: Cornell University Press, 1978), 38. McLuhan addresses comics both in the chapter "The Print: How to Dig It" and in a stand-alone chapter on comics. He is aware that it may "contradict popular ideas . . . to point out that the comic books and TV as cool media involve the user, as maker and participant, a great deal" (161). Chatman, in a four-page section called "A Comic Strip Example," analyzes a ten-frame Sunday newspaper comic strip from 1970, *Short Ribs* by Frank O'Neal, which appeared in the *San Francisco Chronicle*. In Chatman's view, "reading out" is qualitatively different from ordinary reading, though so familiar as to seem natural (41).

32. Michael Auping, "Double Lines: A 'Stereo' Interview about Drawing with William Kentridge," in *William Kentridge: Five Themes*, ed. Mark Rosenthal (New Haven, CT: Yale University Press, 2009), 243.

33. See Hillary Chute, "'The Shadow of a Past Time': History and Graphic Representation in *Maus*," *Twentieth-Century Literature* 52, no. 2 (Summer 2006): 199–230, and Art Spiegelman, *Portrait of the Artist as Young %@&*!*, in the reissue of *Breakdowns* (New York: Pantheon, 2008), for further discussion.

34. W. J. T. Mitchell, *Cloning Terror: The War of Images, 9/11 to the Present* (Chicago: University of Chicago Press, 2011), 60.

35. Peter Galison and Lorraine Daston, *Objectivity* (Brooklyn: Zone Books, 2007), 382–383.

36. Alan Sheridan describes Lacan's Real in language apposite to the gutter: "the ineliminable residue of all articulation, the foreclosed element, which may be approached, but never grasped." Alan Sheridan, "Translator's Note," in Jacques Lacan, *Four Fundamental Concepts of Psychoanalysis*, ed. Jacques-Alan Miller (New York: Norton, 1978), 280. See also Chute, *Graphic Women*, 191.

37. See Hillary Chute, "*Ragtime, Kavalier and Clay*, and the Framing of Comics," *Mfs: Modern Fiction Studies* 54. no. 2 (Summer 2008): 268–301.

38. Bruzzi, *New Documentary*, 10.

39. However, while Hirsch sees that *Maus* accomplishes this in part through its incorporation of photography alongside drawing, in my view comics on its own, because of its gap-and-frame form, offers this "permeability." See Marianne Hirsch, "Family Pictures: *Maus*, Mourning, and Post-Memory," *Discourse* 15, no. 2 (Winter 1992–1993): 11, 8–9.

40. James Agee and Walker Evans, *Let Us Now Praise Famous Men* (1941; repr., New York: Mariner Books, 2001), 12. Other classic word-and-image photographic documentary texts of the period include Margaret Bourke-White and Erskine Caldwell, *You Have Seen Their Faces* (New York: Viking, 1937) and Richard Wright, with art direction by Edwin Rosskam, *12 Million Black Voices* (New York: Viking, 1941), which combines Wright's prose with photographs selected from Farm Security Administration files.

41. Gitelman, *Paper Knowledge*, 1.

42. Stott, *Documentary Expression and Thirties America*, xi.

43. John Berger, "Drawn to That Moment," in *Berger on Drawing* (Aghabullogue, Ireland: Occasional Press, 2005), 72; italics added.

44. John Grierson, "The Documentary Producer," *Cinema Quarterly* 2, no. 1 (1933): 8. Grierson, a British documentary film producer, is credited with first using the term *documentary* in its contemporary sense in a film review in 1926. He later wrote the essay "The Documentary Producer" in *Cinema Quarterly* in 1933, in which he offered his definition about creative treatment. Although Grierson's career was in film, he was not tied to the film iteration of documentary, even claiming, "The documentary idea is not basically a film idea at all" (quoted in Stott, *Documentary Expression and Thirties America*, 14). The *Oxford English Dictionary* dates *documentary* (from the French *documentaire*) to 1827, citing Bentham's phrase "documentary evidence" in *The Rationale of Judicial Evidence*.

45. Stott, *Documentary Expression and Thirties America*, 5, credits it simply as "a 1967 definition."

46. Ibid., 7.

47. Art Spiegelman speaking at New York University/New York Institute of the Humanities symposium "Second Thoughts on the Memory Industry," May 7, 2011.

48. André Bazin, "Ontology of the Photographic Image," in *What Is Cinema?*, trans. Timothy Barnard (1958; repr., Montreal: Caboose, 2009), 7.

49. For more on the epistemic virtue and rise of mechanical objectivity as a "*procedural* use of image technologies," see Galison and Daston, *Objectivity*, 121.

50. Bazin, "Ontology of the Photographic Image," 9.

51. See Daniel Morgan, "Rethinking Bazin: Ontology and Realist Aesthetics," *Critical Inquiry* 32 (Spring 2006): 443–481. Morgan offers an especially deft close reading of Bazin's denial of ontological distinction between image and object. Morgan's reading of Bazin underscores that "realism" is not a lack of style, as some read Bazin, but rather a process or mechanism. To the extent that Morgan highlights that "the nature of the medium becomes the basis for the artwork" (471), he and I arrive at the same place.

52. Bazin, "Ontology of the Photographic Image," 11.

53. Joel Snyder and Neil Walsh Allen, "Photography, Vision, and Representation," *Critical Inquiry* 2, no. 1 (Autumn 1975): 169.

54. Barthes's diagnosis: "From a phenomenological viewpoint, in the Photograph, the power of authentication exceeds the power of representation." Roland Barthes, *Camera Lucida: Reflections on Photography*, trans. Richard Howard (New York: Hill and Wang, 1981), 89.

55. Sontag laments that while the photographic image "cannot be simply a transparency of something that happened," a photograph is "supposed not to evoke, but to show. This is why photographs, unlike handmade images, can count as evidence." Susan Sontag, *Regarding the Pain of Others* (New York: Picador, 2003), 46–47. In the courtroom, the fascinating inverse of this is the fact that many legal proceedings are barred from being documented by mechanical means, such as film or photography, while courtroom sketches are allowed. In the United States, courtroom sketching goes back at least to the Salem witch trials; it is a genre made popular in France in the nineteenth century by figures such as Honoré Daumier. For a rejoinder to Sontag's discussion of "posing" photographs, particularly in the case of Roger Fenton, see Errol Morris, *Believing Is Seeing (Observations on the Mysteries of Photography)* (New York: Penguin 2011), and Ron Rosenbaum, "A Wilderness of Errol," *Smithsonian*, March 2012, 10–13.

56. Bazin, "Ontology of the Photographic Image," 10.

57. Berger, "Drawn to That Moment," 70.

58. John Berger, "Lobster and Three Fishes: A Dialogue between John and Yves Berger," in *Berger on Drawing* (Aghabullogue, Ireland: Occasional Press, 2005), 124.

59. Barthes, *Camera Lucida*, 91, 90.

60. See the Tate Museum's explanation of a "time-based medium" in "Conservation—Time-Based Media," www.tate.org.uk/about/our-work /conservation/time-based-media#art.

61. Tom Gunning, "The Art of Succession: Reading, Writing, and Watching Comics," *Comics and Media: A Critical Inquiry Book*, ed. Hillary Chute and Patrick Jagoda (Chicago: University of Chicago Press, 2014), 40.

62. Spiegelman, *MetaMaus*, 166. "Whatever is dramatic in a comic can be stopped with the blink of an eye," Spiegelman points out—a reader can choose when to disengage (170). For Sacco, film has the aspect of "fill[ing] the sight by force" that Barthes worries about with photography (Barthes, *Camera Lucida*, 91). Sacco also worries that the viewer's experience of film is fairly passive: "It's all there for you think about. Well, does the director mean this or that? You can have those little debates, but ultimately, your brain is sedentary in a certain sense and just sort of absorbs it" (telephone interview with Joe Sacco, June 29, 2005). For more on the connection/disconnection between comics and film, see Chute, *Graphic Women*, 8–9, and Hillary Chute, "Comics as Literature? Reading Graphic Narrative," *PMLA* 123, no. 2 (2008): 452–465.

63. Roland Barthes, "The Third Meaning," *Image-Music-Text*, trans. Stephen Heath (New York: Hill and Wang, 1977), 52–68.

64. Ibid., 62.

65. Ibid., 53. Unlike so-called obvious meaning, which is characterized by its clarity and is "*closed* in its evidence, held in a complete system of destination" (for instance, Barthes writes, in every Eisenstein film the obvious meaning is Revolution), the third, obtuse meaning is "one [meaning] 'too many,' the supplement that my intellection cannot succeed in absorbing, at once persistent and fleeting, smooth and elusive . . . greater than the pure, upright, secant, legal perpendicular of the narrative" (ibid., 54–55).

66. Ibid., 66.

67. Ibid.

68. Ibid., 55.

69. In Europe, as Mila Bongco, among others, has noted, "comics have long made broad inroads into highbrow culture, especially in France and Belgium and Germany where comics for adults have been published steadily. . . . Without having to go underground, French comics took on a highly critical sociological and political character in the 1960s and 1970s. University degrees on this topic may be had in France, Germany, Belgium, and Italy. . . . At the Sorbonne, comics as a distinct discipline was institutionally introduced by the Institut d'Art et d'Archéologie as early as 1972." Mila Bongco, *Reading Comics: Language, Culture, and the Concept of the Superhero in Comic Books* (New York: Garland, 2000), 13.

70. Michael Taussig, *I Swear I Saw This! Drawings in Fieldwork Notebooks, Namely My Own* (Chicago: University of Chicago Press, 2011), 11.

71. Ibid., 53.

72. Ibid., 34; see also esp. chap. 4. Taussig contrasts drawing to photography, asserting that a camera "gets in the way" between him and other people and that drawing is "even more magical than the much-acclaimed magic of photography" (25). In his attention to how people are encouraged to draw as children and find this same activity devalued as adults, Taussig's work rhymes with cartoonist Lynda Barry's recent books on child and adult drawing and the work of the hand. See Lynda Barry, *What It Is* (Montreal: Drawn and Quarterly, 2008); Barry, *Picture This: The Near-Sighted Monkey Book* (Montreal: Drawn and Quarterly, 2010); and Barry, "Car and Batman," *Comics and Media: A Critical Inquiry Book*, ed. Hillary Chute and Patrick Jagoda (Chicago: University of Chicago Press, 2014), 11–19.

73. Kentridge had a brief career as a political newspaper cartoonist for the *Rand Daily Mail* in 1985. See Sean O'Toole, "Cartooning No Fun for Kentridge," *Mail and Guardian*, February 25, 2011, http://mg.co.za/article/2011-02-25 -cartooning-no-fun-for-kentridge; Rosalind Krauss, "'The Rock': William Kentridge's Drawings for Projection," *October* 92 (Spring 2000): 3–35; Auping, "Double Lines."

74. For instance, Annette Wieviorka's highly informative *The Era of the Witness*, trans. Jared Stark (Ithaca, NY: Cornell University Press, 2006) tracks witnessing in many forms across the twentieth century, but not in drawing.

75. Krauss, "'The Rock,'" 25.

76. Walter Benjamin, "Painting, or Signs and Marks," in *Walter Benjamin: Selected Writings, 1913–1926*, ed. Marcus Bullock and Michael W. Jennings (Cambridge, MA: Belknap Press, 2004), 84.

77. Elaine Scarry, *The Body in Pain: The Making and Unmaking of the World* (New York: Oxford University Press, 1985), 281, 292. Scarry writes: "A material or verbal artifact is not an alive, sentient, percipient creature, and thus can neither itself experience discomfort or recognize discomfort in others. But though it cannot be sentiently aware of pain, it is in the essential fact of itself the objectification of *that awareness*; itself incapable of the act of perceiving, its design, its structure, *is the structure of a perception*" (289). It is important in Scarry's analysis that while we can note the presence of the body in the artifact, we can also note the making of human bodies into artifacts themselves (see Scarry's discussion of Marx, for instance, on 244). See also Benjamin, "Painting, or Signs and Marks."

78. Joshua Brown, "Of Mice and Memory," *Oral History Review* 16, no. 1 (Spring 1988): 98.

79. Kentridge, quoted in Auping, "Double Lines," 244; italics added.

80. Clark Coolidge and Philip Guston, *Baffling Means: Writings/Drawings by Clark Coolidge and Philip Guston* (Stockbridge, MA: o●blek editions, 1991), 13.

81. John Berger, "Janos Lavin's Diary," in *Berger on Drawing* (Aghabullogue, Ireland: Occasional Press, 2005), 102.

82. W. J. T. Mitchell, *What Do Pictures Want? The Lives and Loves of Images* (Chicago: University of Chicago Press, 2005), 59. See also J. Hillis Miller, *Illustration* (Cambridge, MA: Harvard University Press, 1992); Daniel Ferrer, "Genetic Criticism in the Wake of Barthes," in *Writing the Image after Roland Barthes*, ed. Jean-Michel Rabaté (Philadelphia: University of Pennsylvania Press, 1997), 221.

83. Mitchell, *What Do Pictures Want?*, 68.

84. Ibid., 63.

85. John Berger, "Distance and Drawing," in *Berger on Drawing* (Aghabullogue, Ireland: Occasional Press, 2005), 115.

86. Art Spiegelman, "Comics Are to Art What Yiddish Is to Language," *Forward*, July 12, 2002.

87. Kentridge, quoted in Auping, "Double Lines," 231.

88. Benjamin Buchloh, "Raymond Pettibon: Return to Disorder and Disfiguration," in *Raymond Pettibon: A Reader*, ed. Ann Temkin and Hamza Walker (Philadelphia: The Museum, 1998), 228.

89. Spiegelman, *MetaMaus*, 49.

90. Sontag, *Regarding the Pain of Others*, 24.

91. Ibid., 47, 46.

92. On the "impossibility" of witnessing, see, for instance, Primo Levi, *The Drowned and the Saved*, trans. Raymond Rosenthal (New York: Vintage, 1988), and Giorgio Agamben, *Remnants of Auschwitz: The Witness and the Archive*, trans. Daniel Heller-Roazen (New York: Zone Books, 2002).

93. Gilles Peress speaking at New York University/New York Institute of the Humanities symposium "Second Thoughts on the Memory Industry," May 7, 2011.

94. Wieviorka, *The Era of the Witness*, 88. However, as she notes, the practice of recording testimony became common after World War I.

95. For a discussion of Sacco's *Palestine* within the discourse of human rights, see Wendy Kozol, "Complicities of Witnessing in Joe Sacco's *Palestine*," *Theoretical Perspectives on Human Rights Literature* (New York: Routledge, 2012), 165–179. In her view, *Palestine* points the way toward "representational forms that engage with the challenge of viewing human rights crises" (167). She argues that Sacco provides "ethical spectatorship," in which "forms of representation . . . foreground the dialogic interactions between ethical looking and the role of spectacle in transnational visual witnessing of human rights crises" (166).

96. Daniel Loick's talk "Terribly Upright: Pathologies of Juridicism," Mahindra Humanities Center, Harvard University, February 14, 2013, and his discussion with me about "juridicism" and ethics helped me to clarify Sacco's work.

97. Taussig, *I Swear I Saw This*, 70.

98. Ibid., 89.

99. Berger, "Drawn to That Moment," 71.

100. Viktor Shklovsky, *Theory of Prose*, trans. Benjamin Sher (Normal, IL: Dalkey Archive Press, 1990).

101. Krauss, " 'The Rock,' " 35.

102. Kozol, "Complicities," 166. Kozol next considers the formal elements— through Joe Sacco's work—that structure what she calls "the witnessing gaze," which is mobilized by possibilities for "ethical spectatorship." See also Wendy Kozol, *Distant Wars Visible: The Ambivalence of Witnessing*

(Minneapolis: University of Minnesota Press, 2014), particularly "Skeptical Documents: Toward an Ethics of Spectatorship."

103. Jacques Rancière, *The Emancipated Spectator*, trans. Gregory Elliott (New York: Verso, 2009), 7; Sontag, *Regarding the Pain of Others*, 111.

104. Marcel Ophüls's 1971 documentary *The Sorrow and the Pity* also ranks among the most famous verbal-visual texts of World War II.

105. As Miriam Hansen points out in "*Schindler's List* Is Not *Shoah:* The Second Commandment, Popular Modernism, and Public Memory," *Critical Inquiry* 22 (Winter 1996): 300, a prominent criticism is "that it violates the taboo on representation *(Bilderverbot)*, that it tries to give an 'image of the unimaginable.'" "Image of the unimaginable" is Gertrud Koch's phrase, quoted in J. Hoberman et al., "*Schindler's List:* Myth, Movie and Memory," *Village Voice*, March 29, 1994, 25. In the same *Village Voice* piece, filmmaker Ken Jacobs criticizes "counterfeit-reality movies" such as *Schindler's List*, suggesting that horror would be more ethically represented with "obvious stand-ins for the real thing. Like [Spiegelman's] drawings of mice, alluding to, indicating, without attempting to represent." Agreeing with Jacobs, Spiegelman, a participant as well, suggests that transparently realistic representation (of traumatic history) offers itself unproblematically as voyeuristic entertainment (27). Spiegelman does not necessarily view realistically drawn comics as problematic, however; for instance, when he was comix editor of *Details* magazine, he commissioned Sacco's piece "The War Crime Trials" (1998).

106. Felman quoted in Claude Lanzmann, "The Obscenity of Understanding: An Evening with Claude Lanzmann," in *Trauma: Explorations in Memory*, ed. Cathy Caruth (Baltimore: Johns Hopkins University Press, 1995), 201.

107. Lanzmann, "The Obscenity of Understanding," 204. In contradistinction to Spiegelman and Sacco, both of whom are riveted in a literal, functional way to the project of understanding through what Sacco calls "visual questions," Lanzmann writes of the figure of blindness: "This blindness was for me the vital condition of creation. Blindness has to be understood here as the purest mode of looking, of the gaze, the only way not to turn away from a reality which is literally blinding" (204).

108. Caruth, *Unclaimed Experience*, 37; Andreas Huyssen, "Of Mice and Mimesis: Reading Spiegelman with Adorno," *New German Critique* 81 (Fall 2000): 67. Hansen, in "*Schindler's List* Is Not *Shoah*," uses the term "bank" to describe the deployment of images in *Schindler's List*. Gertrud Koch's view

in "'Against All Odds' or the Will to Survive: Moral Conclusions from Narrative Closure," *History and Memory* 9, no. 1 (Spring/Summer 1997), 399, is that "pictorial representations evoke special interest because they serve our need to unveil the unseen (including the past we were not a part of)."

109. For instance, high and low, art and kitsch, esoteric and popular, and—the terms that particularly interest Hansen—modernism and mass culture.

110. Hansen, "*Schindler's List* Is Not *Shoah*," 302.

111. Felman and Laub, *Testimony*, xv.

112. Ibid., 34. See Theodor Adorno, "After Auschwitz; Meditations on Metaphysics," *Negative Dialectics*, trans. E. B. Ashton (New York: Continuum, 2000), 300–318. One of Felman's crucial moves is to reject the putative inflexibility of Adorno's widely cited proclamation that "to write poetry after Auschwitz is barbaric" (Adorno, "Cultural Criticism and Society," in *Prisms*, trans. Samuel and Sherry Weber [Cambridge, MA: MIT Press, 1981], 33–34). Felman adopts this sticking point as an entryway into evaluating the political possibilities of form. She rightly believes this "has become itself (perhaps too readily) a cultural cliché, too hastily consumed and too hastily reduced to a summary dismissal."

113. Theodor Adorno, "Commitment," in *The Essential Frankfurt School Reader*, ed. Andrew Arato and Eike Gebhardt (New York: Continuum, 2000), 312. See also W. J. T. Mitchell, "The Commitment to Form; or, Still Crazy after All These Years," *PMLA* 18, no. 2 (March 2003): 321–325. Mitchell's belief, after the modernist moment of form, in "some new notion of form, and thus a new kind of formalism" (324) also addresses Adorno and, I believe, offers an account of form that itself in part accounts for recent interest in graphic narrative. See also Chute, "Comics as Literature?"

114. For a narratological take on comics's "space between," see Robyn Warhol, "The Space Between: A Narrative Approach to Alison Bechdel's *Fun Home*," *College Literature* 38, no. 3 (2011): 1–20.

115. Felman and Laub, *Testimony*, 5.

116. See Chute, "'The Shadow of a Past Time.'"

117. Taussig, *I Swear I Saw This*, 102.

118. Scott McCloud, "Scott McCloud: Understanding Comics," in *Comic Book Rebels: Conversations with Creators of the New Comics*, ed. Stanley Wiater and Stephen R. Bissette (New York: Fine, 1993), 13.

119. Taussig, *I Swear I Saw This*, 100.

120. Berger's "Drawn to That Moment" further points out that drawings offer space, in general, in a way painting does not: in the spaces in between the lines. In this way, drawing itself has a porousness that the gutter in comics amplifies. Thanks to Brian Rotman for first suggesting the connection to Bergson, and William Cheng and Stanley Tigerman for talking to me about gutters in music and architecture.

121. Krauss's description of Kentridge's drawings for projection, filtered through her reading of Deleuze, also provides an apt description for the movement indicated by the gutter. She writes of "a motion that is never *in* the moving subject but in the relay itself, in the space between two 'nows,' one appearing and one disappearing" ("'The Rock,'" 19).

122. Kentridge, quoted in Auping, "Double Lines," 239.

123. Ibid., 242.

124. Harold Bloom, "Get Lost. In Books," *New York Times*, September 5, 2009.

125. Gary Groth, "Art Spiegelman," *Comics Journal* 180 (1995): 61.

126. Marianne DeKoven, *A Different Language: Gertrude Stein's Experimental Writing* (Madison: University of Wisconsin Press, 1983), 5. "Though we can construe sensible meanings here and there," DeKoven also writes, "with varying degrees of readiness—for Joyce, Woolf, and Beckett we can even find ways, after serious thought, to interpret the whole passage coherently—these constructions can never account more than partially for the writing" (408). Paradigms for evaluating modernist experiment are useful to thinking about the extra-semantic quality of comics. See also Hillary Chute, "Graphic Narrative," in *The Routledge Companion to Experimental Literature*, ed. Brian McHale, Alison Gibbons, and Joe Bray (New York: Routledge, 2012), 407–420.

127. Joe Sacco, Chicago Creative Writing Workshop, University of Chicago, February 8, 2012.

128. On the idea of slow reading, see, for instance, Lindsay Waters, "Time for Reading," *Chronicle of Higher Education*, February 9, 2007; David Mikics, *Slow Reading in a Hurried Age* (Cambridge, MA: Harvard University Press, 2013); John Miedema, *Slow Reading* (Duluth, MN: Litwin Books, 2008); Leah Price, "The Medium Is Not the Message," *TLS*, January 2, 2014.

129. The structure of comics would seem to function against what Rosalind Krauss suggests about grids in art: that they largely "serve as a paradigm or model" for "the antinarrative, the antihistorical." See Krauss, "Grids," in *The Originality of the Avant-Garde and Other Modernist Myths* (Cambridge, MA: MIT Press, 1986), 22.

130. Art Spiegelman interview, New York Is Book Country event, Borders Stage, New York City, October 2, 2004.

131. This comment is applicable to the experience of watching film in a theater; it would exclude recent work on DVD or Internet video, which allows one to easily rewind, review, and transport her view and viewing apparatus. However, I still wish to underscore that the act of reading a book and turning its pages at one's own pace is discrete from the act of looking at a screen, even if one may stop and start at will.

132. Gary Groth, "Joe Sacco, Frontline Journalist: Why Sacco Went to Gorazde: Interview with Joe Sacco," *Comics Journal, Special Edition*, Winter 2002, 67.

133. Telephone interview with Joe Sacco, June 29, 2005.

134. Michael Rothberg, *Traumatic Realism: The Demands of Holocaust Representation* (Minneapolis: University of Minnesota Press, 2000), 2; Hayden White, "Historical Emplotment and the Problem of Truth," in *Probing the Limits of Representation: Nazism and the "Final Solution,"* ed. Saul Friedlander (Cambridge, MA: Harvard University Press, 1992), 42; italics added.

135. White, "Historical Emplotment," 41.

1. HISTORIES OF VISUAL WITNESS

Epigraph: Art Spiegelman, *MetaMaus* (New York: Pantheon, 2011), 100. Used by permission.

1. Alissa Rubin, "Horror Is a Constant, as Artists Depict War," *New York Times*, August 28, 2014; Janis Tomlinson, *Goya's War: Los Desastres de la Guerra* (Claremont, CA: Pomona College Museum of Art, 2013), 4. McCullin's Vietnam War photojournalism is the subject of John Berger's brief but important 1972 "Photographs of Agony," in *About Looking* (New York: Vintage, 1980), 41–44.

2. See Ellen Gamerman, "Goya's Pop-Culture Moment," *Wall Street Journal*, September 25, 2014, for a recent survey of fine artists inspired by Goya. See also Siri Hustvedt, *Living, Thinking, Looking: Essays* (New York: Picador,

2012), 329. For analysis on the Chapman brothers' aspirationally shocking responses to Goya, such as in the famous "Sensation" show, see Philip Shaw, "Abjection Sustained: Goya, the Chapman Brothers and the *Disasters of War*," *Art History* 26, no. 4 (2003): 479–504.

3. Robert Hughes quoted in Terry Zwigoff, dir., *Crumb*, Superior Pictures, 1994.

4. R. Crumb, "R. Crumb's Universe of Art," in *The R. Crumb Handbook*, ed. Peter Poplaski and R. Crumb (London: MQ Publications, 2005), 432; Françoise Mouly and Art Spiegelman, eds., *Read Yourself RAW* (New York: Pantheon, 1987). *Read Yourself RAW*'s contents page opens with a vertical list of dedications assembled by various *RAW* artists. Goya's name joins entries like "Every Russian Constructivist" and Kurt Schwitters.

5. See for example, Andrea Frisch, *The Invention of the Eyewitness: Witnessing and Testimony in Early Modern France* (Chapel Hill: University of North Carolina Press, 2004), which argues that "historical, political, social, and technological factors contributed to the slow, unsystematic emergence of the modern notion of eyewitness testimony as a monologic discourse of first-person experiential knowledge" (12).

6. Callot's pupil Abraham Bosse popularized the *échoppe* by writing about it in his 1645 *Traicté des Manieres de Graver*, the first "competent description" of the tools and techniques of etching. See William M. Ivins Jr., *Prints and Visual Communication* (Cambridge, MA: Harvard University Press, 1953), 16.

7. A. Hyatt Mayor, *Prints and People: A Social History of Printed Pictures* (New York: Metropolitan Museum of Art, 1971), n.p. [456].

8. Edwin de T. Bechtel, *Jacques Callot* (New York: George Braziller, 1955), 6. There is debate about whether Mahler misattributed the reference to Callot.

9. Theodore K. Rabb, *The Artist and the Warrior: Military History through the Eyes of the Masters* (New Haven, CT: Yale University Press, 2011), 83. This is connected, as Rabb suggests, with the rise of new kinds of warfare, including gunpowder.

10. Ibid., 96, 102. This study understands "documentary" as a more porous and potentially openly aesthetic category than Rabb's use of it in this context. Pieter Brueghel the Elder changed the spelling of his name in 1559 to Bruegel. I refer to him as Bruegel, but I will honor the spelling of critics I cite who refer to him as Brueghel when their ideas are under direct discussion.

11. See Antony Griffiths, "Callot: Miseries of War," in Antony Griffiths, Juliet Wilson-Bareau, and John Willett, *Disasters of War: Callot, Goya, Dix* (London: South Bank Centre, 1998), 12.

12. Ivins, *Prints and Visual Communication*, 73. This distinction is important, as Ivins points out. In writing about the influential Callot, he notes, "So few of the original prints by men who were not primarily painters are remembered."

13. Sarah B. Kirk and Britt Salvesen, *The Incisive Imagination: Jacques Callot and His Contemporaries* (Milwaukee: Milwaukee Art Museum, 2004), 20.

14. Mayor, *Prints and People*, n.p. [459–460].

15. On Callot's reported refusal—he is said to have claimed he would rather cut off his thumb—see Bechtel, *Jacques Callot*; Diane Wolfthal, "Jacques Callot's *Miseries of War*," *Art Bulletin* 59, no. 2 (1977): 222–233; Esther Averill, *Eyes on the World: The Story and Work of Jacques Callot* (New York: Funk and Wagnalls, 1969); and Katie Hornstein, "Just Violence: Jacques Callot's *Grandes Misères et Malheurs de la Guerre*," *Bulletin of the University of Michigan Museums of Art and Archaeology* 16 (2005): 29–48. Hornstein disputes the veracity of the refusal. On commission, Callot had previously created two large-scale, multiple-plate depictions of Louis XIII's military victories in La Rochelle and the Ile de Ré (see Hornstein, "Just Violence").

16. Griffiths, "Callot: Miseries of War," 16.

17. Tom Gunning, "The Art of Succession: Reading, Writing, and Watching Comics," *Comics and Media: A Critical Inquiry Book*, ed. Hillary Chute and Patrick Jagoda (Chicago: University of Chicago Press, 2014), 45.

18. After buying the booklet, the purchaser conventionally could either bind the sheets together between hard covers, potentially adding other small plates, or trim off the margins and paste each sheet into a blank collector's album. Very serious collectors, apparently, had sets printed before the verses were even added, thus ensuring that they owned one of the very first, and freshest, impressions taken from the copper plate. Griffiths, "Callot: Miseries of War," 13.

19. The book of reproductions edited by Howard Daniel, *Callot's Etchings: 338 Prints* (New York: Dover, 1974), is the only source I have encountered that prints English translations alongside each of the plates.

20. Wolfthal, "Jacques Callot's *Miseries of War*," 222. As Wolfthal points out, there is no proof for this attribution, although most Callot scholars agree with it. Marolles's huge collection (estimated at 123,000 engravings) is now

a major part of the Cabinet des Estampes in the Bibliothèque Nationale in Paris; Griffiths, "Callot: Miseries of War," 13.

21. The plates for the *Small Miseries of War* were discovered after Callot's death and published in 1635 by Israel Henriet.

22. This translates as "The Miseries and Misfortunes of War. Portrayed by Jacques Callot, Lorraine nobleman. And brought to light by Israel his friend. At Paris 1633 with privilege of the king."

23. For more on Henriet, see Averill, *Eyes on the World*. Paris was the only French-speaking location where the market for prints was large enough that Henriet could support himself (Griffiths, "Callot: Miseries of War," 13). The "king's privilege" was a copyright of sorts for which printmakers and publishers needed to apply, and which prevented others from copying or selling the image for a specific period of time (Kirk and Salvesen, *The Incisive Imagination*, 7).

24. Kirk and Salvesen, *The Incisive Imagination*, 20.

25. Wolfthal, "Jacques Callot's *Miseries of War*," 222.

26. See also Hornstein, "Just Violence," 44.

27. See Wolfthal, "Jacques Callot's *Miseries of War*," 233.

28. Hornstein, "Just Violence," 34. Hornstein's is the only essay of which I know in which any analysis of the verses plays a substantial role. She points out that when they are mentioned, which is rarely, it is usually to dismiss them as mediocre. However, she cites one scholar, Marie Richard, who praises the verse because it "does nothing" to detract from the etching, and also because it "testifies to the author's sensibility to the rhetoric of his era: stances, sonnets, odes, and hymns, found for example in the works of Charles Beys, Boisrobert or Chapelain."

29. Rabb, *The Artist and the Warrior*, 83.

30. Susan Sontag, *Regarding the Pain of Others* (New York: Picador, 2003), 43.

31. Paul Hogarth, *The Artist as Reporter* (London: Studio Vista, 1967), 9.

32. Hornstein, "Just Violence," 34.

33. Jed Perl, "Line Sublime: The Artist Who Raised Printmaking to Its Heights," *New Republic*, May 27, 2013, 51, 52.

34. Hornstein, "Just Violence," 37. See also Geoff Mortimer, *Eyewitness Accounts of the Thirty Years' War 1618–48* (New York: Palgrave, 2002).

35. Wolfthal, "Jacques Callot's *Miseries of War*," 224.

36. Hornstein, "Just Violence," 34–35. How much one ought to consider the images of *The Miseries of War* to be of historical record has long been a subject of debate. Hornstein, as many do, characterizes one of the values of the *Miseries* as its confounding of "the slippery divide between people who enact wartime violence and those who suffer from it," and she disputes the use of the series as an "indexical illustration" of harsh tactics employed by soldiers (33, 34).

37. See Wolfthal, "Jacques Callot's *Miseries of War*," 225.

38. Bechtel, *Jacques Callot*, 33.

39. Wolfthal, "Jacques Callot's *Miseries of War*," 223, 225; Perl, "Line Sublime," 52.

40. Hilliard Goldfarb, "Callot and the Miseries of War: The Artist, His Intentions, and His Context," in *Fatal Consequences: Callot, Goya, and the Horrors of War* (Hanover, NH: Hood Museum of Art and Dartmouth College, 1990), 18.

41. Wolfthal, "Jacques Callot's *Miseries of War*," 70.

42. Perl, "Line Sublime," 52.

43. Ibid., 54.

44. Averill, *Eyes on the World*, 1.

45. Robert Hughes, *Goya* (New York: Alfred A. Knopf, 2003), 7.

46. As Hughes notes, Goya did not have international fame in his lifetime. While he was not celebrated in France, the country where he died at age eighty-five, he was admired by Manet and Delacroix among others for his prints.

47. Language in this definition is from Randall Harrison's useful *The Cartoon: Communication to the Quick* (Beverly Hills, CA: Sage, 1981), 16.

48. See Hughes, *Goya*, 23, 128–129 for further discussion of Goya's exposure to Martínez's collection. Goya stayed with Martínez in Cadíz in 1792 when he was convalescing from an illness that resulted in his deafness.

49. Hughes, *Goya*, 216, 47.

50. Ibid., 255.

51. Thomas Crow, "Tensions of the Enlightenment: Goya," in Stephen Eisenman et al., *Nineteenth Century Art: A Critical History* (London: Thames and Hudson, 2011), 92.

52. The French Imperial Army employed Mamelukes, Egyptian mercenaries, who were also known for unrestrained vicious action in war. See Philip Hofer, "Introduction," in Francisco Goya, *The Disasters of War* (New York: Dover, 1967), 1; Juliet Wilson-Bareau, *Goya: Drawings from His Private Albums* (London: Hayward Gallery, 2001), 49; Crow, "Tensions of the Enlightenment," 94; and Hughes, *Goya*, 303–304, on Goya's motives for keeping the *Disasters* private.

53. Over the next four decades, as Tomlinson reports in *Goya's War* (110), the work was known only to a small group of collectors; Goya had pulled prints from various plates as artist's proofs, and these circulated in a very limited way. Tomlinson's account is useful; despite a large body of art historical criticism on Goya, few sources explain how the *Disasters* actually came to be published by the Royal Academy.

54. Tomlinson, *Goya's War*, 110.

55. Hughes, *Goya*, 304.

56. *The Sleep of Reason* is directly influenced, Hughes points out in *Goya* (73–74), by Giovanni Battista Tiepolo's title page image for *Scherzi di Fantasia*, which features owls surrounding an un-inscribed stone slab. Goya's print conspicuously fills in the empty space with words. See Sigmund Freud, "A Note upon the 'Mystic Writing Pad,'" *The Standard Edition of the Complete Psychological Works of Sigmund Freud*, trans. James Strachey in collaboration with Anna Freud (London: Hogarth Press, 1961), 19:227–232.

57. Amusingly, the curators of a 2014 Goya show at the Museum of Fine Arts in Boston chastely read this word-and-image painting as asserting that "only Goya was worthy of this commission" (Stephanie Stepanek, ed., *Goya: Order and Disorder* [Boston: Museum of Fine Arts, 2014], 11), while Hughes reads it as Goya's fantasy of the famously beautiful duchess's sexual desire for him (*Goya*, 162). Even two words can set into play many ambiguous meanings. And Manuela B. Mena Marqués's analysis of Goya's inventive and shifting signatures demonstrates how he made it a self-conscious graphic element within an image; see her "Word and Image," in *Goya: Order and Disorder*, ed. Stephanie Stepanek (Boston: Museum of Fine Arts, 2014), 67–83.

58. Shaw, "Abjection Sustained," 485.

59. The actual execution of the captions for the published prints would have been done by a specialist at the Royal Academy, carefully mimicking Goya's placement and his style of handwriting. Juliet Wilson-Bareau, *Goya's Prints:*

The Tomás Harris Collection in the British Museum (London: Trustees of the British Museum, 1981), 49.

60. There are eight surviving sketchbooks. The collection of Goya's sketchbooks is Wilson-Bareau, *Goya: Drawings from His Private Albums*. While Wilson-Bareau gives the sketchbooks, or albums, descriptive titles, she works off of the system established by Eleanor Sayre of lettering the albums A-H.

61. For recent attention to cartoonists' sketchbooks, a staple of cartooning practice, see Steven Heller, *Comics Sketchbooks: The Private World of Today's Most Creative Talents* (London: Thames and Hudson, 2012), and Julia Rothman, *Drawn In* (Beverly, MA: Quarry Books, 2011). Hughes believes the idea of captioning must have come from the English caricatures Goya studied in Cadíz (*Goya*, 172–173). On Goya as a creator of sketchbooks, see Wilson-Bareau, *Goya: Drawings from His Private Albums*, 11–12. Wilson-Bareau notes that it is unknown why or when he "had the idea of making drawings in a bound album," but it was not a Spanish custom. Goya had acquired a pocket notebook in Italy in 1770 or 1771, and started a sketchbook again at the age of fifty, in 1796, "[beginning] an entirely original artistic practice" (11).

62. Alison Sinclair, "Disasters of War: Image and Experience in Spain," in *The Violent Muse: Violence and the Artistic Imagination in Europe, 1910–1939*, ed. Jana Howlett and Rod Mengham (Manchester: Manchester University Press, 1994), 78.

63. Hughes, *Goya*, 216.

64. Ibid., 272, 273.

65. See Janis A. Tomlinson, *Francisco Goya y Lucientes, 1746–1828* (London: Phaidon, 1994), 193. As Hofer sums it up, "We believe many of the *Desastres* subjects were really seen by him, others depicted from eye witness accounts" ("Introduction," 2).

66. Hughes, *Goya*, 255.

67. Goya also produced two paintings depicting munitions manufacture from his trip to Zaragoza.

68. Sontag, *Regarding the Pain of Others*, 45.

69. In a different context, scholars have written about this dynamic in spectacle lynching in the United States. See Jacqueline Goldsby, *A Spectacular Secret: Lynching in American Life and Literature* (Chicago: University of

Chicago Press, 2006); Dora Apel and Shawn Michelle Smith, *Lynching Photographs* (Berkeley: University of California Press, 2007).

70. Joe Sacco, Chicago Creative Writing Workshop, University of Chicago, February 8, 2012.

71. In my reading, Callot's "Scene of a Pillage," plate 4, offers a similar visual technique that may have influenced Goya.

72. *Witches in the Air* was a commission for the Duke and Duchess Osuna, a family with whom Goya was close. Such fantastical subjects were often desired by *ilustrados*—Spain's Enlightenment intellectuals. Hughes notes that part of the resonance of this image in late eighteenth-century Spain "would have been a reminder of a primary Christian image, the Resurrection of Christ, which it morally inverts—the men are on the ground, refusing to see a diabolic event, being the equivalent of the sleeping tomb guardians in a Resurrection, who have failed to witness one" (*Goya*, 155).

73. See Hughes, *Goya*, 293 for an explanation of the ambiguity of this image.

74. See ibid., 289 for a discussion of "remedy" and the *Disasters*.

75. Ibid., 176.

76. Sontag, *Regarding the Pain of Others*, 44.

77. Henry Vizetelly helped to develop the illustrated newspaper as a venue for actual visual reporting, particularly after the huge success of the paper's first use of artists to make reportorial drawings of the state visit of Queen Victoria to Scotland in 1841; Hogarth, *The Artist as Reporter*, 16. The *Illustrated London News* sought to be distinct from "penny dreadfuls," which offered special illustrated editions devoted to sensational crimes. See Christopher Hibbert, *The Illustrated London News: Social History of Victorian Britain* (London: Angus and Robertson, 1975) for a useful history of the paper; for analyses of illustrated periodicals vis-à-vis constructing nations, see Peter W. Sinnema, *Dynamics of the Pictured Page: Representing the Nation in the Illustrated London News* (Brookfield: Ashgate, 1998), and Michèle Martin, *Images at War: Illustrated Periodicals and Constructed Nations* (Toronto: University of Toronto Press, 2006). See also Celina Fox, *Graphic Journalism in England during the 1830s and 1840s* (New York: Garland, 1988).

78. Other important early pictorial papers include *Vsemirnaya Illyustratziya* in St. Petersburg in 1868 and *Graphic* in London in 1869. Joe Sacco, "Down! Up! You're in the Iraqi Army Now," *Harper's*, April 2007, 47–62.

79. Hogarth, *The Artist as Reporter*, 24.

80. Ibid., 26.

81. John Stauffer, "The 'Terrible Reality' of the First Living Room Wars," in *War/Photography: Images of Armed Conflict and Its Aftermath*, ed. Anne Wilkes Tucker and Will Michels (New Haven, CT: Yale University Press, 2012), 81. Stauffer calls the Crimean War (1853–1856) and the Civil War (1861–1865) the "first living room wars," referring to Michael J. Arlen's 1966 famous term describing the televisual saturation of the Vietnam War.

82. On Fenton's photograph, see Errol Morris, *Believing Is Seeing (Observations on the Mysteries of Photography)* (New York: Penguin, 2011); Sontag, *Regarding the Pain of Others*; and Stauffer, "The 'Terrible Reality,'" among others,

83. See David Tatham, *Winslow Homer and the Pictorial Press* (Syracuse, NY: Syracuse University Press, 2003), and William P. Campbell, *The Civil War: A Centennial Exhibition of Eyewitness Drawings* (Washington, DC: National Gallery of Art, 1961). Homer executed a range of kinds of images of the Civil War. He started as a war correspondent in October 1861, embedded with the Army of the Potomac for *Harper's Weekly*.

84. See Alan Trachtenberg, *Reading American Photographs: Images as History, Mathew Brady to Walker Evans* (New York: Hill and Wang, 1989), 84.

85. For Civil War visual reporting, see William S. Thompson, *The Image of the War: The Pictorial Reporting of the American Civil War* (Baton Rouge: Louisiana State University Press, 1994). For an account of American antebellum pictorial journalism in venues such as *Harper's* and *Frank Leslie's*, see Joshua Brown, *Beyond the Lines: Pictorial Reporting, Everyday Life, and Crisis of Gilded Age America* (Berkeley: University of California Press, 2002).

86. Hogarth, *The Artist as Reporter*, 61. Titles include *Deadly Earnest* (1917), *Every Man His Own Football* (1919), *Adversary* (1919–1921), and *Bankruptcy* (1919–1924).

87. Antony Griffiths, Juliet Wilson-Bareau, and John Willett, *Disasters of War: Callot, Goya, Dix* (London: South Bank Centre, 1998).

88. As Thomas Compère-Morel notes, Dix's name is linked with German Expressionism, Impressionism, Cubism, Dadaism, and Neue Sachlichkeit (New Objectivity), but his originality across movements is linked to the discourse of war. Thomas Compère-Morel, "One against All," in Otto Dix, *Der Krieg* (Milan: 5 Continents Editions, 2003), 7.

89. However, a selection of twenty-four of the etchings priced much more cheaply sold well. See John Willett, "Dix: War," in Griffiths et al., *Disasters of War: Callot, Goya, Dix,* 65.

90. Willett, "Dix: War," 59; Philippe Dagen, "The Morality of Horror," in Otto Dix, *Der Krieg* (Milan: 5 Continents Editions, 2003), 18.

91. Dagen, "The Morality of Horror," 9.

92. *Fortune* magazine, which began in 1930, commissioned Walker and Agee's *Let Us Now Praise Famous Men* in 1936. Founder Henry Luce went on to relaunch *Life* magazine in 1936. Hogarth's *The Artist as Reporter* offers a thorough survey of *Fortune* and *Life* (72–80).

93. Many artists sketched on the spot while reporting, and subsequently developed their work into paintings, which were always reproduced in color. Painting portfolios usually ran as features of several pages every three or four issues. Hogarth, *The Artist as Reporter,* 74.

94. Ibid., 73.

95. Sontag, *Regarding the Pain of Others,* 24–25.

2. TIME, SPACE, AND PICTURE WRITING IN MODERN COMICS

Epigraph: Art Spiegelman, presentation of the lifetime Achievement Award to Will Eisner at the 2002 National Foundation for Jewish Culture awards gala. Used by permission.

1. Neither Darger nor Philip Guston, discussed at the end of this chapter, lived to see the works I discuss in print, although they are both now available (Darger's in bits and pieces). Not surprisingly, then, both are perhaps more associated with the fine art world (largely the realm of the singular object) than with the print world of comics, although both have produced enormously influential work for opening up comics vocabularies.

2. Quoted in Scott McCloud, *Understanding Comics: The Invisible Art* (New York: HarperCollins, 1993), 17. For more on Goethe, see Kunzle's detailed chapter "Töpffer" in his *The History of the Comic Strip,* vol. 2, *The Nineteenth Century* (Berkeley: University of California Press, 1990). Doug Wheeler, Robert L. Beerbohm, and Leonardo De Sá, in "Töpffer in America," *Comic Art* 3 (2003): 40, claim that Goethe's reflections on Töpffer were "known to the literate." However, Goethe's favorable impressions of Töpffer's picture-novels were not published until two years after Goethe's

death in 1832; Goethe's editor, Eckermann, and friend Frédéric Soret compiled these impressions into a long article, which was posthumously published in *Kunst und Alterthum*, the journal Goethe edited and co-wrote.

3. "Goethe thought that Töpffer's [*sic*] invention might spread out from the small circle of initiates it had already charmed and become a new mode of cultural reconciliation—a popular form that could make a big, anonymous society feel like a family." Adam Gopnik and Kirk Varnedoe, *High and Low: Modern Art Popular Culture* (New York: Museum of Modern Art, 1993), 153.

4. Kunzle, *The History of the Comic Strip*, 65.

5. David Kunzle, "Rodolphe Töpffer's Aesthetic Revolution," in *A Comics Studies Reader*, ed. Jeet Heer and Kent Worcester (Jackson: University Press of Mississippi, 2009), 22. Kunzle points to examples where Töpffer's frame further helps to establish the continuity between word and image, such as when the frame itself grows a skull, as in *M. Crépin*, or vocalizes the squealing of a cat in jagged lines, as in *Vieux Bois* (23, 22).

6. David Kunzle, *Rodolphe Töpffer: The Complete Comic Strips* (Jackson: University Press of Mississippi, 2007), xiv.

7. Kunzle, "Rodolphe Töpffer's Aesthetic Revolution," 22.

8. Thierry Smolderen, *The Origins of Comics: From William Hogarth to Winsor McCay*, trans. Bart Beaty and Nick Nguyen (Jackson: University Press of Mississippi, 2014), 28. Along these lines, Töpffer is often considered a modernist *avant la lettre*. See Kunzle, "Rodolphe Töpffer's Aesthetic Revolution." Jed Perl deems Töpffer part of the pre-history of Surrealism in "A Fine Line: Rodolphe Töpffer's Squiggles and Squibs," *Harper's*, July 2008, 83–87.

9. Chris Ware, "Strip Mind: Among Other Things, Rodolphe Töpffer Invented the Graphic Novel," *Bookforum*, April/May 2008, 45. The poster Ware drew was for "Comics: Philosophy and Practice," held in May 2012 at the University of Chicago.

10. Rodolphe Töpffer, *Enter: The Comics: Rodolphe Töpffer's Essay on Physiognomy and The True Story of Monsieur Crépin*, trans. and ed. E. Wiese (Lincoln: University of Nebraska Press, 1965), 5. In *Art and Illusion: A Study in the Psychology of Pictorial Representation* (Princeton: Princeton University Press, 1969), E. H. Gombrich discusses Töpffer's "Essay on Physiognomy" at length and comes up with what he calls "Töpffer's law" in his chapter on caricature: that people everywhere detect not only human faces, but also par-

ticularly "a definite character and expression . . . [to] be endowed with life, with a presence" (342).

11. Hillary Chute, "Art Spiegelman, Part 1: From Töpffer to Pulitzer to a 'Budding Cartoonist,'" *Print*, June 20, 2008, www.printmag.com/article/art _spiegelman_interview_part1.

12. This description is from Kunzle, *Rodolphe Töpffer: The Complete Comic Strips*, xiv. See also Kunzle, *Father of the Comic Strip: Rodolphe Töpffer* (Jackson: University Press of Mississippi, 2007), 78, which quotes Töpffer's own account of his process.

13. Kunzle, *Rodolphe Töpffer: The Complete Comic Strips*, 78.

14. See Töpffer's "Essay on Physiognomy," in *Enter: The Comics*, for an example of his commentary on Hogarth.

15. Stephen Burt, "Wonder Worlds," *Artforum* 52, no. 10 (Summer 2014): 316. Hogarth is a starting point in the view of theorists and cartoonists alike. See, for example, Smolderen, *The Origins of Comics*; Art Spiegelman, "Briefest Taste," in *Dangerous Drawings: Interviews with Comix and Graphix Artists*, ed. Andrea Juno (New York: Juno Books, 1997).

16. For a comparison of comics "shot" techniques with film camera techniques, see John Fell, *Film and the Narrative Tradition* (Berkeley: University of California Press, 1986). Fell focuses predominantly on McCay's work, arguing that film imitated McCay's *Little Nemo in Slumberland* strip. See also Spiegelman, "Briefest Taste," 28–31, on cross-cutting.

17. Spiegelman, "Briefest Taste," 31.

18. Kunzle, *The History of the Comic Strip*, 349.

19. This language is from a letter Goethe dictated to Soret, which he sent to Töpffer in January 1831. Quoted in Kunzle, *Father of the Comic Strip*, 52.

20. Tom Gunning, "The Art of Succession: Reading, Writing, and Watching Comics," *Comics and Media: A Critical Inquiry Book*, ed. Hillary Chute and Patrick Jagoda (Chicago: University of Chicago Press, 2014), 20.

21. John Carlin, in *Masters of American Comics*, ed. John Carlin, Paul Karasik, and Brian Walker (New Haven, CT: Yale University Press, 2006), 180.

22. See Ian Gordon, *Comic Strips and Consumer Culture 1890–1945* (New York: Smithsonian Institution Press, 1998); Bill Blackbeard and Martin Williams, *The Smithsonian Collection of Newspaper Comics* (New York: Smithsonian

Institution Press, 1977); Brian Walker, *The Comics: Before 1945* (New York: Abrams, 2004); Carlin, Karasik, and Walker, eds., *Masters of American Comics*; Judith O'Sullivan, *The Art of the Comic Strip* (College Park: University of Maryland Art Gallery, 1971); Albert Boime, "The Comic Stripped and Ash Canned: A Review Essay," *Art Journal*, 32, no. 1 (Autumn 1972): 21–25, 30.

23. The strip started in 1907 as *A. Mutt*.

24. Gopnik and Varnedoe, *High and Low*, 167.

25. *Dream of the Rarebit Fiend* appeared two to three times a week, and in a larger format on Saturdays.

26. Tim Blackmore, "McCay's McChanical Muse: Engineering Comic-Strip Dreams," *Journal of Popular Culture* 32, no. 1 (Summer 1998): 32–33.

27. McCay was fascinated by voracious consumption: in his 1921 animated film *The Pet*, a woman adopts a cute, small, non-species specified, generic pet (which looks somewhat like a bear or dog with elephant ears), names it Cutey, and then watches in increasing horror as it eats and grows, chomping up the table, the house, and the city before being shot down by planes, like King Kong roughly thirty years later.

28. André Breton, *Manifestoes of Surrealism*, trans. Richard Seaver and Helen R. Lane (Ann Arbor: University of Michigan Press, 1972), 26. There is a large discourse around comics, especially those by McCay and George Herriman, as protomodernist. For instance, Michael Kimmelman says that George Herriman's *Krazy Kat* "unfolds in a desert landscape whose surrealism . . . beat Surrealists to the punch" (Kimmelman, "See You in the Funny Papers," *New York Times*, October 13, 2006).

29. Carlin also notes: "Though most Americans were not fully aware of modern art until the Armory show in 1913, they had already seen the essence of modernism in McCay's works without knowing it. McCay utilized many of the hallmarks of modernism—figures in motion, twentieth-century machines, and modern urban architecture—in much the same way as later Cubist and Futurist painters" (*Masters of American Comics*, 27).

30. Scott Bukatman, "Comics and the Critique of Chronophotography, or 'He Never Knew When It Was Coming!,'" *Animation: An Interdisciplinary Journal* 1, no. 1 (2006): 83. See also Scott Bukatman, *The Poetics of Slumberland: Animating Spirits and the Animated Spirit* (Berkeley: University of California Press, 2012). McCay factors, too, in Bukatman's essay "Sculpture,

Stasis, the Comics, and *Hellboy*," *Comics and Media: A Critical Inquiry Book*, ed. Hillary Chute and Patrick Jagoda (Chicago: University of Chicago Press, 2014), 104–117.

31. The film, also known as the *Edison Kinetoscopic Record of a Sneeze*, was made as publicity to accompany an article in *Harper's* about the Kinetoscope. The Kinetoscope is an early motion picture exhibition device that created the illusion of movement by conveying a strip of perforated film bearing sequential images over a light source with a high-speed shutter.

32. Trains are one of the clearest signifiers of the machine age's conflict with the agrarian world.

33. Bukatman, "Comics and the Critique of Chronophotography," 101.

34. Marianne DeKoven, *Rich and Strange: Gender, History, Modernism* (Princeton: Princeton University Press, 1991), 25.

35. Gunning, "The Art of Succession," 21.

36. Fell, *Film and the Narrative Tradition*, 91.

37. Gunning, "The Art of Succession," 21.

38. Ibid., 26.

39. Stephen Best and Sharon Marcus, "Surface Reading: An Introduction," *Representations* 108, no. 1 (Fall 2009): 1–21.

40. McCay also used crayon and wash to create his images.

41. That McCay re-created events as told by survivors is reported by Annabelle Honess Roe, *Animated Documentary* (New York: Palgrave Macmillan, 2013), 4, among others, but details are few, such as whether this was through already published newspaper accounts or interviews he conducted.

42. Roe, *Animated Documentary*, 7.

43. John Canemaker, *Winsor McCay: His Life and Art*, rev. ed. (New York: Abrams, 2005), 195.

44. Daniel McKenna, "Impression and Expression: Rethinking the Animated Image through Winsor McCay," *Synpotique* 2, no. 2 (Fall 2013): 17.

45. *The Sinking of the Lusitania* is strongly, openly pro-America and anti-Germany; it even calls for "avenging" the deaths of the *Lusitania* civilians in one of its title cards. McCay publicly, perhaps bravely, broke with Hearst, his employer, in advocating U.S. involvement in the war. The notion of

"documentary," then, is clearly not one shaped by "objectivity" as a value. As Paul Wells describes the film in *Animation and America* (New Brunswick, NJ: Rutgers University Press, 2002), 34, there is "no sense of objectivity but there is an engagement with 'reality.'"

46. I disagree with Roe's notion (*Animated Documentary*, 8) that McCay makes no distinction between live action and animation in terms of ability to show reality; he actually underscores the different ontologies of media forms.

47. Today, the socialist wordless novel tradition is carried on by artists such as Eric Drooker, who has published two wordless novels (one received an American Book Award) and illustrated the poems of Allen Ginsberg. See Eric Drooker and Allen Ginsberg, *Illuminated Poems* (New York: Thunder's Mouth Press, 1996). Drooker claims that "Howl" was in part inspired by Lynd Ward's work from the 1930s. See "Eric Drooker Unmasked: An Interview by Chris Lanier," *Comics Journal* 253 (June 2003): 107.

48. Nückel's book *Destiny* appeared in America in 1930, published by Farrar and Rinehart; Patri's *White Collar*, about the Depression, was published in 1940. See Martin S. Cohen, "The Novel in Woodcuts: A Handbook," *Journal of Modern Literature* 6, no. 2 (April 1977): 171–195; David Beronä, *Wordless Books: The Original Graphic Novels* (New York: Abrams, 2008); Malcolm C. Salaman, *The Art of the Woodcut: Masterworks from the 1920s* (Mineola, NY: Dover, 2010); and George A. Walker, ed., *Graphic Witness: Four Wordless Graphic Novels* (Buffalo, NY: Firefly, 2007) for histories of major woodcut artists.

49. Eric Bulson, "Wordless Legacy," review of *Six Novels in Woodcuts* by Lynd Ward, *TLS*, December 16, 2011, 27.

50. Lynd Ward, *Storyteller without Words: The Wood Engravings of Lynd Ward with Text by the Artist* (New York: Abrams, 1974), 20.

51. Masereel, like Ward after him, also illustrated texts, including a 1967 German edition of Marx and Engels's *Manifesto of the Communist Party* (1967; repr., New York: International Publishers, 1983).

52. Mann quoted in Will Eisner, *Graphic Storytelling and Visual Narrative* (Tamarac, FL: Poorhouse Press, 1996), 1; Thomas Mann, "Introduction," trans. Joseph M. Bernstein, in Frans Masereel, *Passionate Journey: A Novel Told in 165 Woodcuts* (New York: Penguin, 1988).

53. Eisner, *Graphic Storytelling and Visual Narrative*, 141.

54. For a detailed discussion of the different panel sizes in *Vertigo*, see Michael Joseph, "Introduction," in *Vertigo: A Graphic Novel of the Great Depression—An Exhibition of the Original Woodblocks and Wood Engravings by Lynd Ward*, exhibit catalog, Special Collections and University Archives, Rutgers University, 27, 30.

55. Ibid., 29.

56. Ibid., 3.

57. As Joseph points out (ibid., 18), most depictions of a timepiece before the very end of the book are accompanied by an image of An Elderly Gentleman.

58. See ibid., 3, on Ward's "hypertextual strategy of reproducing particular images and homologous designs."

59. Ibid., 7.

60. Ward, *Storyteller without Words*, 204. Ward's further descriptions of the 1930s invoke a form of collective trauma: "In this extremity it was probably not surprising that the most sensitive and concerned young people seriously questioned the future they could look forward to and what would be the substance of their remaining years. Many also questioned the morality and wisdom of bringing children into a world that had already proved how many hazards it could provide for the newborn—how many varied fates it held in store for those who had the audacity to survive babyhood" (ibid., 192).

61. Eisner, *Graphic Storytelling and Visual Narrative*, 141.

62. Art Spiegelman, "Reading Pictures," in *Lynd Ward: Six Novels in Woodcuts* (New York: Library of America, 2010), 7.

63. Eisner, *Graphic Storytelling and Visual Narrative*, 141.

64. Joseph, "Introduction," 21, 3.

65. Ward quoted in Cohen, "The Novel in Woodcuts," 194.

66. Eisner, *Graphic Storytelling and Visual Narrative*, 141.

67. Henry Darger, "The Child Slave Rebellion," in *RAW: Required Reading for the Post-Literate*, ed. Françoise Mouly and Art Spiegelman (New York: Penguin Books, 1990), 174.

68. See http://folkartmuseum.org/darger; the museum also houses the Henry Darger Study Center.

69. See the discussion of Darger's "sequelating"—proposing continuation beyond would-be endings—in Michael Moon, *Darger's Resources* (Durham, NC: Duke University Press, 2012), 5–6.

70. Some of the paintings measure twelve feet in width; Darger drew and painted on large pieces of butcher paper glued together.

71. Moon, *Darger's Resources*, ix.

72. Henry Darger, *Art and Selected Writings*, ed. Michael Bonesteel (New York: Rizzoli, 2001), 43, 44.

73. Ibid., 47.

74. Moon, *Darger's Resources*, 12.

75. The crowded scene, with some victims in the trees, is evocative of Callot, with whom Darger may have been familiar. Moon points out that Darger, the son of a German immigrant, may have been aware of traditions relating to conveying the suffering of the Thirty Years' War.

76. Bradford Wright, *Comic Book Nation: The Transformation of Youth Culture in America* (Baltimore: Johns Hopkins University Press, 2001), 143.

77. Roger Sabin, *Adult Comics: An Introduction* (New York: Routledge, 1993), 154.

78. Michael Barrier and Martin Williams, eds., *The Smithsonian Book of Comic-Book Comics* (Washington, DC: Smithsonian Institution Press, 1981), 295, 296.

79. J. Hoberman, *Vulgar Modernism: Writing on Movies and Other Media* (Philadelphia: Temple University Press, 1991), 38. Kurtzman left the magazine in 1956. For a useful history of *Mad*, see Maria Reidelbach's *Completely Mad: A History of the Comic Book and Magazine* (Boston: Little, Brown, 1991).

80. Gopnik and Varnedoe, *High and Low*, 212.

81. Paul Buhle, *From the Lower East Side to Hollywood: Jews in American Popular Culture* (London: Verso, 2004), 195. Buhle has paid significant attention to the comics since the 1960s.

82. Tom De Haven, "The Comics: What a Novel Idea!," lecture, Rutgers University. New Brunswick, NJ, April 24, 2003.

83. Hoberman, *Vulgar Modernism*, 38. Hoberman calls vulgar modernism the "particular sensibility that is the vulgar equivalent of modernism itself," 33. He

writes, "I am not thinking so much of Pablo Picasso's interest in the *Katzen-jammer Kids,* Francis Picabia's affinity with Rube Goldberg . . . I mean a popular, ironic, somewhat dehumanized mode reflexively concerned with the specific properties of its medium or the conditions of its making. Conscious of its position in the history of (mass) culture, the sensibility to which I refer developed between 1940 and 1960 in such peripheral corners of the 'culture industry' as animated cartoons, comic books, early morning TV" (32–33).

84. Harvey Kurtzman, *The Comics Journal Library: Harvey Kurtzman: Interviews with the Pioneering Cartoonist* (Seattle: Fantagraphics, 2006), 109.

85. Quoted in Stephen E. Kercher, *Revel with a Cause: Liberal Satire in Postwar America* (Chicago: University of Chicago Press, 2006), 108.

86. Whereas Kurtzman, a writer-artist, often collaborated on his comic book stories, these were presented by him as the comics auteur. For more on Kurtzman, see Denis Kitchen and Paul Buhle, *The Art of Harvey Kurtzman: The Mad Genius of Comics* (New York: Abrams, 2009).

87. Gary Groth, "The Jules Feiffer Interview," *Comics Journal* 124 (1988), www.tcj.com/the-jules-feiffer-interview/6.

88. A 1960 short animated film version of *Munro,* which Feiffer wrote and storyboarded, won an Academy Award.

89. Hillary Chute, "Bookforum Talks with Jules Feiffer," *Bookforum,* September 2, 2013, www.bookforum.com/interview/12232.

90. Greg Hunter, "'It Was a Complete Revolution for Me': A Conversation with Jules Feiffer," *Comics Journal,* August 25, 2014, www.tcj.com/it-was-a-complete-revolution-for-me-a-conversation-with-jules-feiffer.

91. Bayard Rustin, "Foreword," in Jules Feiffer, *Feiffer on Civil Rights* (New York: Anti-Defamation League of B'nai B'rith, 1966), 8.

92. Kenneth Tynan, "Introduction by Kenneth Tynan," in Jules Feiffer, *Sick, Sick, Sick* (London: Collins, 1959).

93. Chute, "Bookforum Talks with Jules Feiffer."

94. Feiffer won the Pulitzer Prize in 1986 for his "editorial cartooning" in the *Voice.*

95. Chute, "Bookforum Talks with Jules Feiffer."

96. The result was the Comics Magazine Association of America Comics Code. See Amy Kiste Nyberg, *Seal of Approval: The History of the Comics Code*

(Jackson: University of Mississippi Press, 1998), the definitive book on the history and implementation of the code, and Wright, *Comic Book Nation*, chap. 6.

97. As Robert Fiore points out, no comic book—with the exception of those published by Dell, which printed Walt Disney titles—"stood a chance of being sold or distributed" without the Code Authority's seal of approval, and "the Code was universally despised by comics fans." Robert Fiore, "Comics for Beginners," in *The New Comics: Interviews from the Pages of The Comics Journal*, ed. Gary Groth and Robert Fiore (New York: Berkley Books, 1988), 5.

98. A rich body of literature exists on Wertham, a Vienna-born, left-leaning liberal with a psychiatric practice in Harlem who had testified in *Brown v. Board of Education* and was a passionate collector of art from Goya to John Heartfield, Lyonel Feininger, and George Grosz, figures revered by many contemporary cartoonists. See Gopnik and Varnedoe, *High and Low*; Martin Barker, "Frederic Wertham—the Sad Case of the Unhappy Humanist," in *Pulp Demons: International Dimensions of the Postwar Anti-Comics Campaign*, ed. John A. Lent (Madison, NJ: Fairleigh Dickinson University Press, 1999): 215–233; Gordon, *Comic Strips and Consumer Culture*; Bart Beaty, *Fredric Wertham and the Critique of Mass Culture* (Jackson: University Press of Mississippi, 2005); David Hajdu, *Ten-Cent Plague: The Great Comic-Book Scare and How It Changed America* (New York: Picador, 2008); Nyberg, *Seal of Approval*.

99. Art Spiegelman, "Intro," in Harvey Kurtzman, *Harvey Kurtzman's Jungle Book* (Princeton, WI: Kitchen Sink Press, 1988), ix.

100. Marc Leepson, "Doonesbury's Garry Trudeau," *VVA Veteran*, July/August 2010, www.vva.org/veteran/0606/trudeau.html.

101. Garry Trudeau, *But This War Had Such Promise* (New York: Holt, Rinehart, and Winston, 1973).

102. Reprinted in Patrick Rosenkranz, *Rebel Visions: The Underground Comix Revolution, 1963–1975* (Seattle: Fantagraphics, 2002), 212.

103. Terry Zwigoff, dir., *Crumb*, Superior Pictures, 1994.

104. *The Complete Zap*—including a new issue—was released in 2014 for $500 by Fantagraphics, and earned the history of *Zap* major retrospective features in venues such as the *New York Times* and the *Chicago Tribune*.

105. There are several detailed, fascinating histories of the underground comics movement. I offer my own brief account in Hillary L. Chute, *Graphic*

Women: Life Narrative and Contemporary Comics (New York: Columbia University Press, 2010), 13–26. See Rosenkranz, *Rebel Visions*; Dez Skinn, *Comix: The Underground Revolution* (New York: Thunder's Mouth Press, 2004); and Mark James Estren, *A History of Underground Comics* (Berkeley, CA: Ronin Press, 1993).

106. Art Spiegelman, "An Afterword," in *Breakdowns* (New York: Pantheon, 2008).

107. Ibid.

108. For more on comics as experimental and my reading of Crumb and Spiegelman, see Hillary Chute, "Graphic Narrative," in *The Routledge Companion to Experimental Literature*, ed. Brian McHale, Alison Gibbons, and Joe Bray (New York: Routledge, 2012), 407–420.

109. This issue also offers Spiegelman's "Ace Hole, Midget Detective," an eight-page riff on hard-boiled detective fiction completed in 1974, in which each character is drawn with a different implement.

110. Spiegelman offered his own analysis of "Don't Get Around Much Anymore" in "Guided Tour," first published in 1978. See "Don't Get Around Much Anymore: A Guided Tour," republished in Art Spiegelman, *From Maus to Now* to Maus to Now: *Comix, Essays, Graphics and Scraps* (Palermo: La Centrale dell'Arte, 1998), 7–9.

111. Spiegelman, "Briefest Taste," 8.

112. See Andrei Molotiu, *Abstract Comics: The Anthology, 1967–2009* (Seattle: Fantagraphics, 2009), for a recent take.

113. Quoted in Debra Bricker Balken, *Philip Guston's Poor Richard* (Chicago: University of Chicago Press, 2001).

114. Quoted in Arthur C. Danto, "Dick (Nixon) Heads," *The Nation*, October 1, 2001, 34.

115. Danto, "Dick (Nixon) Heads," 33.

116. Andrew Graham-Dixon, "A Maker of Worlds: The Later Paintings of Philip Guston," in *Philip Guston Retrospective* (Fort Worth, TX: Modern Art Museum of Fort Worth, 2003), 58.

117. Bill Berkson, "Pyramid and Shoe: Philip Guston and the Funnies," in *Philip Guston Retrospective* (Fort Worth, TX: Modern Art Museum of Fort Worth, 2003), 71.

118. As Berkson details, Crumb poked fun at the speculations of influence in an issue of *Weirdo* from 1983, where he directly copied Guston's famous "Cyclops heads" or bean-shaped heads on the front and back cover, with the tagline "A Fine Art Piece of Business (What Does It Mean?)." See Berkson, "Pyramid and Shoe," 70–71.

119. Balken, *Philip Guston's Poor Richard*, 98.

120. Philip Guston, "On the Nixon Drawings," in *Philip Guston: Collected Writings, Lectures, and Conversations*, ed. Clark Coolidge (Berkeley: University of California Press, 2011), 228.

3. *I SAW IT* AND THE WORK OF ATOMIC BOMB MANGA

Epigraph: William Kentridge, "The Artist's Voice: William Kentridge," at the ICA Boston, April 8, 2014. Used by permission.

1. Debates about images and suffering were at a pitch in 1972, as my colleague Deborah Nelson has pointed out, even removed from the explicit context of war. That was the year of the first major retrospective of the photographer Diane Arbus—which provoked Susan Sontag's harsh critique of its visual ethics—as well as John Berger's famous essay inspired by photographs of the Vietnam War, "Photographs of Agony," in *About Looking* (New York: Vintage, 1980).

2. See Michael Arlen, *The Living-Room War* (New York: Viking, 1969), which collects many essays on television and the Vietnam War. This concept is also satirized in titles such as *If You Don't Like the War, Switch the Damn Thing Off!* by foreign correspondent Jack Cahill (Don Mills, ON: Musson, 1980).

3. Eldad Nakar, "Framing Manga: On Narratives of the Second World War in Japanese Manga, 1957–1977," in *Japanese Visual Culture: Explorations in the World of Manga and Anime*, ed. Mark W. MacWilliams (Armonk: M. E. Sharpe, 2008), 196.

4. "We saw Vietnam as an element of the Cold War," Robert S. McNamara, the former secretary of defense, states simply in the documentary *The Fog of War*. "Not what they saw it as: a civil war." See Errol Morris, dir., *The Fog of War*, Sony Classics, 2003.

5. The concept of "mechanical objectivity," a "*procedural* use of image technologies" oriented away from the interpretive, is discussed in Peter Galison and Lorraine Daston, *Objectivity* (Brooklyn: Zone Books, 2007), 121.

6. Keiji Nakazawa, *Hiroshima: The Autobiography of Barefoot Gen*, ed. and trans. Richard H. Minear (New York: Rowman and Littlefield, 2010), 35.

7. See Adam L. Kern, *Manga from the Floating World: Comicbook Culture and the Kibyōshi of Edo Japan* (Cambridge, MA: Harvard East Asian Monographs, 2006), 12. His subject is *kibyōshi*, yellow-covered booklets containing visual-verbal narrative art central to the mid-Edo period. He argues this form is "one of the earliest if not *the* earliest comic books for adults in Japanese literary history" (11). Kern traces the use of the term *manga* to *kibyōshi* artist Santō Kyōden, and claims Hokusai, whom he knew, got the term from Kyōden. In any case, it was Hokusai, one of the world's most public faces of Japanese art, who popularized the term. For the complexities around Hokusai's various names, see Edmund de Goncourt, *Hokusai* (New York: Parkstone International, 2012), 9.

8. See Ronald Stewart, "Manga as Schism: Kitazawa Rakuten's Resistance to 'Old-Fashioned' Japan," in *Manga's Cultural Crossroads*, ed. Jaqueline Berndt and Bettina Kümmerling-Meibauer (New York: Routledge, 2013), 27–49, for use of the term *manga* in this context. On the earthquake, see also Gennifer Weisenfeld, *Imaging Disaster: Tokyo and the Visual Culture of Japan's Great Earthquake of 1923* (Berkeley: University of California Press, 2002). Sharon Kinsella discusses the emergence of short political comics and cartoons of the 1920s, especially those influenced by Marxism, in *Adult Manga: Culture and Power in Contemporary Japanese Society* (Honolulu: University of Hawai'i Press, 2000), 21–22.

9. However, there was didactic manga published in the run-up to the Pacific War and during wartime. Kinko Ito describes the anti-American and anti-British current affairs magazine *Manga* (first issue October 1940) and how manga artists were enlisted to draw pro-war manga, especially for leaflets, after the war began. Kinko Ito, "Manga in Japanese History," in *Japanese Visual Culture: Explorations in the World of Manga and Anime*, ed. Mark W. MacWilliams (Armonk: M. E. Sharpe, 2008), 34.

10. Nakar, "Framing Manga," 177–178. See also Tessa Morris-Suzuki, *The Past within Us: Media, Memory, History* (New York: Verso, 2005) on nonfictional historical postwar manga.

11. Tezuka's "Record," executed in a humorous, exaggerated style, features a protagonist with the author's name who has fanciful encounters with characters such as the "God of Manga." Tezuka (1928–1989) published further autobiography after Nakazawa's appeared, including *The Paper Fortress* (1974), about his experience during a firebombing in Osaka. Mizuki's longer work

about his time serving in the Imperial Army, *Onward toward Our Noble Deaths* (first published in Japan in 1973 as *Soin gyokusai seyo!*), is classified by its English-language publisher as "fictionalized memoir." The stories in Tatsumi's *Good-Bye* appeared in various publications, including Japanese *Playboy*, and were collected in 2008. While Tatsumi mentions in an interview that a character representing himself as a boy appears in *Good-Bye*, this character is unnamed and makes only a brief appearance (Adrian Tomine, "Q&A with Yoshihiro Tatsumi," in *Good-Bye*, trans. Yuji Oniki [Montreal: Drawn and Quarterly, 2008]). His first autobiographical work, *A Drifting Life*, was published in Japan in 2008 and was translated into English in 2009.

12. Generally, *gekiga* manga uses conventions that are more realistic than mainstream popular manga, and its subject matter tends toward the gritty and everyday. See Shige Suzuki, "Manga/Comics Studies from the Perspective of Science Fiction Research: Genre, Transmedia, and Transnationalism," in *Comics Worlds and the Worlds of Comics: Towards Scholarship on a Global Scale*, ed. Jaqueline Berndt (Kyoto: International Manga Research Center, Kyoto Seika University, 2010), 67–84. *Gekiga* as a genre was initially tied closely to manga rental bookstores *(kashihon-ya)*, which flourished in the postwar period, as a whole range of manga work outside of the major industry magazines could be borrowed for a modest fee. When the rental libraries waned, new avant-garde publications such as *Garo* (1964–2002) picked up the slack. *Garo* contributor Yoshiharu Tsuge, a cult figure in Japan, also published in Spiegelman and Mouly's *RAW* in the United States ("Red Flowers" in 1985, and "Oba's Electroplate Factory," published in the same issue with Henry Darger in 1990).

13. "The Tragedy of a Planet" was serialized in *Shukan Shōnen Jump* in August 1969. See Kenji Kajiya, "How Emotions Work: The Politics of Vision in Nakazawa Keiji's *Barefoot Gen*," in *Comics Worlds and the Worlds of Comics: Toward Scholarship on a Global Scale*, ed. Jaqueline Berndt (Kyoto: International Manga Research Center, Kyoto Seika University, 2010), 245–261, for a comparison of the perspective adopted by its frames as compared to *Barefoot Gen*. Kajiya sees that "tragedy" establishes more "objective," even allegorical views, while Nakazawa's work reveals what the protagonist witnessed.

14. For an applicable discussion of modes of self-presentation in Japanese novels, particularly the "I-novel," see Tomi Suzuki, *Narrating the Self: Fictions of Japanese Modernity* (Stanford, CA: Stanford University Press, 1996). One might consider the abovementioned works by Tezuka, Mizuki,

and Tatsumi to be *watakushi*, a genre mingling fiction and reality for self-exploration.

15. Shige Suzuki argues that the now stereotypical manga style popularized by Tezuka of drawing people with big eyes and a small mouth is possibly attributable to Disney: "the dominance of such a style is the product of cultural hybridity in Japan's modern and postwar period" ("Manga/Comics Studies," 72). See also Ryan Holmberg, "Tezuka Osamu and American Comics," *Comics Journal*, July 16, 2012, on Tezuka and Disney sources. For an overview of Tezuka, see Natsu Onoda Power, *God of Comics: Osamu Tezuka and the Creation of Post–World War II Manga* (Jackson: University Press of Mississippi, 2009).

16. See Rie Nii, "My Life: Interview with Keiji Nakazawa, Author of 'Barefoot Gen,'" Part 6, Hiroshima Peace Media Center, July 27, 2012, www .hiroshimapeacemedia.jp/?p=24128; Nakazawa, *Hiroshima*, 109. *Kamishibai* was at its height before World War II, in the 1930s; today it is almost extinct as an art form. In its frames and sequences, *kamishibai* has resonances with comics. See Eric Peter Nash, *Manga Kamishibai: The Art of Japanese Paper Theater* (New York: Abrams Comicarts, 2009).

17. See Faythe Levine and Sam Macon, eds., *Sign Painters* (New York: Princeton Architectural Press, 2013), which includes an interview with Green and a foreword by Ed Ruscha. Glenn Adamson points out in his introduction to that volume (18) that while the traditions of sign painting can be seen as in decline, they are still going strong in Latin America, West Africa, India, and China.

18. Nakazawa, *Hiroshima*, 147.

19. Nakazawa does not mince words. A recurring phrase in the autobiography indicating his disgust is that he "almost puked," as when a fellow manga artist tells Nakazawa his work is too cruel and shocking for children. "I was aghast and nearly puked," Nakazawa writes. "How can I associate with these worthless people?" (*Hiroshima*, 164).

20. Nakazawa, *Hiroshima*, 146–147. Also Rie Nii, "My Life: Interview with Keiji Nakazawa, Author of 'Barefoot Gen,'" Part 10, Hiroshima Peace Media Center, July 30, 2012, www.hiroshimapeacemedia.jp/?p=24161.

21. Nakazawa, *Hiroshima*, 147.

22. Alan Gleason, "The Keiji Nakazawa Interview," *Comics Journal* 256 (October 2003): 46.

23. Nakazawa, *Hiroshima*, 151.

24. Keiji Nakazawa, "A Note from the Author," in *Barefoot Gen, Vol. Two: The Day After*, trans. Project Gen (San Francisco: Last Gasp, 2004), n.p.

25. Herbert P. Bix, "Japan's Delayed Surrender: A Reinterpretation," in *Hiroshima in History and Memory*, ed. Michael J. Hogan (Cambridge: Cambridge University Press, 1996), 115. Censorship in occupied Japan, which included scientific and nonscientific material related to the bomb, has been written about widely; relevant titles include Monica Braw, *The Atomic Bomb Suppressed: American Censorship in Japan 1945–1949*, Lund Studies in International History (Malmö, Sweden: Liber International, 1986); Laura Hein and Mark Selden, eds., *Censoring History: Citizenship and Memory in Japan, Germany, and the United States* (Armonk: M. E. Sharpe, 2000); Laura Hein and Mark Selden, eds., *Living with the Bomb: American and Japanese Cultural Conflicts in the Nuclear Age* (Armonk: M. E. Sharpe, 1997). For censorship in the U.S. media specifically, see Jiyoon Lee's overview "A Veiled Truth: The U.S. Censorship of the Atomic Bomb," *Duke East Asia Nexus* 3, no. 1 (2011), and Robert Jay Lifton and Greg Mitchell, *Hiroshima in America: Fifty Years of Denial* (New York: Grosset/Putnam, 1995). Christine Hong discusses how the U.S. public was "carefully shielded in the early post-war years from graphic images of human ruin" and suggests that the "non-centrality" of Hiroshima in the U.S. imagination can be understood as connected to "the initial withholding of visual evidence of the bomb's horrific human impact." See Hong, "Flashforward Democracy: Exceptionalism and the Atomic Bomb in *Barefoot Gen*," *Comparative Literature Studies* 46, no. 1 (2009): 126. The Civil Censorship Detachment (CCD), established by the U.S. General Headquarters (GHQ), under the auspices of General Douglas MacArthur, started its work in September 1945.

26. See Gleason, "The Keiji Nakazawa Interview," 47. In Nakazawa's view, "It was a magazine that the PTAs and good parents of the world would likely target as bad, as 'dirty'" (*Hiroshima*, 155). See also Nii, "My Life," Part 10 ("I approached a publisher known for publishing erotica").

27. That Nakazawa created this genre is widely recognized, including by him: "In one week I completed *Pelted by Black Rain*, the first atomic bomb manga" (*Hiroshima*, 152). A limited number of manga about the consequences of the bomb were published before "Pelted by Black Rain," but not by survivors; these are surveyed in Masashi Ichiki, "Embracing the Victimhood: A History of the A-Bomb Manga in Japan," *International Journal of Asia Pacific Studies* 7, no. 3 (September 2011): 35–52. For instance, Sanpei Shirato's *The*

Vanishing Girl (1958) is about *hibakusha* and victimization. Ichiki points to the fact that Nakazawa's work was the first that actually used realities about the bomb and its consequences to reinvent genres and to innovate them, rather than to subsume "the bomb" as a plotline to existing formulas.

28. Nakazawa, *Hiroshima*, 155. In 1966, the same year Nakazawa drew "Pelted by Black Rain," Masuji Ibuse's novel *Black Rain*, a much less politicized work, was published in Japan and became a classic of "atomic bomb literature"; it remains Japan's best-known work of that genre. see John Whittier Treat, *Writing Ground Zero: Japanese Literature and the Atomic Bomb* (Chicago: University of Chicago Press, 1995), 261. *Black Rain* popularized the "Hiroshima maiden" theme. Takayuki Kawaguchi argues that Nakazawa's later *Barefoot Gen* is a form of resistance to turning the category of "A-bomb literature" into a genre in the victimized mode of *Black Rain*. See Kawaguchi, "*Barefoot Gen* and 'A-Bomb Literature': Re-recollecting the Nuclear Experience," trans. Nele Noppe, in *Comics Worlds and the Worlds of Comics: Toward Scholarship on a Global Scale*, ed. Jaqueline Berndt (Kyoto: International Manga Research Center, Kyoto Seika University, 2010), 234–245. See also Lisa Yoneyama, *Hiroshima Traces: Time, Space, and the Dialectics of Memory* (Berkeley: University of California Press, 1999), and Ryuko Kubota, "Memories of War: Exploring Victim-Victimizer Perspectives in Critical Content Based Instruction in Japanese," *L2 Journal* 4, no. 1 (2012): 37–57, on the feminization of victimhood (and the "victimizing" of femininity). See Treat, *Writing Ground Zero* for a lengthy discussion of Ibuse and an authoritative survey of atomic bomb literature.

29. The "black" series appeared in July 1968, August 1969, September 1969, and May 1970, respectively, all in *Manga Punch*, excepting the last, which was in *Manga Pocket Punch*.

30. See Yu Itō and Tomoyuki Omote, "*Barefoot Gen* in Japan: An Attempt at Media History," in *Reading Manga: Local and Global Perceptions of Japanese Comics*, ed. Jaqueline Berndt and Steffi Richter (Leipzig: Leipziger Universitätsverlag, 2006), 21–38, for a detailed media history of manga venues in the 1960s and 1970s. *Shōnen Jump* began as a biweekly in June 1968 and became a weekly in October 1969. The "peace" series by Nakazawa includes, among others, "Suddenly One Day," "Something's Up," and "Song of the Red Dragonfly."

31. Itō and Omote, "*Barefoot Gen* in Japan," 23, 24; Nakazawa, *Hiroshima*, 157. Nakazawa describes that "mail poured in virtually every day, from all over Japan. . . . No matter what the age group, more than half the letters spoke of

shock at the subject matter: 'The atomic bomb as you drew it in *Suddenly One Day*—is that fact? I didn't know that the atomic bomb caused such enormous destruction'" (*Hiroshima*, 157).

32. Rie Nii, "My Life: Interview with Keiji Nakazawa, Author of 'Barefoot Gen,'" Part 11. Hiroshima Peace Media Center. July 30, 2012. http://www.hiroshimapeacemedia.jp/?p=24168.

33. Nakazawa, *Hiroshima*, 158.

34. Titles include "Our Eternity," "Song of Departure," "Song of the Wooden Clappers," and "One Good Pitch." Nakazawa went on to create twenty-two separate manga titles about the atomic bomb during his career; see Ichiki, "Embracing the Victimhood."

35. This autobiographical series continued in *Boys' Jump Monthly* until August 1974, with five *mangaka* drawing stories. These include "I Must Hustle!" by Akio Chiba, "Lone-Wolf Manga General" by Hiroshi Motomiya, "Blue Kaleidoscope of Manga" by Shotaro Ishinomori, "That's a Gag!" by Fujio Akatsuka, and "Tale of the Ragged Studio" by Fujio Fujiko. Many of the contributing artists had experienced war, although this did not feature as largely as in Nakazawa's *I Saw It* (Itō and Omote, "*Barefoot Gen* in Japan," 25).

36. Thank you to Leonard Rifas for pointing out the importance of editors in this context.

37. Etymologically, *Ore Wa Mita* can mean both "I saw it" and "I was there." Most precisely, it means something that is a combination: "I was there and I saw it with my own eyes." Thank you to Julia Ortner for her explanation.

38. I cite this translation throughout the chapter. Thank you to Adam Kern and Ogi Fusami for facilitating a scan of the original Japanese black-and-white version. This version of *I Saw It* is collected in *Genbaku to inochi* (Tokyo: Kin-No-Hoshi Sha, 2013). *I Saw It* is also collected in English in *The Mammoth Book of Best War Comics*, ed. David Kendall (New York: Carroll and Graf, 2007), opening the volume as the first story of twenty-six. In his introduction to *I Saw It*, Kendall remarks that it is "credited as the first instance of comics being used to describe horrific factual events" (15).

39. John Hersey, *Hiroshima*, new ed. (New York: Vintage, 1989). The entire contents originally appeared as "Hiroshima" in the *New Yorker*, August 31, 1946.

40. EduComics publisher Leonard Rifas details this and other circumstances surrounding the American production of *I Saw It* in his fascinating "Glo-

balizing Comic Books from Below: How Manga Came to America," *International Journal of Comic Art* 6, no. 2 (Fall 2004): 138–171.

41. The most comprehensive sources for the publication/translation of *Gen* are Rifas, "Globalizing Comic Books from Below," and Berndt and Richter, eds., *Reading Manga* (and in that volume particularly Roger Sabin, "*Barefoot Gen* in the US and UK: Activist Comic, Graphic Novel, Manga," for English editions, and Itō and Omote, "*Barefoot Gen* in Japan," for Japanese serialization).

42. See Rifas, "Globalizing Comic Books from Below," and Crumb's endorsement on the *Gen* volumes published by Last Gasp.

43. Ferenc Morton Szasz, *Atomic Comics: Cartoonists Confront the Nuclear World* (Reno: University of Nevada Press, 2012), 114.

44. See Berndt and Richter, eds., *Reading Manga*, for *Gen* as a global text; see also Sabine Fiedler, "*Nudpieda Gen—Hadashi no Gen* in an International Speech Community," in that volume (59–76) on the Esperanto version.

45. See Susan Napier, *Anime: From* Akira *to* Princess Mononoke: *Experiencing Contemporary Japanese Animation* (New York: Palgrave, 2001) for an analysis favorably comparing the 1983 *Barefoot Gen* film with 1988's *Grave of the Fireflies*, Japan's other widely known anime about World War II. See Itō and Omote, "*Barefoot Gen* in Japan," for a discussion of the adoption of *Barefoot Gen* in schools. See also Thomas LaMarre, "Manga Bomb: Between the Lines of *Barefoot Gen*," in *Comics Worlds and the Worlds of Comics: Towards Scholarship on a Global Scale*, ed. Jaqueline Berndt (Kyoto: International Manga Research Center, Kyoto Seika University, 2010), 281.

46. Joichi Ito, "An Anniversary to Forget," *New York Times*, August 7, 2005.

47. See Kawaguchi, "*Barefoot Gen* and A-Bomb Literature," among others on this aspect. I disagree with Hong's argument in "Flashforward Democracy," although it is one of the few rigorous English-language essays on *Gen*, that the narrative "retroactively valorizes US Occupation pedagogy" (139).

48. Nakazawa, *Hiroshima*, 9.

49. LaMarre, "Manga Bomb," 302.

50. Inundated with complaints, the municipal government retracted the restriction after six months ("Widow of 'Barefoot Gen' Creator Says Manga Sends Positive Message," *Asahi Shimbun*, August 27, 2013). Keiji Nakazawa,

Barefoot Gen, Vol. Ten: Never Give Up, trans. Project Gen (San Francisco: Last Gasp, 2009).

51. Page numbers refer to the English-language translation published in 1982 by EduComics, although the comic book is actually unpaginated. The translators of the English-language edition flipped the order of the panels on each page to stay true to the narrative sequencing of the original work and to accommodate the Western convention of reading left to right across a page, although they did not flip the order of the images within the frames.

52. This insight is from José Alaniz, "Trauma and Disability in Comics," paper presented at the Comics Pedagogy Symposium, University of Oregon, Eugene, OR, October 24, 2014.

53. Yoneyama, *Hiroshima Traces*, 85.

54. Japan Broadcasting Corporation, ed., *Unforgettable Fire: Pictures Drawn by Atomic Bomb Survivors*, trans. World Friendship Center, Hiroshima (New York: Pantheon, 1977).

55. Nakar, "Framing Manga," 184.

56. *The Hiroshima Panels*, minus "Nagasaki," which is permanently exhibited in that city, have a dedicated gallery in Tokyo, the Maruki Gallery. See http://www.aya.or.jp/~marukimsn/english/indexE.htm. See Kyo Maclear's chapter on *The Hiroshima Panels*, "Witnessing Otherwise," in her *Beclouded Visions: Hiroshima-Nagasaki and the Art of Witness* (Albany: SUNY Press, 1998), particularly on their use of the human figure.

57. Mark Vallen, "The Hiroshima Panels," *Art for a Change: Events, Theory, Commentary* (blog), August 6, 2005, http://art-for-a-change.com/blog/2005/08/hiroshima-panels.html.

58. More proximate to Nakazawa's style is the Marukis' less well-known, now out-of-print 1950 book of drawings, *Pika-don* (excerpted as illustrations for Kenzaburo Oe's *Hiroshima Notes*). *Pika-don* was censored during the occupation. See Ogi Fusami, "*Barefoot Gen* and *Maus*: Performing the Masculine, Reconstructing the Mother," in *Reading Manga: Local and Global Perceptions of Japanese Comics*, ed. Jaqueline Berndt and Steffi Richter (Leipzig: Leipziger Universitätsverlag, 2006), 78.

59. Frederik L. Schodt, *Manga! Manga! The World of Japanese Comics* (New York: Kodansha International, 1983), 22.

60. Kajiya, "How Emotions Work," 247. "Inexorable art of witness" is Spiegelman's description of *Barefoot Gen*. See Art Spiegelman, "Barefoot Gen:

Comics after the Bomb," in Keiji Nakazawa, *Barefoot Gen: A Cartoon Story of Hiroshima* (San Francisco: Last Gasp, 1987), n.p. Here Kajiya, too, is writing about *Barefoot Gen*, but his phrase is even more applicable to the earlier work *I Saw It*.

61. W. J. T. Mitchell, "Comics as Media: Afterword," in *Comics and Media: A Critical Inquiry Book*, ed. Hillary Chute and Patrick Jagoda (Chicago: University of Chicago Press, 2014), 259. See also W. J. T. Mitchell, "Metamorphoses of the Vortex: Hogarth, Turner, and Blake," in *Articulate Images: The Sister Arts from Hogarth to Tennyson*, ed. Richard Wendorf (Minneapolis: University of Minnesota Press, 1983), 125–168. Mitchell argues that "the vortex can help us to understand the manner in which images have a history that involves their changing significance, not just as representations of objects, but as the underlying forms or constitutive structures in which particular images achieve intelligibility" (125–126). "Empathetic doodling," a phrase Mitchell borrows from Chris Ware, refers to cartooning.

62. In only one instance does Nakazawa fail to depict the moment of actual mark-making when his love of comics is the subject. In a panel detailing his conflict around leaving his ill mother in Hiroshima to move to Tokyo, he draws Keiji staring at a comics composition, his right hand resting on the table but arranged awkwardly close to his body, creating a conspicuous gulf between body and paper, as if the hand is unwillingly restrained (*I Saw It*, 37).

63. Itō and Omote, "*Barefoot Gen* in Japan," 26.

64. The ten volumes came out from Last Gasp between 2004 and 2009. Previously, only the first four volumes were readily available.

65. In the introduction to his prose autobiography, Nakazawa repeats this claim, as elsewhere: "It's true. [My life is] the same life as in *Barefoot Gen*. I'm the model for Gen. *Barefoot Gen* is based on fact" ("A Note from the Author," xxiv). This is also clarified in Gleason, "The Keiji Nakazawa Interview," 50.

66. Keiji Nakazawa, *Barefoot Gen, Vol. Three: Life after the Bomb*, trans. Project Gen (San Francisco: Last Gasp, 2005), 52–54.

67. Kajiya, "How Emotions Work," 246–247.

68. Keiji Nakazawa, *Barefoot Gen, Vol. Nine: Breaking down Borders*, trans. Project Gen (San Francisco: Last Gasp, 2009), 120–123.

69. One might say, as we will also see in Chapter 5 with Sacco's work, that Seiji's project is in bearing witness to the existence of concrete others (specified

individuals) rather than generalized others (equal moral agents who are dis-embedded and disembodied). See Seyla Benhabib, "The Generalized and the Concrete Other: The Kohlberg-Gilligan Controversy and Moral Theory," in *Situating the Self: Gender, Community, and Postmodernism in Contemporary Ethics* (New York: Routledge, 1992).

70. Paul Virilio, *War and Cinema: The Logistics of Perception*, trans. Patrick Camiller (London: Verso, 1989).

71. Donald M. Goldstein, Katherine V. Dillon, and J. Michael Wenger, *Rain of Ruin: A Photographic History of Hiroshima and Nagasaki* (Washington, DC: Brassey's, 1995), 54. One could consider these images technically photograms—images created by placing objects directly on the surface of light-sensitive materials. William Henry Fox Talbot called them "photogenic drawings"; Man Ray, who produced them from the 1920s through the 1940s, called them "rayographs." See Virilio, *War and Cinema*, 81; Akira Mizuta Lippit, *Atomic Light (Shadow Optics)* (Minneapolis: University of Minnesota Press, 2005), 94.

72. Lippit, *Atomic Light*, 94, quotes this passage from Virilio's *War and Cinema*, 81.

73. Lippit, *Atomic Light*, 94. Lippit also argues that the bomb made the Japanese cities themselves into cameras: "The atomic explosions in Hiroshima and Nagasaki turned those cities, in the instant of a flash, into massive *cameras*; the victims grafted onto the geography by the radiation, *radiographed*" (50).

74. Lippit, *Atomic Light*, 109, 95, 32. In Lippit's view, psychoanalysis, X-ray, and cinema have provided a mode of avisuality, and this interest attaches in his readings, say, to the figure of the invisible in Japanese film as a response to atomic devastation. Lippit's book is startlingly brilliant. It indicates, however, a pattern of academic distance from what we might think of, contra avisuality, as visuality with images. Even academics studying images can display what seems like a fear of what images do and how they are received, as in Jacques Khalip and Robert Mitchell, eds., *Releasing the Image: From Literature to New Media* (Stanford, CA: Stanford University Press, 2011), whose editors record a desire to be "released" from the regime of the image and what they deem the "representationalism" and "ocularcentrism" it can propose.

75. Elaine Scarry, *The Body in Pain: The Making and Unmaking of the World* (New York: Oxford University Press, 1985), 238.

76. Keiji Nakazawa, *Barefoot Gen, Vol. Seven: Bones into Dust*, trans. Project Gen (San Francisco: Last Gasp, 2008), 173; Keiji Nakazawa, *Barefoot Gen,*

Vol. Eight: Merchants of Death, trans. Project Gen (San Francisco: Last Gasp, 2008), 253.

77. Steven Okazaki, dir., *White Light/Black Rain*, HBO, 2007. Little Boy had inscribed on its shell, among other inscriptions, "Greetings to the Emperor from the men of the *Indianapolis*."

78. Nakazawa, unlike many manga artists, and even in his later fictional work, insists on the auteur model also promoted by American underground cartoonists: "A true cartoonist does both the story and the pictures himself" (Gleason, "The Keiji Nakazawa Interview," 46).

79. Lippit, *Atomic Light*, 120.

80. Yoshihiro Tatsumi, "Hell," in *Good-Bye*, trans. Yuji Oniki (Montreal: Drawn and Quarterly, 2008), 13–41.

81. Spiegelman's introduction, "Barefoot Gen: Comics after the Bomb," written in 1990, appears in the first two volumes of the ten-volume series published by Last Gasp. These two volumes are the most known and translated outside of Japan.

82. Michael Silverblatt, "The Cultural Relief of Art Spiegelman," *Tampa Review* 5 (Fall 1992): 36.

83. LaMarre, "Manga Bomb," 268.

84. Ibid., 276.

85. Ibid., 282. LaMarre, however, understands his difference from Eisenstein's view in his emphasis on the plastic line as also having active transformational properties: "The plastic line is precisely a line that both gives way and bounces back, both bends and springs back."

86. Ibid., 292.

87. See ibid., 277, for LaMarre's concept of the structural line. Structural lines are also recognizable in the *mecha* style, which LaMarre suggests is associated with neutral depictions such as architecture in Nakazawa's work, and also with war manga in general and its detailed depictions of machines and vehicles (ibid., 293–299).

88. Ibid., 299.

89. Spiegelman, "Barefoot Gen: Comics after the Bomb"; LaMarre, "Manga Bomb," 292.

90. LaMarre, "Manga Bomb," 300.

91. Ibid., 304 (italics added); see also 300.

92. Sheng-Mei Ma, "Three Views of the Rising Sun, Obliquely: Keiji Nakazawa's A-Bomb, Osamu Tezuka's Adolf, and Yoshinori Kobayashi's Apologia," in *Mechdademia 4: War/Time*, ed. Frenchy Lunning (Minneapolis: University of Minnesota Press, 2009), 186.

93. Keiji Nakazawa, *Barefoot Gen, Vol. Five: The Never-Ending War*, trans. Project Gen (San Francisco: Last Gasp, 2007), 215.

94. Bill Randall, "Lost in Translation: From Lives to Abstractions in the Blink of a Child's Eye," *Comics Journal* 256 (October 2003): 56.

95. Kawaguchi, "*Barefoot Gen* and 'A-Bomb Literature,'" 243.

96. Randall, "Lost in Translation," 53.

97. Ma, "Three Views," 187.

98. Laura Wexler, "'I Saw It': The Photographic Witness of Keiji Nakazawa's *Barefoot Gen*," paper presented at the panel "Picturing Photography in Graphic Memoirs," Modern Language Association, Boston, January 2013. The military photographs to which Wexler refers are best seen in Erin Barnett and Philomena Mariani, eds., *Hiroshima: Ground Zero 1945* (New York: International Center for Photography, 2011), and were first published in a 1947 classified report titled "The Effects of the Atomic Bomb on Hiroshima, Japan." Adam Levy's fascinating essay "Hiroshima: Lost and Found" in *Hiroshima: Ground Zero* describes how the owner of the Deluxe Town Diner in Watertown, Massachusetts, discovered many of these photographs, previously classified, in a discarded suitcase in the trash.

99. See Thierry Groensteen, *The System of Comics*, trans. Bart Beaty and Nick Nguyen (Jackson: University Press of Mississippi, 2007). Thank you to Chris Pizzino for suggesting that this concept can be seen as a jointing.

100. Clark Coolidge and Philip Guston, *Baffling Means: Writings/Drawings by Clark Coolidge and Philip Guston* (Stockbridge, MA: o•blek editions, 1991), 13.

101. Reprints of the original editions of the *Japan Punch*, which was published in Yokohama, are now collected in ten volumes published by Yushodo. For a detailed discussion of Wirgman, see John Clark, *Japanese Exchanges in Art, 1850s–1930s, with Britain, Continental Europe, and the USA* (Sydney: Power Publications, 2006). Japanese editors and artists came to work on *Japan Punch*, and a subsequent publication, *Marumaru Chimbun*, was started by Japanese in 1877.

102. Hiroshi Odagiri, "Manga Truisms: On the Insularity of Manga Discourse," in *Comics Worlds and the Worlds of Comics: Toward Scholarship on a Global Scale.* ed. Jaqueline Berndt (Kyoto: International Manga Research Center, Kyoto Seika University, 2010), 64.

103. Kern, *Manga from the Floating World*, 129. See Shunsuke Tsurumi, *A Cultural History of Postwar Japan* (New York: KPI, 1987) for more on Asahi newspapers and American and Japanese serialization.

104. Frederik L. Schodt, "Henry Kiyama and *The Four Immigrants Manga*," in Henry (Yoshitaka) Kiyama, *The Four Immigrants Manga: A Japanese Experience in San Francisco, 1904–1924*, trans. Frederik L. Schodt (Berkeley, CA: Stone Bridge Press, 1999), 7–18. Schodt translated the book in 1999, and points out how its 1931 publication predates the first "true" American comic book with all-new material, 1935's *New Fun Comics*. Schodt discusses *The Four Immigrants Manga* as a "'bridge work' in the sense that it showed how Japanese artists had early on adopted American formats" (7). It is also a bridge work in straddling two languages and two countries in its production history, as Mayumi Takada points out in "*The Four Immigrants Manga* and the Making of Japanese Americans," *Genre*, Winter 2006, 128. The book is unusual in mixing languages, sometimes even in the space of a single speech balloon. Schodt points out that its intended audience is other first-generation immigrants living in California, for whom this mixing would be familiar (16).

105. For more on handscrolls and conventional reading practices, see Masako Watanabe, *Storytelling in Japanese Art* (New York: Metropolitan Museum of Art, 2011).

106. Schodt, *Manga! Manga!*, 33.

107. For more detailed histories of Japanese caricatural and visual-verbal art practices and genres, see Jean-Marie Bouissou, "Manga: A Historical Overview," in *Manga: An Anthology of Global and Cultural Perspectives*, ed. Toni Johnson-Woods (New York: Continuum, 2010), 17–33; Robin E. Brenner, *Understanding Manga and Anime* (Westport, CT: Libraries Unlimited, 2007); Ito, "Manga in Japanese History"; John Lent, "Japanese Comics," in *Handbook of Japanese Popular Culture*, ed. Richard Gid Powers and Hidetoshi Kato (New York: Greenwood Press, 1989), 221–242; Schodt, *Manga! Manga!*; Tsurumi, *A Cultural History of Postwar Japan*. Some scholars, among them Kern, resist the idea that older forms resulted in Japan's current manga culture, while acknowledging parallels (Kern, *Manga from the Floating World*, 131). See also Paul Gravett, "Japanese Spirit, Western Learning," in

Manga: Sixty Years of Comics Culture (London: Lawrence King, 2004), 18–23; Kinsella, *Adult Manga*; Roger Sabin, *Adult Comics: An Introduction* (New York: Routledge, 1993), and Stewart, "Manga as Schism."

108. Miné Okubo, *Citizen 13660* (1946; repr., Seattle: University of Washington Press, 1983).

109. Okubo's approximately 200 illustrations, which appear above typeset text, were created, as she explains, for exhibition, and each image is signed. Fascinatingly—Okubo's work merits closer attention than this chapter affords—she effectively made audiences take stock of her draftsmanship as a documentary practice. Okubo is self-conscious as a documentarian, stating as such in the book (*Citizen 13660*, 53, 206), and she was received as one. In 1945 the *New York Times* noted an exhibit of her "documentary paintings and drawings," and in 1981 *Citizen 13660* was received as supplement to her oral testimony to the U.S. Commission on Wartime Relocation and Internment of Civilians (xi). An even earlier work appearing in a similar format of sketches and typeset text is Taro Yashima's memoir *The New Sun* (New York: Henry Holt, 1943), which details the persecution in Japan of dissidents, himself included. See Deborah Gesenway and Mindy Roseman, *Beyond Words: Images from America's Concentration Camps* (Ithaca, NY: Cornell University Press), 1987, for a study of images created in internment camps. See Sarah Dowling, "'How Lucky I Was to Be Free and Safe at Home': Reading Humor in Miné Okubo's *Citizen 13660*," *Signs: Journal of Women in Culture and Society* 39 no. 2 (Winter 2014), for an analysis of Okubo's own surveillance of the camps as documentarian.

110. Buck Rogers, for instance, a Great War veteran, accidentally gets preserved for 500 years by unidentified "radioactive gas"; see Szasz, *Atomic Comics*, 16. Szasz also discusses these comics' mixed but generally positive attitudes toward atomic energy (18–19).

111. Szasz, *Atomic Comics*, 21, 19.

112. Ibid., 38, 39.

113. Educational comics began in 1943 and blossomed with publisher Max Gaines's *Picture Stories from the Bible* (Old Testament). These comics, some of which took on the atom bomb directly, are certainly a genre of nonfiction, but as an expressly didactic one that tried to simplify wartime and nuclear history, they fall outside of the context of documenting and witnessing that I investigate here.

114. Szasz, *Atomic Comics*, 70.

115. Harvey Kurtzman and Wally Wood's "Atom Bomb!," *Two-Fisted Tales* 1, no. 33 (May-June 1953), is a rare, even if fictional, instance of the depiction from a Japanese perspective of destruction caused on the ground in Nagasaki. Kurtzman wrote the story, and Wally Wood drew and inked it.

116. The magazine produces, in fact, a particularly sharp discordance in the choice of image to frame the prose content. The cover is a colorful scene of groups of people in the midst of enjoying outdoor recreational activities in-cluding sailing, swimming, golf, tennis, croquet, baseball, horseback riding, reading, and baseball, while inside the magazine is a report that ex-plicitly details the ruination, violence, sickness, and despair caused by the atomic bomb from the point of view of six ordinary Hiroshima residents. The cover, significantly, provides an *aerial view* of an American population going about their business on a summer day—a view that, however indirectly, re-minds one of Hiroshima surveilled from the sky. Michael Yavenditti claims that "the decision to devote the entire issue to 'Hiroshima' came too late to change the tranquil picnic-scene cover," while some advertisements were vetted at the last minute ("John Hersey and the American Conscience: The Reception of 'Hiroshima,'" *Pacific Historical Review* 43, no. 1 [1974]: 24–49). Mouly, the current art editor of the *New Yorker*, suggests that the cover was intentional: "That's what William Shawn [who was co-managing editor in 1946], when he became editor, really wanted—he wanted incendiary jour-nalism. But he never flagged it on the cover, never gave an indication it was there. He wanted to have images on the cover that would just be a quiet mo-ment" ("Talk on *Blown Covers*," in *Comics and Media: A Critical Inquiry Book*, ed. Hillary Chute and Patrick Jagoda [Chicago: University of Chicago Press, 2014], 189). See Werner Sollors, "Holocaust and Hiroshima: American Ethnic Prose Writers Face the Extreme," *PMLA* 118, no. 1 (January 2003): 56–61, for an analysis of the advertisements that did appear.

117. Northrop Frye, *Northrop Frye on Literature and Society, 1936–1989*, ed. Robert D. Denham (Toronto: University of Toronto Press, 2002), 314.

118. As Leonard Rifas observes, "Judging from the evidence in the comix, a sense that mainstream society was rocketing forward on a fundamentally suicidal, insane trajectory toward world destruction, created a rationale for 'dropping out' more fundamental than the war in Vietnam" ("Politics of Comix," un-published manuscript, 2014), 14.

119. See Chris York and Rafiel York, *Comic Books and the Cold War 1946–1962* (Jefferson, NC: McFarland, 2012); Bradford Wright, *Comic Book Nation: The Transformation of Youth Culture in America* (Baltimore: Johns Hopkins University Press, 2001); and Szasz, *Atomic Comics*. Christopher Pizzino points

out that the atomic comics that caught on were ones that made atomic radiation seem safe: *Spider-Man*, in which Spidey's neighborliness is a value, was an instant hit, while *The Hulk*, featuring an angry outcast, took a long time to catch on ("Atomic Adventures: How Comics Absorbed the Bomb," lecture, University of Georgia, April 2014).

120. Rifas, "Politics of Comix," 21, 19.

121. Helen Swick Perry, *The Human Be-In* (New York: Basic Books, 1970), 61. Part of Perry's quotation is also cited in Rifas, "Politics of Comix."

122. Peter Poplaski and R. Crumb, *The R. Crumb Handbook* (London: MQ Publications, 2005), 394.

123. See Rifas, "Politics of Comix"; Leonard Rifas, "Cartooning and Nuclear Power: From Industry Advertising to Activist Uprising and Beyond," *PS: Political Science and Politics*, April 2007, 255–260, for accounts of *All-Atomic Comics* and other anti-nuclear comics.

124. Green, quoted in Patrick Rosenkranz, *Rebel Visions: The Underground Comix Revolution, 1963–1975* (Seattle: Fantagraphics, 2002), 4.

4. *MAUS*'S ARCHIVAL IMAGES AND THE POSTWAR COMICS FIELD

Epigraph: Georges Didi-Huberman, *Images in Spite of All: Four Photographs from Auschwitz*, trans. Shane B. Lillis (2008; repr., Chicago: University of Chicago Press, 2012), 182. Page reference is to the 2012 edition. Reprinted by permission of the University of Chicago Press. Copyright © 2008 by the University of Chicago.

1. For more on *Binky*, see the introduction to Hillary L. Chute, *Graphic Women: Life Narrative and Contemporary Comics* (New York: Columbia University Press, 2010), and the updated edition of *Binky Brown Meets the Holy Virgin Mary*, which includes Green's afterword (San Francisco: McSweeney's, 2009).

2. Justin Green, "Panel: Comics and Autobiography. With Phoebe Gloeckner, Justin Green, Aline Kominsky-Crumb, Carol Tyler," in *Comics and Media: A Critical Inquiry Book*, ed. Hillary Chute and Patrick Jagoda (Chicago: University of Chicago Press, 2014), 90.

3. Tom De Haven, "The Comics: What a Novel Idea!," lecture, Rutgers University. New Brunswick, NJ, April 24, 2003.

4. Art Spiegelman, personal correspondence, August 20, 2014.

5. Green, "Afterword," in *Binky Brown Meets the Holy Virgin Mary* (San Francisco: McSweeney's, 2009), 53.

6. Green, "Panel," 86.

7. Art Spiegelman, "An Afterword," in *Breakdowns: Portrait of the Artist as Young %@&*!* (New York: Pantheon, 2008).

8. Art Spiegelman, "Introduction: Symptoms of Disorder/Signs of Genius," in Justin Green, *Justin Green's Binky Brown Sampler* (San Francisco: Last Gasp, 1995), 6. In *Funny Aminals*, Terry Zwigoff is listed as the editor, despite the fact that Justin Green is routinely identified by cartoonists as the editor. Zwigoff went on to become the director of the acclaimed films *Crumb* and *Ghost World*. According to Crumb, Zwigoff shed his editorial role out of disappointment with the tenor of many of the contributions: "None of the stories were expressions of his original editorial concern for the well-being of innocent animals. . . . Terry abdicated his position and wanted nothing more to do with it." Robert Crumb, *The Complete Crumb Comics Volume 9: R. Crumb versus the Sisterhood!* (Seattle: Fantagraphics, 1992), viii. Green may have then taken over.

9. Joseph Witek, *Comic Books as History: The Narrative Art of Jack Jackson, Art Spiegelman, and Harvey Pekar* (Jackson: University Press of Mississippi, 1989), 110; see also Art Spiegelman, *MetaMaus* (New York: Pantheon, 2011), 135.

10. Art Spiegelman, *Portrait of the Artist as a Young %@&*!*, in *Breakdowns: Portrait of the Artist as a Young %@&*!* (New York: Pantheon, 2008).

11. There are several comics adaptations of *The Metamorphosis*, including by R. Crumb and Peter Kuper.

12. Quoted in Stephen Tabachnick, "Of *Maus* and Memory: The Structure of Art Spiegelman's Graphic Novel of the Holocaust," *Word and Image* 9, no. 2 (April–June 1993): 155. For a recent analysis of "Josephine" in the context of Jewishness, see David Suchoff, *Kafka's Jewish Languages: The Hidden Openness of Tradition* (Philadelphia: University of Pennsylvania Press, 2011).

13. Giorgio Agamben, like Spiegelman, has incisively objected to the designation "Holocaust" on the basis of the term's semantic history that connects it to the biblical *olah*, "burnt offering," implying a Christian justification; see Agamben, *Remnants of Auschwitz: The Witness and the Archive*, trans. Daniel Heller-Roazen (New York: Zone Books, 2002), 28. In order to maintain consistency with the lexicon that Spiegelman's *Maus* itself establishes in the record of its conversations between Spiegelman and his survivor

father, however, I will use the term here while acknowledging its problematic status. For Spiegelman's view, see *MetaMaus*, 74, 101.

14. On Bourke-White's photo, "Liberation of Prisoners at Buchenwald, April 15, 1945," see Marianne Hirsch, *The Generation of Postmemory: Writing and Visual Culture after the Holocaust* (New York: Columbia University Press, 2012), 30. This photograph quickly became iconic but was not published in the initial May 7, 1945, edition of *Life*, with its report titled "Atrocities," which published other Bourke-White images of Buchenwald and famous images of the camps and their victims. It first appeared in the December 26, 1960, special double issue, "25 Years of Life." See Ben Cosgrove, "Behind the Picture: The Liberation of Buchenwald, April 1945," *Life* online, http://life.time.com /history/buchenwald-photos-from-the-liberation-of-the-camp-april-1945/#1.

15. Transcripts from Vladek and Art Spiegelman's 1972 interview sessions can be found in *MetaMaus*. Spiegelman points out he was able to do all of his outside research in a few weeks at the library because there was not a large amount available in English (*MetaMaus*, 43).

16. Gary Groth, "Art Spiegelman," *Comics Journal* no. 180 (1995): 95.

17. Hillary L. Chute, *Outside the Box: Interviews with Contemporary Cartoonists* (Chicago: University of Chicago Press, 2014), 20.

18. Examples include Jillian Tamaki's "Domestic Men of Mystery," *New York Times*, June 20, 2010, and R. O. Blechman's "The Birth of the Croissant and the Bagel," *New York Times*, April 6, 2009.

19. Gar Alperovitz and Jeff Faux, "Our Future: Centralization of Decentralization?" with untitled illustration by Art Spiegelman, *New York Times*, January 5, 1976.

20. The link between underground comics and film warrants much greater attention than it has been given. Spiegelman was active in the Collective for Living Cinema in New York City, where he gave his first illustrated lecture on the history of comics, and later on in Anthology Film Archives. He appeared in underground filmmaker George Kuchar's *The Devil's Cleavage* (1973), and Kuchar contributed comics to two titles edited by Spiegelman and Bill Griffith, *Short Order Comix* (1974) and *Arcade* (1975).

21. Art Spiegelman, "Real Dream: 'A Hand Job,'" *Arcade: The Comics Revue*, no. 1 (San Francisco: Print Mint, 1975), n.p.

22. Jared Gardner, "Autography's Biography: 1972–2007," *Biography* 31, no. 1 (Winter 2008): 16.

23. See, for instance, ibid., 8.

24. For a more detailed description of this work, see Hillary Chute, "Comics as Archives: Meta*MetaMaus*," *e-misférica* 9, nos. 1–2 (Summer 2012).

25. Bacon's drawings of Auschwitz's Crematorium II—also drawn by Spiegelman in *Maus*—were used as evidence in the Adolf Eichmann trial in 1961. Spiegelman was among a group of writers and artists who protested the Auschwitz-Birkenau Memorial and Museum's refusal to return Babbitt's work, commissioned by Josef Mengele, to her; she was unaware her paintings had survived until 1973. See Steve Freiss, "Return of Auschwitz Art Sought," *New York Times*, September 20, 2006. After the war, Babbitt, born Gottliebová, married Art Babbitt, the longtime Disney animator who created the character Goofy.

26. This group, the Zeichenstube (graphic department), was discovered. Philip Rosen and Nina Apfelbaum, *Bearing Witness: A Resource Guide to Literature, Poetry, Art, Music, and Videos by Holocaust Victims and Survivors* (Westport, CT: Greenwood Press, 2002), 122, 138.

27. David Mickenberg, Corinne Granof, and Peter Hayes, *The Last Expression: Art and Auschwitz* (Evanston, IL: Northwestern University Press, 2003), 79.

28. See Stephen Feinstein, "Art from the Concentration Camps: Gallows Humor and Satirical Wit," *Journal of Jewish Identities* 1, no. 2 (July 2008): 53–75, on playing cards, stamps, and other "humorous" genres of creation; Mickenberg, Granof, and Hayes's comprehensive *The Last Expression* on illustrated fairy tales, among other forms of expression; and Hirsch and Spitzer's fascinating analysis of a surviving tiny book (less than an inch long and half an inch wide) in *The Generation of Postmemory*.

29. Feinstein, "Art from the Concentration Camps," 55.

30. Susan Sontag, *On Photography* (New York: Farrar, Straus and Giroux, 1977), 20.

31. Laura Jockusch's *Collect and Record! Jewish Holocaust Documentation in Early Postwar Europe* (New York: Oxford University Press, 2012) offers a fascinating history of Jewish Holocaust documentation in early postwar Europe with particular attention to the formation of commissions and documentation centers. Jockusch makes the important point that the "augmented attention to memory toward the end of the twentieth century left earlier Holocaust testimony projects largely forgotten and created the misconception that *all* testimony was belated" (11). However, Jockusch does not focus on any early postwar visual testimony such as we see in Spiegelman's archive.

32. "Master Race" greatly affected Spiegelman, who wrote about it in an EC comics fanzine called *Squa Tront* in 1975. An earlier, panel-by-panel analysis of "Master Race" is reprinted in Art Spiegelman, *From Maus to Now to Maus to Now: Comix, Essays, Graphics, and Scraps* (Palermo: Sellerio-La Central dell'Arte, 1998). See also Art Spiegelman, "Ballbuster: Bernard Krigstein's Life between the Panels," *New Yorker*, July 22, 2002.

33. In the "Anja's Bookshelf" section of the *MetaMaus* DVD, Spiegelman provides sample images of this range of work, including full scans of the two most important pamphlets. Spiegelman provides access to Mala Spiegelman's thirty-page translation of *The Destruction of the Jews of Sosnowiec*—a document that is mostly written out longhand on stationery of the local Hadassah chapter but includes a few typed pages. He gives Mala a place in *Maus*'s romantic history of artifacts by offering her translation as an artifact, a singular document, and not simply as translated content.

34. While *Maus* details Vladek Spiegelman's exit from the camps in great detail based on his testimony, it conspicuously does not offer details about Anja Spiegelman's journey from the camps. "Searching for Memories of Anja," a section I helped to assemble for *MetaMaus* based on Spiegelman's research archive, indicates from interviews Spiegelman conducted with Anja's friends who were with her during the war that she went from Auschwitz to camps including Gross-Rosen, Ravensbrück, and a camp identified as "Malhoff," which may have been Malchow, a camp system that existed on the terrain of the Ravensbrück camp.

35. Little information is available on Osynka. The survivor and author Stefan Petelycky claims Osynka was known in the camps as Petro Balij, and identifies his number, 57321. Stefan Petelycky, *Into Auschwitz, for Ukraine* (Kingston, ON: Kashtan Press, 1998).

36. Spiegelman, *MetaMaus*, 49.

37. J. Hillis Miller, *The Conflagration of Community: Fiction before and after Auschwitz* (Chicago: University of Chicago Press, 2011), 225, 171.

38. After the first volume of eight issues, Penguin Books took over publication, switching the size of the magazine to match the pages of its most famous feature, *Maus*.

39. See Spiegelman, *MetaMaus*, 78–79. In Spiegelman's account, Pantheon agreed to publish the first half only after the highly unusual appearance of a positive review of *Maus*, a small-press comics work in progress, in the *New York Times Book Review* (see Ken Tucker, "Cats, Mice, and History—the

Avant-Garde of the Comic Strip," *New York Times Book Review*, May 26, 1985). At the time of Tucker's article, six installments of *Maus* had appeared in *RAW*.

40. There is a growing body of critical work on Salomon. See, for instance, Ernst van Alphen, *Caught by History: Holocaust Effects in Contemporary Art, Literature, and Theory* (Stanford, CA: Stanford University Press, 1997); Mary Lowenthal Felstiner, *To Paint Her Life: Charlotte Salomon in the Nazi Era* (Berkeley: University of California Press, 1997); Griselda Pollock, *Encounters in the Virtual Feminist Museum: Time, Space and the Archive* (New York: Routledge, 2007); Michael P. Steinberg and Monica Bohm-Duchen, eds., *Reading Charlotte Salomon* (Ithaca, NY: Cornell University Press, 2006); Claudia Barnett, "Painting as Performance: Charlotte Salomon's *Life? Or Theatre?*" *TDR: The Drama Review* 41, no. 7 (2003): 97–126; Deborah Schultz and Edward Timms, "Charlotte Salomon: Images, Dialogues and Silences," *Word and Image: A Journal of Verbal/Visual Enquiry* 24, no. 3 (2008): 269–281; and Julia Watson, "Charlotte Salomon's Memory Work in the 'Postscript' to 'Life? Or Theatre?'" *Signs* 28, no. 1 (2002): 409–420.

41. Spiegelman, *MetaMaus*, 50–51.

42. Alfred Kantor, "Introduction," in *The Book of Alfred Kantor* (New York: Schocken, 1971), n.p.

43. Spiegelman, *MetaMaus*, 53.

44. Art Spiegelman, "*MetaMaus* Outtake," interview with Hillary Chute, New York, August 4, 2008.

45. In addition to his work produced in the camps, Kościelniak created two highly informative suites of drawings shortly after the war, one depicting Auschwitz and one Birkenau, called "The Prisoner's Day."

46. Spiegelman, *MetaMaus*, 49–50; italics added.

47. Janina Struk's *Photographing the Holocaust* (London: I. B. Tauris, 2004) surveys the range of camp photography, including the internal Nazi strictures on photographic documentation, often broken by the SS, and prisoner participation.

48. Spiegelman, *MetaMaus*, 138.

49. Rosenthal produced three extant booklets. Along with *Mickey in Gurs*, the Centre de Documentation Juive Contemporaine in Paris owns *A Day in the Life of a Resident, Gurs Internment Camp 1942*. They were donated to the CDJC in Paris by the Hansbacher family in 1978; no information about the donors or how they came to be the owners of the booklets is available. A

Small Guide through Gurs Camp 1942, a third booklet, is at the Skovgaard Museum in Viborg, Denmark. It is part of the collection of Elizabeth Kasser (1910–1992), a Swiss nurse who lived in Gurs as a member of a welfare organization during the war. Kasser's collection of inmate art, either bought by her or given to her, was donated to the Skovgaard Museum in 1986. While all are reportage in comics form, in only one is Mickey Mouse the protagonist. See Pnina Rosenberg, "*Mickey Mouse in Gurs*—Humour, Irony and Criticism in Works of Art Produced in the Gurs Internment Camp," *Rethinking History* 6, no. 3 (2002): 273–292 for descriptions of Rosenthal's other two booklets from 1942.

50. Feinstein, "Art from the Concentration Camps," 71. See Mickenberg, Granof, and Hayes, *The Last Expression*, the only source I know of that reprints *Mickey au Camp de Gurs* in full. It also offers English translation from the French, which I cite in this chapter.

51. Rosenthal, *Mickey in Gurs*, n.p. [7]; repr. in Mickenberg, Granof, and Hayes, *The Last Expression*.

52. See Walter Benjamin's essay "Karl Kraus" (1931), in *Walter Benjamin: Selected Writings, Vol. 2: Part 2 (1931–1934)* (Cambridge, MA: Harvard University Press, 2005).

53. Lisa Naomi Mulman, *Modern Orthodoxies: Judaic Imaginative Journeys of the Twentieth Century* (New York: Routledge, 2012), 93.

54. Spiegelman, *MetaMaus*, 132.

55. "By going back to Little Orphan Annie's eyes—letting the reader discover the expression reading into that face, as one always does with comics—it all actually becomes a lot more open to one's inner sets of associations. In other words, you've got to do the work the same way you do when you're reading prose"; Spiegelman, *MetaMaus*, 150. Scott McCloud writes in *Understanding Comics: The Invisible Art* (New York: HarperCollins, 1993) about this comics phenomenon as "amplification through simplification" (30) or "filling up" (37).

56. For more on the style of *Maus* as a narrative and political choice, see Hillary Chute, "'The Shadow of a Past Time': History and Graphic Representation in *Maus*," *Twentieth-Century Literature* 52, no. 2 (Summer 2006): 199–230. For the work that went into the creation of Spiegelman's style, see Spiegelman, *MetaMaus*.

57. Brian Boyd, *On the Origin of Stories: Evolution, Cognition, and Fiction* (Cambridge, MA: Harvard University Press, 2009), 389, xi. Boyd also writes on Spiegelman in "Art and Evolution: Spiegelman's *The Narrative Corpse*,"

Philosophy and Literature 32 (2008): 31–57, claiming that evolutionary anthropologists have shown that "entities that cross intuitive ontological boundaries arrest our attention and persist in our memory" (39). This notion is suggestive for thinking about the cross-discursive form of comics and its effect as documentary evidence.

58. J. Hillis Miller calls *Maus* "the most vivid . . . account I know of what preceded Auschwitz for Jews in a city like Sosnowiec" (*The Conflagration of Community*, 172).

59. Spiegelman, *MetaMaus*, 42.

60. Art Spiegelman, "Four Maus Notebooks," *MetaMaus* DVD (New York: Pantheon, 2011). Also central to Agamben's *Remnants of Auschwitz* is the question of what survival is: "Is there a humanity of human beings that can be distinguished and separated from human beings' biological humanity?" (55). Agamben addresses this most thoroughly, through Primo Levi, in analyzing the status of the *Muselmann* (the weakest inmates) in the Nazi camps. Four of Spiegelman's *Maus*-era notebooks, very scantily redacted, are available as scans on *MetaMaus*'s DVD supplement.

61. Chute, *Graphic Women*, 2.

62. Jean-Luc Nancy, *The Ground of the Image*, trans. Jeff Fort (New York: Fordham University Press, 2005), 48.

63. Art Spiegelman and Hillary Chute at the 92nd St. Y, New York, October 6, 2011, www.youtube.com/watch?v=Vnb2D4FySro.

64. Nancy, *The Ground of the Image*, 21.

65. An image, especially in the context of this book, is often visual, but not definitionally so: an image could be auditory, for example, as Nancy mentions in ibid., 32.

66. Ibid., 33.

67. Shoshana Felman and Dori Laub, *Testimony: Crises of Witnessing in Literature, Psychoanalysis, and History* (New York: Routledge, 1992), xv.

68. Nancy, *The Ground of the Image*, 49; italics added.

69. Art Spiegelman, *The Complete Maus: Maus: A Survivor's Tale*, 25th anniversary ed. (New York: Pantheon, 2011), 85.

70. Spiegelman, *MetaMaus*, 185. Spiegelman attaches the idea of narrative as geography to Klaus Wyborny, a German avant-garde filmmaker (183–184).

71. Ibid., 166.

72. Miller, *The Conflagration of Community*, 171.

73. Ibid., 172. For more on the temporal and spatial experiment in Spiegelman's work as a register of traumatic history, see Chute, "'The Shadow of a Past Time,'" and Hillary Chute, "Temporality and Seriality in Spiegelman's *In the Shadow of No Towers*," *American Periodicals* 17, no. 2 (2007): 228–244.

74. Miller, *The Conflagration of Community*, 173, 174.

75. Nancy, *The Ground of the Image*, 36; Miller, *The Conflagration of Community*, 183.

76. Pages similar to 227 occur throughout *Maus*, such as the page from "Prisoner of War" that opens with a diagram of moving mountains to valleys and concludes with a classic montage panel of silhouetted workers (58). Spiegelman also struggled to find ways to visually transmit what he came to think of as "vertical" information, such as the food routinely served at certain times of day in Auschwitz, using what he calls "horizontal" information, such as physical action, which can be mapped intuitively in comics (*MetaMaus*, 211–212).

77. Spiegelman, *MetaMaus*, 59.

78. See ibid., 57–59 for a discussion of researching the toilets at Auschwitz. Spiegelman had been able to verify by visiting Auschwitz I, where Vladek hid, that the barracks had real toilets and plumbing, since it had been a soldiers' garrison during World War I. In Auschwitz II–Birkenau, the toilets were holes set in long planks.

79. Art Spiegelman, "Don't Get Around Much Anymore: A Guided Tour," republished in Art Spiegelman, *From Maus to Now to Maus to Now: Comix, Essays, Graphics and Scraps* (Palermo: La Centrale dell'Arte, 1998), 8.

80. See John Bender and Michael Marrinan's recent *The Culture of Diagram* (Stanford, CA: Stanford University Press, 2010), which suggests that formal characteristics of the diagram include "reductive renderings, usually executed as drawings, using few if any colors; they are generally supplemented with notations keyed to explanatory captions" (7). Judi Freeman points out that the abstract logic of the diagram was seen as an important prerequisite of mass production, and as a model for reproducibility was a subject of intrigue to Dadaists and Surrealists, who hoped to alter and subvert this representation of "ultimate realism." Freeman, *The Dada and Surrealist Word-Image* (Cambridge, MA: MIT Press, 1989), 92.

81. Spiegelman, *MetaMaus*, 150.

82. Ibid., 59.

83. Ibid.

84. Ibid., 60.

85. The "camps themselves were the execution of representation," in Nancy's view. "*Execution* in both senses of the word, that is, both its completion (through a presentation saturated with itself) and its exhaustion without remainder." Therefore "what forbids representation in this sense is the camp itself" (*The Ground of the Image*, 47).

86. Spiegelman, *MetaMaus*, 59.

87. Harvey Blume, "Art Spiegelman: Lips: Interview by Harvey Blume," *Boston Book Review*, 1995, 4.

88. "Most definitions of STORY leave me cold," Spiegelman writes in the 1977 introduction to *Breakdowns*. "Except the one that says: 'A complete horizontal division of a building . . . [From the Medieval Latin HISTORIA . . . a row of windows with pictures on them.]'" See also Art Spiegelman, *In the Shadow of No Towers* (New York: Pantheon, 2004).

89. Among these Didi-Huberman most vehemently rejects are the views of Gérard Wajcman and Lanzmann. Didi-Huberman glosses the "three concomitant hyperboles" of the thesis of the unimaginable as follows: (1) if we want to *know* something of the Shoah, we will have to get rid of images; (2) if we want to convoke a proper *memory* of the Shoah, we will have to dismiss all images; (3) *ethics* disappears wherever the image appears. Georges Didi-Huberman, *Images in Spite of All: Four Photographs from Auschwitz*, trans. Shane B. Lillis (Chicago: University of Chicago Press, 2008), 158.

90. Spiegelman, *MetaMaus*, 55.

91. Didi-Huberman, *Images in Spite of All*, 16.

92. Ibid., 105.

93. See Marianne Hirsch and Diana Taylor, "CFP: On the Subject of Archives, *e-misférica* 9.1," posted September 20, 2011, http://discardstudies.com/2011/09/20/cfp-on-the-subject-of-archives.

94. I make this point and others about the relation of comics and archives in "Comics as Archives."

95. Additionally, one learns in *MetaMaus* that Anja suffered many miscarriages before giving birth to Art; his existence did not feel ordained to his parents, or to him.

96. Art Spiegelman, "Prisoner on the Hell Planet," *Short Order Comix* no. 1 (San Francisco: Head Press, 1972).

97. See Chute, *Graphic Women*; Chute, "Comics as Archives."

98. See Marianne Hirsch, "Postmemory's Archival Turn," in *The Generation of Postmemory: Writing and Visual Culture after the Holocaust* (New York: Columbia University Press, 2012), 227–249, for a further discussion of Foster and contemporary art practice.

99. Jared Gardner, "Archives, Collectors, and the New Media Work of Comics," *Mfs: Modern Fiction Studies* 52, no. 4 (Winter 2006): 788.

100. Anne Golomb Hoffman, "Archival Bodies," *American Imago* 66, no. 1 (Spring): 5–6.

101. Quoted in Gardner, "Autography's Biography," 804.

102. Agamben, *Remnants of Auschwitz*, 158.

103. Elisabeth R. Friedman, "Spiegelman's Magic Box: *MetaMaus* and the Archive of Representation," *Studies in Comics* 3, no. 2 (2012): 277. Friedman argues that Agamben and Derrida occupy a similar view of the archive as unable to archive "affective traces," and she also argues that *Maus* disproves Agamben's view of the unarchivability of testimony (279). She points out that *Remnants of Auschwitz* concludes by reprinting testimonies from *Muselmänner*, which actually do constitute an archive: "*Maus* suggests that Agamben's view of testimony, while defined in opposition to the traditional archive, may also contain within it a new theory of the archive" (289).

104. Spiegelman quoted in Chute, "The Shadow of a Past Time"; see that essay for more on this connection.

105. Spiegelman, *MetaMaus*, 73.

106. *MetaMaus*, an archival book about a book about archives, is in many ways a mirrored object; the central interview portion of the book also ends with the Spiegelman family headstone (234). For a reading of *Maus*'s last page, see Chute, "The Shadow of a Past Time," 2006.

107. Art Spiegelman, "Art Spiegelman," in *Dangerous Drawings: Interviews with Comix and Graphix Artists*, ed. Andrea Juno (New York: Juno Books, 1997), 12.

108. Spiegelman, *MetaMaus*, "Four Notebooks."

109. Friedman, "Spiegelman's Magic Box," 278–279.

5. HISTORY AND THE VISIBLE IN JOE SACCO

Epigraph: Edward Said, "Homage to Joe Sacco," introduction to *Palestine*. © 1993, 1994, 1995, 1996, 2001 Joe Sacco. All rights reserved. Used by permission.

1. Recent discussions of the genre include Kristian Williams, "The Case for Comics Journalism," *Columbia Journalism Review*, March/April 2005, 1–4; Amy Kiste Nyberg, "Theorizing Comics Journalism," *International Journal of Comic Art* 8, no. 2 (Fall 2006): 98–111; Benjamin Woo, "Reconsidering Comics Journalism: Information and Experience in Joe Sacco's *Palestine*," in *The Rise and Reason of Comics and Graphic Literature: Critical Essays on the Form*, ed. Joyce Goggin and Dan Hassler-Forest (Jefferson, NC: McFarland, 2010), 166–177; and Dirk Vanderbeke, "In the Art of the Beholder: Comics as Political Journalism," in *Comics as a Nexus of Cultures*, ed. Mark Berninger, Jochen Ecke, and Gideon Haberkorn (Jefferson, NC: McFarland, 2010).

2. Mary N. Layoun, "Telling Stories in *Palestine*: Comix Understanding and Narratives of Palestine-Israel," in *Palestine, Israel, and Politics of Popular Culture*, ed. Rebecca L. Stein and Ted Swedenburg (Durham, NC: Duke University Press, 2005), 319.

3. Sacco did not receive an advance for his works *Palestine* or *Safe Area Goražde*, while he did receive a Guggenheim grant for *The Fixer*. While cartoonists Phoebe Gloeckner and Alison Bechdel have won since Sacco did in 2001, at the time he was awarded the fellowship, he did not win in a nonfiction category, as Bechdel did in 2012—he won in the fine arts category.

4. See Joe Sacco, "Comics as Journalism," Dedmon Lecture, University of Chicago, February 7, 2012. See also Nation Institute, "About Our Prizes," www .ridenhour.org/about_our_prizes.html. In 2012 Sacco won the PEN Center USA's Graphic Literature Award for Outstanding Body of Work. That PEN even has a Graphic Literature Award is a sign of the new prominence of the form.

5. Sacco's other books include the collections *Bumf Vol. 1*, a work of very dark fantastical satire steeped in presidential history (Seattle: Fantagraphics, 2014); *Notes from a Defeatist* (Seattle: Fantagraphics, 2003), which gathers his early work; *War's End: Profiles from Bosnia 1995–1996* (Montreal: Drawn and

Quarterly, 2005), which collects two short pieces, "Soba" and "Christmas with Karadzic"; *But I Like It* (Seattle: Fantagraphics, 2006), a volume of music posters and stories; and refurbished, deluxe special editions of *Palestine* (Seattle: Fantagraphics, 2007) and *Safe Area Goražde* (Seattle: Fantagraphics, 2012). He also contributed comics to a history of the labor movement, *From the Folks Who Brought You the Weekend* (New York: New Press, 2001).

6. See Tom Gunning, "The Art of Succession: Reading, Writing, and Watching Comics," *Comics and Media: A Critical Inquiry Book*, ed. Hillary Chute and Patrick Jagoda (Chicago: University of Chicago Press, 2014), 38.

7. Gary Groth, "Joe Sacco, Frontline Journalist: Why Sacco Went to Gorazde: Interview with Joe Sacco," *Comics Journal, Special Edition*, Winter 2002, 61.

8. Nancy K. Miller, "Cartoons of the Self: Portrait of the Artist as a Young Murderer," *M/E/A/N/I/N/G* 12 (1992): 393.

9. Alicia Erian, "Covering Wars, Embedded in the Graphic Novel," *Journal News* 3 (August 2003): 3E.

10. Sacco's family moved to Australia when he was a child and then to Los Angeles before settling in Oregon. Sacco's journalism degree came from a U.S. institution, the University of Oregon, but he lived on and off in Malta after college, drawing the first Maltese comic series, a romance, *Imhabba Vera* (True Love).

11. In *Footnotes in Gaza* Sacco conspicuously draws himself using his Maltese passport. Sacco now has dual citizenship with Malta and the United States. *Goražde*'s chapter "America Man" details a fascinating encounter in which a Bosnian man questions Sacco's motives on the basis of his Americanness. Sacco, who often refers to himself as southern European, recently told an interviewer, "I'm more American than anything else, but there's a fair amount of European in me. . . . I'd say I'm probably more transatlantic than anything else." Rebecca Tuhus-Dubrow, "Joe Sacco: *January* Interview," *January Magazine*, June 2003.

12. Joe Sacco, "More Women, More Children, More Quickly: Malta 1935–43 as Recollected by Carmen A. Sacco" (1990), in *Notes from a Defeatist* (Seattle: Fantagraphics, 2003), 132–153. This title of this twenty-one-page piece is a reference to Stanley Baldwin, the former British prime minister, who stated in 1932, "The only defense is offense, which means that you have to kill more women and children more quickly than the enemy if you want to save yourselves" (quoted in *Notes from a Defeatist*, 132).

13. Tom Wolfe, "The New Journalism," in *The New Journalism*, ed. Tom Wolfe and E. W. Johnson (New York: Harper and Row, 1973), 52.

14. For the classic work on New Journalism, see ibid., 50. See also Michael L. Johnson, *The New Journalism: The Underground Press, the Artists of Nonfiction, and Changes in Established Media* (Lawrence: University Press of Kansas, 1971); and Nicolaus Mills, ed., *The New Journalism: A Historical Anthology* (New York: McGraw-Hill, 1974). Wolfe's introduction to the 1973 collection, which he also coedited, is a useful explanation of the context out of which New Journalism arose. He describes a cultural overreverence for the novel in the 1950s and the concomitant view that journalism, the output of vaunted war correspondents excluded, was a devalued form of writing for "day laborers": "There was no such thing," he writes, "as a *literary* journalist working for popular magazines or newspapers" (8). After Gay Talese began "novelistic" reporting in *Esquire* in 1962, Wolfe and others joined the ranks to experiment with literary techniques in the arena of journalism. The shorter pieces of the early 1960s gave rise to the significant long-form genre experiments of the mid- to late 1960s that definitively changed the landscape, such as Truman Capote's "nonfiction novel" *In Cold Blood*, published as a book in 1966, and Norman Mailer's *The Armies of the Night*, from 1968, with its subtitle *History as a Novel/The Novel as History*.

15. Tuhus-Dubrow, "Joe Sacco"; Jennifer Contino, "Pieces of War," *Sequential Tart*, www.sequentialart.com/archive/oct01/sacco.shtml. Sacco uses a tape recorder for interviews and a point-and-shoot camera for reference shots, both tools that he conspicuously draws into his comics, revealing his means of producing the story we are reading. Sacco transcribes his own tapes. He also keeps thorough "journalism notes," which he then rigorously cross-indexes by name and by subject. Sacco maintains three separate kinds of notebooks for his reporting: interview notebooks, "field diaries" (separate from journalism notes), and spare notebooks into which he sketches. For a provocative discussion of the ethnographic field notebook as "a type of modernist literature" and one that "serves as a means of witness," see Michael Taussig, *I Swear I Saw This! Drawings in Fieldwork Notebooks, Namely My Own* (Chicago: University of Chicago Press, 2011).

16. David Rieff, "Bosnia beyond Words: Review of *Safe Area Gorazde* by Joe Sacco," *New York Times Book Review*, December 24, 2000, 7.

17. Layoun, "Telling Stories in *Palestine*," 315, 317. Layoun describes *Palestine* as working synecdochically, showing "partial and particularized images" that stand in for the larger picture. Sacco's graphic narratives are driven by his interviews and conversations and by his own observations, and are also

threaded through with historical information such as maps, direct quo-
tations from politicians, and summaries of peace treaties, accords, and
policies. Sacco's works take the time to narrate historical backdrops to the
stories and testimonies that they materialize. In *Palestine* (Seattle: Fantagraphics, 2003), he gently indicts his readership by naming the episode in
which he explains the historical outlines of the Israel-Palestine conflict "Re-
mind Me." After detailing the look of his own days in the refugee camp of
Balata, he begins a paragraph, "Do we really need to talk about 1948?" before
presenting a timeline of 1948's crucial events (41). Sacco's view is neither too
close, eliding large-scale transformations, nor too wide and delocalized.

18. Peter Galison, "Ten Problems in History and Philosophy of Science," *Isis*
99 (2008): 120.

19. Sacco placed himself in the orbit of classic New Journalism by illustrating
the cover for the Penguin Classics Deluxe Edition of Ken Kesey's 1962 book
One Flew over the Cuckoo's Nest (New York: Penguin Classics, 2007); the
front and back cover in Sacco's version are discrete comic strips. Kesey was
famously profiled by Wolfe in *The Electric Kool-Aid Acid Test* (1968). Yet
Sacco is critical of some of New Journalism's later efforts: "later they became
entertainers" (Joe Sacco, Chicago Creative Writing Workshop, University
of Chicago, February 8, 2012).

20. Fredric Jameson, *The Political Unconscious: Narrative as a Socially Symbolic
Act* (Ithaca, NY: Cornell University Press, 1981), 102.

21. Art Spiegelman, *In the Shadow of No Towers* (New York: Pantheon, 2004).

22. Quoted in David D'Arcy, "Profile: Art Spiegelman's Comic Book Journalism," NPR *Weekend Edition*, June 7, 2003, transcript, 1.

23. Kristine McKenna, "Brueghel in Bosnia," *LA Weekly*, January 8, 2004.

24. Sacco, Chicago Creative Writing Workshop.

25. Nicholas Mirzoeff, *Watching Babylon: The War in Iraq and Global Visual
Culture* (New York: Routledge, 2005), 27.

26. Groth, "Joe Sacco, Frontline Journalist," 63. The French cartoonist Jacques
Tardi adapted three of Céline's novels into comics, including the book that
inspired Sacco: *Voyage au Bout de la Nuit* (1988), along with *Casse-pipe*
(1989) and *Mort à Crédit* (1991). Tardi's celebrated 1993 *C'était la Guerre des
Tranchées*, a history-laden take on World War I, was published in English as
It Was the War of the Trenches, trans. Kim Thompson (Seattle: Fantagraphics,
2010). Tardi's *Maus*-like nonfiction graphic narrative, based on his father's

experience, *Moi, René Tardi, Prisonnier de guerre au Stalag IIB*, appeared in France in 2014.

27. Edward Said, "Homage to Joe Sacco," in Joe Sacco, *Palestine* (Seattle: Fantagraphics, 2001), v.

28. See Brian Edwards, "Jumping Publics: Magdy El Shafee's Cairo Comics," *Novel: A Forum on Fiction* 47, no. 1 (2014): 67–89. In this essay on Egyptian cartoonist Magdy El Shafee, author of the recently translated *Metro*, Edwards claims El Shafee was directly influenced by this specific page of *Palestine*, particularly its dense form (77–78).

29. Sacco's work brings attention to certain kinds of spectacles and their contexts. Mirzoeff argues the contemporary condition is in fact one of "modern anti-spectacle that dictates that there is in fact nothing to see and one must keep moving, keep circulating, and keep consuming" (*Watching Babylon*, 28). The intensive work of slowing a reader down and visually situating her in space (as against constant movement) positions Sacco's work as counter to the "keep moving" modality.

30. Said, "Homage," iv, v.

31. Naseer Aruri, quoted in Sacco, *Palestine*, n.p.

32. Said, "Homage," ii; Spiegelman is quoted in Gary Groth, "Art Spiegelman," *Comics Journal* no. 180 (1995): 61.

33. Said, "Homage," v. While Said's use of the word "detain" may be charged, framing and politicizing Sacco's work as a textual counterattack to the material Israeli detainment of Palestinians, his introduction to *Palestine* does not clarify or expand on this notion.

34. Joe Sacco, telephone interview, June 29, 2005.

35. Sacco, "Comics as Journalism."

36. See Wendy Brown, *States of Injury: Power and Freedom in Late Modernity* (Princeton: Princeton University Press, 1995), particularly "Wounded Attachments."

37. Seyla Benhabib, "The Generalized and the Concrete Other: The Kohlberg-Gilligan Controversy and Moral Theory," in *Situating the Self: Gender, Community, and Postmodernism in Contemporary Ethics* (New York: Routledge, 1992).

38. Nicholas Mirzoeff, *The Right to Look: A Counterhistory of Visuality* (Durham, NC: Duke University Press, 2011).

39. Aryn Bartley, in "The Hateful Self: Substitution and the Ethics of War," *Mfs: Modern Fiction Studies* 54, no. 1 (Spring 2008): 50–71, groups Michael Herr, author of the celebrated first-person Vietnam account *Dispatches* (New York: Knopf, 1977) together with Sacco, both proponents of New Journalism. Against the rhetorical stance of objectivity adopted by "official journalism," she praises their self-critiquing self-awareness in the arena of "the ethics of representing war" (52). But like many interested in ethics and trauma, she ignores the significance of the difference/addition of visual form in the transmission of the experience of the witness—and of the journalist. Bartley lauds the two journalists' attention to "languages of the other," but the crucial distinction in Sacco's work is in its presentation of images generated by, as well as depicting, the testifying other.

40. Many of the images Sacco highlights in his work have new relevance after 9/11 and the war on terror. For more on images and terror, see W. J. T. Mitchell, *Cloning Terror: The War of Images, 9/11 to the Present* (Chicago: University of Chicago Press, 2011).

41. Edward Said, *After the Last Sky: Palestinian Lives*, photographs by Jean Mohr (New York: Pantheon, 1985).

42. "Christmas with Karadzic," Sacco's story about December 1995, when he tracked down the former president of the Republika Srpska, Radovan Karadzic (who was indicted for war crimes in the Bosnian War, including ordering the Srebrenica massacre, and was a fugitive from 1996 to 2008), is a sustained work about the production of journalism as such, including, in Sacco's view, the moral feelings that are supposed to accompany such work. See also Andrea A. Lunsford and Adam Rosenblatt, "Critique, Caricature, and Compulsion in Joe Sacco's Comics Journalism," in *The Rise of the American Comics Artist: Creators and Context*, ed. Paul Williams and James Lyons (Jackson: University Press of Mississippi, 2010), 68–87.

43. Wolfe's New Journalism manifesto names four devices, on each of which comics journalism has a unique purchase: scene-by-scene construction, realistic full dialogue, "third-person point of view" in addition to the first-person view of the journalist, and the recording of the everyday details within a scene. Comics can deepen all of these; it is, at least in the world of print, the echt New Journalism, the culmination of imagination and investigation outlined during the Vietnam War. During the 1960s, as New Journalism became something with articulable values, comics also reinvented itself in the underground, without commercial strictures, as a serious form for self-expression. Both movements flourished—and today meet in work such as Sacco's.

44. In "Case for Comics Journalism," 4, Williams celebrates how comics necessarily creates "an overlay of subjective and objective storytelling." "Objectivity," of course, is a concept with a history, and as Peter Galison and Lorraine Daston have recently demonstrated, it is not identical to accuracy.

45. Hillary Chute, "Interview with Joe Sacco," *The Believer*, June 2011, 49.

46. Sacco, "Comics as Journalism."

47. Dick Doughty writes, "As a graphic artist, Sacco does not have the troubles that come from trying to use a camera. His mind is his camera—still, video, and sound all in one. He illustrates not only what he sees, but all he is told, and he does it superbly." "Sacco: 'Palestine: In the Gaza Strip' and 'Palestine: A Nation Occupied,'" *Journal of Palestine Studies* 27, no. 2 (Winter 1998): 99.

48. Charles Baudelaire, "The Modern Public and Photography," in *Classic Essays on Photography*, ed. Alan Trachtenberg (New Haven, CT: Leete's Island Books, 1980), 88.

49. Orayb Aref Najjar, "Cartoons as a Site for the Construction of Palestinian Refugee Identity: An Exploratory Study of Cartoonist Naji al-Ali," *Journal of Communication Inquiry* 31, no. 3 (July 2007): 256.

50. In 2012 the *Guardian* began a series, "Drawing the Revolution," featuring cartoonists from Algeria, Tunisia, Egypt, and Syria. See www.guardian.co .uk/commentisfree/series/drawing-the-revolution.

51. Chute, "Interview with Joe Sacco," 51.

52. Quoted in Joan Mandell, "Naji al-Ali Remembered," *MERIP Middle East Report* 149 (November-December 1987): 26; Kasim Abid, dir., *Naji al-Ali: Artist with a Vision*, Icarus Films, 1999.

53. See Najjar, "Cartoons as a Site," 282, on a refugee camp exhibit and other uses of al-Ali's imagery today. See also the Palestine Poster Project, which archives a 2010 poster that features a photograph of graffiti of al-Ali's signature character on the Israeli security wall, along with many other posters featuring his imagery that were produced after his death: www.palestineposterproject.org /special-collection/artists-and-collectives/naji-al-ali.

54. Associated Press, "Palestinian Journalist Dies of Wounds in London," *New York Times*, August 30, 1987.

55. For more on the meeting, see Abid's film documentary *Naji al-Ali: Artist with a Vision*.

56. Najjar, "Cartoons as a Site," 256.

57. Leila Abdelrazaq, *Baddawi* (Charlottesville, VA: Just World Books, 2015).

58. Al-Ali drew for the Lebanese paper *as-Safir* as well as the Kuwaiti paper *at-Tali'a al-Kuwaitiya*, in addition to the international edition of the Kuwaiti paper *al-Qabas*.

59. Hanthala's first appearance was in the July 13, 1969, edition of the Kuwaiti paper *al-Siyassah* and became al-Ali's signature, appearing in every subsequent cartoon.

60. Najjar's essay documenting al-Ali's influence includes a 2004 photograph taken by its author of T-shirts of Hanthala (with the words "Free Palestine") for sale and "holding their own" against Che Guevara T-shirts and scarves of Yasser Arafat and Hamas's Sheikh Ahmad Yassin in the West Bank ("Cartoons as a Site," 259). Few scholarly works exist in English on al-Ali or on Palestinian cartooning. Sadam Issa, from the University of Wisconsin–Madison, received a Library of Congress grant recently to complete a work on Palestinian political cartoons from 1948 to 2009. Allen Douglas and Fedwa Malti-Douglas's valuable *Arab Comic Strips: Politics of an Emerging Mass Culture* (Bloomington: Indiana University Press, 1994), the first and only book-length study in English, does not include analysis of al-Ali.

61. Joe Sacco, "Introduction," in Naji al-Ali, *A Child in Palestine: The Cartoons of Naji al-Ali* (London: Verso, 2009), viii.

62. See also "Shahid," *Brill Encyclopaedia of Islam* (Brill Online Reference Works), 1–8. Agamben discusses this etymology briefly in *Remnants of Auschwitz* (26–27).

63. The idea underlying the early Christian use of the term, which is ultimately the source for the English word, is that by dying for Christ, one bears witness to the truth of the Gospel.

64. Lori Allen, "The Polyvalent Politics of Martyr Commemorations in the Palestinian *Intifada*," *History and Memory* 18, no. 2 (Fall/Winter 2006): 107–138. As Allen points out, these posters, which attest to the regularity of death, are semiotically complex and track the process by which people become icons. See also Laleh Khalili's *Heroes and Martyrs of Palestine: The Politics of National Commemoration* (Cambridge: Cambridge University Press, 2007). For one succinct account of the history of the uses of photography in Palestine—and the argument that it was only in the 1980s and 1990s that photography was largely used for Palestinian self-determination instead of colonial rule and surveillance—see Michket Krifa, "Image-Making: Culture and Photography in the Arab World," lecture, Baker Institute for

Public Policy, Rice University, May 3, 2005, www.youtube.com/watch?v
=4HoqXuN1Xhg. On contemporary Palestinian art generally, see Samia
Halaby, *Liberation Art of Palestine: Palestinian Painting and Sculpture in
the Second Half of the 20th Century* (New York: H.T.T.B., 2001).

65. Marjane Satrapi enacts this same zoom across historical events in the
opening of her book *Persepolis*, trans. Mattias Ripa and Blake Ferris (New
York: Pantheon, 2003). See Hillary L. Chute, *Graphic Women: Life Narrative
and Contemporary Comics* (New York: Columbia University Press, 2010), 143.

66. As Spiegelman explains, his interest in comics is because the medium "[al-
lows] artists to be the visual commentators, rather than photographers" (Gary
Groth, "Art Spiegelman," *Comics Journal* no. 181 [1995]: 115).

67. Joe Sacco, *Safe Area Goražde: The War in Eastern Bosnia 1992–1995* (Seattle: Fantagraphics, 2000), 126. *Goražde* is explicitly about visual media even
as it tracks the relative scarcity, compared to other areas of Bosnia, of news
cameras in the enclave during the war. It particularly highlights video as a
documentary form, from Sacco's friend Edin recording damage with a cam-
corder to a tape of amateur footage of violence that circulates around
Goražde and is for sale for journalists. Sacco disparages the tape in a comparative media moment, revolted by "the video procession of dead children
and shrieking parents" even as he subsequently draws dead children and
shrieking parents described to him in a doctor's testimony (121).

68. As James Chandler asks, "Is this an act of representing a kind of Homeric
blindness that allows him to see things others can't see? Is it the idea that
his eyes reflect rather than see the world? Or are these empty spaces peep
holes for us ourselves to see the world afresh?" Chandler, introduction to
"Public Conversation: Joe Sacco and W. J. T. Mitchell," *Comics and Media:
A Critical Inquiry Book*, ed. Hillary Chute and Patrick Jagoda (Chicago: University of Chicago Press, 2014), 53. In my reading, this blankness amidst so
much visual elaboration and political and aesthetic pressure on the act of
seeing is a surface mark of Sacco's desire to cede the stories he solicits to
others—to highlight, superficially at least, a modesty through formlessness
in the face of others' experiences.

69. Jane Taylor noted the forensic practice in South African morgues of drawing
bodies as opposed to photographing them in her lecture "UBU and the Truth
Commission," Franke Institute for the Humanities, University of Chicago,
November 16, 2010.

70. The special editions of Sacco's *Palestine* and *Goražde* chart his drawing process. In a huge bird's-eye view of Goražde (seen in the book on pages 30–31),
he avows, "I wanted to put each building in its right place" (special edition,

n.p.). Hitchens makes note of how Sacco's comics form "makes me remember that distinctive Bosnian architecture—the gable ends and windows—with a few deft strokes. You know where you are, in other words, and it's not in some generic hotspot." Christopher Hitchens, "Introduction," in Sacco, *Safe Area Goražde*, vi.

71. Ibid., v.

72. William Hogarth, *The Analysis of Beauty*, ed. Ronald Paulson (1753; repr., New Haven, CT: Yale University Press, 1997). See Thierry Smolderen, "Why the Brownies Are Important," *Coconino World*, www.old-coconino.com/s_classics/pop_classic/brownies/brow_eng.htm.

73. Smolderen, "Why the Brownies Are Important," 11. Joseph Koerner's "Unmasking the World: Bruegel's Ethnography," *Common Knowledge* 10, no. 2 (Spring 2004): 220–251, characterizes the difference between Bosch and Bruegel: Bosch "saw the worlds that humans make as unreal and therefore contemptible," whereas Bruegel, in my view much like Sacco, "would see them as contingent and therefore intriguing" (222). To the extent that some critics see Bruegel's focus on everyday life as populist, despite the difference of painting, another point of comparison obtains. See Valentin Denis, ed., *All The Paintings of Pieter Bruegel*, trans. Paul Colacicchi (New York: Hawthorn Books, 1961). Art critic Robert Hughes, author of *Goya*, famously named Crumb the modern era's Bruegel. While Sacco and Crumb work in different genres, one can recognize in both the idiom of ethnography, a documenting of the human condition, albeit in different registers.

74. McKenna, "Brueghel in Bosnia"; Sacco, Chicago Creative Writing Workshop.

75. Groth, "Joe Sacco, Frontline Journalist," 65.

76. Joe Sacco, in "Public Conversation: Joe Sacco and W. J. T. Mitchell," 57.

77. Comics' formal spaciousness allows Sacco to present details in his work that would otherwise have vanished from history; he documents what gets dropped in the broad strokes of political and war reportage, such as how people cut and stacked wood in Goražde, or precisely how people in Goražde put together paddle-wheel generators jerry-rigged from refrigerators and cars. "I recognize this isn't the type of thing that's going to make it in the newspaper," Sacco says, noting that these details would be "lost." "Joe Sacco: Presentation from the 2002 UF Comics Conference," *Imagetext* 1, no. 1 (Spring 2004): 17–18. www.english.ufl.edu/imagetext/archives/volume1/issue1/sacco. Further, comics journalism, in offering visual backgrounds in addition to textual information, may include recurring details that go unremarked in

the written narrative but amplify the atmosphere Sacco seeks to convey (while also transmitting relevant information).

78. The Office of the United Nations High Commissioner for Refugees is mandated to coordinate international action to protect refugees.

79. Koerner, "Unmasking the World," 247.

80. In all of his comics journalism, Sacco pulls back at some point and displays the topography of place. Perhaps the single most successful moment in *Palestine* is a wordless double spread bird's-eye view of the Jabalia refugee camp that appears in the middle of the book. Jeff Adams, in *Documentary Graphic Novels and Social Realism* (New York: Peter Lang, 2008), 128, points out the similarity between this image and Bruegel's drawing *The Kermess of Hoboken*.

81. "Interview with Joe Sacco," *Egg: The Arts Show*, PBS, 2002, transcript at http://www.pbs.org/wnet/egg/303/sacco/interview.html.

82. Said, "Homage" to Joe Sacco.

83. Michael Silverblatt, "The Cultural Relief of Art Spiegelman," *Tampa Review* 5 (Fall 1992): 32.

84. Gary Groth, "Joe Sacco, Frontline Journalist," 67.

85. Andreas Huyssen, "Of Mice and Mimesis: Reading Spiegelman with Adorno," *New German Critique* 81 (Fall 2000): 82; Joseph Witek, *Comic Books as History: The Narrative Art of Jack Jackson, Art Spiegelman, and Harvey Pekar* (Jackson: University Press of Mississippi, 1989), 111.

86. Scott McCloud, *Understanding Comics: The Invisible Art* (New York: Harper-Collins, 1993), 37, 36.

87. Roland Barthes, *Camera Lucida: Reflections on Photography*, trans. Richard Howard (New York: Hill and Wang, 1981), 26, 41. 40.

88. For instance, Liliane Weissberg asserts, "The Holocaust aesthetics no longer centers on the scream, but on its absence"; see her "In Plain Sight," in *Visual Culture and the Holocaust*, ed. Barbie Zelizer (New Brunswick: Rutgers University Press, 2001), 26. In "Representing the Holocaust in Fiction," in *Emotion in Postmodernism*, ed. Gerhard Hoffman and Alfred Hornung (Heidelberg: Universitätsverlag C. Winter, 1997), Rüdiger Kunow, after Berel Lang, discusses the concept of an "aesthetic radical of representation." He writes, "During the last decade the project to translate the 'moral radical' into an *aesthetic radical of representation*, representing the Holocaust under the shadow of its unrepresentability had gained new momentum" (252).

89. Cathy Caruth, *Unclaimed Experience: Trauma, Narrative, and History* (Baltimore: Johns Hopkins University Press, 1996), 11. Caruth believes this reshuffling of frames of knowledge is generated by trauma: "Through the notion of trauma . . . we can understand that a rethinking of reference is aimed not at eliminating history but at resituating it in our understanding, that is, at precisely permitting *history* to arise where *immediate understanding* may not" (11).

90. Joe Sacco, *The Fixer: A Story from Sarajevo* (Montreal: Drawn and Quarterly, 2003), 51.

91. The body of writing on this common practice is thin. See Howard Tumber and Frank Webster, *Journalists under Fire: Information War and Journalistic Practices* (Thousand Oaks, CA: Sage Publications, 2006); and Jessica Wanke, "Fixers, Inc.," *American Journalism Review*, February/March 2009, which is more of a lifestyle piece than a critical assessment.

92. Joe Sacco, "Joe Sacco: Presentation."

93. The figure of Neven, who was born in Sarajevo to a Muslim mother and Serb father and was raised as a Serb, points helpfully to the Serb/"Chetnik" (Serb nationalist) distinction and to the difficulty of easy assignation of political position based on ethnic background. As a soldier, Neven was a sniper for Ismet Bajramovic, known as "Celo," an infamous warlord leading an armed cell of the Green Berets. Celo committed suicide in 2008.

94. Shortly afterward, Sacco devotes an entire page to a single haunting image of the Bosnian parliament skyscrapers with the upper floors of one of the buildings on fire. A single question, floating near the top of the burning building, asks, "Who will defend Sarajevo?" (page 35). This image is clearly evocative of photos and video stills of the World Trade Center on 9/11. Sacco plays here on readers' prior knowledge of one global disaster through its widely circulating images, and the discrepancy in global attention to other world-historical events.

95. Sacco discussed this in a conversation with Mitchell: "No words are necessary at all if you want to create that mood. You don't want to talk about that mood. You want the reader to have that mood." "Public Conversation: Joe Sacco and W. J. T. Mitchell," 57.

96. Although less conspicuous, similar clouds also appear in *Palestine* and *Safe Area Goražde* (in the latter see, for instance, 166, 167, 169, 170, 179, 183, 217) as well as in *Footnotes in Gaza*, usually in serious scenes, like battles, in which the visuals sharing the space have historical resonance and are drawn with great precision. Mitchell, in conversation with Sacco, called them "psychic clouds" ("Public Conversation: Joe Sacco and W. J. T. Mitchell," 57). They are the projection of a psychic landscape.

97. Shoshana Felman and Dori Laub, *Testimony: Crises of Witnessing in Literature, Psychoanalysis, and History* (New York: Routledge, 1992), xv.

98. Neven will soon don sunglasses in this episode, obscuring his eyes even more completely than they are throughout the body of the book.

99. Neven's comment on responsibility and seeing is reminiscent of Herr's *Dispatches*, a major influence on Sacco that also provides the epigraph for Caruth's title chapter in *Unclaimed Experience:* "It took the war to teach it, that you were responsible for everything you saw as you were for everything you did. The problem was that you didn't always know what you were seeing until later, maybe years later, that a lot of it never made it in at all, it just stayed stored there in your eyes" (*Dispatches*, 20).

100. For a discussion of memory as "an act in the *present* on the part of a subject who constitutes herself by means of a series of identifications across temporal, spatial, and cultural divides," see Marianne Hirsch, "Projected Memory: Holocaust Photographs in Personal and Public Fantasy," in *Acts of Memory: Cultural Recall in the Present*, ed. Mieke Bal, Jonathan Crewe, and Leo Spitzer (Hanover, NH: University Press of New England, 1999), 7.

101. The last page of *Maus* is graphically similar, featuring an overlay stamping the gutter that bisects the page.

102. Joe Sacco, telephone interview, June 29, 2005.

103. Felman and Laub, *Testimony*, 2, 16.

104. Joe Sacco, telephone interview, June 29, 2005.

105. Felman and Laub, *Testimony*, 41.

106. Caruth's definition of trauma is anchored in address: trauma, for her, is "always the story of a wound that cries out, that addresses us in the attempt to tell us of a reality or a truth that is otherwise not available" (*Unclaimed Experience*, 4).

107. Sacco worked with two Israeli researchers to locate documents in Hebrew. His editor at Metropolitan Books, Riva Hocherman, an Israeli, also did translation for *Footnotes*.

108. Joe Sacco, *Footnotes in Gaza* (New York: Metropolitan, 2009).

109. Edward C. Holland, in " 'To Think and Imagine and See Differently: Popular Geopolitics, Graphic Narrative, and Joe Sacco's 'Chechen War, Chechen Women,' " *Geopolitics* 17, no. 1 (2012): 477, compares a prose history of the Gaza Strip unfavorably to *Footnotes* and praises Sacco for tracing how 1956 "resonates (and in some cases doesn't resonate) into the present."

110. As in all of his work, which features fixers Sameh *(Palestine)*, Edin *(Safe Area Goražde)*, and Neven *(The Fixer)*, among others, Sacco makes Abed's role in facilitating his work an explicit part of the story.

111. The location where the jug sits in the 1956 image is where we see the jutting side mirror of a moving taxicab in the 2003 image, indicating forward motion and the reflection of the past.

112. For the history of Manet's famous series, which he completed between 1867 and 1869, see John Elderfield, *Manet and the Execution of Maximilian* (New York: Museum of Modern Art, 2006).

113. As in all of Sacco's work, narration—from a witness or from the author, in boxes or unbordered—is further distinct from speech within the frame, which occurs in balloons, by virtue of the fact that speech from within the frame appears entirely in uppercase letters.

114. Sacco's detailed portrayal of the butchering of a bull for the feast warrants greater attention than I can give it in this context; it is a fascinating portion of the text, a place where the book deliberately slows down. And while the feast is a positive moment of Palestinian tradition and ritual, the section's gruesome level of bodily detail is connected to the book's focus on sentience and the body.

115. Sacco's drawings are, in a sense, loosely comparable to reenactments in film. Errol Morris is the contemporary documentary filmmaker who has made reenactments famous, particularly in his groundbreaking *The Thin Blue Line* (IFC Films, 1988). When *The Thin Blue Line* was released in 1988, there was resistance to it as a "documentary" because of its reenactments, which illustrated conflicting testimonies about a murder. The film, which eventually helped secure the release of suspect Randall Dale Adams, was marketed instead as "nonfiction."

116. The photocopy of the UNRWA report from the United Nations archive appears with a 10 percent screen, so on the page it has a different tone from the white backgrounds of the panels. Unlike cartoonists such as Alison Bechdel, who are known for re-creating archival typeset documents, Sacco in this instance actually scans the photocopy onto his page.

117. See page 382, also the first page of the last chapter of one of the book's two major sections.

118. Patrick Cockburn, "'Footnotes in Gaza' by Joe Sacco: 'They Planted Hatred in Our Hearts,'" *New York Times Book Review*, December 24, 2009.

119. As Sacco points out in this chapter, though, however muddled and inconclusive the document is, "the refugees' claim in the U.N. report dovetails with the eyewitness testimony Abed and I gathered many years later. Namely: the fighting had stopped; the men were unarmed; they did not resist" (page 118).

120. The chapter in the "Rafah" section "Casualties among the Mob," a phrase of Golda Meir's describing the Rafah incident, details how news of massacres was received in Israel, where David Ben Gurion rejected a proposal to debate the Rafah incident in the Knesset. See Sacco, *Footnotes in Gaza*, 376 and Appendix 1: "Documents and Sources."

121. See Christopher Harker, "Different (Hi)stories, Different Gazas," *Geopolitics* no. 16 (2011): 475, for a characterization of Sacco's work specifically as against "singular History." *Footnotes* was in part inspired by a brief mention, although perhaps not an actual footnote, in Noam Chomsky's *The Fateful Triangle* (see Sacco's foreword in *Footnotes in Gaza*, ix).

122. For more on comics as mapping and charting—and in particular as what Edward Tufte calls a "time-series display"—see Hillary Chute, "Comics Form and Narrating Lives," *Profession*, 2011, 107–117.

123. Elaine Scarry, *The Body in Pain: The Making and Unmaking of the World* (New York: Oxford University Press, 1985), 50.

124. Anonymous sources are yet particularized by identifying numbers—Anonymous 4, for example.

125. Emmanuel Levinas, *Totality and Infinity: An Essay on Exteriority*, trans. Alphonso Lingis (Pittsburgh: Duquesne University Press, 1969), 198, 199; for an important description of this ethics, see "Section III: Exteriority and the Face," 187–253. See also Emmanuel Levinas, Emmanuel Levinas, *Ethics and Infinity: Conversations with Philippe Nemo*, trans. Richard A. Cohen (Pittsburgh: Duquesne University Press, 1985), particularly the section "The Face" (83–92). Levinas here notes, crucially, the excess of signification of the face: it does not suggest an authentic "character" in the typical sense, a content that is "a correlate of knowing," but rather is "meaning all by itself. . . . It is uncontainable" (86–87).

126. Judith Butler, *Frames of War: When Is Life Grievable?* (London: Verso, 2009), 77.

127. Jean Hillier and Emma Rooksby, *Habitus: A Sense of Place* (Burlington: Ashgate, 2002), 3.

128. Bechdel's process of creating comics, in which she poses herself as the bodies she wants to draw in a digital photograph that she then uses as a reference

shot, makes clear one way that cartoonists inhabit the others they draw. See Chute, *Graphic Women*.

129. Interview with Joe Sacco, January 20, 2009, New York.

130. "Public Conversation: Joe Sacco and W. J. T. Mitchell," 65. On inhabitation, see also Sacco's most recent interview with Gary Groth, "Joe Sacco on *Footnotes in Gaza*," *Comics Journal* 301 (2011): 401–402.

131. See Chute, *Graphic Women*, particularly the chapter "Materializing Memory."

132. Peter Galison and Lorraine Daston, *Objectivity* (Brooklyn: Zone Books, 2007), 414.

133. Holland, "'To Think and Imagine and See Differently,'" 112.

134. Lawrence Weschler, *Shapinsky's Karma, Boggs's Bills, and Other True-Life Tales* (San Francisco: North Point Press, 1988), 59. Weschler's phrase describes his view of *Maus*.

CODA

1. CBSNews.com, "Picture the Power of Images," May 11, 2004. See also Marianne Hirsch, "Editor's Column: Collateral Damage," *PMLA* 119, no. 5 (October 2004): 1209–1215, which incisively addresses Rumsfeld's comment. The artist Susan Crile, in her series "Abu Ghraib," has made drawings of twenty of the famous photographs with chalk, pastel, and charcoal on paper, highlighting the iconicity of photography and the textured materiality, in this case haunting, produced by drawing.

2. Michael Kimmelman, "A Startling New Lesson in the Power of Imagery," *New York Times*, February 8, 2006.

3. Judith Butler, "Photography, War, Outrage," *PMLA* 120, no. 3 (May 2005): 827.

4. Jytte Klausen, *The Cartoons That Shook the World* (New Haven, CT: Yale University Press, 2009), 19.

5. Art Spiegelman, "Drawing Blood: Outrageous Cartoons and the Art of Outrage," *Harper's*, June 2006, 43–52.

6. NBC News, "Charlie Hebdo Attack: Pen Becomes Defiant Symbol of Freedom," January 8, 2015.

7. Joe Sacco, "On Satire—a Response to the Charlie Hebdo Attacks," *Guardian*, January 9, 2015.

8. Art Spiegelman and Joe Sacco, "Only Pictures?" *The Nation*, March 6, 2006.

9. Spiegelman, "Drawing Blood," 43.

10. Joseph Brean, "Art Spiegelman: Politically Correct Fever Grips Canada," *National Post*, April 1, 2008.

11. Patricia Cohen, "Yale Press Bans Images of Muhammad in New Book," *New York Times*, August 12, 2009.

12. Jed Finley and Larry Milstein, "Paris Attacks Prompt Reexamination of 2009 Yale Press Controversy," *Yale Daily News*, January 13, 2015.

13. Noah Feldman, "Paris Gunmen Were Old-Style Terrorists." *Bloomberg View*, January 7, 2015.

14. See Cartoon Movement's blog *Comics Journalism*, ed. Tjeerd Royaards, http://blog.cartoonmovement.com/comic-journalism.

15. Gary Panter, *SatiroPlastic: Drawings by Gary Panter* (Montreal: Drawn and Quarterly, 2001).

16. See, for instance, Etsuo Suzuki and Yoko Miyawaki, *Edu-Manga: Anne Frank* (Gardena, CA: Digital Manga Publishing, 2002); Sid Jacobson and Ernie Colón, *Anne Frank: The Anne Frank House Authorized Graphic Biography* (New York: Hill and Wang, 2010). For an excellent survey of comics about Anne Frank, see C. R. Ribbens, "War Comics beyond the Battlefield: Anne Frank's Transnational Representation in Sequential Art," *Comics Worlds and the Worlds of Comics: Towards Scholarship on a Global Scale*, ed. Jaqueline Berndt (Kyoto: International Manga Research Center, Kyoto Seika University, 2010), 291–233. See also Henry Gonshak, "Beyond *Maus*: Other Holocaust Graphic Novels," *Shofar* 28, no. 1 (2009).

17. Shane Denson, Christina Meyer, and Daniel Stein, eds., *Transnational Perspectives on Graphic Narratives* (New York: Bloomsbury, 2013). John Lent, the founder of the *International Journal of Comic Art*, has also edited book collections on comics from around the world, including *Cartooning in Africa*, *Cartooning in Latin America*, *Southeast Asian Cartoon Art*, and the forthcoming *Asian Comics*. See also, among others, the important exhibit catalogue *Africa Comics* (New York: The Studio Museum in Harlem, 2006); Anne Rubenstein, *Bad Language, Naked Ladies, and Other Threats to the Nation: A Political History of Comic Books in Mexico* (Durham, NC: Duke University Press, 1998); Wendy Suyi Wong, *Hong Kong Comics* (New York: Princeton Architectural Press, 2002); Cynthia Roxas, *A History of Komiks of the Philippines and Other Countries* (Manila: Islas Filipinas Pub. Co, 1985);

Karline McLain, *India's Immortal Comic Books: Gods, Kings, and Other Heroes* (Bloomington: Indiana University Press, 2009); José Alaniz, *Komiks: Comic Art in Russia* (Jackson: University Press of Mississippi, 2010); Ann Miller, *Reading Bande Dessinée: Critical Approaches to French-language Comic Strip* (Chicago: Intellect, 2007).

18. Unlike Sacco and Mumford, Archer did not actually travel to Iraq, and so works less in the tradition of the artist-reporter than in a new kind of multi-media reporting that is based both in traditional methods and online news gathering. See Dan Archer, "The Nisoor Sqaure Shootings," *Multiple Journalism*, http://multiplejournalism.org/case/the-nisoor-square-shootings.

19. Lebanon's *Samandal* also publishes collections that have both Arabic-language comics and English-language comics (neither are translated). See the 2010 collection, whose English-language title is *Picture Stories from Here and There (Samandal)* (Beirut: Creative Commons, 2012).

20. Jeffrey Skoller, "Introduction to the Special Issue: Making it (Un)real: Contemporary Theories and Practices in Documentary Animation." *Animation* 6, no. 3 (2011): 211.

21. Marcus Brogdan, "Joe Sacco's 'Footnotes in Gaza' Is a Bookshelf Lightning Rod," *Los Angeles Times*, December 27, 2009.

22. Nicholas Mirzoeff, *The Right to Look: A Counterhistory of Visuality* (Durham, NC: Duke University Press, 2011), 5.

23. See Rupert Bazambanza, *Smile through the Tears: The Story of the Rwandan Genocide*, trans. Lesley McCubbin (Jackson's Point, ON: Soul Asylum Poetry, 2007); Jean-Philippe Stassen, *Deogratias: A Tale of Rwanda*, trans. Alexis Siegel (New York: First Second, 2000).

24. Eric Hayot, *On Literary Worlds* (Oxford: Oxford University Press, 2012), 7. See also David Herman, "Narrative Worldmaking in Graphic Life Writing," in *Graphic Subjects: Critical Essays on Autobiography and Graphic Novels* (Madison: University of Wisconsin Press, 2011).

25. Hillary L. Chute, *Outside the Box: Interviews with Contemporary Cartoonists* (Chicago: University of Chicago Press, 2014), 137.

26. See Jodi Rudoren and Fares Akram, "Artists' Work Rises from the Destruction of the Israel-Gaza Conflict," *New York Times*, August 16, 2014.

27. Paul Gravett, "Coco Wang: Comics Made in China," May 26, 2014 (first published in *Art Review Asia*, vol. 3), www.paulgravett.com/articles/article/coco_wang1.

ACKNOWLEDGMENTS

The first thank-you goes to Mark Brokenshire, my research assistant, without whom this book would never have been finished on schedule. I am extremely lucky to work with someone as capable, smart, and sympathetic as Mark; he tirelessly assisted the completion of *Disaster Drawn*, and went the extra mile at every possible opportunity. Thank you, too, to other research assistants with whom I worked on this book over the years: Jonah Furman, Daniel Rivera, and Kim Buisson. I am deeply grateful to all those who read chapters and offered suggestions: Noah Feldman, Anna Henchman, Heather Keenleyside, Eric Slauter, David Elmer, Marianne DeKoven, Peter Galison, James Mulholland, Brian Norman, Patricia Chute, Mark Brokenshire, Daniel Rivera, Joe Ponce, Chris Pizzino, Leonard Rifas, Jeremy Stoll, Tamar Abramov, and Bill Brown. Additionally, I would like to express my profound gratitude to the American Academy of Arts and Sciences, where I was a visiting scholar in 2012–2013, and where I received helpful feedback from an excellent interdisciplinary group of friends and colleagues (S.N.N. forever!).

This book was sharpened by the responses of audiences at lectures at which I presented work in progress, including at Australian National University (for an IABA conference keynote); Boston University; California State University, Long Beach; Dartmouth College; Freie Universität Berlin; Harvard University; Northern Illinois University; Oberlin College; Penn State University; Rutgers University; Stanford University; University of

Hawai'i, Manoa; University of Michigan; University of Missouri; University of Oregon; University of Wisconsin–Madison; Vanderbilt University (particular thanks to Juliet Wagner at Vanderbilt's Film Theory and Visual Culture Seminar for asking me about the *Lusitania*); and Yale University. At the University of Chicago I benefited from speaking at the Franke Institute for the Humanities and from presenting at the American Literatures and Cultures workshop (special thanks to James Rosenow for suggestions about figures, which I adopted). I have benefited enormously from the intellectual community at the University of Chicago, and in particular from stimulating conversations with my colleagues W. J. T. Mitchell (an extraordinary model both professionally and personally), Eric Slauter, Bill Brown, Debbie Nelson, Elaine Hadley, Tom Gunning, Jim Chandler, Patrick Jagoda, Linda Zerilli, and Hamza Walker, in addition to many others. Thank you to my graduate students in The Vietnam War in American Culture (Winter 2015) and Documentary: Aesthetics and Evidence (Spring 2015) for so compellingly engaging my thinking about the topic of this book. Thanks also to Doug Lavin for talking to me in Cambridge about ethics.

I started thinking about this book more than a decade ago, and I am grateful to the people who helped me conceptualize its concerns early on (and have continued to do so): Marianne DeKoven, Carolyn Williams, Harriet Davidson, Richard Dienst, Marianne Hirsch, and Nancy K. Miller. I am indebted, too, to Sidonie Smith for inviting me to speak at the Presidential Forum at the MLA in Los Angeles in 2011; I am gratified to have joined Marianne Hirsch, Nancy K. Miller, Leo Spitzer, Leigh Gilmore, Gillian Whitlock, Julia Watson, and others whose scholarship I admire in that programming. Gillian in particular has given me the opportunity to try out ideas from this book, and I appreciate her valuable ongoing feedback. My continued conversations with Art Spiegelman and Joe Sacco, cartoonists whose comics inspired this book—and inspired my fascination with comics in the first place—are profoundly meaningful to me; thank you for your support of this work.

At Harvard University Press, it has been an exceptional honor to work with Lindsay Waters, whose guidance and friendship over the years mean a lot to me. Thank you to Shanshan Wang for ushering the book in; to Amanda Peery for her consummate professionalism and patience in taking it through the later stages; and to its designers, Jill Breitbarth and Lisa Roberts. The staff of the Visual Resources Center at the University of Chicago, and especially Bridget Madden, has been constant in its support of this project and has helped me considerably; I am fortunate the center exists. Nell Pach proofread the manuscript. Melody Negron and Sue Warga attentively saw it through production. Jonah Furman prepared the index. Adam Kern, Alan Gleason, and Ogi Fusami helped me track down Japanese resources; Sarah Wenzel, of the University of Chicago Library, supplied many references. Dana Bryaska kindly translated Ukrainian into English. I am hugely grateful to Joe Sacco for, among many other things, his permission to use an image from *Safe Area Goražde* for the cover. And for decisive aesthetic advice at the last minute, I thank Noah Feldman and Chris Ware.

INDEX

Bazin, André, 20–21, 274n51
Beach, August F., 88
Bechdel, Alison, 19, 142, 192, 342n116, 343n128
Bechtel, Edwin de T., 42, 49
Benjamin, Walter, 25, 176, 262
Berger, John, 18, 21, 27, 31
Bergson, Henri, 35
Berkson, Bill, 108, 302n118
Bix, Herbert, 116
Blake, William, 28, 52
Bloom, Harold, 36
Blume, Harvey, 186
Bluth, Don, 169
Bosch, Hieronymous, 216, 338n73
Bourdieu, Pierre, 249
Bourke-White, Margaret, 158, 320n14
Boyd, Brian, 177
Boys' Jump, 116, 117, 118, 151, 156
Brady, Mathew, 65
Brakhage, Stan, 160
Breton, André. *See* Surrealism
Brown, Joshua, 25
Brown, Wendy, 205
Bruegel the Elder, Pieter (also Brueghel), 42, 200, 216–217, 220, 283n10, 338n73, 339n80
Bruzzi, Stella, 7, 17, 18
Buchloh, Benjamin, 28
Buck Rogers, 146, 316n110
Buhle, Paul, 96
Bukatman, Scott, 77, 84
Burt, Stephen, 73
Butler, Judith, 249, 256

Callot, Jacques, 8, 40, 41–51, 62; as influence, 8, 16, 41–42, 50, 66, 89; *Miseries of War*, 41–51
Canemaker, John, 76
Captain America, 12
Carderera, Valentín, 54

Caricature, 70, 75, 108, 126, 128, 145, 288n61, 292n10
Cartoon Movement (publisher), 260, 345n14
Caruth, Cathy, 32, 223, 270n20, 340n89, 341n99, 341n106
Ceán Bermúdez, Juan Agustín, 53, 54
Céine, Louis-Ferdinand, 202, 332n26
Censorship, 100–103, 256–258
Chabon, Michael, 12, 100
Chapman, Jake and Dinos, 40, 283n2
Charlie Hebdo, 256–257, 259–260
Chatman, Seymour, 16, 272n31
CIA, 116
Citizen Kane, 11
Civil War (U.S.), 10, 21, 65
Cockburn, Patrick, 246
Colbert, Stephen, 97
Comics: as counterarchive, 205, 234–235, 243–254; and documentary, 1–2, 6–7, 14–19; form, 4, 19–24, 25–28, 29–34, 35–38; and witness, 29, 31
Comics Code, the, 99, 102, 299n96
Comics journalism, 50, 63–67, 157; Francisco Goya, 41, 56–59; Joe Sacco, 37, 197–198, 206, 208–210, 217, 224, 228, 247; Muhammad cartoons controversy, 260–262
Compère-Morel, Thomas, 66, 290n88
Coolidge, Clark, 26, 108, 143
Crimean War, 10, 63, 64, 271n23, 290n81
Critical Inquiry (journal), 22
Crow, Thomas, 52
Crumb, Robert, 107–108, 121, 149–150, 153, 214; *Funny Aminals*, 151, 154–157; *Zap Comix*, 40, 72, 103–105, 147, 300n104
Cubism, 86

334n43; and comics, 98–99, 102–103, 154, 200, 259, 317n118
Village Voice (newspaper), 97, 98, 279n105
Virilio, Paul, 134

Waltz with Bashir, 87, 262
Wang, Coco, 264–265
War: Art Spiegelman, 156, 157–162, 178; and comics, 5, 7–14, 28, 103, 142; Francisco Goya, 28, 53–54, 62; Harvey Kurtzman, 95–96; Henry Darger, 93, 94; Jacques Callot, 46; Joe Sacco, 199, 200; and journalism, 40, 41, 60, 63–67, 255–256, 259, 261; Jules Feiffer, 97–98; Keiji Nakazawa, 113, 114, 117, 118, 121, 122, 126; Winsor McCay, 87
Ward, Lynd, 89–92
Ware, Chris, 72, 292n9, 311n61
Waud, Alfred, 65
Wertham, Fredric, 100, 300n98
Weschler, Lawrence, 254
Wexler, Laura, 142, 314n98
Wharton, Francis, 19
White, Hayden, 38
Wieviorka, Annette, 30, 276n74
Wilde, Oscar, 89
Williams, Martin, 95
Wilson-Bareau, Juliet, 54, 288n61

Wirgman, Charles, 143
Witek, Joseph, 156, 220, 268n7
Witness: Art Spiegelman, 157–164, 172, 174, 178, 179, 189–191, 194; and comics, 2, 4, 24–25, 28–36, 38, 39–41, 55, 58, 69–71, 111–112, 141–142, 169, 176, 212, 257, 260–262, 265; and documentary, 7, 145–146; Francisco Goya, 51, 54, 55, 56, 58–60; Henry Darger, 93–94; Jacques Callot, 42, 45, 47, 50; Joe Sacco, 198, 199, 205–206, 207, 233–242, 245, 254; and journalism, 63–67; Keiji Nakazawa, 111–112, 115, 118, 122, 125–128, 132; Philip Guston, 107–108; and trauma, 36, 50–51, 262, 264; and war, 5, 8, 14, 41–43, 45; Winsor McCay, 87, 88
Wolfe, Tom, 199, 331n14, 334n43
Wolfthal, Diane, 44, 45, 47, 49, 50, 284n20

Yellow Kid, The, 11
Yoneyama, Lisa, 124

Z (cartoonist), 261
Zakaria, Fareed, 259
Ziadé, Lamia, 261
Zola, Emile, 89
Zwigoff, Terry, 151, 319n8